jazz styles

MARK C. GRIDLEY

Case Western Reserve University

prentice-hall, inc. englewood cliffs, new jersey 07632

Library of Congress Cataloging in Publication Data

Gridley, Mark C 1947–
    Jazz styles.

    1. Jazz music.   2. Style, Musical.   3. Jazz
musicians.   I. Title.
ML3561.J3G67   785.4'2   77-8580
ISBN   0-13-509877-7 pbk.
ISBN   0-13-509885-8 case

© 1978 by Prentice-Hall, Inc., Englewood Cliffs, N.J. 07632

Printed in the United States of America

10   9   8   7   6   5   4   3   2

Prentice-Hall International, Inc., *London*
Prentice-Hall of Australia Pty. Limited, *Sydney*
Prentice-Hall of Canada, Ltd., *Toronto*
Prentice-Hall of India Private Limited, *New Delhi*
Prentice-Hall of Japan, Inc., *Tokyo*
Prentice-Hall of Southeast Asia Pte. Ltd., *Singapore*
Whitehall Books Limited, *Wellington, New Zealand*

CONTENTS

iv

part V APPENDIX 283

PREFACE

This book is intended as a guide to appreciating jazz as well as an introduction to most styles which have been documented on records. Almost two-thirds of the jazz history which is available to us on records has been made since 1940 because jazz recording did not begin until 1917. Therefore, approximately two-thirds of the styles discussed here are post-1940 styles.

The text is meant for high school through adult level readers. No technical knowledge of music is required for understanding the contents. The only musical notation included is a section of optional illustrations at the back of the book called "For Musicians."

Any individual or class using this book should listen to as much jazz, both recorded and live, as possible. The book will be an effective guide only if reading is accompanied by extensive listening. The book's coverage is neither comprehensive nor encyclopedic, but acquisition of the cited records approximates a comprehensive introduction to the most significant styles of jazz.

Acknowledgments Without the contributions of Harvey Pekar this book could never have reached its present form. He has had a far-reaching influence on both its content and organization through his detailed reviews and revisions of many drafts. His precise knowledge, perceptive ear, and indefatigable record collecting have been indispensable to my work on the book, and I am profoundly grateful to him.

Several friends have collaborated with me on particular sections of the book. Harvey Pekar worked on "What Is Jazz?", "Swing," "Bop," "Ornette Coleman," and the sections on Lennie Tristano and Sun Ra;

Charlie Braman contributed to the sections on Miles Davis, Weather Report, and Herbie Hancock; Bill Dobbins to the sections on Miles Davis, Ornette Coleman, Herbie Hancock, Chick Corea, and Keith Jarrett. Ernie Krivda assisted with the chapters "What Is Jazz?" and "John Coltrane"; Andrew White and J. C. Thomas also helped with the Coltrane chapter. The responsibility for any faults the book may have rests with me alone, however.

I am grateful to friends for bringing about five very significant events in my affair with jazz: Alan Sist for introducing me to Miles Davis's *Kind of Blue* and *Miles Ahead* and Charlie Parker's *Now's the Time;* my parents for giving me *Duke Ellington at His Very Best;* my brother for giving me Miles Davis's *E.S.P.* and Cannonball Adderley's *Mercy, Mercy, Mercy;* John Garra for exposing me to Coltrane's *Giant Steps;* and Dave Laura for acquainting me with Ornette Coleman's music.

I deeply appreciate the assistance of Charlie and Bill Braman, Kay Cremer, Kathy Miadock, and those friends listed below who volunteered their time to help me with the huge process of editing and rethinking mountains of raw manuscript:

Al Arters
Art and Virginia Benade
Chris Colombi
Bill Dobbins
Dave Greenwald
Mr. and Mrs. F. W. Gridley
Rex Hesner
Ed Hurley
Ernie Krivda
Ben Littenburg
Willis Lyman
Greg Matteson
Moryt Milo
Jeff Papez
Joyce Reimer
John Richmond
Alan Sherwin
J. C. Thomas
Phil Weinacht
Jack Witt
and the students who have taken my jazz courses during the past five years

I also wish to thank the musicians who patiently answered my questions in person, by phone, and by mail:

Bob Bohinc
Dave Brewer
Sal Cardello
Bob Curnow
Bill Dobbins
Bill Evans
Joe Farrell
Bill Gidney
Dizzy Gillespie
Benny Goodman
Jamie Haddad
Skip Hadden
Herbie Hancock
Don Heckman
Cleve Huff
Drene Ivy
Hank Kahout
Val Kent

Stan Kenton
Ron Kozak
Don Krahn
Ernie Krivda
Bud La Bianca
Abe Laboriel
Joey Lovano
Willis Lyman
Peter Martin
Pat McCarty
Bob McKee
Al McKibbon
John McNamara
Pat Meighan
Gerry Mulligan
Gus Oswald
Ron Papaleo
Jeff Papez
Jaco Pastorius
Larry Patrick

Ray Porrello, Jr.
Gary Queen
John Ross
Al Russ
Bob Sambrosky
Mike Sexton
Fred Sharp
Alan Sherwin
Wayne Shorter
Paul Smith
Ron Smith
George Steckler
Richard Straub
Al Vinci
Andrew White
Tony Williams
Karl Zahtilla
Joe Zawinul
Elmer Zelman
George Zorko

The book's content reflects the substantial influence of musicians with whom I performed long before the first draft was begun.

Drew Abbott
Dick Borden
Bill Bryan
Bob Budson
Stuart Carr
Warrick Carter
Bob Chase
Maurice Crane
Jim DeCamp
Scott Durbin
Bruce Early
Frank East
Dale Eli
Bill Faunce
Rick Ferretti
Andy Goodrich
Greg Hopkins
Gerry Kalber
Al Kaplan
Jim Kay
Cary Kilner
Paul Kirby

Adam Koslofsky
Mike Kuhl
Greg Matteson
Bob McDonald
Mike McGaw
Bill Meyer
Mike O'Sullivan
Cam Phillips
Keith Pollock
Mike Rehner
Mike Richer
Les Rout
Bud Spangler
Glen Stevenson
Bob Strand
Fred Trost
Roy Valenti
Lyle Velte
Frank Vocjek
Keith Warnick
George West
Larry Wocjek

For class-testing one of my drafts, I thank Bill Dobbins, of the Eastman School of Music; Professor Curtis Wilson, Chairman, Department of Black Studies; Professor Julius Drossin, Chairman, Department of Music; C. A. Colombi, Jr., Lecturer in Jazz History; and the students of Music 441: History of Jazz, Cleveland State University, Cleveland, Ohio.

Special thanks are due Dr. John Suess, Chairman of the Music Department, Case Western Reserve University, for his continued enthusiasm in hiring me to create and teach the jazz courses for which the book is written.

The book's instrument sketches and cover art were developed from the work of Pat McCarty, who is a bass trombonist of symphony orchestra caliber as well as a creative illustrator.

Bill Anderson, who has spent years keeping up with the snowballing jazz record market, updated and proofread the discography.

I am very grateful to Marty Hanks, Pat Berry, Kathy Miadock, and Jeanine Graham for typing preliminary drafts without pay. I am indebted to Evelyn Gonyon, Emily McCarty, Cheryl Taylor, Janice Lynch, Betty Hickle, Betty Slonaker, Ruth Twaddell, Trudy Sansbury, Shirline Williams, and Ester Schultz for the patience and concentration they directed at translating my atrocious handwriting into a typewritten manuscript.

The photos of musicians in the text reflect the great generosity of Bill Smith of *Coda Magazine* and Duncan Schiedt.

chapter 1
INTRODUCTION

Jazz is a broad stream of musical styles which originated in America. Though primarily urban, black music, jazz is played by all races and can be found in some rural areas as well as in more than half of the world's major cities.

An essential element of jazz is improvisation. This means that each performance represents an original and spontaneous creation. Improvisation is a very demanding activity which requires highly sophisticated talents. Even though improvisation has been common in non-European music and in pre-twentieth century European music, jazz stands out as the most developed and most common improvisational style in the twentieth century.

Jazz has affected a number of other contemporary musical idioms. Its tonal, melodic and rhythmic devices are evident in various works by such symphony orchestra composers as Aaron Copland, Ned Rorem, Maurice Ravel, Erik Satie, Milton Babbitt, and Darius Milhaud.

Though they are essentially different styles, jazz and rock sprung from some of the same roots and have occasionally influenced each other. During the late 1960s, jazz was simultaneously influencing and being influenced by rock. Motown rock performances often employed jazz-flavored accompaniment figures arranged for combinations of trumpet, trombone and saxophone. Certain popular rock groups—notably Chicago (previously known as The Chicago Transit Authority) and Blood, Sweat, and Tears—have employed jazz orchestration techniques. Some of their performances have also contained improvised solos with jazz flavor. Both the Motown style and that of Blood, Sweat, and Tears and Chicago helped spread the adoption of jazz elements in popular music of the 1970s. That same period saw certain tone colors and rhythmic devices from rock incorporated into jazz by Miles Davis, Herbie Hancock, Chick Corea and others.

Jazz has had a significant impact on popular music in general. Combo and big band jazz styles, and, to a limited extent, jazz improvisation itself, have been employed in the music for stage shows and in the accompaniments for pop singers and dancers. Entertainment modeled on the Las Vegas stage show forms a large part of night club, concert hall and television fare, and musicians with jazz backgrounds write, conduct and perform the music for many of these productions.

The influence of jazz on Broadway musical shows is extensive. Jazz flavor is displayed in accompaniments, especially the melodic figures assigned to trumpets, trombones and saxophones. The style of drumming employed in most Broadway pit orchestras is also a jazz-influenced style.

Jazz is quite evident in film and television music. Henry Mancini's compositions for the *Peter Gunn* television series and for films such as "The Pink Panther" were loaded with jazz elements, and this has been widely imitated. In fact, a large portion of men writing background music for films and television have extensive jazz experience. Among those who had jazz careers before entering this side of the music industry are Oliver Nelson, Pete Rugolo, Benny Golson, Benny Carter, Lalo Schifrin, J. J. Johnson and others. And many jazz musicians have written for films in addition to maintaining active performing careers (Duke Ellington, John Lewis, Herbie Hancock and others).

Despite its sweeping influence on contemporary music all the way down to television commercials and "piped-in" background music, the popular appeal of jazz has been limited. Even the most popular jazz musicians have been unable to match the followings enjoyed by stars such as Bing Crosby, Frank Sinatra, Eddy Arnold, Elvis Presley, the Beatles, Stevie Wonder and others. It is easy to see why a musician, whatever his style, would be unable to compete with the popular attraction of a Frank Sinatra or a Stevie Wonder. But the fact is that jazz groups usually fail to compete with even the average pop group. Most jazz groups are not only less popular than the pop groups which pack concert halls and sell albums by the millions; they are even less popular than most out-of-town and local pop groups which play in night clubs and neighborhood taverns. Jazz radio and television programming is also quite rare.

Jazz playing is clearly more a skill than a profession. A large number of people play jazz as a hobby. In fact, there is a group that calls itself The Docs of Dixieland, a band of physicians who have reworked the name of a popular New Orleans group, The Dukes of Dixieland. Only a small proportion of people who play jazz actually earn a living from it, and usually these manage only for limited periods in their lives. Jazz careers tend to be short and to be frequently interrupted. In most major American cities, there are only a few full-time jazz musicians. Many excellent jazz musicians must earn the main portion of their incomes as salesmen, postal workers, teachers, or in other ways.

Jazz musicians frequently take non-jazz musical jobs in order to support themselves. Such jobs are found in bands which accompany stage shows, circuses, and so forth. The same musicians may also be found recording non-jazz soundtracks for radio and television commercials, movie music, or accompaniments for pop singers. Many of these players are good jazz musicians. Some have been jazz innovators. You may not believe this, but some jazz musicians, including a few names you would recognize, also play school proms, wedding receptions, cocktail parties and bar mitzvahs. And almost all musicians of all styles have tutored students, at one time or another, as a source of income.

The music business, in general, is capricious, no matter what the style. Support of the arts has been sporadic throughout history, and twentieth-century America is no exception. But because of the massive publicity given to financially successful singers and musicians, the public often mistakenly assumes that music is financially a very rewarding profession. The truth is that careers in entertainment can be filled with dazzling riches, but usually nonsinging musicians who simply work at their art and never have a hit record are quite average breadwinners. So, considering the amount of preparatory practice for each paid hour of performance, their earnings are quite modest. When it comes to the average instrumentalist in classical music and jazz, we find that garbage collectors, mailmen, and factory workers earn more stable incomes, which are often larger.

Despite its status as an obscure music in America, jazz has had large and devoted followings in Europe and Japan. I have heard intensely emotional accounts of the personal hardships which East Europeans and Russians have had to suffer to obtain jazz records, to hear jazz on the radio, and even to play jazz.

It is ironic that American record collectors must often send to Japan or Europe for recordings of American jazz musicians because the record companies here neglect to keep certain albums in print and refuse to reissue valuable historical items. In fact, the market for jazz is so large in places outside of America that the first recordings by innovative American jazz musicians are sometimes made by foreign companies. A number of great American jazz musicians have spent years in Europe because their music was received more sympathetically there than at home. And some actually moved to Europe permanently.

The first jazz books and magazines appeared in Europe, not in the United States. Some of the best jazz journalists have been European. Leonard Feather is from England. André Hodeir is French. Joachim Berendt is German. Even during the 1960s a larger variety of jazz magazines was published in England than in America. The leader in discography—that field which keeps track of all the records issued, their recording dates, musicians' names, tune titles, alternate versions and alternate catalog numbers—was Jorgen Grunnet Jepsen, who lived in Denmark. The biggest listing of premodern jazz was published by Brian Rust in England.

The amount of study that European writers have devoted to American jazz is voluminous. Yet, even during the 1960s, the number of American colleges and universities which paid respectful attention to jazz was negligible. In the eyes of most university music professors and wealthy patrons of the arts, jazz was still classed with popular music. They felt that it lacked seriousness and was not deserving of the financial or academic attention received by symphony orchestra music. (In fact, the general term for music played by symphony orchestra musicians is "serious music.")

The Present Book In the 1970s, however, American colleges and government have shown increasing interest in jazz. The present volume is in fact a part of that development, since it grew out of a jazz course which I taught at Case Western Reserve University. It represents an attempt to organize and present basic information about jazz. Specifically, the book is an introduction to important jazz styles and performers from 1917, with particular emphasis on jazz since 1940.

Although it is very difficult to generalize about music, certain recognized styles, such as swing, bop, and West Coast, can be described. Some of the following chapters are devoted to important musicians like Duke Ellington and John Coltrane. These chapters are not biographies. They are descriptions of styles as important as those named for such "chronological" eras as swing and bop. It just happened that certain important styles became attached more to musician names than to era names. But, of course, as in the era descriptions, the music within musician-named categories also includes several different approaches to jazz. Labels are used here only for the sake of expediency; they do not signify any hard and fast rules for defining jazz or pigeonholing musicians.

Much of the text is organized chronologically. Although I do not think a knowledge of jazz history is essential to the appreciation of jazz, an historical approach provides the most expedient means of organizing a wide range of diverse styles. It allows generalizations to be made about particular sounds, and about the players who employed those sounds. Many players fail to fit precisely in any single style. But a particular performer's playing often will have enough in common with a given style to justify mentioning him in the discussion which treats that style.

In thinking about jazz history, it is important to remember that in most periods several major styles coexisted, and each style had many offshoots. Many characteristics of one style may also exist in the style which chronologically preceded it and in that which followed. The music of some players may combine elements of several different styles. But, because such a player must be included in one chapter or another, his work is placed with that of other styles which are not entirely the same as his. In some cases he will be labelled as a transitional figure.

As you explore the musical relationships between styles you will discover a remarkable continuity. Some developments occurred so smoothly that contemporary observers were actually unaware of them until they had already happened. Few revolutions occur in music. Changes appear radical only to people not deeply involved with the elements of the styles as their proportions are being altered.

Although styles tend to flow one from another, jazz history cannot be accurately described as a single stream, evolving from Dixieland to swing to bop and so forth. Some offshoots from major styles began streams of their own which, in turn, remixed with major streams. It is important to remember this when you read the style descriptions which follow. A multitude of styles exists. Some styles emerge from a mixing of various proportions of several preceding styles. A few styles come from single, extremely original, jazz improvisers. If you realized how many styles were omitted from this book in spite of the large quantity it treats, the diversity of jazz would boggle your mind.

The reader may find a problem in coordinating the descriptions here with actual performances by the players described. Players often change their styles. By the time you hear an artist in person, he may have assumed a style so unlike the one he was previously known for that you might not recognize it—either from the description given in this book or from his records. Unfortunately, there is no solution to this problem. I have tried to describe each player's creative peak, and, if he evolved more than one significant style, I have tried to mention them.

Big Bands   A word should be said about my treatment of big bands. Substantial interest exists in the big band music of Benny Goodman, Glenn Miller, Tommy Dorsey, Count Basie, Duke Ellington, Charlie Barnet, Stan Kenton, Woody Herman, Buddy Rich, Thad Jones–Mel Lewis, Maynard Ferguson, Don Ellis, Harry James and others. Most of their music, however, is prewritten and, therefore, not stressed here as much as that of the soloists because the essence of jazz is improvisation.

To discuss big bands properly would require extensive musical notations of big band arrangements. This would take us beyond the nontechnical scope of this book. I have attempted, as in the Duke Ellington chapter, to describe some big band sounds in words. But a true appreciation of the big band styles can be found only by playing the recordings and studying notations of their arrangements.

Jazz is primarily improvised music. Many lines improvised by jazz musicians compare favorably well with lines written by classical composers. Many of saxophonist Charlie Parker's improvisations, for example, are as intricate and well conceived as parts of Beethoven's compositions. Rarely, however, is the work of jazz *arrangers* as creative as that of the best classical composers. In my opinion, though, many arrangements by Duke Ellington, Gil Evans, and Sun Ra do compare well with work in the classical field. Furthermore, Ellington's, Evans's, and Sun Ra's work sensitively integrates jazz improvisation with written music. Ellington will be the only arranger discussed at length.

Treatment of the Various Instruments

Trumpet, saxophone, and piano are stressed more than any other instruments in this book. The complex contribution of the bass and drums is extremely difficult to describe. For this reason, my lack of words regarding them should not be interpreted as a lack of interest or a feeling that they lack importance. All instruments must be heard to be appreciated, but bass and drums require especially concentrated listening in order to appreciate their sound in jazz. And this is especially true of most pre-1960s recordings, where they cannot be heard as easily as saxophones and trumpets.

Flute, violin, guitar, organ, trombone, clarinet, and vibraharp are not extensively treated because they have not attracted players who contributed concepts as far reaching as those of trumpeters, pianists, and saxophonists. The less common instruments have had extremely capable improvisers. But none has had a stream of improvisers of the caliber that the saxophone has had in Coleman Hawkins, Lester Young, Charlie Parker, John Coltrane, and Ornette Coleman, or that the trumpet has had in Louis Armstrong, Dizzy Gillespie, and Miles Davis, or that the piano has had in Earl Hines, Art Tatum, Bud Powell, Bill Evans, and McCoy Tyner. One sign of a major force is the influence a musician has on players of instruments different from his own. Trumpeter Louis Armstrong influenced the improvisational styles of saxophonists, trombonists, pianists and guitarists. Saxophonist Charlie Parker influenced the styles of trumpeters, pianists, guitarists, vibraharpists and flutists. But how many trombonists or guitarists have shaped the improvisational styles of leading saxophonists and trumpeters?

It is important to note that the musicians dealt with in this book probably represent fewer than five percent of all jazz musicians. Not only did these men manage to get their names known to jazz fans, but they also made their livings from jazz for at least a few years of their lives. For every one of the musicians discussed here, there are several other solid improvisers, not necessarily innovators or important stylists, who have not managed to surface to the public eye and were not able to make their livings playing jazz.

When reading an outline of jazz history, you must remember that the central figures did not create their innovations entirely by themselves. Nor did they invent a style simply by consolidating the one or two primary influences I have listed for them. Their work instead reflects the result of many influences, their own ideas, *and* chance occurrences. Additionally, it may reflect techniques which they picked up from musicians in their own home towns. (Not all come from New York City!) Many of the musicians who influenced greats-to-be were obscure, part-time players who never got much attention. In reading interviews, we often come across names of local musicians and legendary characters unknown to us. Whenever you come across a name like that and say "Who?", remember that the name might represent a very strong player who is far superior to many well-known players.

basics of jazz

Part One is an introduction to the basic elements of jazz. The first chapter examines four possible definitions of jazz. The discussion revolves around two important characteristics of jazz: improvisation and jazz swing feeling.

The next chapter introduces useful techniques for listening to a variety of jazz styles. In fact, some of the suggestions have such broad application that they will help the listener get more out of music in general. There is an outline of the standard roles of the piano, bass, and drums in a jazz combo. Then the skills which are required of the jazz improviser are detailed. Throughout the chapter there are references to the unwritten rules which make it possible to produce a respectable jazz performance without rehearsal, using players who are unfamiliar with each other. In this connection, there is an examination of tune forms and how they provide the harmonies for jazz improvisation and influence the form that solos take.

An understanding of musical terms will heighten your comprehension of the remaining material, although a technical knowledge of music is *not* required for you to read and understand any of the remaining chapters.

If you find any of the following terms unfamiliar, you might find it helpful to read Chapter 17, "Elements of Music" in the back of the book before continuing.

tempo	tone center
meter	tonal
rhythm	mode
measure	chromatic
quarter note	atonal
syncopation	polytonal
waltz	bluesy quality
eighth note	flat third
polyrhythm	flat fifth
swing eighth note	flat seventh
legato	blue note
staccato	major
dotted eighth note	minor
sixteenth note	chord
dotted eighth-sixteenth figure	chord progression
eighth note triplet	twelve-bar blues progression
scale	sixteen-bar blues
octave	chord voicing
fourth	voicing in fourths
fifth	orchestration
key	scoring
bridge	blues poetry
turnaround	tone color
verse	intonation
chorus	vibrato
	thirty-two-bar forms

chapter 2
WHAT IS JAZZ?

The word jazz has a variety of meanings, encompassing a broad, changing stream of styles. Definitions of jazz tend to be controversial, partly because people hold different concepts of what jazz is and partly because jazz depends on improvisation, which is often very difficult to notate. The inflections in pitch, variations in tone color, and rhythmic nuances in jazz improvisation must be notated in order to describe and define jazz. This has not been done. The changes which have taken place throughout the history of jazz and the existence of many different jazz styles also make it difficult to arrive at an adequate definition. But there are some traits which characterize jazz of several different eras. Two of these traits are improvisation and jazz swing feeling.

IMPROVISATION
To improvise is to compose and perform simultaneously. A great deal of improvised music is spontaneous, unrehearsed, not written down beforehand. Popular synonyms for the verb improvise include ad lib, fake, ride, and jam. Some of the vitality typical of a jazz performance may be due to its spontaneity. Jazz musicians are so conscious of spontaneity and originality that they try to never improvise in a given context the same way twice. Several versions of a tune played by a soloist during one recording session may be quite different from one another.

For most people, improvisation is an essential element of jazz, and musicians occasionally use the word jazz as a synonym for improvisation. For example, in a music publisher's brochure describing big band arrangements, a note might be included to the effect that "only the tenor saxophone part requires jazz." Or a musician's contractor might phone a player requesting that he play jazz trumpet chair in a big band, meaning the player will be the only man in the trumpet section required to improvise.

The inexperienced listener may have difficulty in differentiating what has been written or memorized beforehand from what is being improvised. If a performance sounds improvised it quite often is, but the best improvisations are so well constructed that they sound almost like written melodies. Many jazz fans solve the problem by knowing that, in most performances when a tune itself ends, what follows is improvised. It is all improvised until that same tune begins again. In the case of large jazz ensembles where written arrangements are required and the players sit down in front of music stands, the audience knows that a player is improvising when he stands up alone and solos. Most of the remaining music in that case is read from written arrangements. And, of course, any lines played in unison by several players must have been prepared beforehand, not improvised in performance.

Do not let the emphasis on improvisation lead you to think that small jazz groups are without arrangements. Even before the wide-scale use of written arrangements began with the big bands, such early figures as Jelly Roll Morton provided written arrangements for their men. And in bands not using written arrangements, many passages were agreed upon in advance. Introductions and endings were occasionally rehearsed, memorized, and used again and again. Some early groups worked out elaborate, unwritten arrangements. These arrangements sometimes competed in quality with the improvisations they framed. Of course, arrangements themselves are very often improvised during a performance also.

SWING FEELING The following discussion presents several different views regarding what jazz is. Some of the views allow music which bears no jazz swing feeling to be called jazz. Some views allow nonimprovised music to be called jazz. As a foundation for describing jazz swing feeling, elements are listed which I think contribute to swing feeling in performances of both jazz and non-jazz styles.

If music makes you want to dance, clap your hands, or tap your feet, it is what many people call swinging music. This effect can be achieved in performances of rock, classical, country, or any kind of music. The word swing has probably been used most in relation to jazz performances, but it describes that feeling which any musical style can project: the feeling that the group sound is getting off the ground.

Music that keeps a relatively steady beat, is performed well and with great spirit, seems buoyant. In that sense, many non-jazz performances can be described as swinging. But to specify the unique ways in which an effective jazz performance swings, we must outline both the general characteristics of swinging and those characteristics specific to jazz swing feeling.

Swing is a rhythmic phenomenon which is the sum of several easily defined factors and a few subtle, almost indefinable factors. During the following discussion, the term swing should not be confused with its use as a label for an era in American popular music that began during the 1930s and continued until the late 1940s (swing era, swing bands, King of Swing, etc.). It is also not to be confused with its occasional use as a synonym for jazz itself.

Swing in the General Sense

One of the easily defined factors contributing to the phenomenon of swing feeling is constant tempo. In jazz, a steady beat is usually maintained, whereas in certain styles of symphonic music the tempo may fluctuate somewhat in accordance with the conductor's wishes. I believe that constant tempo brings a certain momentum to music and that this momentum is essential to swing feeling. (The constant tempo factor in swing feeling is not recognized or accepted by those who feel that swing feeling is achieved partly by slight alterations in tempo and nonsynchronization of players.)

Another easily defined element of swing feeling is cohesive group sound. This is achieved when every member's playing is precisely synchronized with that of every other member. The different members need not be playing the same rhythms in unison, but each player must execute the rhythms of his part precisely in relation to the beat and the other group members. A group cannot swing if its members are not playing together. Note that this is a rhythmic concept only. You can play out of tune and still swing.

Saying a performance swings often means simply that the group is maintaining constant tempo and that its rhythmic parts are precisely synchronized. But it also indicates that the music is played with a rhythmic lilt.

A less definite characteristic common to music already bearing constant tempo and cohesiveness is a subtle, almost undefinable rhythmic lilt. Musicians sometimes refer to it as an edge or a buoyancy. This subtle rhythmic lilt is also referred to as a good rhythmic groove. In fact, verbs derived from the nouns, swing and groove, are commonly used ("The band is swinging tonight." "That pianist is really grooving.") In the sense of rhythmic lilt, edge, or buoyancy, swinging in music is quite similar to the meaning of swinging socially. It simply denotes pleasure, having a good time ("It was a swinging party"). This lilt, or buoyancy, must occur consistently in the playing of all group members for a group sound to swing. But an unaccompanied solo performer can also swing and a single member of an unswinging ensemble can swing, too.

The spirit with which a group plays also contributes to swing feeling. The general public occasionally uses the word jazz to convey the meaning of spirit. To "jazz up" and to "liven up" are often used interchangeably. "Jazzy" clothes are gaudy or extroverted clothes.

Music that swings, then, is characterized by constant tempo, cohesive playing, and is performed with rhythmic lilt and spirit.

Perhaps a successful performance of any kind of music swings if it conveys a feeling of life and energy which compels the listener to respond. But the description of a performance as swinging depends on the perception of the individual. Listeners tend to disagree when asked whether a certain performance swings. This description of swinging applies not only to jazz, but also to performances of polkas, waltzes, flamenco music, Gypsy music, marches, blue grass, rock, and classical music. "Swing in the general sense" can describe the feeling achieved by a good performance of any music.

Swing in the Jazz Sense   For jazz to swing, it must possess those characteristics already described for swinging in general. But jazz is somehow different. Jazz swings more, perhaps. Or at least it swings differently. Jazz swings in additional ways. These additional ways can again be described in terms of several straightforward factors and a few subtle, almost undefinable factors.

One important element in jazz swing feeling is the preponderance of syncopated rhythmic figures (see "Elements of Music" chapter). Syncopation often takes the form of accenting a note just before or just after a beat. Part of the rhythmic style that characterizes jazz swing feeling is a tendency to play not exactly on the beat, but just slightly before or after it. The tension generated by members of a group tugging at opposite sides of the beat may be part of jazz feeling. Laying back, playing slightly behind the beat, gives a relaxed feeling, and it occasionally lends a soulful mood to the music. The laid back tendency applies particularly to the playing of syncopations. Presented with a notated syncopation, a classical musician would probably play it slightly earlier than a jazz player. *Timing* is the single most identifiable dimension along which the listener may judge a player's degree of jazz feeling. Tone quality, pitch and note selection all seem secondary to his mastery of constant tempo, syncopation and the *swing eighth*.

Another factor contributing to the special kind of swing in jazz is the swing eighth (see Chapter 17).

Certain quick, precisely controlled deviations in pitch, tone color and vibrato, including characteristic ways of beginning and ending notes, are essential to jazz feeling (see Figure 2.1). Their effect is soulful or jazzlike. The changes in pitch and tone color are embellishing devices which are timed precisely. In fact, you can often identify a novice player by an ill-timed scoop or bend. These inflections are learned by imitation and have not yet been accurately notated for musicians to read from written manuscripts, although attempts have been made, and musical notation is used to indicate their use. In performance of notated inflection, the precise sound is subject to widely varying interpretation.

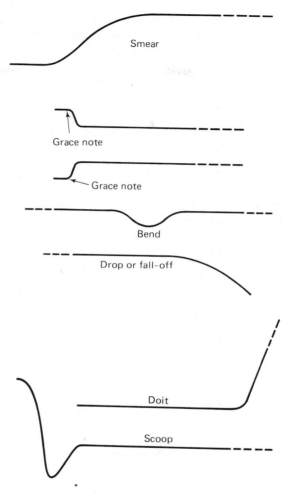

Figure 2.1. Possible visualizations of tonal inflections common to jazz (all are essentially graphs of pitch against time).

There is also a component of swing feeling which applies specifically to jazz lines. The continuous rising and falling motion in a jazz line provides alternation of tension and relaxation. Melodic elements of tension and relaxation are numerous and can be described only in relation to the context in which they occur. Generalizations could be made about how melodic devices create and resolve tension, but such a discussion would be too lengthy to undertake here.

Jazz swing feeling is composed of all elements of general swing feeling (constant tempo, cohesive playing, rhythmic lilt, and spirit), together with those qualities especially important for jazz (syncopation, swing eighths, attacks and releases, tonal inflections, and the ebb and flow of tension in a jazz line).

Again it is important to recognize that listeners disagree about whether a performance swings at all and, if so, how much. If beauty is in the eye of the beholder, swing must be in the ear of the listener. Within jazz swing feeling, there are different types of swing, also. For example, Basie swings differently from Miles Davis; Ellington swings differently from Basie, even though he was from the same era.

Not all players associated with jazz swing with equal facility. Some players sound stiff, stilted, or just plain awkward. Many pre-Louis Armstrong players and even some of his own post-1928 group members fit that category. Armstrong's clarinetist Johnny Dodds and trombonist Kid Ory were influential early jazz players, yet neither of them swung in any way near that of Armstrong. The first jazz group to make a record, the Original Dixieland Jazz Band, sounded stiff when compared to the relaxed yet precise way Armstrong executed syncopated rhythmic figures. Even one of the five most influential saxophonists in jazz history, Coleman Hawkins, did not swing with the lilt of many lesser players. Hawkins definitely swung, but not as easily as some other saxophonists.

Some of the post-1968 music of Miles Davis-led and Miles Davis-inspired groups, some of the post-1960 music of Sun Ra, much of the post-1965 music of John Coltrane and nearly all the post-1966 music of Cecil Taylor does not have conventional jazz swing feeling. The question of whether those performances qualify as jazz (in spite of their jazz roots) is controversial.

DEFINING THE JAZZ MUSICIAN: FOUR VIEWS

1) For many people, a musician need only be associated with the jazz tradition to be called a jazz musician. He may fall into this category even though he neither improvises nor swings. Defining a jazz musician by association alone is circular, but unavoidable in this discussion.

2) For many other people, a musician must play with jazz swing feeling in order to be called a jazz musician. In fact, for these people a musician need only swing in order to qualify as a jazz musician. These people tend to say, "Jazz is a feeling more than anything else."

3) For some people, a musician need only be able to improvise. Of course, the people who define jazz this way overlook the Indian, rock, and selected pop musicians who also improvise.

4) Probably the most common definition is that which requires the musician both to improvise and swing in the jazz sense in order to qualify as a jazz player.

Much music can be sorted according to the two categories of swing (swing in the general sense and jazz swing feeling) and the four approaches to identifying the jazz musician.

Applications of the Four Definitions

Of course, a great deal of music which is not jazz is improvised. Numerous musicians associated with Indian music, African music, rock, American popular music, as well as classical music improvise. The music of India is like jazz in several ways. Much of it is improvised, there is much syncopation, and a performer creates his own personal style. The native music of Africa is also like jazz. It employs improvisation; there is much syncopation. It is characterized by extensive repetition of rhythmic and melodic figures. Question-and-answer format is common (also known as call and response, leader and chorus, or antiphonal form). And two or more moving parts create a complex rhythmic fabric. Some solos at rock performances are improvised (although many are rehearsed over and over, memorized and played almost the same each time). Pop singers often improvise embellishments in the tunes they sing, adding their own personal nuances. J. S. Bach, Franz Liszt and other classical composers were excellent improvisers.

As interesting as many of these improvisations are, few people would claim that this music is jazz just because it is improvised. The musicians improvise without jazz swing feeling. Their music might definitely swing in the general sense, but the absence of jazz swing feeling is critical.

George Gershwin's "Rhapsody in Blue" is a written piece with no improvisation. The piece is often performed by symphony orchestra musicians whose playing does not swing in the jazz sense. Yet some people consider "Rhapsody in Blue" to be jazz. This is probably because its syncopated rhythmic and melodic figures give it a jazz flavor. Another reason is that the band which first performed the piece was Paul Whiteman's, a band billed as a jazz group. Jazz musicians did not, however, consider it primarily a jazz band. It swung only stiffly, and rarely did such jazz members as cornetist Bix Beiderbecke and saxophonist Frankie Trumbauer improvise more than a very short solo. So perhaps the only way a performance of "Rhapsody in Blue" would qualify as jazz is by association with the jazz tradition. If it were called jazz because of its syncopations and bluesy melodic figures, any performance of a jazzy piece should also be called jazz. (If Paul Whiteman's band did swing, and the pianist did improvise some portion of "Rhapsody in Blue," then such a hypothetical performance would qualify as jazz by our fourth definition.)

Several Stan Kenton big band performances contain no improvised solos (Robert Graettinger's "City of Glass," a Kenton LP of Christmas carols, an album of national anthems, etc.). Yet the band is associated with the jazz tradition and can swing in the jazz sense if it chooses. Kenton's musicians are capable of both improvising and swinging, but on these albums they are not improvising and sometimes not swinging either. Note that famous jazz bands such as those of Duke Ellington and Count Basie also have occasionally recorded pieces containing no improvisation (Ellington's 1944 recording of "Black, Brown and Beige"). However, that was very rare. Usually the bands featured several swinging improvised solos as integral parts of every piece, and every member swung the rhythmic figures in the written arrangements. It is not rare for the Kenton band to play music containing no improvisation. But by our fourth definition, an improvisationless performance by a swinging jazz band does not qualify as jazz.

Some players associated with jazz swing quite well but do not improvise (for example, the nonsolo members of big bands playing written arrangements which require swing feeling). Some swing well but improvise only a little. Some swing but improvise poorly, lacking originality or authority in their lines. Many cocktail pianists (usually accompanied by a bassist and drummer) working hotel bars fit this latter category. Many pianists and guitarists who work primarily accompanying singers and many hornmen in the orchestra pits of Broadway shows also fall under that classification.

Most people do not associate the names Guy Lombardo or Lawrence Welk with jazz. That is probably because most of Lombardo's and Welk's music is outside of the swing band category. It is what, during the 1940s, was called the sweet band category. Yet both Guy Lombardo and Lawrence Welk have at various times had good jazz soloists with their bands. Those soloists did not play often, but they did occasionally improvise swinging jazz solos. Here then is an example of jazz (fourth definition) in what, by association alone (first definition), is definitely a non-jazz context.

Lukas Foss and John Cage are mid-twentieth century composer-performers who employ improvisation in their pieces. Their music is associated primarily with symphony orchestra composers and musicians, the category most people call classical music. (Classical is also a term attached to the period of music during which Mozart, Haydn, and Beethoven were active: the second half of the eighteenth and the early part of the nineteenth centuries.) The improvised portions of their pieces rarely swing in either the general sense or in the jazz sense. Because the music is improvised, someone might want to call it jazz by our third definition. But the music of Foss and Cage is an example of improvisational music which very few people, if any, ever call jazz.

Several important musicians of what was considered the avant-garde during the 1950s and 60s play with unusual rhythmic style. Pianist Cecil Taylor and saxophonists Ornette Coleman and Albert Ayler were all said to have lacked jazz swing feeling. They definitely swung, however, in the general sense of the term (constant tempo, cohesive playing, rhythmic lilt, spirit). These musicians were also definitely associated with the jazz tradition (first definition) and their music was largely spontaneous (third definition). Yet, many listeners refused to call them jazz musicians. Perhaps those listeners were using our fourth definition.

Many of the post-1968 Miles Davis groups and their offshoots (Weather Report, for instance) swing only in the general sense of the term. They do not swing in the jazz sense. Yet the music is skillfully improvised, played by men who can swing in the jazz sense if they wish, and who are intimately associated with the jazz tradition. Can their music be called jazz? If one applies the fourth definition (swings in jazz sense and is improvised), it cannot be called jazz. But it does qualify as jazz by our first and third definitions (associated with jazz tradition and improvised).

Singers Singers are not discussed in this book, but it is interesting to classify them according to the four definitions. The first definition, association with the jazz tradition, is not especially useful because most American popular singers are associated with jazz at some time during their careers. A great deal of pop music has been influenced by jazz, and the rhythm sections, composers, arrangers, and conductors for most non-rock pop singers have had jazz backgrounds. The Las Vegas, Hollywood, and New York pop scenes are filled with jazz musicians trying to make a living by accompanying singers and dancers. The bands on TV talk shows of Steve Allen, Mike Douglas, Merv Griffin, Dick Cavett, and Johnny Carson are staffed by many jazz performers. Singers appearing with these bands could, by association alone, be called jazz singers by our first definition.

The first talking film, "The Jazz Singer," starred Al Jolson; a subsequent remake starred Danny Thomas. But neither man was particularly associated with jazz. The word jazz and, apparently, the term jazz singer had such broad connotations that a film about a vaudeville singer was named "The Jazz Singer."

By our second definition (performing with jazz swing feeling is sufficient qualification) countless singers qualify as jazz singers. Again, of course, the opinion that a singer's work bears jazz feeling is a personal one.

Our third definition, which requires only that a musician improvise, would also place countless singers in the jazz category. However, although pop singers tend to improvise when developing their personal interpretation of a song, they usually perform it almost the same way every time after settling into an agreeable version. That subsequent lack of spontaneity would probably exclude many of these pop singers.

Singers who improvise and swing are jazz singers by the fourth definition. A simple index of these criteria is called scat singing, a form of vocal improvisation which employs nonsense syllables such as Oo, bop, dwee, shebam, koo, skee, ya, etc. Scat singers improvise swinging jazz lines in the manner of trumpeters and saxophonists. Singers who fall into this category include Louis Armstrong, Carmen McRae, Ella Fitzgerald, Jackie Cain, Roy Kral, Jackie Paris, Cleo Laine, Dave Lambert, Mark Murphy, Jon Hendricks, Sarah Vaughan, Leon Thomas, Urszula Dudziak, Dee Dee Bridgewater, Joe Williams, Irene Kral, Sammy Davis, Jr., Eddie Jefferson, Mel Torme, and Betty Carter.

Nearly all non-rock pop singers have had some association with jazz, but there are a few whose association with jazz is so strong that most people do not hesitate to call them jazz singers. Among those I think of immediately are Bessie Smith, Ma Rainey, Ethel Waters, Mamie Smith, Billie Holiday, Mildred Bailey, Jimmy Rushing, Anita O'Day, Nat King Cole, Billy Eckstine, Dinah Washington, Frank Sinatra, Nancy Wilson, Lou Rawls, Johnny Hartman, Vic Damone, Ray Charles, Nina Simone, Helen Merrill, and Peggy Lee.

SUMMARY Improvisation can be defined. Jazz swing feeling transcends verbal definitions, but its essence is quite obvious to the listener who takes time to compare examples of different musical styles. The term swing in subsequent chapters usually refers to jazz swing feeling.

A definition of jazz requiring both improvisation and jazz swing feeling would exclude most popular music, all classical music, most rock, and some improvisationless pieces by otherwise jazz-oriented groups (Stan Kenton, Duke Ellington, Count Basie) and much of the new music that sprung from the jazz tradition during the 1960s and 70s (Cecil Taylor, Ornette Coleman, Albert Ayler, Weather Report, post-1968 Miles Davis). That same definition includes not only the music of Louis Armstrong, Charlie Parker, Clifford Brown, most of Ellington, Basie, Miles Davis, etc., but also thousands of performances by countless musicians from the late 1920s on into the future. This book examines music from each of the four categories, but most of the book is devoted to that of the fourth category.

chapter 3
APPRECIATING JAZZ IMPROVISATION

Listening to jazz improvisation is a demanding task. But with knowledge and practice, it can also be one of the most pleasurable experiences available to your ears. To appreciate what the jazz improviser does requires knowing some of what he knows. So, in addition to suggesting listening techniques, this chapter provides descriptions of the roles of different instruments in a jazz combo, the skills possessed by an improviser, alternatives available to the improviser and, finally, an introduction to chord progressions and tune construction.

For this information to have any meaning, you should periodically get a record or tape and carefully listen for the aspects being discussed. At the end of each section, or at least as often as every five paragraphs, you should stop reading, and listen carefully to at least one good example of the music. Listen for the concepts you most recently read about. This book means little without the actual music it describes. If you plan to read the book as you might read a novel or as you would read a textbook about economics or history, you are doing yourself a disservice. This book is a guide. Try not to fall into the easy trap of treating it as the content of learning itself. Only a small part of the content of learning is found in this book. The primary content of your learning is in hearing the music. The book is intended to make jazz more comprehensible by improving your listening skills. The most important section of the book is the guide to records and record collecting. You ought to buy at least one record recommended for each chapter before reading that chapter.

Before reading the description of instrument roles which follows, get a record or tape made between the middle 1950s and the late 1960s, on which only horn (sax, trumpet, or trombone), piano, bass, and drums are playing. It is important to find a recording on which the bassist and drummer are clearly audible. If you do not already have or know about a record that meets these criteria, glance at the following list of suggestions:

1) Anything Sonny Stitt recorded after 1969.
2) Miles Davis albums made for Columbia, entitled *E.S.P.*, *Sorcerer*, *Someday My Prince Will Come*, *Kind of Blue*, *Basic Miles*, *Milestones*.
3) Any Freddie Hubbard or Lee Morgan records made for Blue Note.
4) J. J. Johnson records made for Columbia, entitled *Blue Trombone*, *J. J. Inc.*, *First Place*, *Really Livin'*.

First, listen to a selection as you normally would. Then listen an additional four times to that same selection: *first*, concentrate on every sound but drums and cymbals; *second*, listen carefully to the soloist and bassist; *third*, ignore the soloists and listen only to the piano, bass, and drums; and *fourth*, ignore everything except the interaction between the chords the pianist is playing and notes of soloists. Finally, listen four more times, each time concentrating on a single performer.

You may find it helpful to hum the original tune to yourself while listening to the improvisations which are based on its chord changes. Synchronize the beginning of your humming with the beginning of a solo chorus and maintain the same tempo as the performer. You might hear snatches of the original tune embedded in the improvisation, and you will begin to hear the chord changes more clearly. You will become aware of two compositions based on the same chord changes: the original tune and the improvised melody.

Try to imagine a graph of the solo line. The horizontal dimension of the graph represents the passage of time. The vertical dimension represents highness and lowness of pitch. Your graph can be embellished by colored shapes and textures representing the accompanying sounds of piano chords, drums, cymbals, bass, and so on. The solo line itself can include all the ornamentations soloists employ: scoops, bends, shakes, doits, drops, smears, trills, vibrato, changes in tone color, changes in sharpness of attack, and changes in loudness (see Figure 3.1).

You might be able to imagine layers of sound, one on top of another, all moving forward in time, each layer representing a different instrument. Once you become skilled in visualizing separate sounds,

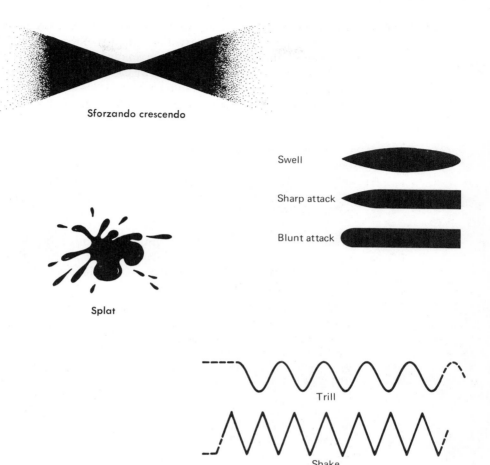

Sforzando crescendo

Swell

Sharp attack

Blunt attack

Splat

Trill

Shake

Figure 3.1. Possible visualizations of tone perceptions.

you will begin to observe relationships between those sounds. That, together with hearing chord changes, is an important step in appreciating the interaction between musicians which is so essential to jazz.

Hearing the improvised lines of a jazz soloist as melodies in themselves should help you enjoy the music of most pre-1960s improvisers. Much of the music after that period requires sensitivity to mood and certain specific elements of music. There is less emphasis on clear-cut melody and accompaniment. Sometimes the mood alone may be the single most prominent aspect. The music of Sun Ra, Cecil Taylor, and post-1968 Miles Davis is especially accessible to listeners who are attuned to variations in mood, interesting tone colors, and rhythms. Most

jazz, however, can usually be appreciated for a combination of qualities: mood, melody, and particular elements of the sound itself.

Try listening to every note in a soloist's improvisation. You might
not be able to detect each note in fast passages, especially those played
by saxophonist John Coltrane or pianist Oscar Peterson. But with
repeated listening and close concentration, you should eventually be
able to hear every note. If this proves difficult for you, do not be upset.
Most people can improve their listening skills with practice. It is not
uncommon for professional musicians to require repeated listenings
before they can account for every note in complex, up-tempo improvisations. Some musicians require years of listening before they appreciate the content of a particular style. Given proper exposure, your ears
will get better and better.

**INSTRUMENT
ROLES**

What follows is a general description of some instrument roles that
developed during the 1930s and 40s. These roles have to some extent
become standardized, although since the 1960s certain jazz groups
have made innovations in the use of instruments, so that the roles have
not been strictly maintained.

Jazz is partly an ensemble art. The soloist and rhythm section
combine to form an ensemble which, though described here in terms
of separate roles, attempts to play as a single unit. The *rhythm section*
is a group of players, improvising together, who both accompany and
inspire the soloist. They provide a setup or a springboard for his lines
and can make or break his effectiveness. The following discussion is
intended to clarify the role of each instrument in the rhythm section.

The rhythm section usually consists of string bass or electric bass
guitar (see Figure 3.2), drums (see Figure 3.3), and an instrument
which plays chords, such as a piano or guitar. An organ can be substituted for both the bass and chord instrument, because bass lines can
be played on the organ by means of foot pedals. But in spite of this
advantage, most jazz organists actually play bass lines with the left
hand, using the foot pedals for assistance. This technique restricts the
organist to a single hand for playing chords and, consequently, no
extra hand for chording behind his own right hand solos. The poor
pianos and poor sound systems often furnished by night clubs compel
many groups to carry their own portable electric piano or electric
organ. Carrying an organ has the additional advantage of saving salary
for one man, the bassist, because an organist can supply bass lines
together with chords.

Bass

The bassist plucks one note per beat with occasional embellishments
added (see Chapter 18 for notations of typical bass lines). Many
bassists pluck the second and fourth notes of each measure harder
than the first and third, thus contributing to the creation of a swing

Figure 3.2. Acoustic string bass violin and electric bass guitar. The electric bass can be differentiated from the solid body electric guitar because the bass has four tuning pegs, one for each string, and the guitar has six.

feeling. The bassist keeps the beat and gives buoyancy and a low register component to the group sound. This style of playing is called **walking bass.** The notes played by the bass are chosen from important notes of the chord progression or notes compatible with these chords. The bass clarifies a chord progression by playing its most important notes. Good walking bass lines make musical sense by themselves. In fact, some soloists consider walking bass to be the single most essential sound in the rhythm section. They would play without drums or chording instrument before they would play without walking bass.

Some bassists fill in silences with musical remarks, almost as though they were talking with the rest of the group (sometimes called "broken time"). In some post-1960 groups, these musical remarks have become more important than the beat. The role of the bassist has changed, and

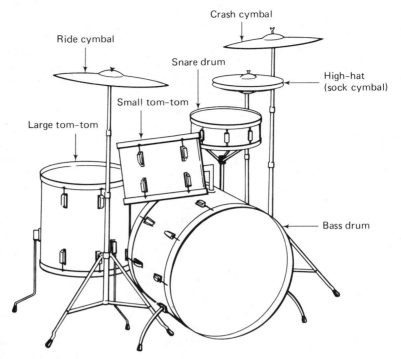

Figure 3.3. Audience view of drum set.

now he is involved in musical conversations as intricate as those typically carried on simultaneously between trumpet, trombone, and clarinet during Dixieland jam sessions. This kind of bass playing requires a good deal of discretion and originality, in part because it does not have the thirty year tradition that walking bass can rely on.

Some bassists employ a variety of techniques in their work. Occasionally a bassist will pluck two strings at the same time. That is called a double stop. Or he might strum his four strings as though his bass were a guitar (although a guitar has six strings). In symphony orchestras, the bass sound is usually extracted by a bow drawn across the strings in the manner of a saw cutting through wood. This technique is called *arco*. Jazz bassists employ it also but not as often as plucking. A few bassists have developed solo styles using the arco technique.

Piano The pianist plays chords in a syncopated fashion, providing harmonies and rhythms which complement and support the soloist. These chords are usually played in the middle of the piano keyboard, a pitch range that is easy to hear (see Chapter 18 for notations of typical piano accompaniments). What the pianist does underneath a soloist is called **comping** (ac**comp**anying or **comp**lementing). While playing the chorded rhythms that constitute comping, the pianist uses both hands to play chords. But when taking his own solo, he uses his left hand to comp while his right hand plays melodic lines.

Comping is supposed to enhance the solo line, and it also inspires the soloist, suggesting chords and rhythms for use in his improvisation. The pianist must be inventive when he comps, without getting in the soloist's way. That is a difficult task, requiring a great deal of discretion. Sometimes the pianist may drop out if he feels that the soloist would sound better without him. Piano comping must also relate to the drummer's kicks and prods. Ideally, the pianist and drummer will kick and prod the soloist in some integrated (or perhaps unison) fashion. The members of the rhythm section are constantly providing an accompaniment for the ever-changing melodic and rhythmic directions of the soloist's improvisation. They also underscore rhythms in written melodies and ensemble figures.

Comping and soloing are two separate skills. Many pianists who have mastered and may be innovative in one area, may not be as proficient in the other. Numerous styles of comping exist. Certain broad categories can be assigned to different ten-year periods. But even within eras, drastic differences in comping styles are evident.

Drums   The drummer uses his right hand to play rhythms which provide both regular pulse and swing feeling just as the bass often does. The drummer plays these rhythms on the *ride cymbal*, which is suspended to his right over the drum set (see Figure 3.4).

These rhythms are called ride rhythms. Occasionally they consist of one stroke per beat (ching, ching, ching, ching), played in unison with the walking bass, but usually they are more complicated (see Chapter 18 for notations of common ride rhythms), for example, ching chick a

Figure 3.4. Drums.

ching chick a ching chick a ching OR ching ching ching chick a ching OR ching chick a ching chick a ching chick a chick a ching, etc.). The drummer may play ride rhythms on other parts of his set, too. In fact, before the ride cymbal came into common use, ride rhythms were played on the snare drum and high-hat cymbals. Note that the drummer's right hand is not limited to playing the ride cymbal. He can use it on any part of his set, but the ride cymbal gets more of its attention.

The drummer's left hand is free to accent and color the group sound by striking the *crash cymbal,* suspended over the drums to his left, or by striking his *snare drum,* on a stand close to his lap (see Figure 3.4). The sounds made by striking the snare drum and crash cymbal are often called "fills" because they fill in a musical gap left by the soloist. The crash cymbal has a more diffuse, splashy sound than the ride cymbal. The snare drum has a crisp, crackling sound. The *small tom tom,* suspended over the bass drum, and the *large tom tom,* sitting on the floor to the player's right, are also available for accent and coloration.

Accentuating the swing feeling achieved by the bassist's emphasis of the second and fourth beats in each measure, the drummer plays those same beats by pressing his left foot on a pedal which closes two cymbals together making a "chick" sound. This apparatus is called a *high-hat* or *sock cymbal* (see Figure 3.5). The high-hat will produce

Figure 3.5. Open high-hat, closed high-hat.

a "chick" sound if the pedal is depressed and held in closed position for a second. It can then be opened and closed again for another "chick" sound. A "ching" sound, almost like a chord, can be achieved by bringing the cymbals together just long enough for them to strike each other, and then releasing them to resonate. All this is done by means of the high-hat's foot pedal. The high-hat can also be struck with sticks, wire brushes, or mallets, all of which produce different sounds (see Figure 3.6). The high-hat cymbals can be struck when they are closed or open. The drummer may drag the stick from top-down direction or down-up. Each cymbal in the unit can also be struck independently. Any part of any cymbal can be struck; each part produces a different sound.

The drummer uses his right foot to press a pedal which, in turn, causes a mallet to strike the *bass drum* (see Figure 3.7). The drummer usually plays the bass drum lightly on all four beats of each measure, and he also uses it for accents.

This is the basic drum set. Most drummers have additional instruments (extra cymbals, tom toms, timbales, rattles, cow bell and wood block).

The drummer can create a huge variety of sounds, depending on what drum or cymbal he strikes, how hard he strikes it, and what part of the surface is struck. Striking the center of the cymbal creates a sound different from that produced by striking half-way out to the edge which, in turn, is unlike striking the edge itself. The sound also varies according to what means are used to initiate it: sticks, wire brushes, mallets, and bare hands all produce different effects (see Figure 3.6).

Figure 3.6. Sticks, brushes, mallets.

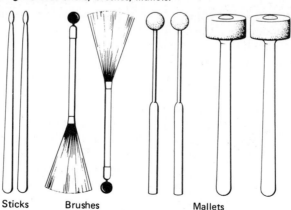

Sticks   Brushes   Mallets

Figure 3.7. Bass drum—foot pedal.

A drummer can be recognized on a record by the particular instruments he plays and the characteristic ways in which he strikes them. No two drummers have the same cymbal sound, and each drummer has his personal way of tuning his drums, which he does by tightening the drum heads (the plastic or animal hide striking surfaces) by means of adjustment bolts. Drummers acoustically dampen portions of their drumheads by attaching gauze and tape. They tune cymbals by critical placement of tape on the underside, by drilling holes in them or by cutting slices out of them. To produce a "sizzle" sound they often drill holes in a cymbal and attach rivets that fly up and down when the cymbal is struck; another technique, which does not require drilling, is to hang a large key chain across the top of the cymbal which bounces when the cymbal is struck.

Cymbals on a bandstand often appear old and dirty. Very few drummers polish their cymbals because the sound of the cymbal will be changed if any part of its surface is removed, whether it be dirt, corrosion, or the brass itself. Many drummers actually let new cymbals age to provide a certain tone.

Even though they come in various brands, thicknesses, and diameters, there is not enough standardization to guarantee perfect cymbals for every drummer. Drummers will spend years looking for cymbals which give them the sound they desire. Many drummers collect cymbals, using certain ones for certain jobs, depending on the sound required. When required to play on someone else's drum set, a jazz drummer often removes its cymbals and uses his own. No one knows as much about cymbals as the master jazz drummer.

A drummer's sticks are similar in importance to the saxophonist's reeds. Sticks come in different sizes and weights and are made of various materials. Drummers are quite particular about their sticks.

The drummer not only keeps time and colors the group sound, but he kicks and prods the soloist in ways that relate to rhythms the pianist and bassist are using. He also underscores rhythms in the ensemble lines of tunes and arrangements. The conception of jazz drumming changed radically during the 1960s so that in many groups the drummer was as much in the forefront as those instruments traditionally defined as melody instruments. The amount of interplay between drummers and other group members began to equal the amount of interplay previously expected only among front line instruments (trumpet, clarinet and trombone) simultaneously improvising in Dixieland jam sessions.

Prior to the 1960s, most drummers were primarily required to state the tempo in obvious ways, thus keeping time for the group. All group members are supposed to keep time independently, but with the drummer stating the beat strongly, drummers were considered the propulsive force. Some of the more adventuresome groups of the 1960s took advantage of the fact that group members kept time independent of the drummer. These groups still kept time, but did not require the drummer to state the beats. He was free to color the sound orchestrally.

The 1970s saw a large number of combos using two or more drummers. In some performances, all would play color, but in many, one would be explicitly stating the beats while the others were coloring the sound. Hornmen also played percussion instruments in many of these groups.

Similar changes occurred in the role of the bass during that period. Bassists played more melody than during the 1950s, and they were far more interactive rhythmically than when they had been involved exclusively in walking.

Soloist All jazz improvisers, soloist and rhythm section included, possess the skill of strict timekeeping. When it is said that the rhythm section keeps time for the band, you might assume that constant tempo would not be maintained without a rhythm section, but that is not the case at all. Much jazz was originally dance music, so you might say that the rhythm section was keeping time to make the beat obvious for dancing. The improvising soloist, as well as all the other players, keeps time to himself with a kind of "mental metronome." The ability to keep perfect time with rhythmic vitality enables a soloist to swing without a rhythm section or in spite of a bad one. When the rhythm section is good, it acts as a kind of springboard for the soloist and enhances his sound.

The improvising soloist learns to be aware of a number of important events. Although he cannot possibly be conscious of all of them all the time, he does manage to respond intuitively to most of them. Much successful jazz improvisation is largely the result of ultra-high-speed intuition. Here are a few things the improvising soloist tries to do:

1) *Remember the chord changes common to the tune he is playing.* Occasionally, when the improviser is at a jam session or sitting in with a strange group, he may not know the chord progressions of the tune being played. He might know the melody, but be unsure of some of the progressions. Or he might be requested to play a tune he once knew but whose progressions he has forgotten. In these cases, he listens to the rhythm section and determines the chord changes while he improvises. He can usually guess some of the progressions because he knows certain patterns which recur in hundreds of tunes. He can also determine the chords by listening to other soloists use them. And even if he does know a tune, he cannot always predict the chord progressions the rhythm section will play. A tune can often be harmonized in several different ways which are quite unlike each other. Altering chord progressions, reharmonization, is very common in jazz.

2) *Create phrases compatible with the chord changes.* Both the style of jazz and the individual player determine what notes are compatible with the chord changes. The concept of compatibility is very broad. For example, notes that are definitely compatible for modern jazz of the 1940s are often not at all compatible for jazz of the 1920s, but the final decision rests with the improviser.

3) *Edit* his work so that each improvisation represents a clear musical statement.

4) *Think ahead* so that the phrases will fit together well.

5) *Remember what he has played* so that self-duplication does not occur.

6) *Swing* with the tempo of the piece.

7) *Respond to the rhythmic figures of his accompanists* so that a healthy interaction will occur instead of a monologue.

8) Keep loudness at a level which will *project* out beyond the sound of the band to the audience.

9) *Play in tune and with the desired tone quality.*

10) *Remember how long he has been soloing* so that he can stop before he uses up the time left for other soloists.

11) *Play in the mood of the piece.*

12) *Create something personal and original.*

Rarely are an improviser's lines totally fresh and original. There are recurring themes in the improvisations of every jazz musician. Along with tone color, these themes help us identify an improviser's style. Using recurring themes is an accepted practice. In fact, aspiring jazz musicians are often advised to collect favorite "licks" or "riffs," those very themes and fragments which will later recur in his music and help us identify him. Most improvisers tend to play bits and pieces of lines they have played before, melodic figures they have practiced, and pet phrases of other improvisers. An improviser may actually play portions of a solo he remembers from another musician's recording. (When phrases are lifted intact from another improviser's work, we can often differentiate them from the original by differences in inflection, tone color, and precision.) Sometimes an improviser will quote snatches of a pop tune or a classical piece. The bits and pieces that constitute a solo may not themselves be original, but the way in which they are combined often is.

Jazz improvisations can be very intimate, personal creations. This is especially obvious when a soloist uses his instrument almost as an extension or substitute for his own voice. Pianists, guitarists and vibraharpists can often be heard humming the lines they are playing. Pianists Keith Jarrett and Oscar Peterson are noted for humming their lines as they play. Drummers can often be seen mouthing their rhythmic figures. Guitarists George Benson and Toots Thielemans purposely incorporate such devices into their styles. Benson scat sings lines in unison with his guitar picking. Toots whistles in unison with his guitar. Bassist Slam Stewart hums his lines in octave unison with his bowed bass playing; so does Major Holley. Saxophonist-flutists Yusef Lateef, Roland Kirk, Dewey Redman, Jeremy Steig and others hum and blow their horns at the same time. The different tone colors a musician creates in this way are part of his personal style.

ALTERNATIVES AVAILABLE TO THE IMPROVISER

Describing what an improvising soloist does must take into account the actual playing situation. Let us examine a few alternatives suggested by three different situations: playing alone, playing with chord instruments, and playing according to chord changes and constant tempo. The following descriptions are separated only for the sake of clarity. The rules listed in each category are not binding and they are not necessarily exclusive to that category. The player probably never thinks in these terms either. He responds intuitively to the requirements of each situation.

If he is playing alone and not required to follow chord changes or keep time, he is free to play anything that comes to mind:

1) He can organize his notes in a melodic sequence or

2) just place them in a haphazard way.

3) He can use notes common to a single key,

4) switch keys occasionally, or

5) play in no key at all.

6) He can group his notes in a way that implies a tempo, or

7) use no tempo of any sort, either stated or implied.

8) He can play loudly or softly at will.

If he is playing with chord instruments (piano, guitar, etc.), but not necessarily improvising on a tune or chord changes:

1) He must play notes which are compatible and in tune with the the other sounds.

2) His notes should not make the ensemble sound cluttered—they must have clarity and balance.

3) He must sequence his notes so that they fit with what preceded them and what is likely to follow. This means paying attention to both the construction of his own line and its relationship to the lines of the other performers. The more he plays with the same musicians, the better he will be able to predict what those musicians are likely to play from moment to moment. That knowledge will increase his ability to construct lines compatible with theirs.

4) He must adjust the loudness of his playing in response to the group sound. Sometimes he may suddenly play louder or softer for the sake of contrast.

5) He might play melodically with such strength that he surfaces to the forefront of the ensemble sound, or

6) he might choose, at any moment, to play notes and rhythms which are subsidiary to those of another group member. Those sounds might help create an ensemble texture instead of a solo line.

If an improviser is playing according to chord changes and constant tempo:

1) His lines must reflect the direction set by the chord progression.

2) He must maintain the tempo of the piece, and

3) swing in that tempo, letting the steadiness of tempo give momentum to his improvisation.

4) He must play notes that fit with the underlying chords. Improvisers are free, however, to initiate lines that deviate from an otherwise strictly defined chord progression. But if the line is to sound good, the improviser's accompanists must listen and instantly follow suit. Frequently a hornman initiates the deviation and the pianist responds with appropriate chords. Or

a pianist can suggest alterations in harmony by what he plays. Then the hornman picks up the direction, and the ensemble works together with the alteration. Soloists can also play notes which are incompatible with the underlying chords, while the rhythm section maintains the preset progression. This is called playing "against the changes," and is used quite effectively by some soloists.

Giving the Improviser a Chance

Since jazz is a spontaneous music, dependent on both the inspiration of the soloists and the simultaneous inspiration of musicians in a group, its quality can vary drastically from performance to performance. It is rare for all group members to be equally inspired at the same time. So if you listen to a jazz group playing in a night club, you ought to stay through at least two sets. Give yourself a good chance to hear their best moments. For the same reason, it is also a good idea to hear them on several different nights.

SKILLS POSSESSED BY THE IMPROVISER

Spontaneous music is not totally spontaneous creation. Extensive preparation is required. Before a musician can improvise coherent lines with jazz feeling, he must undergo much training. Some is formal, but most is informal. Jazz players spend years practicing their instruments and learning tunes and the chord changes to them.

Near-effortless command of an instrument is the constant goal of a jazz player, because the ability to play virtually any musical idea that comes to mind, and to play it immediately, is related to instrumental proficiency. It is not unusual for a player to practice by himself for more than two hours a day, and some average four hours a day, five to six days per week. In other words, they play every spare minute. In addition to practicing scales and exercises, the jazz musician invents, collects and develops phrases he might later use during improvisation. He tries out rhythmic variations of his favorite phrases. He practices to achieve fluency in different keys, in different registers of his instrument, and in different tempos and rhythmic styles.

Jazz musicians are quite versatile. A majority of modern jazz musicians play more than one instrument. Even if they never perform publicly on their second instrument, this versatility gives them a great depth of experience and understanding.

To adequately and creatively respond to the harmonies produced by a rhythm section, a soloist must be well acquainted with the piano keyboard. The keyboard provides a means for seeing and hearing relationships between melody and harmony at the same time. Most post-1945 jazz musicians know the keyboard well. Many trumpeters, saxophonists, guitarists, bassists, and trombonists actually play piano well. Some drummers also have a solid familiarity with keyboard harmony. A few drummers are accomplished pianists.

Nearly every saxophonist plays clarinet, and, since the 1960s, most play flute also. He also plays saxes other than the kind he is known for. Most saxophonists are capable of performing on soprano, alto, tenor, and baritone sax.

Tenor saxophonist Stan Getz has played bass and bassoon as well as piano. Pianist Lennie Tristano has played clarinet and tenor sax; tenor saxophonist John Coltrane has played E-flat alto horn (a brass instrument); both trumpeter Bobby Hackett and tenor saxophonist Paul Gonsalves have played guitar; tenor saxophonist Coleman Hawkins played cello; pianist Bill Evans has played violin and flute; trumpeter Fats Navarro, pianists Wynton Kelly and Horace Silver all played saxophone. A large number of hornmen and pianists play drums.

To respond in a split second to the rhythm section, the improvising soloist must have an extremely quick and keen ear for pitch and rhythm. This ability also helps him imagine a note or phrase and immediately play it. Jazz musicians are so quick to perceive and respond to subtle nuances in style and group direction that they can usually play a respectable performance the first time they work with an unfamiliar group.

Tonal memory is another forte of the jazz musician. He is able to hear a note or phrase, remember it, and then accurately play it back. It is not uncommon to hear an improviser incorporating phrases from the solo that immediately preceded his. Soloists in big bands often quote ensemble figures in their improvisations. Some can incorporate back-up riffs so well that their solo has as much continuity with the whole piece as a written arrangement.

A jazz musician has to remember hundreds of tunes and chord progressions. He must be as familiar with pop tunes and jazz standards as he is with his native language, perhaps more so. The convenience of knowing many of the same tunes helps musicians play together without rehearsal.

Another helpful skill is that of recognizing chord progressions quickly. Many jazz musicians can play a tune from memory after hearing it only a few times, and they often improvise solos compatible with the tune's chord progression after hearing it only once or twice.

As long as musicians listen to each other and interact flexibly, they can play well together. Keeping constant tempo and following agreed-upon chord progressions can help, but the most important ingredient in a good ensemble is each musician's sensitivity to the requirements of the musical situation. An examination of how improvisation relates to chord progressions appears later, but it is important to know that in a performance based on preset chord progressions, each group member is aware of the portion of the tune going by at each moment, whether or not he is actually playing at that moment. This claim also applies to the drummer, a player who need not necessarily know the actual chords.

Even though improvisation is their primary skill, most jazz musicians can also read music. Not all musicians in past jazz history could read, but the widespread use of written arrangements for big bands during the 1930s and 40s made reading an important skill. This was not necessarily true for drummers and bassists, however. Arrangers tended to write only chord symbols for bassists instead of particular notes. And because arrangers of the 30s and 40s did not know how to write for drums, they often provided no music for drummers at all. So most drummers did not have the same opportunity that hornmen had to become sharp sight readers.

Basically, the skills of reading and writing music can be described as four levels:

1) The ability to read music accurately if allowed to practice or look it over ahead of time. Many people call that "reading music."

2) The ability to play a piece of music correctly the first time it is seen. This is called "sight-reading." Musicians simply term this skill "reading." When musicians say someone reads, they usually mean he is capable of sight reading. Playing a tune correctly the first time it is seen is called sight reading. This skill is possessed by all symphony orchestra musicians and by most jazz musicians, but, at least during the 1950s and 60s, it was not a common skill among pop singers or in rock and country and western groups. The ability to sight read saves rehearsal time because it is easier to learn a new piece by reading it than by trial and error ("by ear"). Some people go so far as to say that a player "is not a real musician unless he reads music." I do not agree. Many players who are both instrumentally proficient and compositionally creative are unable to read music. Before 1940, many jazz musicians were less than sharp sight readers.

3) The ability to make up an original tune and correctly notate it: "writing music" or "composing." Actually the act of making up a tune is "composing"; notation is more specialized. But the term "writing music" usually refers to the process of making up a tune, and not necessarily to writing it down for musicians to play. Many people who are said to write music actually cannot write down their ideas. In other words, there are composers who cannot read or write music. Pop singers and rock musicians often make up songs and then pay a skilled musician to write them down (not for the singers or rock musicians themselves, but for copyright, sales, and publication—the singers and rock musicians usually teach songs to each other by ear).

4) The highest level of music reading and writing is the ability to listen to someone else's music and then correctly notate it. This

skill is possessed by people who write down jazz solos they hear on records.

During the 1950s and 60s, it was rare to find rock groups or country groups who could quickly notate their own work or sight read some-one else's. Some pop singers can read music, but most are unable to sight read. But it is not at all uncommon for jazz musicians to both compose and notate their own tunes. Some jazz players have written every tune on every album they have recorded. It is not unusual to find a jazz saxophonist or pianist who has written more than one hundred original tunes. Nearly all jazz improvisers are also composers. Though many of them never write a memorable tune, some become so good at writing that they are more important to jazz as tune writers or band arrangers than as improvising players. Most jazz musicians occa-sionally write down their improvisations in the form of tunes. Few of the tunes become famous in jazz history, but all serve as vehicles for improvisation.

CHORD PROGRESSIONS AND TUNE CONSTRUCTION

To appreciate what the jazz improviser does, it helps to know a little of what he knows. In most pre-1960s jazz, the improviser's knowledge of forms, coupled with adherence to a few unwritten rules, allowed him to put together a performance without any rehearsal because (a) con-stant tempo was maintained, (b) musicians knew many of the same tunes in the same keys, (c) the standard chord changes of these tunes were followed, and (d) traditions regarding the sequence of tune and solos were adhered to.

When a jazz group plays a twelve-bar blues, the entire tune is usually played twice by everyone. Then the soloists improvise on the chord progression of the twelve-bar blues. One complete twelve-bar progression is called a chorus. Each soloist ordinarily improvises for several choruses. When he ends his improvisation, another soloist takes over. If anybody misses an entrance or overlaps into someone else's chorus, the chord changes just keep moving along so that the whole group stays together. That twelve-bar progression and the tempo at which it is played is law. After all the solos are taken, the whole group concludes by playing the entire tune twice more.

Some tunes were written in the form of four eight-measure sec-tions. If the piece were in meter of four, and most were, you could imagine each section as a thirty-two beat section (eight measures of four beats per measure). In notating the chords, musicians use a verti-cal line to separate each group of four beats. That line is called a bar line. We used the term in our description of twelve *bar* blues. The form which has four, eight measure sections is called a thirty-two bar form because it has thirty-two measures in all, each measure separated from the other by a bar line.

The most common arrangement of thirty-two measure forms is one which uses two eight-bar sections, one called the A section, the other called the B section, release, inside, bridge or channel. The A section is played twice in succession. Then the B section is inserted, followed by the A section again. The sequence is *AABA*, and thousands of standard pop tunes of the 1920s, 30s, 40s, and 50s were thirty-two bars long in the AABA form.

When jazz musicians played a tune of that form, they played its melody once before and once after the solo improvisations. Each solo adhered to the tune's chord progression so that a repeating sequence of AABA was followed over and over again without interruption. Rarely was a beat omitted or a measure omitted. The cycle continued AABAAABAAABA etc.

What musicians meant by the term **chorus** was simply that segment of a solo which used the entire thirty-two measure AABA chord progression or entire twelve measure blues progression. A soloist might take only a chorus or perhaps take ten to twenty choruses. The number of choruses he was assigned indicated the duration of his solo. Then he ended on the thirty-second measure of some chorus and was immediately followed by another soloist who started on the first measure of the next chorus. (He ended on the twelfth measure if a blues progression was used.) Sometimes a soloist stops improvising in the middle of a chorus, usually at the end of an eight-measure section. Another player immediately takes up where the previous player has left off, and the AABA form remains unchanged.

Soloists sometimes trade eight-measure sections with each other: one musician improvises on the first eight measures, another on the second eight, and so on. This is called **trading eights.** The same thing is done with four-measure sections and is called **trading fours.** Trading fours is especially convenient in the twelve-bar blues, which is made up of three four-bar phrases.

In jazz styles of the 1940s and 50s, it is common for drummers to trade eights or fours with the rest of the group. A soloist, accompanied by the rhythm section, plays for four or eight bars, and then the entire band drops out while the drummer improvises alone for four or eight bars. This pattern repeats over and over so that various soloists are trading fours or eights with the drummer. The form of the tune and its tempo are maintained throughout that sequence, even though no chords or melodies are played during the drum solos. That is how the entire band can begin playing again, precisely after four or eight measures. Each musician is silently counting the beats and thinking of the chord changes passing while he is not playing. At the end of four or eight bars, each musician knows exactly where he is in relation to the beats and chord changes, no matter how complex and unpredictable the intervening drum solo has been.

When a single member or an entire section of a band plays as though the tempo were twice as fast as it actually is, this is referred to as **double-timing.** This means that, although the tempo remains the same, twice as many notes are played on each beat and in such a way as to give the feeling that the tempo has doubled. For example, in double time the walking bass may be playing eighth notes, whereas ordinarily it is playing quarter notes.

The opposite of double-timing is **half-timing.** In half-timing the tempo remains the same, but the note values become twice as long, so that the tempo seems to be slower, half as fast as the absolute rate at which chords are passing.

Half-timing is rare, but double-timing is quite common. During the 1950s and 60s improvisations on ballads were often played in double time. After the tune was played in its original tempo, solo improvisations followed, nearly always in double-time, as though the improvisers wanted to swing hard and were impatient with the slowness of the original tempo. Chord progressions in these performances moved at the same absolute rate during solos as during the tune itself, but the improvisations seemed twice as fast as the tune.

Double-timing is also common in Latin American jazz because the beat in that music is usually subdivided into eighth notes instead of quarter notes. Rock of the 1960s is often in double-time, and some is actually in quadruple-time. In quadruple-time the beat is divided into four equal parts (sixteenth notes). Young dancers during the early 1960s often requested "fast music" when in fact they did not want up-tempo performances at all. They wanted rock in double-time or quadruple-time feel. To the dancers, it was fast.

Another device related to double-time and half-time is **pseudo rubato.** The term "rubato" means to play in a rhythmically free manner without adhering to a strict tempo. In symphonic pieces where a conductor is used, the rates at which passages are performed can be slowed and quickened by the conductor. The tempo is freely manipulated by him. The style is called rubato. During the 1960s, especially in the Bill Evans trio and the Miles Davis quintet, certain passages had the feeling of rubato style, yet they were adhering to passage of chords at the tempo which was set in the beginning of the performance. The musicians were not stating the beats by use of bass drum on all four beats, sock cymbal closing on second and fourth beats, walking bass or ride rhythms. The tempo was there, but it was not obvious. It was not a true rubato, but it felt like one. (True rubato was occasionally employed by these musicians also.)

Another manipulation that often leads the listener to believe mistakenly that the tempo has changed is the **stop-time solo break.** Its name "stop-time" implies that the tempo stops when all group members except the soloist stop playing. Actually, however, the tempo and constant passage of chords is maintained, but since everyone except the soloist has stopped playing, we perceive the tempo as suspended (or "the time has stopped"). Breaks are especially effective as springboards for solo choruses. Often, groups finish the opening melody statement with a two-measure break for the first soloist. Many tunes end with a long note held for one or two measures, and this "empty space" in the melody furnishes a good opportunity for a solo break. In other words, a combo might stop playing during the last two measures of a thirty-two-bar tune, giving the soloist for the next chorus a two-measure break to launch his improvisation. If the piece is a twelve-bar blues, the solo break takes place in the eleventh and twelfth measures. But solo breaks are not restricted to the last two bars of a chorus. Trumpeter Louis Armstrong and other early jazz musicians made frequent use of stop-time breaks within the main part of a chord progression. "Wild Man Blues" is traditionally played with such internal breaks.

Other standard alternatives are also available to aid unrehearsed performances. For example, **introductions** are optional. But if a piece is to include one, the performers have at least four stock alternatives:

1) Use the final four or eight measures of the tune, and let the rhythm section rework and play it without the hornmen.

2) Have the rhythm section improvise a common four- or eight-measure progression and, at the same time, a line compatible with it.

3) Use an introduction that the entire group knows (from a famous recording of the tune, for example) thus including the hornmen in addition to the rhythm section.

4) Let the rhythm section play a one, two, or four bar figure (called a vamp) over and over until the hornmen feel like starting the tune.

Other alternatives exist, but these four seem the most common.

Endings are handled in similar ways. A few of the standard alternatives include:

1) End immediately on the last bar of the tune with no extra notes.

2) Improvise a *ritard* for the last three or four bars, and then sustain the final chord.

3) Sustain a chord or rest while a soloist takes a *cadenza* (an improvisation out of context), then follow it with a final, sustained chord.

4) Repeat the last four bars of the tune, thus creating a tag, and then sustain the tune's final chord.

5) Use a well-known ending.

6) Let the rhythm section play a vamp followed by a final chord.

7) Have the rhythm section improvise some common progression and end with it.

Other styles of ending also exist, but most fall into one of these categories.

Although the tune is usually played as written, before and after the improvised solos, jazz performers occasionally omit the melody statement. In 1936, a group including tenor saxophonist Lester Young and pianist Count Basie recorded a pop tune called "Shoe Shine Boy" without playing its melody. The entire performance consisted of improvisations on the chord progressions of "Shoe Shine Boy" without playing its melody. Alto saxophonist Charlie Parker and trumpeter Dizzy Gillespie employed the same technique on a 1950 recording called "Leap Frog," and Parker gave a similar treatment to "Cosmic Rays" in 1953. In 1951, trumpeter Miles Davis recorded improvisations on the chord progressions of Parker's "Confirmation"; he entitled his performance "Denial." Davis's 1951 "Bluing" was a twelve-bar blues without a melody. Davis released another performance without a melody line in 1954, calling it "No Line." He later recorded several performances without melodies or strictly set chord progressions ("Flamenco Sketches" and "All Blues" on *Kind of Blue* and "Country Son" on *Miles in the Sky*).

Once a progression had begun, its chords and its tempo remained in charge of the situation, providing the organization principles for the entire musical event. Strangers could play with each other and be instantly compatible. Musicians from different eras could play with each other, using the tempo and chord progression as a common unifying principle.

During the 1960s and 70s, much jazz departed from the tradition of improvising within fixed chord progressions and chorus lengths. Alto saxophonist Ornette Coleman and tenor saxophonist Albert Ayler pioneered such improvisatory practices. Miles Davis also explored those techniques with tenor saxophonist Wayne Shorter and pianist Herbie Hancock. The Davis group's "Hand Jive" (*Nefertiti*) and "Dolores" (*Miles Smiles*) performances contain prewritten melodies but do not use the chord progressions or lengths of those melodies as strict guides for improvised solos. Their recordings of "Freedom Jazz Dance" and "Ginger Bread Boy" (*Miles Smiles*) also contain improvisations which do not adhere strictly to the chord progressions and chorus lengths of tunes. Much improvisation in jazz-rock groups of the 1970s also rejected the restrictions of eight-bar and twelve-bar progressions in favor of spontaneously developed forms and of extended improvisation stemming from a single scale or chord.

PART II

premodern jazz

This is the first unit which deals directly with jazz styles. The first chapter begins with a discussion of the musical sources that contributed to the beginnings of combo jazz. There is an introduction to the music of Louis Armstrong, Sidney Bechet, Bix Beiderbecke, and what strong soloists of early New Orleans, Chicago, and New York jazz are known to us through phonograph records. The swing era is described in three chapters which cover big bands and swing era giants Duke Ellington and Count Basie. Coleman Hawkins, Lester Young, and Art Tatum are discussed, and there are brief introductions to the work of a number of other distinctive soloists and bandleaders. Much of the Ellington chapter is devoted to an appreciation of how composition and improvisation were blended in his band. The Basie chapter discusses how the playing of his rhythm section fostered modern jazz swing feeling; Basie's use of "comping" is described, as well as the playing of his soloists, notably Lester Young, who paved the way for several styles of modern jazz improvisation.

TABLE 4.1. Early Jazz Musicians—A Partial Listing

Trumpet

Buddy Bolden
Freddie Keppard
Joe "King" Oliver
Louis Armstrong
Wingy Manone
Red Nichols
Bix Beiderbecke
Tommy Ladnier
Henry "Red" Allen
Joe Smith
Bubber Miley
Charlie Teagarden
Jabbo Smith
Nick LaRocca
Paul Mares
George Mitchell
Sidney DeParis
Muggsy Spanier
Phil Napoleon
Wild Bill Davidson
Mutt Carey
Bobby Hackett

Trombone

Kid Ory
J. C. Higginbotham
Miff Mole
Jack Teagarden
Fred Robinson
Charlie Green
Jimmy Harrison
Charlie Irvis
Joe "Tricky Sam"
   Nanton
George Brunis
Bill Rank
Tommy Dorsey
Glenn Miller
Wilbur DeParis
Eddie Edwards
Honore Dutrey

Composer—Arranger

Jelly Roll Morton
Kid Ory

W. C. Handy
Clarence Williams
Fats Waller

Clarinet and Saxophone

Johnny Dodds
Sidney Bechet
Jimmy Noone
Frank Teschemacher
Benny Goodman
Albert Nicholas
Barney Bigard
Omer Simeon
Alphonse Picou
Mezz Mezzrow
Jimmy Strong
Sidney Arodin
Darnell Howard
Leon Rappolo
Buster Bailey
Don Redman
Bud Freeman
Floyd Towne
Coleman Hawkins
Jimmy Dorsey
Hilton Jefferson
Stomp Evans
Charlie Holmes
Larry Shields
Pee Wee Russell
Adrian Rollini
Don Murray
Tony Parenti
Izzy Friedman
Min Leibrook
Cecil Scott
Frankie Trumbauer
Edmond Hall
Gene Sedric
George Lewis

Bass

Pops Foster
Wellman Braud
John Lindsay

Violin

Joe Venuti

Piano

James P. Johnson
Fate Marable
Jelly Roll Morton
Willie "The Lion" Smith
Fats Waller
Lil Hardin Armstrong
Pete Johnson
Clarence Williams
Meade Lux Lewis
Albert Ammons
Cripple Clarence Lofton
Cow Cow Davenport
Elmer Schoebel
Pinetop Smith
Jimmy Yancey
Earl Hines
Frank Signorelli
Fletcher Henderson
Joe Sullivan
Jimmy Blythe
Henry Ragas

Guitar and Banjo

Lonnie Johnson
Johnny St. Cyr
Elmer Snowden
Eddie Lang
Eddie Condon

Drums

Baby Dodds
Papa Jack Laine
Paul Barbarin
Zutty Singleton
Sonny Greer
Dave Tough
George Wettling
Ben Pollack
Andrew Hilaire
Chauncey Morehouse
Gene Krupa
Vic Berton
Ray Bauduc

chapter 4

EARLY JAZZ: COMBO JAZZ PRIOR TO THE MIDDLE 1930s

Jazz is the result of a gradual blending of several musical cultures which occurred over a period of a few centuries. The fusion was first recognizable as jazz around the beginning of the twentieth century, but the music did not swing in the jazz sense until the late 1920s and early 30s.

Turn-of-the-century New Orleans was a port city in which the diversified musical cultures of African slaves, Europeans, as well as sailors from many parts of the world came together. It provided an ideal place for the blending of African and European musical influences which was to become jazz.

Jazz began as a conglomerate of many styles and continued to absorb new influences and be diversified itself. It drew from twentieth-century classical music during the 1940s, from the music of India during the 1960s, and, during the 1970s, from the pop music form called rock.

Native African music is rhythmically more complex than early jazz. Jazz did not exhibit comparable rhythmic complexity until the modern jazz of the 1940s developed through the work of Dizzy Gillespie and Charlie Parker. Writers on jazz have sometimes stated that jazz rhythm and improvisation stem from African music, and that jazz harmony developed from European music. In reality, this situation is more complicated. Premodern jazz sounded rhythmically similar to popular music and was not nearly so complex as native African music. Not all jazz rhythm is African and not all jazz harmony is European. The concept of improvisation was neither exclusively African nor European. At the time jazz originated, improvisation was becoming less and less common in European classical music, but improvisation had been an important element as recently as one hundred years before New Orleans jazz was first recorded.

Nobody knows for certain how jazz originated because its development began long before jazz recordings were made. Very little jazz was recorded or written down before 1917, and its sources are not thoroughly documented. Although the earliest recordings, together with statements by people who lived during those formative pre-1917 years provide us with some clues, the evidence is sketchy. The probable origins of jazz include African music of many styles, European popular and classical music, British, French, Spanish, Irish, and Italian folk music, cries of street vendors, as well as work songs and field hollers sung by laborers to ease their jobs. That large number of styles probably contributed to the formation of jazz as well as to other musical forms which also influenced jazz: the blues, ragtime, march music, and popular songs.

The blues is primarily a kind of vocal music, partly derived from Afro-American religious music and work songs. It has had a great influence on jazz and has also become a major source for long-lived pop music forms variously called blues, rhythm and blues (often shortened to "r and b"), and rock and roll (often shortened to "rock"). The Afro-American vocal approaches so important in the blues might have provided sources for the unique tonal inflection used by jazz hornmen. Afro-American singing has rich, deep tone colors and an extensive variety of tonal inflections.

Instrumental jazz tone colors and tonal inflections might have originated partly in imitation of the varied tonal inflections of African singing, the robust sonorities of the Negro voice, inflections of pitch and its soulful delivery.

West African singing might also account for the blue notes in jazz because much West African vocal music employs a five-note scale instead of the seven-note scale (see Chapter 17). Afro-Americans might have compromised certain intervals and the intonation of those intervals in the process of adapting to the seven-note scale. This is only a theory, but if you listen to recordings of native West and Central African singing, you might notice melodic tendencies in the direction of what, in the jazz sense, is called bluesy.

Ragtime is primarily a form of written piano music. It does not swing in the jazz sense. However, piano rags provided the melodies and harmonies for numerous early jazz combo recordings; Scott Joplin's "Maple Leaf Rag" is an example. The highly syncopated quality of piano rags leads me to believe that early jazz obtained much of its syncopated, rhythmic character by way of ragtime. Ragtime itself probably originated through both African and European musical traditions. (Its syncopations are thought to stem partly from polyrhythmic African drumming.) The huge popular success of Scott Joplin's "The

Entertainer," as background music for the film "The Sting," brought this turn-of-the-century written piano music to the attention of millions. Ragtime is also a term generally applied to early jazz combo music.

March music might have provided the emphatically steady beat and the compositional forms employed by early jazz combos. Many early jazz pieces resemble marches: "The Chant," "Steamboat Stomp," "Dixieland Jass Band One-Step," and "High Society," for example. March music also influenced the instrumentation of jazz combos and the methods of early jazz drumming. Marching bands were a prominent aspect of the musical scene in turn-of-the-century New Orleans. Many early jazz musicians, including performers like Louis Armstrong, were active in bands used for street parades and funerals.

The similarity of early jazz to European **dance music** is also strong. The forms and even some of the melodies for many early jazz pieces were lifted from music written for a dance called the quadrille. European music played a strong part in the musical culture of New Orleans, and elements of European dance music could easily have been absorbed in the evolution of jazz.

Popular songs have provided formats for much jazz improvisation. Early jazz musicians often began improvising simply by embellishing the melodies of pop tunes. Eventually the embellishments became as good as and more important to a performance than the tunes themselves. In some performances, all that remained was the original tune's spirit and chord progressions. What is today called improvising was referred to by early jazz musicians as "messin' around," embellishing, "jassing," "jazzing up."

Though much jazz developed in New Orleans, it was not until New Orleans jazz musicians traveled to Chicago and New York that jazz was recorded.* Sometimes the music's originators made those records, but often their imitators got there first. The group generally credited with making the first recording of jazz was the **Original Dixieland Jazz Band** (*The Original Dixieland Jazz Band*), sometimes labeled Original Dixieland Jass Band, a white group led by trumpeter Nick LaRocca. They recorded "The Dixieland Jass Band One-Step," "Livery Stable Blues," "Ostrich Walk," and several other selections in 1917 (see Figure 4.1). The Original Dixieland Jazz Band may not have improvised very much in these performances. A large part of the music sounds as though it has been worked out in advance. It is possible that the ODJB employed a larger proportion of improvisation in their

---

* Though some early jazz was recorded by portable machines in New Orleans and many early jazz records came from Richmond, Indiana's Gennett Record Company.

Figure 4.1. Original Dixieland Jass Band (also called Original Dixieland Jazz Band), 1916. Left to right: Tony Spargo [Sbarbaro, Sparbaro] (drums), Eddie Edwards (trombone), Nick La Rocca (trumpet), Alcide Nunez (clarinet), Henry Ragas (piano). *Duncan Schiedt*

nightclub performances of these same tunes than in their studio versions. Perhaps the awareness that every note recorded would be permanently on display moved these musicians to record only their most carefully prepared work.

The band usually cited as strongest in New Orleans jazz was a black group led by trumpeter **Joe "King" Oliver.** He worked with several New Orleans bands and in 1918 moved to Chicago, where he worked with several more bands before finally forming his own. Oliver's **Creole Jazz Band** was an all-star New Orleans group which, at various times, had most of the best black New Orleans players (*Louis Armstrong and King Oliver, King Oliver's Jazz Band, 1923*).

More than half of all jazz musicians and nearly all the influential innovators in jazz have been black. There have been strong white players such as cornetist Bix Beiderbecke; trombonists Miff Mole, Jack Teagarden, and Kai Winding; pianists Al Haig, and George Shearing; clarinetists Benny Goodman, Artie Shaw, and Buddy Defranco; tenor saxophonist Stan Getz, and others. But only a few white players have been influential innovators: pianist Lennie Tristano, alto saxophonist Lee Konitz, pianist Bill Evans, and bassist Scott LaFaro are among them.

It was in Chicago that important black New Orleans musicians were recorded in the early 1920s. What is usually referred to as New Orleans style is probably not the music that was played between 1900 and 1920 in New Orleans—we have never heard that music because it was not recorded—but rather the music recorded by New Orleans musicians between 1923 and the early 1930s in Chicago. These players, though born and trained in New Orleans, were older and likely to have played differently in Chicago than they had in New Orleans. A major difference is that, according to interview data and a few early records, the earliest forms of jazz placed great emphasis on collective improvisation, with all group members playing at the same time. These early bands tried to have every player simultaneously creating phrases which complemented every other player. We are told that it was common to have performances in which no single instrument took the lead. For many listeners, the greatest appeal of early jazz (or Dixieland, as it has been called) is the activity of several horn lines occurring simultaneously without getting in each other's way. This improvising of complementary lines strongly impressed numerous observers in pre-1920s New Orleans. Eventually, however, roles developed whereby a clarinet would play multi-noted figures ornamenting trumpet lead, and a trombone would play simpler figures outlining the chord notes, filling in low harmony and creating lower pitched motion.

The black Chicago musicians, most of whom were displaced New Orleans players, strayed from a collective approach to improvisation in favor of a style which featured solos in addition to collective passages. The skills of the improviser who was required to solo dramatically were somewhat different from those of the improviser required to blend with the collectively improvised phrases of other players. The delicate balance and sensitive interplay of collective improvisation which characterized the earliest form of jazz was, to a certain extent, discarded during the Chicago period of the New Orleans players. Musicians of subsequent eras who played Dixieland tried to recapture the essence of those very special skills which make successful collective improvisation possible.

Jelly Roll Morton was another famous figure in early jazz. He earned his living as a solo pianist in New Orleans. Later he moved to Chicago where he made a series of recordings with his combo called Morton's Red Hot Peppers (see Figure 4.2).

The recordings Morton produced are tightly arranged and carefully polished. Jelly Roll was the most sophisticated composer-arranger in early New Orleans-style jazz. One of his tunes, "King Porter Stomp," was made famous by the Fletcher Henderson and Benny Goodman big bands in the swing era.

Jelly Roll Morton shared some of the personnel who played in King Oliver and Louis Armstrong recording sessions: trombonist Kid Ory, clarinetist Johnny Dodds, drummer Baby Dodds, and Johnny St. Cyr

Figure 4.2. Jelly Roll Morton and his Red Hot Peppers, 1926. Left to right: Andrew Hilaire (drums), Kid Ory (trombone), George Mitchell (trumpet), John Lindsay (bass), Morton (piano), Johnny St. Cyr (banjo), Omer Simeon (clarinet). *Duncan Schiedt*

on banjo and guitar. In the context of Morton's leadership, these players sounded different than when playing with King Oliver and other leaders. Morton's pieces were elaborate compositions instead of just simple arrangements with lots of improvisation.

Trumpeter George Mitchell also lent his intelligent solos to many Morton recordings. Mitchell was one of the best early trumpeters. He had come to Chicago from Louisville, Kentucky, in 1919. Mitchell was a soloist on Morton's most compositionally adventurous recordings, "The Chant" and "Black Bottom Stomp," made in 1926 (*King of New Orleans Jazz*).

CHICAGO VERSUS NEW ORLEANS

During the 1920s Chicago was the center for a very active jazz scene, which could be separated into three main categories. One was the transplanted New Orleans black musicians who were constantly performing and recording. Another contained their white New Orleans counterparts, the New Orleans Rhythm Kings (Friar's Society Orchestra). These two groups of musicians were influencing a third group of younger white musicians, many of whom were Chicago natives. This young white jazz community developed what was called the Chicago style, or the Chicago school. Its music was modeled on the New Or-

TABLE 4.2. The New Orleans and Chicago Jazz Styles—Representative Musicians

New Orleans	Chicago
Joe "King" Oliver	Muggsy Spanier
Bunk Johnson	Jimmy McPartland
Freddie Keppard	(Austin High School)
Buddy Bolden	Frank Teschemacher
Louis Armstrong	(Austin High School)
Sidney Bechet	Dave Tough
Jimmy Noone	Bud Freeman
Kid Ory	(Austin High School)
Baby Dodds	Joe Sullivan
Johnny Dodds	Mezz Mezzrow
Zutty Singleton	Eddie Condon
Pops Foster	Gene Krupa
Johnny St. Cyr	
Lonnie Johnson	
Omer Simeon	
Pops Foster	
Jelly Roll Morton	
Honore Dutrey	
Albert Nicholas	
Barney Bigard	

leans style, but sounded less relaxed. Several of these musicians (Jimmy McPartland, Frank Teschemacher, and Bud Freeman) had attended the same Chicago high school, Austin High. They were often called the Austin High Gang—this included Dave Tough, who attended Wayne High (*The Chicagoans "The Austin High Gang" 1928–30*). In addition to the Austin High Gang, the white Chicago scene included Muggsy Spanier, Gene Krupa, Eddie Condon, Mezz Mezzrow, Joe Sullivan, and Ben Pollack, the Chicago-born drummer with the New Orleans Rhythm Kings who became a prominent band leader during the 1920s.

Eventually the Chicago musicians and the transplanted New Orleans musicians mixed with New York musicians. By the late 1920s a strong New York scene had developed in addition to the thriving Chicago scene. Key performers in the early combo jazz of New York included trumpeter Red Nichols, trombonist Miff Mole, and violinist Joe Venuti (*Thesaurus of Classic Jazz*). By the 1930s most of the original Chicagoans had moved to New York.

Many of the Chicago-style players became prominent figures in the next jazz era, the swing era. Benny Goodman and Gene Krupa began their careers playing Dixieland in Chicago (*A Jazz Holiday*). Some big swing bands of the 1930s attempted to orchestrate the style of Dixieland. Singer Bob Crosby had such a big band. The small contingent of it was called the Bobcats, several members of which had worked in Ben Pollack's groups. (With the Bobcats were bassist Bob Haggart and trumpeter Yank Lawson, who, during the 1970s, were joined by tenor saxophonist Bud Freeman, trumpeter Billy Butterfield and others to form the World's Greatest Jazz Band. For the 1970s, that group was one of the most polished organizations of Chicago-style veterans. Their style extended from the Bobcats and its orchestrated Dixieland.)

Between 1933 and 35, two other famous swing era figures, trombonist Tommy Dorsey and clarinetist-alto saxophonist Jimmy Dorsey, also employed a big band Dixieland format. The Dorseys became better known as swing bandleaders despite their roots in the Dixieland style.

Early jazz has been identified by many labels which lack standard use. Certain labels have definite meanings for some jazz scholars and musicians, but these labels are not uniformly applied by everyone. Chicago jazz and New Orleans jazz are two of these terms. Ragtime, gut bucket, barrelhouse, Dixieland, classic jazz, and traditional jazz are others. These terms tend to be applied to solo piano styles and combo jazz, to include both black and white musicians, and to refer to music produced by old New Orleans and Chicago veterans as well as revivalist groups.

Early jazz took many forms and appeared in several geographic regions in addition to New Orleans and Chicago. By the middle 1920s, New Orleans musicians had performed in Los Angeles, New York, San Francisco, Europe, and numerous other places. Due to the absence of musical notations and acoustic recordings, we cannot be sure whether any of these places had jazz before New Orleans players traveled there. It is possible, however, that jazz sprang up in places other than New Orleans because there were other American cities in which a blending of West African slave cultures and European cultures occurred.

THE SOLOISTS Another idea to keep in mind is that jazz can be played on any instrument. The human voice is an extremely adaptable instrument which undoubtedly played a significant role in the development of jazz. And jazz does not require marching band instruments typical of New Orleans street parades and funeral processions. Violins, guitars, pianos, and banjos—all have been vehicles for jazz improvisation. (The banjo itself is considered an instrument of African origin.)

Piano We know that jazz piano styles were evolving in places other than New Orleans prior to 1920. In fact, some of the strongest jazz pianists of the 1920s were from the East Coast. Many of them played unaccompanied solo piano. Early jazz piano may have developed apart from jazz band styles.

Early jazz piano styles probably evolved from ragtime. Playing ragtime did not always necessitate reading or memorizing written music. Once the style had been absorbed, there were undoubtedly skilled pianists who could improvise original rags and embellish pre-written ones. A very powerful style which might have its roots in ragtime piano was **stride style.** Stride piano makes use of percussive, striding, left-hand figures in which low bass notes alternate with mid-range chords together with very active right-hand playing. (Technically: stride style left hand consists of playing a bass note on the first and third beats and a mid-range chord on the second and fourth beats of each measure.) Together, the two hands produced music which you might imagine as a small orchestra with a driving rhythm section. The style is very demanding for the pianist. Because the sound is difficult to describe, I suggest you listen to James P. Johnson's 1921 "Carolina Shout" (*The Smithsonian Collection of Classic Jazz*), his 1930 "You've Got to Be Modernistic" (*The Encyclopedia of Jazz on Records, Vol. 1*), or something by Willie "The Lion" Smith (see Figure 4.3).

One of the best known products of the stride piano style was New York-born Fats Waller. Though his jazz contributions have been overlooked because of his reputation as a popular entertainer, Waller played with excellent technique and a bouncing swing feeling which he used to create countless lighthearted and joyful performances. As-

Figure 4.3. James P. Johnson, father of stride piano style. *Duncan Schiedt*

pects of Waller's style were continued in the playing of pianist-band-leader Count Basie. Waller wrote hundreds of tunes, the most familiar of which are "Ain't Misbehavin'," "Honeysuckle Rose," "Squeeze Me," and "Jitterbug Waltz."

In addition to ragtime and stride styles, early jazz piano developed **boogie woogie.** A prime characteristic of boogie woogie is the subdivision of each beat in the left-hand figures so that, in a measure of four beats, there are actually eight pulses in each measure ("eight to the bar"). If you hear a record of boogie woogie, you will have no trouble recognizing it immediately because it has been revived so many times that it has become a well-known and popular jazz piano style. Pianist Pinetop Smith actually entitled one of his tunes "Boogie Woogie" (*The Encyclopedia of Jazz on Records, Vol. 1*), and this piece was later adapted and popularized by trombonist Tommy Dorsey's swing era big band. The earliest leading boogie woogie pianists include Meade Lux Lewis (1929 "Honky Tonk Train Blues"), Pete Johnson, Albert Ammons, and Cow Cow Davenport (*Smithsonian Collection*).

Boogie woogie overlaps with another style in which there are eight pulses per bar, **honky tonk.** The terms honky tonk and boogie woogie are sometimes used interchangeably, but they often designate quite separate styles. The term honky tonk sometimes indicates an early rock and-roll style of guitar and piano playing which was extremely simple, repetitious, and technically undemanding. (Note: Many pieces recorded during the 1960s and 70s whose titles and lyrics contain the words "boogie" or "honky tonk" do not fit the meanings described here. Like much language in rapidly changing pop music, the meaning of these two terms depends on the user and the period of history.)

Cornet-Trumpet

In the early years of jazz the cornet was much more widely used than the trumpet. The trumpet's and cornet's tones and ranges are quite similar, and many listeners cannot tell the two instruments apart. Their appearance is also a confusing factor, but one distinguishing feature is the apparent length. The tubing of the cornet, although equal in length to that of the trumpet, is organized so that it looks shorter and stubby (see Figure 4.4). Some old jazz cornets are especially compact-looking.

The prime difference between trumpet and cornet, a difference that is difficult to see, is that the inside of the cornet's tubing is cone-like whereas the trumpet's is more cylinder-like. The technical term for the inside diameter is bore. So it is said that cornets have a primarily conical bore and trumpets have a primarily cylindrical bore. Although the instruments are played in almost the same way, their mouthpieces are slightly different. The tone color of the cornet is said to be mellow, and that of the trumpet is said to be more brilliant.

Except for Nat Adderly and Thad Jones, most modern players usually use trumpet instead of the cornet. Before 1927 nearly all jazz

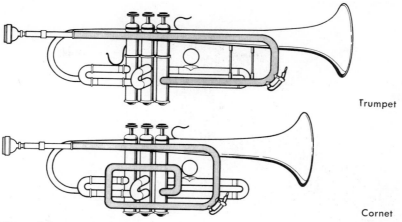

Trumpet

Cornet

Figure 4.4

trumpeters used the cornet, but after 1926 they began to adopt the trumpet. The 1930s and early 40s was a period of transition between the two instruments: every band had a so-called trumpet section, but in at least two famous bands, Duke Ellington's and Fletcher Henderson's, the trumpet section sometimes contained more cornets than trumpets. I prefer to ignore this problem and label most cornetists as trumpeters for the following reasons: (a) most listeners cannot detect the difference in sound; (b) it is often impossible to determine from recording data whether a player was using trumpet or cornet on a particular session; (c) the only player I am fairly certain used cornet exclusively throughout his career was Bix Beiderbecke; and (d) trumpet tone colors in jazz vary across a range far greater than that which separates the most pure of cornet from trumpet tones, and actually encompasses the pure tones of both.

Although the general public of the 1960s probably knew him more as the grinning entertainer who popularized the Broadway show theme "Hello Dolly," trumpeter **Louis Armstrong** is most significant to jazz history as a tremendously innovative force of the 1920s. His command of the trumpet was probably greater than that of any preceding jazz trumpeter. With warmth and assurance, Armstrong improvised melodic lines with a large, brassy tone and what, for the 1920s, was a remarkable high range. The sustained high note was one of his most effective dramatic devices.

Armstrong made his lines sound very natural. His work was thoughtful without sounding calculated. He was a master of pacing; he was always thinking ahead, calmly forging sensible lines which had both the flow of spontaneity and the stamp of finality. A superb sense of drama was evident in his double-time solo breaks and in his high-note endings. He also managed to break away from the melody of a piece and improvise original lines compatible with the tune's chord progressions. Armstrong's 1927 "Savoy Blues" and "Hotter Than That"

Figure 4.5. Louis Armstrong, age 70, July 4, 1970. *Bill Smith, Coda*

and his 1928 "West End Blues" show him to be a master craftsman (see Figure 4.5).

But Armstrong's most significant contribution was something else: he was one of the first jazz musicians to play with what became known as jazz swing feeling. Most jazz musicians before Armstrong played with enthusiasm, but seemed rhythmically stiff. Of course, their playing was not stiff when compared with march music or symphonic music, but it was stiff compared with Armstrong's. He loosened and relaxed the stiff approach, gave jazz lines a buoyancy and influenced the adoption of the swing eighth note (see Chapter 17).

Armstrong's early work is documented by recorded solos with numerous bands including King Oliver's, Clarence Williams's, Carroll Dickerson's and Fletcher Henderson's. But what have become his classic recordings were made by combos that he organized specifically for recording sessions rather than for tour. The records carried group names like "The Hot Five" and "The Hot Seven." The personnel from one Hot Five to another occasionally varied, but the instrumentation remained fairly constant: trumpet, piano, trombone, clarinet, and banjo or guitar. Usually there were no drums. His Hot Sevens were Hot Fives augmented by guitar, banjo, or tuba and drums.

Among the musicians on these early recordings were pianist Lil Hardin (Armstrong's wife, and pianist for King Oliver's band), pianist Earl Hines (see Figure 4.6), as well as former New Orleans associates: trombonist Kid Ory, clarinetist Johnny Dodds, guitarist Lonnie

Figure 4.6. Earl "Fatha" Hines, age 65. *Bill Smith, Coda*

Johnson, guitarist-banjoist Johnny St. Cyr, drummer Baby Dodds (brother of Johnny Dodds), and drummer Zutty Singleton (*Armstrong and Hines-1928, The Genius of Louis Armstrong, The Louis Armstrong Story, Vols. 1–4, The Smithsonian Collection of Classic Jazz*).

Through his melodic and rhythmic innovations, Armstrong directly influenced generations of jazz musicians, not only trumpeters, but players of all instruments. Armstrong probably influenced his own pianist, **Earl Hines,** who, prior to meeting Armstrong, had developed a system of right-hand playing, phrasing lines like a trumpet player. Some of his improvisations swung like Armstrong's. Hines also used double-time devices popularized by Armstrong (Earl Hines—*Monday Date*).

Hines voiced some lines in octaves, giving them an extra punch which, when combined with his horn-like phrasing, created what was called Hines's trumpet-style right hand (see Figure 4.7). These devices were not used in all his work, however. He blended stride approaches with flourishes and horn-like figures. Modern jazz piano of the 1940s was greatly indebted to techniques pioneered by Hines.

Jazz piano eventually moved away from the orchestrally pianistic one-man-band style of ragtime and stride to streamlined horn-like lines in the right hand and brief, syncopated chords in the left. (Technical note: Though the use of tenths in a pianist's left-hand style is usually associated first with Teddy Wilson, who emerged as a strong player of

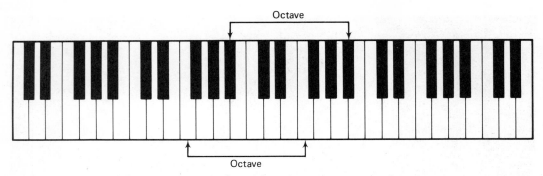

Figure 4.7. Piano keyboard illustration of octave intervals.

the 1930s, this technique was already evident in the 1920s recordings of Hines.)

Henry "Red" Allen was possibly the most harmonically advanced trumpeter of early jazz. Allen did not swing with the ease of Armstrong, but he was more adventurous harmonically. Almost eight years younger than Armstrong, Allen was also from New Orleans, and, like Armstrong, played with King Oliver in Chicago and Fletcher Henderson in New York. Allen's creative peak was during the mid-1930s, whereas Armstrong's was in the late 1920s. Allen can be classed as a transitional figure in the move from early jazz to modern jazz.

Red Allen had a dark, weighty tone and liked the trumpet's low register. His instrumental facility was exceptional, especially for the 1920s. His improvisational conception almost resembled a jazz sax style, a characteristic which later typified another transitional figure in the history of jazz trumpet, Roy Eldridge. Allen seemed to think more about harmonic complexity than about swinging, and though he swung, his timing was not constant. Sometimes he played ahead of the beat in a pre-Armstrong style, sometimes a little behind, like Armstrong himself. He double-timed creatively, and even when he was not double-timing, his phrases seemed based on a double pulse.

Allen anticipated modern jazz in several respects. He simultaneously displayed great authority and relaxation. Sometimes he repeated a phrase several times as though building up tension soon to be released in a stream of original phrases. In spite of his advanced knowledge of chord changes, Allen's lines were not totally modern. He interrupted his phrases to treat chords separately, and his improvisations clearly reflected the form of the tune, whereas modern jazz tended to openly reflect less and less of the chord changes and a tune's form. Allen's masterpiece was his 1935 recording of "Body and Soul" in which he demonstrated his most important characteristics as a jazz performer. He double-timed through much of his improvisation without sounding strained, though that same solo would certainly have been difficult for any other trumpeter of the period (*Luis Russell and His Louisiana Swing Orchestra, Trumpeter's Holiday*).

Figure 4.8. Bix Beiderbecke, age 18, August 30, 1921. *Duncan Schiedt*

Jabbo Smith was another innovative trumpeter whose style spanned the early jazz period and the swing era. He had outstanding proficiency and used a brassy, cutting tone and fast vibrato. Smith attacked his notes percussively and liked to place his lines in the trumpet's high register, higher than almost any other early trumpeter. That high range was essential to the outgoing style he developed. By the late 1930s, he could handle complex chord changes and improvise long, saxophone-like lines, as on his 1938 "Rhythm In Spain." In those respects, he was a precursor of Roy Eldridge (*Jazz Makers '38–40*).

A great white trumpeter-composer-bandleader from Iowa who can be classified with neither the New Orleans groups nor the Chicago groups, was **Bix Beiderbecke** (see Figure 4.8). He and Armstrong were the leading trumpeters during the late 1920s and early 1930s. Beiderbecke was almost as original and creative as Armstrong, but he had less command over his instrument and a bit cooler sound. Bix used a less brassy, lighter weight tone and had a softer texture than Armstrong. His rhythmic approach was also less outgoing. Like most early jazz players, he did not have pronounced jazz swing feeling when he began performing, but later he developed a swing feeling which approached that of Armstrong.

Beiderbecke joined saxophonist **Frankie Trumbauer** for several classic recording sessions. Their 1927 recordings of "Singin' the Blues" and "A Good Man Is Hard to Find" represent two of the most relaxed, melodic, and tender performances in early jazz. Trumbauer's instrument was a C-melody saxophone, which is approximately a size in between the alto and the tenor. It is capable of a very light-colored, light-weight tone. Trumbauer was a very precise and melodic soloist who employed what was an uncommonly slow vibrato for early jazz. Tenor saxophonist Lester Young, a significant figure in the beginnings of modern jazz, has said that he modeled his own light, cool tenor saxophone sound on the playing of C-melody saxophonist Trumbauer. Like Trumbauer, Young also used a slower vibrato than his contemporaries (*The Bix Beiderbecke Story Vol. 2—Bix and Tram, Smithsonian Collection*).

Beiderbecke was also a pianist and composer. His "In a Mist" is frequently cited as an example of the influence French impressionist composer Claude Debussy had on jazz. It is a very interesting composition which has been orchestrated by numerous jazz arrangers. Beiderbecke's own solo piano recording is especially effective (*The Bix Beiderbecke Story Vol. 3—Whiteman Days*).

Bobby Hackett was a trumpeter who emerged almost ten years after the creative peaks of Armstrong and Beiderbecke. He seems to belong in the early jazz category, however, because his playing had more in common with early trumpet styles than with later ones. Hackett was associated with several types of jazz between the 1930s and 70s. He had the grace and intelligence of Beiderbecke, but he played with a warmer tone and superior instrumental facility. Hackett's playing projected an ease and calm relaxation equaled by few other trumpeters.

Hackett's lines take into account nearly every chord in a progression. The primary notes of a progression are thoughtfully woven into a flowing line. His famous solo on the Glenn Miller big band's "String of Pearls" is an eloquent demonstration of how chord notes can be sequenced to form a logical line. His solo has frequently been written into published arrangements of the tune. It has become so much a part of the piece that trumpeters are usually not allowed to improvise their own solos, but required to quote Hackett's.

Hackett's trumpet style was compatible with a variety of different eras in jazz. He performed in Dixieland groups, swing era contexts, and during the 1950s and 60s he participated in many recordings in the "easy listening," "mood music," or "for lovers only" category (soft, slow trumpet playing with lush string backgrounds). He was a remarkably consistent player. Even in the non-jazz context of "for lovers only" records, he played tastefully (*The Hackett Horn*).

Trombone In ensemble improvisation, trombonists invented low harmony parts and filled in gaps with devices similar to those played by tuba and trombone in marching band music. With clarinet and trumpet filling out the middle and upper registers, trombone contributed to the combo sound in the lower range. When soloing, early trombonists tended toward a jazz trumpet conception to which they added the trombone's unique capacity for smears and slides. Rarely, however, did they play lines as intricate as those of early jazz trumpeters.

Kid Ory was one of the first notable New Orleans jazz trombonists. His husky tone and assertive presence were an important part of several early jazz combos. He had a hard, cutting tone and a percussive attack. His work had a boisterous air about it. Ory was also a composer and group leader. His "Muskat Ramble" (later spelled "Muskrat Ramble") became a jazz standard.

Miff Mole was from New York. He and Jack Teagarden were the leading white trombonists in early jazz. His tone was clear and well contained, and his command of the instrument was possibly the best of all early jazz trombonists. Mole's lines were choppy, with frequent wide leaps of range between notes. Melodically and rhythmically, Mole's conception resembled that of trumpeters Bix Beiderbecke and Red Nichols, men with whom he often recorded (*Thesaurus of Classic Jazz*).

Jack Teagarden was a trombonist from Texas who paid close attention to producing and maintaining a smooth, full tone which was prettier than that of most other premodern trombonists. His work projected a thoughtful, relaxed quality even though some of his favorite phrases were technically demanding. Teagarden's unique feeling and well-formed phrases were an inspiration to the trombonists of modern jazz. His style was possibly as important to jazz trombone history as Armstrong's was to trumpet. His career was long and productive, running from the 1920s until his death in 1964.

J. C. Higginbotham, a trombonist from Georgia, was a few years younger than Mole and had a larger, harder, weightier tone. Higginbotham projected a very hard-driving, confident presence. His solos bore a trumpet conception, sometimes sounding like Armstrong. The rhythms in his phrases were altered so that they did not possess the sameness to which others were prone. He seemed to be treating only one phrase at a time. His work had an overall sense to it. Though 1929 was probably his creative peak, he played until his death in the early 1970s (*Luis Russell and His Louisiana Swing Orchestra*).

Clarinet   Clarinet was more common than saxophone in early jazz. (This situation was drastically reversed during the 1940s when modern jazz emerged. Early jazz combos *without* clarinet were as rare as modern jazz combos with clarinet.) Clarinet usually played countermelodies around the trumpet. Clarinet solos were not usually as dramatic as the trumpet solos. Eventually, however, clarinetists were able to get away from a conception based on embellishment, and by the late 1930s, some early players and many swing era players were capable of dramatic, well-paced solo lines.

Johnny Dodds was one of the leading New Orleans clarinetists who moved to Chicago. He made a large number of recordings with King Oliver, Armstrong and pianist-composer Jelly Roll Morton there. He and Kid Ory were older than Armstrong, and in New Orleans had often hired him as a sideman but in Chicago, after Armstrong had achieved a large reputation, the leader/sideman roles were often reversed. Dodds had an edgy tone and very fast vibrato.

Jimmie Noone was a more polished player than Johnny Dodds and possessed a greater command of the clarinet. Some consider Noone to be the best New Orleans clarinetist. He had a dark, warm, round tone. He often played jumping staccato lines which had a lot of flash and verve. Noone was a favorite performer of leading white Chicago clarinetists Frank Teschemacher and Benny Goodman. Pianist Earl Hines and Noone made an excellent series of recordings in 1928 (*Jimmie Noone and Earl Hines "At the Apex Club"*).

Frank Teschemacher was the leading white Chicago clarinetist. His technique was excellent, and he swung a bit more loosely than Noone. He also had a somewhat lighter tone and slower vibrato (*The Chicagoans "The Austin High Gang," 1928–30*). Teschemacher and Benny Goodman, who became a popular soloist and band leader during the 1930s, both cited Jimmie Noone as a primary influence.

New Orleans clarinetist and soprano saxophonist **Sidney Bechet** was one of the most highly regarded musicians in early jazz. In addition to Armstrong, he was one of the first improvisers to display jazz swing feeling. Like Armstrong, he double-timed and created dramatic solos. Bechet had a big, warm tone with a wide and rapid vibrato. He was a very energetic, hard-driving improviser who played with broad imagination and authority. He died in 1959, having spent a large part of his career in France (see Figure 4.9).

As a soprano saxophonist (see Figure 4.10), Bechet influenced alto and soprano saxophonist Johnny Hodges, who in turn, influenced others. Hodges was featured with the Duke Ellington band for about forty years. His pre-1940s playing displayed some of the double-timing and ebullience of Bechet. For an example of Hodges's double-timing, listen to his solo on Ellington's 1940 recording of "In a Mellotone." For close comparison of the two soprano sax styles, play Bechet's 1938 "Really the Blues" back to back with Hodges's 1938 "Jeep's Blues" and Bechet's 1941 "When It's Sleepy Time Down South" (*Sidney Bechet Jazz Classics Vol. 1*, Sidney Bechet—*Master Musician*) with Hodges's 1938 "Empty Ballroom Blues" (*Hodge Podge*). Hodges later slowed down and smoothed out considerably but retained the smoothness of tone and extremely expressive inflections of pitch which he had learned from Bechet. During the 1960s, the soprano sax was resurrected by modern jazz saxophonist John Coltrane, one of whose tunes was entitled "Blues to Bechet."

Figure 4.9. Sidney Bechet playing soprano sax, age 53, 1950. *Duncan Schiedt*

Figure 4.10. Clarinet and soprano sax. *The Selmer Company*

Rhythm Section   The front line of most early jazz combos included trumpet, clarinet, trombone, and occasionally, saxophone. The rhythm section was made up of several instruments which might include guitar, banjo, tuba, bass saxophone, string bass, piano, and drums. No bands had all these instruments playing at the same time, but most drew some combination from that collection. It was not unusual for early jazz combos to be without string bass, and many early jazz recordings were made without drums. Some groups substituted tuba for string bass (eventually many tuba players learned to play string bass), and some used bass saxophone (see Figures 4.11 and 4.12). Groups often included both guitar and banjo, though some had only one of these. Usually one player alternated between the two instruments. Piano was absent from some recordings and replaced banjo and guitar on others, though usually both piano and banjo or guitar were used (see Figure 4.13).

    The banjo and guitar were often strummed all four beats of each measure. The tuba, bass sax, or string bass played on the first and third of every four beats. That meant they played on only two beats per measure, a style known as "two-beat" rhythm. Sometimes the pianist struck chords in unison with the guitar or banjo, sometimes he played embellishments instead. In many groups, the pianist created countermelodies while the front line instruments were playing melodies and countermelodies of their own. Comping as defined in "Appreciating Jazz Improvisation" did not begin until the late 1930s.

Figure 4.11. Tuba (Besson, BB♭). *The Selmer Company*

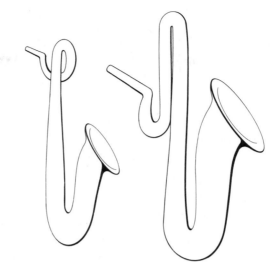

Figure 4.12. Baritone saxophone—Bass saxophone. Key mechanisms are omitted so that the distinctive differences in the sizes of the instruments and the shapes of the looped necks will be more readily apparent.

Figure 4.13. Guitar and banjo (note that the guitar has six tuning pegs, one for each string, and the banjo has four). Guitars appear in a variety of shapes. The one pictured here is a guitar used in early jazz. Electric guitars are usually solid slabs of wood with electronic attachments embedded. Basically, a banjo is a drum with a guitar-like neck and strings. The banjo commonly used in early jazz had four strings, but some banjos have as many as nine strings.

Early jazz drummers are not usually heard on records because early recording equipment was unable to handle the drums. Records were made by playing into acoustic recording horns, which looked like the horn that comes out of the phonograph in the famous picture of a dog listening to "His Master's Voice." The small end of the horn was connected to a cutting needle which made grooves in a cylinder or a disc. A blow to the bass drum or any other loud sound could literally knock the needle off the cutting surface. Many recordings consequently represent working bands minus their drummers. Occasionally you will hear the odd sound of a wood block or finger cymbals. Louis Armstrong's famous 1928 "West End Blues" recording was made with that poor substitute for drums. Not until the 1960s did jazz drummers receive anywhere near accurate recording and reproduction.

Although we do not know exactly how he sounded, we do know what kind of instruments the early jazz drummer played. He did not have a high-hat. He had a floor cymbal apparatus which enabled him to strike a cymbal with a foot pedal, but it did not allow him to achieve the "chick" sound possible with the high-hat. He also had a bass drum, almost marching band size, two to three times as large as that which became popular during the mid-1960s. A snare drum mounted on a stand and a cymbal suspended above the set were also at his disposal. Wood block and cow bell were attached to the bass drum.

New Orleans drummer **Warren "Baby" Dodds** (brother of clarinetist Johnny Dodds) has been credited with pioneering the use of the ride rhythm which he played on the snare drum. Later in jazz history, ride rhythms were played on the high-hat. Eventually, in the 1950s and 60s, they became the primary timekeeping rhythms, and drummers played them on the ride cymbal.

Arthur "Zutty" Singleton, another leading New Orleans drummer, was among the first to use wire brushes to strike his drums. Brushes did not totally replace sticks, but they offered a lighter, softer sound, as well as the capacity to produce sustained sounds if dragged across and around a drum head or cymbal. Zutty also pioneered the use of bass drum on all four beats of each measure. Many drummers had struck the bass drum primarily on the first and third beats. Singleton influenced George Wettling and Sid Catlett. Catlett played a transitional role in jazz, helping jazz drum conceptions move from early jazz to modern jazz.

Most guitarists confined themselves to timekeeping, or, at best, to simple, chorded solos. Solos were difficult to hear, anyway, because guitars had yet to be amplified. But New Orleans guitarist **Lonnie Johnson** did record several interesting, unamplified guitar solos which were not simple, chorded lines, but almost hornlike.

chapter 5
SWING:
THE EARLY 1930s
TO THE LATE 1940s

With the adoption of swing eighths, string bass, high-hat cymbals, and a looser, less stiff rhythmic feeling, jazz began to swing more. This was a gradual change which began during the late 1920s and continued into the 1940s. Jazz from this period is called swing music, and, since much of it was played by bands of ten or more men, it is often called the big band era. Much big band music was not improvised—it was written music—but hundreds of improvising musicians were employed in the big bands, so it was a good era for jazz. Some big bands, especially Count Basie's, placed great emphasis on improvisation, but numerous bands were not as concerned with jazz. These were the "sweet" bands of Guy Lombardo, Lawrence Welk, Blue Baron, Freddy Martin, Wayne King and others. Glenn Miller's, although a swinging band, was also classed in the "sweet" band category. There were big bands prior to the swing era (Fletcher Henderson, Duke Ellington, and Paul Whiteman, for example) and after the swing era (Dizzy Gillespie, Gerald Wilson, Stan Kenton, and Thad Jones–Mel Lewis, for example), but the swing era was a peak for the popularity of this instrumentation.

Though jazz had been danced to for most of its history, it functioned more as dance music during the swing era than before or since. Only occasionally did jazz musicians perform just for listening as later became customary for most jazz groups. Benny Goodman, however, gave a Carnegie Hall concert in 1938, and Duke Ellington began an annual series there in 1943.

During the 1930s and 40s, it seemed that almost every other big name jazz musician was leading or playing in a big band. In fact, big

TABLE 5.1. Swing Style Musicians—A Partial Listing

Composing—Arranging

Fletcher Henderson
Eddie Durham
Benny Carter
Sy Oliver
Don Redman
Duke Ellington
Billy Strayhorn
Eddie Sauter
Will Hudson
Budd Johnson
Edgar Sampson
Jimmy Mundy
Deane Kincaide

Drums

Jo Jones
Sid Catlett
Chick Webb
Gene Krupa
Sonny Greer
Cozy Cole
Louis Bellson
Buddy Rich
Dave Tough
Jimmy Crawford
Ben Thigpen

Trombone

Lawrence Brown
Dickie Wells
Trummy Young
Jimmy Harrison
Benny Morton
Vic Dickenson
Joe "Tricky Sam" Nanton
Bill Harris
J. C. Higginbotham
Jack Jenney
Tommy Dorsey

Saxophone

Coleman Hawkins
Johnny Hodges
Benny Carter
Willie Smith
Chu Berry
Herschel Evans
Dick Wilson
Ben Webster
Lester Young
Georgie Auld
Don Byas
Russell Procope
Illinois Jacquet
Hilton Jefferson
Tab Smith
Flip Phillips
Pete Brown
Buster Smith
Tex Beneke
Jerry Jerome

Boomie Richman
Vido Musso
Ernie Caceres
Earl Bostic
Joe Thomas
Budd Johnson
Jimmy Dorsey

Trumpet

Roy Eldridge
Cootie Williams
Bunny Berigan
Harry James
Buck Clayton
Charlie Shavers
Frankie Newton
Heny "Red" Allen
Oran "Hot Lips" Page
Harry "Sweets" Edison
Rex Stewart
Harold "Shorty" Baker
Jonah Jones
Taft Jordan
Jabbo Smith
Herman Autrey

Clarinet

Benny Goodman
Artie Shaw
Barney Bigard
Woody Herman
Buster Bailey
Jimmy Hamilton

Guitar

Django Reinhardt
Charlie Christian
Eddie Durham
Oscar Moore
Irving Ashby
Al Casey

Piano

Art Tatum
Teddy Wilson
Billy Kyle
Mary Lou Williams
Milt Buckner
Count Basie
Duke Ellington
Nat Cole
Erroll Garner
Clyde Hart
Johnny Guarnieri
Jay McShann
Mel Powell
Jess Stacy

Bass

Walter Page
Jimmy Blanton
John Kirby
Israel Crosby
Wellman Braud

Vibraharp

Lionel Hampton
Red Norvo

Adrian Rollini
Tyree Glenn

Bandleaders

Duke Ellington
Count Basie
Bennie Moten
Benny Carter
Chick Webb
Andy Kirk
Jay McShann
Cab Calloway
Tommy Dorsey
Benny Goodman
Jimmy Dorsey
Glenn Miller
Charlie Barnet
Boyd Raeburn
Woody Herman
Stan Kenton
Gene Krupa
Artie Shaw
Fletcher Henderson
Lionel Hampton
Bunny Berigan
Harry James
Earl Hines
Billy Eckstine
Jimmie Lunceford

bands were more common in the 1930s than jazz combos were in the 1950s and 60s. Big bands provided the popular music medium during the late 1930s that rock combos provided during the 1950s and 60s. The swing era was one of the few periods in jazz history when jazz had wide popular appeal. Count Basie's Decca recording of "One O'Clock Jump" sold over one million copies. Duke Ellington's "Mood Indigo" also did very well.

Like rock combos of the 1950s and 60s, a principal function for swing bands of the 1930s was to provide dance music. In addition nearly every band had at least one singer, and sometimes several. The lyrics of the songs, together with the personality and good looks of the singer, were primary attractions for a sizable portion of the big band audiences. The popular success of jazz during the swing era was partly a result of its appeal to the eyes and feet of fans instead of to the ears alone.

Big Band Instrumentation

Big bands were made up of ten or more musicians whose instruments fall into three categories: brass, saxophones, and rhythm section. The brass section included trumpets and trombones. Although saxophones are also made of brass, they are technically called woodwinds because they originated from instruments traditionally made of wood (clarinet, flute and oboe) and are played in the manner of traditional wooden instruments. Because most saxophonists also play clarinet, and both sax and clarinet have cane reeds attached to their mouthpieces, the sax section was often called the "reed section," a label which was retained in later decades even when saxophonists began adding flute, a non-reed instrument.

The alto and tenor saxophones were the most frequently used saxes, and, by the late 1930s, most bands had also adopted the baritone saxophone (see Figure 5.1). The soprano and bass saxophones were not especially common.

The sax section contained from three to five men. Saxophonists did not usually play one instrument to the exclusion of the others. Some men, for instance, were required to alternate from clarinet to alto and baritone saxophones. Eventually a section of two altos, two tenors, and a baritone became standard. The leader of the sax section, an alto saxophonist, sat in the middle, with the baritone on one end, tenor on the other.

The size of the trumpet section varied from two to five men, three being the standard number during the late 1930s and early 40s. The lead trumpeter was in the middle. The trombone section ranged from one to five men, two or three being standard. The lead trombonist was in the center.

The rhythm section ordinarily contained piano, guitar, bass, and drums. Rhythm guitar remained a part of Count Basie's band through

Figure 5.1. Alto (on left), tenor (on right), and baritone saxophones. *Barry Perlus*

the 1970s, but disappeared from most other big bands during the late 40s. Although the banjo had preceded the guitar in many bands, it dropped out of sight during the 1930s. Tuba had preceded string bass in some bands, but had been abandoned by the mid-1930s. Before the guitar and string bass became firmly established, guitarists were often required to alternate guitar and banjo, while bassists were required to alternately play both tuba (also called brass bass) and string bass (also called bass violin). The pianist in the rhythm section occasionally played melody instead of just chords and embellishments.

The growth of big bands was accompanied by an increase in the use of written arrangements, which had not been necessary with small combos. As bands became bigger, it was more difficult to improvise a respectable performance. Many big bands did succeed in playing without written arrangements, but eventually considerations of convenience and variety forced musicians to learn to read and write arrangements. A newcomer had much less difficulty adapting to a band whose materials consisted of written arrangements rather than memorized routines.

The compositional devices employed in a large portion of the arrangements were quite simple. Melodies were played by the entire band in unison or in harmony. Then jazz improvisation followed, accompanied both by the rhythm section and by figures scored for other members of the ensemble. The melodies and accompanying figures were passed from one section of the band to another. Saxes might state the A section, brass state the bridge, and so forth. In addition to pop tune melodies, arrangements often contained variations on those themes, some of which were actually as good as transcriptions of improvised solos. These were offered as passages for one section of the band to play while another remained silent or accompanied them. Sometimes, portions within the passages were passed back and forth, so that it sounded as though one section of the band posed a question and another section answered it. This technique, also common in other forms and eras of world music, is called question and answer, call and response, or antiphonal (an-TIFF-on-ull) style.

Short, simple, repeated phrases called riffs were used by some big bands as essential elements of their style. At times, different riffs were assigned to various sections of the band, and played antiphonally. Properly timed, these antiphonal passages could swing a band buoyantly and give jazz improvisation a good send-off. Sometimes entire arrangements were based on such riffs. Woody Herman's "Woodchopper's Ball," Count Basie's "One O'Clock Jump" and "Jumpin' at the Woodside" are well-known examples of that technique.

Bandleaders Some of the best swing bands were led by Fletcher Henderson, Count Basie, Duke Ellington, Jimmie Lunceford, Benny Goodman, Chick Webb, Cab Calloway, and Andy Kirk. Following this discussion are entire chapters devoted to Ellington and his musicians (Johnny Hodges, Cootie Williams, Ben Webster, Rex Stewart, etc.), and Basie and his musicians (Hot Lips Page, Buck Clayton, Sweets Edison, Dickie Wells, Lester Young, Herschel Evans, etc.). The Henderson and Ellington bands bridged the gap between the styles of early jazz and the swing approach. Each had begun during the early 1920s and grown larger and more sophisticated by the late 1930s.

A very large portion of great early jazz and swing era improvisers worked with **Fletcher Henderson** between the early 1920s and late 30s (see Table 5.2). Henderson's was an all-star band somewhat comparable to that of the all-star combos led by trumpeter Miles Davis between the late 1940s and late 60s (see Figure 5.2). Together with saxophonist-arrangers Don Redman and Benny Carter, pianist-arranger Henderson created big band arranging techniques which eventually became standard (*A Study in Frustration, The Complete Fletcher Henderson*). His style represented one major stream of big band jazz; Ellington's represented the other. In his arrangements, Henderson pitted saxes against brass. He also perfected techniques of block voicing, in

Figure 5.2. Fletcher Henderson Band, 1928. Left to right: Henderson, Benny Bailey, Benny Carter, Clarence Holiday (guitar), Coleman Hawkins (tenor saxophone), Kaiser Marshall (drums), Cootie Williams, Jimmy Harrison, Bobby Stark, unidentified trombonist, Rex Stewart. *Duncan Schiedt*

which the melody is the top voice of a series of chords in parallel motion (in other words, assigning notes in a chord to different instruments, rhythm of the melody played in unison by the entire band). It produced a thicker sound than if the line were not harmonized. Ellington used block voicing, but he also added an assortment of other special techniques (discussed in the next chapter). Part of Henderson's arranging reputation resulted from the Benny Goodman big band's use of his work on "King Porter Stomp," "Blue Skies," "Down South Camp Meeting," "Sometimes I'm Happy," "Japanese Sandman," "Wrappin' It Up" and "When Buddah Smiles."

TABLE 5.2. Musicians Prominent in the Fletcher Henderson Bands

Trumpet	Saxophone and Clarinet	Trombone
Louis Armstrong	Coleman Hawkins	Jimmy Harrison
Rex Stewart	Chu Berry	Charlie Green
Roy Eldridge	Don Redman	Dickie Wells
Tommy Ladnier	Benny Carter	J. C. Higginbotham
Cootie Williams	Ben Webster	Benny Morton
Joe Smith	Russell Procope	
Bobby Stark	Hilton Jefferson	
Henry "Red" Allen	Buster Bailey	
Emmett Berry	**Bass and Tuba**	
Drums	John Kirby	
	June Cole	
Sid Catlett	Bobby Escudero	
Kaiser Marshall	Israel Crosby	

Jimmie Lunceford was the nonplaying leader of one of the most polished-sounding big bands. His records placed more emphasis on ensemble playing than on improvising; jazz improvisation was more common in the Fletcher Henderson and Count Basie bands. One of Lunceford's biggest strengths was the team of arrangers writing for his band. Will Hudson, Eddie Wilcox, Gerald Wilson, and Sy Oliver all contributed good big band arrangements. Will Hudson's "Jazznocracy" and "White Heat," and Sy Oliver's "Swingin' Uptown" are attractive features which displayed the precise ensemble playing of the band (*The Smithsonian Collection of Classic Jazz, Willie Bryant and Jimmie Lunceford and Their Orchestras*). Sy Oliver later contributed several excellent arrangements to the big band of trombonist Tommy Dorsey. Lunceford also had Jimmy Crawford, one of the best swing era drummers.

Lunceford had good soloists, too. Willie Smith, Lunceford's lead alto saxophonist, is often ranked with Johnny Hodges (see Chapter 6) and Benny Carter (discussed later) as the best swing era altoists. Smith also had an interesting approach to jazz clarinet. Trumpeters Paul Webster, Eddie Tompkins, and Thomas Stevenson contributed solos with large, clear tones and confident, uncluttered conception. Lunceford's primary trombone soloist, Trummy Young, was also considered a better-than-average swing soloist, as was Joe Thomas, Lunceford's primary tenor sax soloist.

A distinctive feature in some Lunceford performances was unusually high trumpet playing. The style soon became essential to the excitement of the big band sound (notably in the work of Cat Anderson in Ellington's band and Maynard Ferguson in the Charlie Barnet and Stan Kenton bands). By the 1960s, the average high-register capability of big band trumpeters had improved considerably over that of early jazz trumpeters.

Clarinetist **Benny Goodman** led one of the most popular jazz-oriented big bands of the swing era (*Carnegie Hall Jazz Concert Vol. 1, The Complete Benny Goodman, Vol. 1, 1935*). The band was a showcase for his swinging, technically impressive clarinet playing (see Figure 5.3). In his performances, he also featured a few innovative swing era figures in small combo format. Guitarist Charlie Christian and pianist Teddy Wilson received much exposure in this way. Also featured by Goodman were tenor saxophonist Vido Musso, trumpeters Cootie Williams (see Chapter 6), Bunny Berigan, Harry James, vibraharpist Lionel Hampton, and drummer Gene Krupa, all of whom led their own bands at one time or another.

Goodman's use of drummer Gene Krupa as a soloist helped emancipate the drummer from his traditional, restricted role as only a time-keeper. Krupa was idolized and widely imitated, although he was not as advanced a rhythm section player as his contemporaries Jo Jones and Sid Catlett. His own rhythm section playing was a driving force in

Figure 5.3. Benny Goodman Band, 1936. Goodman (standing up front playing clarinet), Gene Krupa (drums); trumpets left to right: Nate Kazebier, Pee Wee Erwin, Chris Griffin; Jess Stacy (piano), Allan Reuss (guitar); reeds left to right: Hymie Schertzer and Bill DePew (both playing clarinet, alto sax in lap), Art Rollini (playing clarinet, tenor sax in lap), Dick Clark (playing bass clarinet, tenor sax and clarinet are on stand); trombones left to right: Red Ballard, Murray McEachern; Harry Goodman (bass). *Duncan Schiedt*

the Goodman band sound, however. A well-rehearsed, swinging band, Goodman's group lacked the easy, relaxed rhythmic feeling of the Count Basie band, and also seemed stiffer than the Andy Kirk band.

Another good big band was led by drummer **Chick Webb**. (*The Best of Chick Webb*). Trombonist Jimmy Harrison, trumpeter Taft Jordan, and saxophonists Benny Carter and Hilton Jefferson were all featured by Webb. One of the band's most valuable assets was saxophonist-arranger-composer Edgar Sampson, who composed "Stompin' at the Savoy," "Don't Be That Way," "Blue Lou," and "Lullaby in Rhythm" (all recorded by Benny Goodman).

Singer **Cab Calloway** led one of the most outgoing swing bands (*16 Cab Calloway Classics*). His group was known as a "hot" band and was influenced by Ellington's use of plunger mutes, growl style brass playing, and wailing reeds. Tenor saxophonist Chu Berry's best-known recording, "Ghost of a Chance," was made with the Calloway band. Vibraharpist-trombonist Tyree Glenn, who later joined Ellington, also played with the band. Calloway's rhythm section was excellent, with bassist Milt Hinton and drummer Cozy Cole. Trumpeters Jonah Jones and Dizzy Gillespie both played in the Calloway band. Gillespie contributed arrangements and exciting solo work which forecast the modern jazz he was to soon help launch.

Andy Kirk led one of the few swing bands which approached the easy, relaxed rhythmic style of Count Basie's band (*Clouds of Joy, Instrumentally Speaking*). Kirk's band was not as advanced nor as graceful as Basie's, yet their unpretentious air and simple but effective arrangements are reminiscent of Basie. The band had four first-class soloists: pianist Mary Lou Williams, tenor saxophonist Dick Wilson, and trumpeters Harold "Shorty" Baker and Howard McGhee. Baker was sporadically heard in the Duke Ellington band, and McGhee became a leading modern jazz trumpeter.

Composer-arranger-pianist **Mary Lou Williams** contributed substantially to the Kirk band. Like trumpeter Howard McGhee, she later incorporated elements of modern jazz and developed a style which spanned several jazz eras. Her solos were intelligent, well-executed musical statements that swung more smoothly and flexibly than early jazz piano styles.

Tenor saxophonist **Dick Wilson** had a muscular swing era style which closely resembled that of Coleman Hawkins, but he did not have the large quantity of ideas Hawkins had. (Hawkins is discussed later in this chapter.) He swung more comfortably than Hawkins and seemed a bit more relaxed, but his vibrato was just as fast. Wilson's tone was rougher than that of Herschel Evans (see Chapter 7) or Chu Berry (discussed later).

The **Glenn Miller** band, like hundreds of big bands in the swing era, had a few good jazz improvisers who were capable of swinging and soloing intelligently. Although Miller's band emphasized pretty arrangements and backgrounds for singers and vocal groups, tenor saxophonists Tex Beneke and Al Klink, and cornetist Bobby Hackett sometimes played jazz solos. (It was Hackett who played the famous solo on "String of Pearls.")

Tommy Dorsey developed a method of playing trombone which produced an extremely smooth, clear tone. His high-register work became the model for a later series of highly skilled trombonists who had glossy tones and meticulous technique (Urbie Green, Si Zentner, Carl Fontana, Bill Watrous, Phil Wilson, and others). One of his best big bands had tenor saxophonist Boomie Richman, trumpeter Charlie Shavers, and Sy Oliver, who contributed numerous arrangements ("Easy Does It," "We'll Get It," "Opus 1"). Dorsey also had powerful rhythm sections with such drummers as Louis Bellson, Buddy Rich, and Dave Tough.

Artie Shaw was an exceptionally explorative bandleader (*Artie Shaw Featuring Roy Eldridge, The Complete Artie Shaw, This Is Artie Shaw*). In addition to standard big band instrumentation, he also employed a string quartet (two violins, viola, and cello) in one of his bands, and led a combo, the Gramercy 5 (named for a telephone exchange—it was actually a sextet). Shaw composed some of his own material, which, especially in the string writing, was innovative for

1936. Throughout his career, Shaw had good sidemen: trumpeters Hot Lips Page (see Chapter 7) and Roy Eldridge (discussed next), tenor saxophonist Georgie Auld, pianists Johnny Guarnieri and Dodo Marmarosa. Shaw achieved considerable popularity; his 1940 "Frenesi" recording sold approximately four million copies. Shaw was also an accomplished clarinetist. His tone was bigger and smoother than Goodman's, and his solos were melodically more adventurous. But in spite of his advanced technique, Shaw did not seem to swing as much as Goodman.

Trumpet   Trumpeter **Roy Eldridge** was one of the most advanced improvisers of the swing era. He is often considered a link between swing and modern jazz. Eldridge had a very aggressive style and unprecedented instrumental proficiency. His imaginative choice of notes and sax-like lines provided continuity in the history of jazz trumpet from the style of Louis Armstrong to the modern approach pioneered by Dizzy Gillespie (see Figure 5.4). Listen to his advanced harmonic conception,

Figure 5.4. Roy Eldridge (wearing hat, playing Harmon muted trumpet), age 65, and Clark Terry (playing fluegelhorn), age 56. *Bill Smith, Coda*

pacing, and use of unusual intervals on the 1936 "Blues in C-sharp Minor," recorded with pianist Teddy Wilson and tenor saxophonist Chu Berry. Dizzy Gillespie displayed a pronounced Eldridge influence in his work with the Cab Calloway and Teddy Hill bands.

Eldridge creatively varied the size, texture, and vibrato of his tone. Sometimes it was clear and warm, at other times brittle and edgy. His high-register playing had a sweeping scope; in that register his entrances and syncopations were timed with a rhythmic feeling which suggested the modern jazz inflections that replaced early jazz rhythmic style. He was prominently featured with several big bands, including Fletcher Henderson's (*A Study in Frustration, The Complete Fletcher Henderson*), Gene Krupa's (*Drummin' Man*), and Artie Shaw's (*The Smithsonian Collection of Classic Jazz*). Listen to his blazing "After You've Gone," recorded with the Krupa big band (*Drummin' Man*). His most creative period was probably 1936–38, but he was still performing during the 1970s.

Charlie Shavers was another brassy swing trumpeter with outstanding instrumental proficiency (*Coleman Hawkins and the Trumpet Kings*). He had a brittle tone and quick vibrato. Rhythmically he was not as loose or relaxed as Buck Clayton or Hot Lips Page (see Chapter 7). Shavers improvised interrupted phrases of short, clipped notes, occasionally jumping into the high register for an exciting effect. Toward the middle and late 1940s, when he was in Tommy Dorsey's band, he showed a preference for saxophone-like phrasing and the high register that became standard in modern jazz trumpet.

The swing era had many good trumpeters, some of whom were original improvisers, but not especially famous. One of them was **Frankie Newton** (*Swinging on 52nd Street, Trumpeter's Holiday*). Manipulation of tone color was a primary aspect of the Newton style. He loved to create a variety of effects by use of growl style, an assortment of mutes, variations in rate of vibrato, and so forth. Newton exaggerated tonal effects more than Harry "Sweets" Edison, another trumpeter who also favored a variety of attacks and inflection. Newton's playing was characterized by short melodic fragments and repeated notes rather than the long, well-conceived lines of Roy Eldridge. Newton did have moments in which he maintained an idea over several measures with a skill comparable to Eldridge's, but he did not have as large a tone or as much conceptual continuity as Eldridge.

One of the most famous swing era trumpeters was **Bunny Berigan** (*Bunny Berigan and His Orchestra—the Great Dance Bands of the 30's and 40's*). His 1937 "I Can't Get Started" solo was well loved, and his improvisation in the Tommy Dorsey band's recording of "Marie" was transcribed and included in subsequent arrangements for other bands. Berigan was a very proficient trumpeter with a clear tone and remarkably clean articulation. He could play quite well in the trumpet's lowest register and still maintain a full, consistent tone in the high register. His playing seemed almost effortless because it was so relaxed and assured. Louis Armstrong's approach was evident as a source for Berigan's solo conception.

Saxophone The man generally considered to be the father of jazz tenor saxophone playing is **Coleman Hawkins** (see Figure 5.5). Prior to Hawk's arrival on the jazz scene in the 1920s, the saxophone had not attained much more than novelty instrument stature. Hawk's deep-toned, husky command of the horn brought it recognition. Tenor sax became one of the most popular instruments in jazz. In fact, for many people, tenor saxophone symbolizes jazz.

Hawk not only had a strong command of his instrument, he also had an advanced understanding of chord progressions. His lines reflected all the complexities of a tune's harmony. He devoured complex chord changes and filled his lines with intricate ornamentation, as his 1939 "Body And Soul" recording vividly demonstrates (*Body and Soul: A Jazz Autobiography, Smithsonian Collection*). Modern jazz hornmen of the 1940s and 50s usually had a highly developed understanding of chord progressions and harmony, but the harmonic sophistication displayed in Hawk's solos was unusual in the 1920s and 30s.

From 1923 to 1934, Hawk was a featured soloist with the Fletcher Henderson band (*A Study in Frustration, The Complete Fletcher Henderson*). After that he worked mostly with small groups. Though primarily associated with the swing era, he was also a respected figure at modern jazz sessions of the 1940s. In spite of the fact that he lacked the smoothness and fluid swing of modern jazz soloists, his skill with difficult chord progressions helped him adjust to newer styles. A surging energy continued to flow unquenched from his horn for decades. Hawkins was one of the most intense and consistent saxophone soloists in jazz history.

Hawkins not only influenced his swing era contemporaries—Chu Berry (discussed next), Ben Webster (see Chapter 6), Don Byas (discussed later), Dick Wilson (see Andy Kirk section), and Herschel Evans (see Chapter 7)—but also such modern tenor saxophonists as Sonny Rollins and John Coltrane. His influence declined after the 1940s, but he remained an active performer, exhibiting terrific vitality, until his death in 1969.

Chu Berry was a great tenor saxophonist who was influenced by Hawkins and also played with Fletcher Henderson. Berry had a smoother, more uniform tone quality than Hawkins, swung more gracefully, and created lines which were less ornamented than those of Hawkins. Berry's tone was very deep and full; it just seemed to roll out of his saxophone. Berry became well known for his improvisations on "Ghost of a Chance," which he performed with Cab Calloway's big band (*16 Cab Calloway Classics*).

Figure 5.5. Coleman Hawkins, age 45, 1949. *Duncan Schiedt*

Don Byas, together with Lester Young (see Chapter 7), was more advanced than most swing tenor men and could hold his own with many modern jazzmen of the late 1940s (*The Greatest of Dizzy Gillespie, Smithsonian Collection*). Byas incorporated the harmonic advances made by Hawkins, as well as elements of Art Tatum's complex piano style (discussed later in this chapter). Byas had fire, technical proficiency, harmonic sophistication, and melodic daring. He loved to double-time and run through every note in each chord. More significant was his tendency to add new chords to a tune, and to use both the original and new chords in his improvisations. The richness of his lines easily matches that of many solid 1950s modern jazz saxophonists. Byas swung more easily than Hawkins, but not quite as easily as Lester Young or the modern jazz players of the late 1940s.

It is difficult to classify the Byas style neatly in either the swing or modern period. In fact, some of his best recorded solos were made with modern jazz trumpeter Dizzy Gillespie (1947 "52nd Street Theme"). Two of the most amazing recordings made during the swing era were the 1945 "Indiana" and "I Got Rhythm" performances by bassist Slam Stewart and Byas. These recordings represent the creative peak of Byas's career. The Byas style provided a model for the modern tenor style of Lucky Thompson. Byas remained active for several decades and died in 1973.

Benny Carter, with Willie Smith and Johnny Hodges (see Chapter 6), was one of the leading alto saxophonists of the swing era (*Alto Saxes*). Both Hodges and Carter had rich, deep, full-bodied tones, but the two players had different rhythmic styles. Carter tended to subdivide the beat precisely and evenly into legato eighth notes. Hodges had a more natural rhythmic feel and the placement of notes in relation to the beat was far less obvious in Hodges's playing. Though both Carter and Hodges imparted a luxurious feel to their playing, Carter was more obvious in his constructions, Hodges more subtle. And Hodges had a strikingly original way of placing accents, which set him apart from most swing and early jazz players. His style of accenting was unusual and imaginative, but he made it sound easier and more natural than it was. Both Hodges and Carter swung easily, and Carter paved the way for modern jazz alto sax styles with his intelligently conceived, harmonically oriented solos.

Carter was also a good trumpeter, clarinetist, and a top-notch arranger. He contributed arrangements to several good bands, including his own, Fletcher Henderson's, McKinney's Cotton Pickers, Benny Goodman's, Chick Webb's, and during the 1960s, Count Basie's.

Toward the end of the swing era (early 1940s), tenor saxophonist **Illinois Jacquet** emerged with a style that employed exciting high-note devices. Although at one time considered unmusical by some listeners, Jacquet's high-note devices became central to a number of leading 1960s and 70s saxophone styles, notably Albert Ayler's and John Coltrane's. Ayler and Coltrane incorporated the devices more logically into a solo's framework, however. Jacquet was brought to public attention by his solo on "Flying Home" with the Lionel Hampton big band. He drew from the heavy weight, dark colored tone and style common to Herschel Evans and Dick Wilson, although his lines occasionally displayed elements of Lester Young's rhythmic and melodic conception. Though often found in the context of modern players, Jacquet's playing fits within advanced swing era style (*Illinois Jacquet*).

Piano   **Art Tatum** was one of the most widely admired pianists in jazz history (*Art Tatum Masterpieces, Piano Starts Here, Smithsonian Collection*). Even compared with all the very fast, imaginative modern pianists who have emerged since the 1940s, Tatum still stands out with his incredible power and technical facility (see Figure 5.6). His style contains elements of stride piano combined with horn-like lines. Tatum's playing was quite flowery, with long, fast runs which sometimes overlapped each other. He was important in the development of modern jazz because he became a master at spontaneously adding and changing chords in pop tunes. Another device of his, picked up by

Figure 5.6. Art Tatum, age 39, 1949. *Duncan Schiedt*

modern alto saxophonist Charlie Parker and trumpeter Dizzy Gillespie, was to change keys several times within a phrase and still resolve the harmonic motion, neatly getting out of what often seemed like a precarious position.

The fast lines and added chords of Tatum were a direct influence on tenor saxophonist Don Byas, another swing era figure prominent in the transition from swing to modern jazz. Tatum was also an influence on the innovative modern jazz pianist Bud Powell who, in turn, influenced countless pianists of the 1950s. Oscar Peterson picked up techniques from both Tatum and Powell. Peterson is often compared with Tatum, not because they sound alike, but because Peterson has come closer than anyone else to achieving Tatum's impressive pianistic speed and power.

Tatum was not a band pianist (neither is Peterson), but he appeared as an unaccompanied soloist and as the leader of a piano–bass–guitar combo. His bassist on many recordings was **Slam Stewart,** who was a good timekeeper, a responsive accompanist for Tatum's melodic flights, and an inventive soloist. During solos, Stewart often bowed the strings while he hummed in unison (or in octaves). The combination of voice and bass produced a rough-textured and original tone color.

He humorously slid from note to note, but always managed to make as much melodic sense as most swing hornmen. Stewart's solo playing moved jazz bass a step further away from its rigid role of being only a timekeeper.

With the exception of Tatum, **Teddy Wilson** was probably the most innovative pianist in the swing era (*Teddy Wilson and His All Stars*). He, too, contributed to the development of modern jazz (see Figure 5.7). In fact, his lighter lines probably had a more direct effect on such modern pianists as Al Haig, Hank Jones, and Tommy Flanagan than did Tatum's playing. Wilson could be flowery also, but when he chose to create horn-like lines, he refined the best of Earl Hines. Wilson's work on the 1936 "Blues in C-sharp Minor" (*Teddy Wilson and His All Stars*) provides an excellent demonstration of his precisely executed, intelligently conceived horn lines. The whole feeling of Wilson's sound was that of lightening the early jazz and swing weightiness, and making way for the fleet smoothness and streamlined quality of modern jazz piano soloing and comping.

Figure 5.7. Teddy Wilson (with Arvell Shaw on bass). *Duncan Schiedt*

Wilson was featured in Benny Goodman's small combos (*Carnegie Hall Jazz Concert Vol. 1, The Complete Benny Goodman Vol. 1*) and in his own bands. Like Tatum, Wilson is often mistaken for the type of pianist who usually plays in cocktail lounges and is referred to as a cocktail pianist. This is partly due to the pleasantness of his style. Both Tatum and Wilson influenced countless cocktail pianists but do not themselves fall into this category. As their 1930s and 40s recordings show, melodic meat, variety, swing, and refinement distinguish Wilson and Tatum from the hundreds of less gifted players who have absorbed portions of their styles.

Techniques of Earl Hines were especially evident in the early 1940s work of **Nat Cole** and Erroll Garner, who were also important figures in the transition from swing era styles to modern jazz. Cole was one of the first pianists to extensively incorporate spare, hornlike lines in his playing, which exhibited a lightness not typical of the heavy-handed and flowery styles of premodern jazz. Cole also perfected a style of accompanying in which chords are played in brief, syncopated bursts, a style which eventually became known as comping. (He was later prominent as a pop singer, using the name of Nat King Cole.) Oscar Peterson, Bill Evans, and Horace Silver have all cited Cole as an early influence on their own musical thinking. In fact, Cole had a more pervasive influence than most people realize. His piano style received little attention after he became a popular singer, and it is often overlooked because of that.

Erroll Garner is a unique figure in jazz piano history. It is difficult to classify him as either a swing era or a modern jazz musician, although he attained a very large audience during the height of modern jazz's first wave, and he recorded with alto saxophonist Charlie Parker, a leader in founding modern jazz. Hines's influence was evident in Garner's octave-voiced right hand lines and rhythmic conception. Other aspects of Garner's style were more unique. His left hand usually played a chord on each beat as a rhythm guitarist might, but a bit behind the beat. Some of Garner's piano playing is richly orchestral, less like jazz than like the twentieth-century classical (French Impressionist) music of Claude Debussy and Maurice Ravel.

Though not notably innovative as a creater of melodic lines, **Milt Buckner** influenced pianists of the 1940s through his use of block chording, or the so-called locked-hands style (*Lionel Hampton—"Steppin' Out"*). In this style the pianist plays chords in parallel motion, one chord for each note of the melody. This is in contrast to a style of playing in which one hand plays a single melodic line, while the other plays occasional chords. In locked hands style the pianist uses both hands as though they were locked together, all fingers striking the piano keyboard at the same time. During the late 1940s and early 50s Lennie Tristano, George Shearing, Ahmad Jamal, Oscar Peterson, and others used this technique, as did Red Garland and Bill Evans in the late 1950s. During the 1960s many pianists, including

McCoy Tyner, made use of block chording. Each pianist's technique of block chording, particularly the voicings employed, was a distinctive aspect of his style. James P. Johnson, Willie "The Lion" Smith, and other early pianists had contributed the stride style. Earl Hines was a pioneer in playing horn-like lines. Meade Lux Lewis, Pinetop Smith, Cow Cow Davenport, and others introduced boogie woogie. Tatum had explored reharmonization. Milt Buckner added locked hands style to the list of alternatives available to the modern jazz pianist.

Guitar   During the swing era, guitar was beginning to be viewed as more than a timekeeping member of the rhythm section. Part of this change was due to work done by Charlie Christian and Django Reinhardt. **Charlie Christian** mastered what was then the almost unexplored world of electric guitar (*Charlie Christian, Joe Guy & Lips Page/Trumpet at Minton's, Solo Flight—The Genius of Charlie Christian*). His long, swinging, single-note-at-a-time lines became models for modern jazz guitarists. Some of his phrasing had the fluid swing and freshness of tenor saxophonist Lester Young (see Chapter 7). Christian was featured with the Benny Goodman combos and big band. His work is also available on some amateur recordings of jam sessions with modern jazz trumpeter Dizzy Gillespie and pianist Thelonious Monk. Christian died in 1942 at the age of twenty-one, having been an active influence for no more than three years.

Django Reinhardt was a Belgian Gypsy guitarist who had at least as much influence on modern jazz guitar playing as Charlie Christian. Reinhardt rarely visited America, but his recordings were available here. Prior to Reinhardt, most jazz guitarists had played brief, chorded solos which were quite modest compared to piano and horn solos. Reinhardt had a technical command of his guitar equal to Art Tatum's virtuoso piano technique. In fact, both men were fond of fast, flashy, cleanly executed lines. Reinhardt's playing was ornate and flamboyant with a prominent vibrato (*The Best of Django Reinhardt, Swing It Lightly*). He combined the spirited flavor of Gypsy music with the equally spirited sound of jazz. His lines could have the intelligence of a master composer or simply could be a sequence of flourishes. Like the great modern jazz alto saxophonist Charlie Parker, Django created music which often seemed greater than life.

Reinhardt's influence on American musicians reversed a typical pattern. Being primarily an American art form, jazz was usually exported rather than imported. Although there have been good European jazz musicians since the 1920s (clarinetist Hubert Rostaing; violinists Stephane Grappelly and Jean Luc Ponty; pianists Bengt Hallberg and Martial Solal; bassist Neils Henning Orsted Pedersen, trombonist Albert Mangelsdorff; tenor saxophonists Tubby Hayes and Ronnie Scott, and others), few have influenced American players. (In the late 1960s and 70s, however, several European musicians, including Austrian pianist-composer Joe Zawinul and Czechoslovakian bassist Miroslav Vitous came to the United States and began influencing new developments in modern jazz.)

Reinhardt's style is difficult to classify because its most prominent traits seem to transcend idiom. Considered a part of the swing era, before and during the time of Charlie Christian's activity, he also explored modern jazz concepts in the late 1940s and early 50s.

TABLE 6.1. Duke Ellington Band Alumni—A Partial Listing

Clarinet and Saxophones

Rudy Jackson
Barney Bigard
Jimmy Hamilton
Russell Procope
Willie Smith
Otto Hardwicke
Johnny Hodges
Harry Carney
Ben Webster
Al Sears
Paul Gonsalves
Harold Ashby

Drums

Sonny Greer
Louis Bellson
Sam Woodyard
Rufus Jones

Trumpet

Louis Metcalf
Bubber Miley
Arthur Whetsol
Cootie Williams
Rex Stewart
Taft Jordan
Ray Nance
Willie Cook
Cat Anderson
Clark Terry
Harold "Shorty" Baker
Johnny Coles
Money Johnson

Trombone

Joe "Tricky Sam" Nanton
Lawrence Brown
Juan Tizol
Britt Woodman

Quentin "Butter" Jackson
Tyree Glenn
Buster Cooper

Bass

Wellman Braud
Billy Taylor
Jimmy Blanton
Oscar Pettiford
Wendell Marshall
Jimmy Woode
Aaron Bell
Ernie Shepard

Piano

Duke Ellington
Billy Strayhorn

chapter 6
DUKE ELLINGTON

Duke Ellington is regarded as one of the most outstanding figures in jazz history by hundreds of musicians and jazz journalists. He was not only a bandleader and pianist, but also probably the single most creative and prolific composer-arranger in jazz history. He wrote over a thousand tunes and probably one and one-half times that number of arrangements and rearrangements. He began composing and arranging well before 1920 and continued until his death in 1974. By the late 1970s, with several companies repackaging his past performances, more than 150 Ellington band albums had appeared (see Figure 6.1).

Pianist   Although piano playing was the least of his great talents, Ellington was both a flashy and original solo player in the percussive stride style of James P. Johnson and Willie "The Lion" Smith. As an accompanist he developed a spare manner which framed phrases in arrangements and embroidered the solos of his sidemen. Ellington's piano playing was full of vitality and imagination.

Composer   Ellington wrote many tunes which, with the addition of lyrics, became popular songs, such as "Satin Doll," "Sophisticated Lady," "I'm Beginning to See the Light," "Solitude," "Mood Indigo," and "Don't Get Around Much Anymore." He also wrote hundreds of three-minute instrumentals such as "Concerto for Cootie," "In a Mellotone," and "Black and Tan Fantasy." The lengths of these pieces average three minutes because that was standard time length for one side of a 78 rpm record, the primary recording medium until the early 1950s (*In A Mellotone, This Is Duke Ellington*).

Figure 6.1. Duke Ellington and Billy Strayhorn. *Duncan Schiedt*

Ellington also wrote many longer pieces, including "Creole Rhapsody," "Reminiscing in Tempo," "Harlem," "New World a' Comin'," etc. He even wrote a fifty-minute tone parallel to the history of the American Negro ("Black, Brown and Beige").

Ellington composed and his band played several film scores (movie sound tracks): *Paris Blues, Anatomy of a Murder, Asphalt Jungle, Assault on a Queen,* and *Change of Mind.*

Many of Ellington's pieces depict real personalities: "Bojangles" (the famous black tap dancer, Bill Robinson),* "A Portrait of Bert Williams" (a leading black comic), and "Portrait of the Lion" (Willie "The Lion" Smith, a great stride pianist).

Other pieces paint musical pictures of places and sensations: "Warm Valley," "Harlem Air Shaft," and "Transbluency" (*At His Very Best—Duke Ellington and His Orchestra, The Smithsonian Collection of Classic Jazz, This Is Duke Ellington*). Ellington composed the entire 11½-minute "Perfume Suite" (*The Indispensable Duke Ellington*), not to describe the various labels of the commercial perfumes, but rather to delineate the character a woman assumes under the influence

* Not the "Mr. Bojangles" by Jerry Jeff Walker that became popular during the early 1970s, though both the Ellington piece and the pop tune were inspired by Bill Robinson.

of them. He also put together an album inspired by Shakespeare sonnets: *Such Sweet Thunder*.

Nearly every jazz musician has played at least one Ellington tune during his career. The respect Ellington received from other jazz musicians is demonstrated by the fact that no other jazz composer has had as many albums devoted to his music. A partial list of musicians who made albums of Ellington tunes includes Thelonious Monk, McCoy Tyner, Kenny Burrell, Oscar Peterson, Andre Previn, Chico Hamilton, and Dave Brubeck. Composer-arranger Clare Fischer and trumpeter Dizzy Gillespie also collaborated on an album of Ellington tunes. A vocal group—Lambert, Hendricks, and Ross—recorded an entire LP of transcriptions of famous Ellington recordings; they provided lyrics for both the written and improvised lines.

Ellington's impact was so far-reaching that even Archie Shepp, a tenor saxophonist considered avant-garde during the 1960s, included Ellington tunes in his recordings: "I've Got It Bad and That Ain't Good," "In a Sentimental Mood," "Come Sunday," "Prelude to a Kiss," and "Sophisticated Lady."

Numerous jazz composers have written tunes dedicated to Ellington. Among them are Charles Mingus ("Duke's Choice," recorded in 1957 for Bethlehem records, "Open Letter to Duke," recorded in 1959 for Columbia records), Miles Davis ("He Loved Him Madly," recorded in 1974 for Columbia records), and Dave Brubeck ("The Duke," recorded for Columbia several times by Brubeck during the 1950s and once by Miles Davis and Gil Evans in 1957).

Arranging Style

One of Ellington's greatest skills as an arranger was that of capitalizing on the uniquely personal sounds of individual players. Instead of writing for an anonymous group of instruments ("lead trumpet, second trumpet, third trumpet," etc.) as most arrangers do, he actually wrote parts suited to particular players (Cat Anderson, Cootie Williams, Rex Stewart, etc.). He carried this technique one step further by indicating sections of each piece where certain players were to improvise solos accompanied by prewritten ensemble passages. Ellington matched the improviser with the ensemble so carefully that the resulting sound was unusually effective, and his sidemen improvised so thoughtfully that it was often difficult to know which parts were improvised and which were written.

Ellington led what is called a big band. This is a group of ten or more players consisting of a brass section (including trumpets and trombones), a saxophone section, and a rhythm section. By 1940 Ellington's sax section contained two altos, two tenors, and one baritone saxophone. Prior to the 1940s, Ellington's bands were often smaller (three saxes instead of five, one or two trumpets, one or two trombones). Most of the saxophonists doubled on clarinet, and the baritone saxophonist usually played bass clarinet as well. Ellington's rhythm section included piano (himself), bass, drums, and until 1947, rhythm guitar.

While most arrangers, including Ellington, write passages that pit the sound of one section against that of another (sax section against brass section, for instance), Ellington often wrote passages to be played by combinations of instruments drawn from different sections of the band. This is called voicing (or scoring) across sections. In his 1940 "Concerto for Cootie" (*Smithsonian Collection*), Ellington voiced pizzicato bass notes in unison with the horns. On Ellington's 1940 "Jack the Bear" (*At His Very Best—Duke Ellington and His Orchestra*), bassist Jimmy Blanton played pizzicato melody statements both alone and with horns. Voicing across sections was unusual in most 1930s and 40s big bands; the bass was primarily a member of the rhythm section and rarely played horn parts.

In his 1930 "Mood Indigo," Ellington voiced bass clarinet with muted trumpet and muted trombone; this is an example of combining instruments from three different sections of the band, trumpet section, trombone section, and sax section. Bass clarinet was played by baritone saxophonist Harry Carney (*This Is Duke Ellington*). During the late 1950s, Ellington achieved an unusual color by voicing clarinet (Jimmy Hamilton) with tenor sax (Paul Gonsalves) and fluegelhorn (Clark Terry). The three instruments played unison lines while three trombones accompanied them with punching back-up figures (*Cosmic Scene;* "Newport Up," 1956 *Ellington at Newport;* and "Idiom '59," 1959 *Festival Session*).

Occasionally Ellington added another unique tone color by placing a wordless vocal (also called instrumentalized voice) in an arrangement. His 1927 "Creole Love Call" (*This Is Duke Ellington*), 1946 "Transbluency" (*At His Very Best—Duke Ellington and His Orchestra*), and 1947 "On a Turquoise Cloud" all use wordless vocals. "Transbluency" combines muted trombone with wordless vocal, and, later in the arrangement, clarinet is paired with the vocal. His "On a Turquoise Cloud" blends vocal, clarinet, and muted trombone; vocal, bass clarinet (Harry Carney), and violin (played by trumpeter Ray Nance) are combined in another passage.

One of the Ellington band's first important jobs was playing at the Cotton Club in New York where the floor shows placed great emphasis on "jungle sounds." To create these sounds, Ellington used the growl style associated with trumpeter Bubber Miley and trombonist Joe "Tricky Sam" Nanton. The growls were achieved by a combination of mutes and unorthodox methods of blowing. The most common mute was a plumber's plunger (rubber suction cup, also known as a plumber's helper). This was used to open and close the bell of the horn. Occasionally an additional mute was secured inside the horn's bell, lending a buzz to the sound. Voice-like effects were created by Miley and Nanton in this way. The growl style could be very expressive.

Other elements of the jungle sound were supplied by certain voicings of clarinets. Sometimes everyone in the sax section would be playing clarinet at the same time. Ellington assigned notes to each clarinet which, in combination, produced unusual harmonies and wailing, intensely emotional effects. Together with his unorthodox practice of voicing across sections and his use of the growl styles, these clarinet techniques added to the broad color range of his sophisticated big band arranging style.

Though voicing across sections was one of Ellington's strongest contributions to big band writing style, he also scored imaginative passages that pitted saxes against brass. In the sixth chorus of his 1940 "Cottontail," he pits brass against saxes, assigning musical questions to the brass and answers to the saxes. Then on the bridge, the brass take over and the saxes are silent. On the final A section, trumpets are paired with saxes for the melody statement. The entire arrangement exhibits many typical swing era big band techniques, but all are applied in the unique Ellington manner. There always seems to be a bit more imagination, more variety, and fewer clichés in Ellington's writing. Find a copy of the 1940 "Cottontail" (*This Is Duke Ellington*) recording and listen while you study this guide:

First Chorus

A   Melody stated by saxes and trumpets with rhythm accompaniment.

A   Sax and trumpet melody repeated with trombone section figures added to the accompaniment.

B   Saxes ask musical questions, muted trumpet (Cootie Williams) answers them.

Four-Measure Interlude

This consists of a brief conversation between the sax section and brass section with rhythm accompaniment.

Second Chorus

AA   Improvised tenor sax solo (Ben Webster) with rhythm accompaniment.

B   Tenor sax talks for a while with the brass section.

A   Brass depart, leaving tenor to continue improvising with rhythm section accompaniment.

Third Chorus

AA   Tenor continues improvisation accompanied by rhythm section.

B   Brass return to talk more with tenor sax.

A   Brass depart and tenor finishes his improvisation accompanied by rhythm section.

Fourth Chorus

AA   Brass play alone, accompanied by rhythm section.

B   Improvised baritone sax solo (Harry Carney) accompanied by rhythm section.

A   Improvised piano solo accompanied by rhythm guitar, bass, and drums.

Fifth Chorus

AABA   Sax section plays the whole chorus accompanied by rhythm section.

Sixth Chorus

AA   Brass section shouts questions and sax section answers, accompanied by rhythm section.

B   Brass section takes over loudly with rhythm section steaming forward.

A   Saxes and trumpets play the melody to its end with rhythm section accompaniment and no trombones.

In many ways the Ellington band created its own jazz idiom. Its earliest recordings had characteristics in common with early jazz, and its later recordings displayed elements of swing and modern jazz. But the evolution of the band did not closely mirror the evolution of jazz, or even the evolution of big band jazz. In its style and in jazz history, it is unique.

During the 1940s, Ellington's writing influenced Charlie Barnet's band and Woody Herman's band. Herman's band even recorded with Ellington sidemen. Gil Evans used Ellington techniques in writing for the recordings of Claude Thornhill and Miles Davis. During the 1950s and 60s, Ellington's influence could be heard in the compositions and arrangements of Charles Mingus, Sun Ra, George Russell, Clare Fischer, and Lalo Schifrin. And it is quite likely that his piano style influenced such modern jazz pianists as Thelonious Monk and Cecil Taylor.

Sidemen   Duke Ellington's band was one of the first big bands. In fact, Ellington, Fletcher Henderson, and Don Redman are often considered largely responsible for the birth of big band jazz. Ellington not only helped create the big band idiom, but also led the most long-lived and stable band in jazz. He started in 1923 and never broke up his band. Many players remained with him for twenty to thirty years at a stretch (see Table 6.1). Drummer Sonny Greer remained with Ellington from

1919 until 1951. Baritone saxophonist Harry Carney played with him from 1927 until Ellington's death in 1974. Carney himself died five months later.

Nearly all the members of Ellington's band had strong, unique styles of their own; together they made up an all-star unit. Most of Ellington's soloists were exceptionally deliberate players. Their self-pacing was nearly always tasteful. Thoughtfully constructed improvisations were the rule. In certain arrangements their solos often became crystallized and then recurred almost note for note in subsequent performances. These pieces then became much like written compositions, entirely unimprovised.

Clarinetist **Barney Bigard** and his successor Jimmy Hamilton are considered by some to be as creative as Benny Goodman and other swing era clarinetists. Both Bigard and Hamilton developed unique styles based on their excellent command of the clarinet. (Both men doubled on tenor saxophone, also.) Bigard brought an expansiveness to the feeling of an Ellington piece. His long, sweeping, legato lines swooped and darted through the ensemble sound. Listen to his contributions on Ellington's 1940 "Jack the Bear" and "Harlem Air Shaft" (*At His Very Best—Duke Ellington and His Orchestra*). Or study his improvisation in the 1936 "Clarinet Lament" (*The Ellington Era Vol. 1*), which Ellington wrote especially for him. His was a New Orleans style adapted to the swing era.

Jimmy Hamilton is an original improviser with a style less intense than Bigard's. His sound is well manicured and lighter than most swing clarinet sounds. Hamilton's conception is precise and articulate, with a cool, floating quality that suggests elements of modern jazz. Listen to his work on the 1956 Bethlehem records he made with Ellington (*Duke Ellington—The Bethlehem Years Vol. 1*), the 1956 and 1958 Newport Jazz Festival LPs (*Newport 1958, Ellington at Newport*), and Ellington's 1959 *Festival Session*.

Clarinetist **Russell Procope,** not featured extensively until Hamilton left the band, displayed an excited, thick-toned style with fast vibrato. Procope had played alto saxophone with the John Kirby Sextet before he joined Ellington. Although with Kirby he played in a swing era style, his approach in Ellington's band was far more like New Orleans clarinet than like swing, and his vibrato was as fast as Sidney Bechet's. Listen to his duet with Jimmy Hamilton on Ellington's "The Mooch" (*Hi-Fi Ellington Uptown*), his solo on "Idiom '59" (Ellington—*Festival Session*), or his feature, "Swamp Goo" (*The Greatest Jazz Concert in the World*).

Bubber Miley was a respected contemporary of such outstanding early jazz trumpeters as Tommy Ladnier, Louis Armstrong, Jabbo Smith, Henry "Red" Allen, and Bix Beiderbecke. His plunger muted style lent a very emotional and playful voice to such Ellington recordings as the 1927 "East St. Louis Toodle-Oo" and "Creole Love Call" (*This Is Duke Ellington*).

Miley's successor, **Cootie Williams,** not only carried on the plunger mute sound, but also contributed a warm, lyrical conception in his unmuted solos. He had a huge tone and the inflections of the Armstrong style. Williams was with Ellington from 1929 until 1940 and then rejoined the band in 1962 and remained until Ellington's death in 1974. Ellington wrote his 1936 "Echoes of Harlem" (*The Ellington Era Vol. 1*) and his 1940 "Concerto for Cootie" (*Smithsonian Collection*) to feature Williams. "Concerto for Cootie" was later rewritten with lyrics and became the popular tune "Do Nothin' 'til You Hear from Me." When Cootie returned in 1962, Ellington wrote an entirely new piece called "New Concerto for Cootie."

Rex Stewart played cornet for Ellington from 1934 until 1944. His humorous solos and colorful sounds produced by pressing his cornet valves only half way down (half valve, cocked valve) were characteristic sounds in the Ellington repertory. Ellington wrote "Boy Meets Horn" (*The Ellington Era Vol. 1*) to feature Stewart. He was also featured on "Morning Glory" and Ellington's 1940 "Portrait of Bert Williams." The 1941 "Take the 'A' Train" (*This Is Duke Ellington*) recording contains an improvised Stewart solo which has been copied many times in subsequent versions of the tune by non-Ellington bands, and quoted by Cootie Williams during late 1960s and early 70s performances. (The first solo on "Take the 'A' Train" is Stewart's; the second is by Ray Nance.)

Ray Nance is one of the few violinists in jazz. Listen to his playing on Ellington's "Black, Brown, and Beige" (*At His Very Best—Duke Ellington and His Orchestra*) and "Lonesome Lullaby" (*Duke Ellington—The Bethlehem Years Vol. 1*). Nance is also one of the warmest and most romantic sounding jazz cornetists. He improvised the second solo on the famous 1940 "Take the 'A' Train" (*In A Mellotone*) recording which is so frequently copied. It was also quoted by Cootie Williams during the late 1960s and early 70s.

Cat Anderson is one of a long line of astounding big band trumpeters who play stratospherically high notes. It has been playfully stated that Anderson plays notes so high that only dogs can hear them. Listen to Anderson's work on "Coloratura" in Ellington's 1945 "Perfume Suite" (*The Indispensable Duke Ellington*), Ellington's 1955 "La Virgen de la Macarena" (*Ellington Showcase*), and "Summertime" (*Duke Ellington—The Bethlehem Years Vol. 2*).

Clark Terry is a trumpeter featured by Ellington from 1951 until 1959. He has excellent instrumental facility and a very distinctive, happy, swinging style. He also helped popularize the fluegelhorn, an oversized cornet played in much the same way as trumpet and cornet but with a mellower tone (see Figure 6.2). Terry blows the horn so

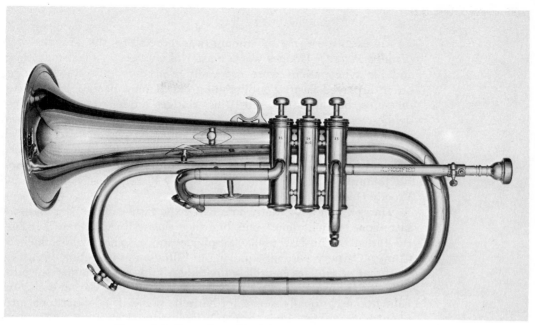

Figure 6.2. Fluegelhorn. *The Selmer Company*

well that he can achieve a brassy edge, whereas most players are unable to overcome the fluegelhorn's naturally soft, stuffy tone color. For examples of Terry's excellent playing, listen to his solo improvisations on the 1956 *Ellington at Newport,* the *Newport 1958,* the 1959 *Festival Session,* and the 1958 *Cosmic Scene,* as well as his own LPs made with trombonist Bob Brookmeyer for Mainstream record company.

The best known of Ellington's sidemen was lead alto saxophonist **Johnny Hodges.** Lead alto refers to the saxophonist who plays the highest notes in the section and who leads the other saxophonists in timing and interpretation of written sax parts.* His solos and his style in leading the sax section were a vital part of the Ellington sound from 1928 until 1970 (with an absence from 1951 to 1955). Hodges produced such an unusually deep and lush tone that his recorded alto sax has sometimes been mistaken for tenor saxophone. He developed a remarkable way of gliding from note to note very gradually and smoothly. It was almost as if his instrument were equipped with a slide, like a trombone. This technique is called portamento, but jazz musicians generally refer to it as smearing. Hodges used it to great advantage in ballad playing. Ellington wrote numerous pieces tailor-made for that well-known Hodges approach.

---

* In Ellington's arrangements the lead sax part was not always given to Hodges. Otto Hardwicke and Russell Procope played lead in some pieces.

An exquisite sense of timing was crucial to the Hodges style (*Hodge Podge*). Hodges was a master of subtlety in tonal inflections, and his syncopations were especially well timed. Pre-1942 Hodges often displayed flashy double-timing like Sidney Bechet, his primary influence, but after the mid-1940s, Hodges tended to lay back very deliberately no matter what the tempo. Nearly every Ellington album features Hodges, and he was such a consistent player that almost all these recordings contain good Hodges playing. Hodges influenced many alto saxophonists, including Tab Smith, Louis Jordan, Earl Bostic, Johnny Bothwell, Willie Smith, Bobby Plater, Charlie Barnet, and Woody Herman.

Harry Carney is usually considered the father of the jazz baritone saxophone, which almost puts him in a class with Coleman Hawkins, the father of the jazz tenor saxophone and a soloist who influenced Carney. Carney's ensemble playing in Ellington's sax section often vied with that of Hodges himself, providing a rock-solid foundation, often as important as that of the band's bassist. Inspired by Carney's playing, Ellington occasionally scored for baritone sax lead. Few baritone saxophonists have been able to match the size and strength of Carney's mammoth, rich sound. He also played clarinet and bass clarinet for Ellington, each of which, in his hands, became a strong, thick-toned voice in the Ellington ensemble. Although primarily an ensemble voice, Carney occasionally received feature numbers, including "Serious Serenade (*Ellington Showcase*), "Frustration" (*Duke Ellington—The Bethlehem Years Vol. 2*), and "Chromatic Love Affair" (*The Greatest Jazz Concert in the World*).

Ben Webster and the saxophonist who took his place seven years after Webster left Ellington, Paul Gonsalves, were two of the most skillful tenor saxophone ballad players to be influenced by the Coleman Hawkins approach. Webster solos on the Ellington recordings of "All Too Soon" (1940), "Just A-Settin' and A-Rockin'" (1941), "I Don't Know What Kind of Blues I've Got" (1941), and "Chelsea Bridge" (1941). He played with a breathy tone and a slow, marked vibrato which was especially distinct at the end of sustained tones. He also employed a hoarse, rasping sound to create a rousing effect in selected portions of a solo, as on the 1941 recording of "Raincheck" (*The Indispensable Duke Ellington*), the 1942 recording of "Mainstem," and the 1941 recording of "Blue Serge" (*In a Mellotone*). For an example of the masculine, laid-back approach to medium-tempo improvisation that Webster developed, listen to Ellington's 1940 recording of "Cottontail" (*This Is Duke Ellington*). Pianist Art Tatum and Webster got together in 1956 and recorded an excellent Verve album of ballads which stands out among Webster's recordings made outside of the Ellington band (*Art Tatum–Ben Webster Group Masterpieces*). But his 1939-43 recordings with Ellington probably represent the peak of his career. He died in 1973, having been an influence on such modern tenor saxophonists as Charlie Ventura, Eddie "Lockjaw" Davis, and Archie Shepp.

Gonsalves began as a disciple of Webster but soon created his own unique style, one aspect of which was a very unusual and fluid conception for medium- and up-tempo playing. His ballad style can be heard in "Laura'" (*The Bethlehem Years Vol. 2*), "Days of Wine and Roses," and "Where or When" (*Ellington Indigos*). He had a soft, diffuse tone without edge. But, in spite of his soft tone, his playing almost had the urgency of John Coltrane's, and Gonsalves's choice of notes was so unusual that it is amazing he could deliver them as fluently as he did. Listen to "Take the 'A' Train" on Ellington's 1950 *Hi-Fi Ellington Uptown*, and his solos on the 1956 *Ellington at Newport, Newport 1958,* 1958 *Cosmic Scene,* and 1959 *Festival Session.* Gonsalves played with Ellington from 1951 until his death ten days before Ellington's in 1974.

Trombonist **Joe "Tricky Sam" Nanton** was master of the growl style. With his plumber's plunger and unorthodox blowing, he came very close to pronouncing words with his trombone. From 1926 until his death in 1948, Nanton gave Ellington a provocative sound to voice in arrangements, as in the 1940 "KoKo" (*Smithsonian Collection*). Quentin "Butter" Jackson perfected the growl style in Ellington's band from 1948 to 1959 and carried it with him into the modern Thad Jones–Mel Lewis band of the 1970s. Al Grey played a similar role in Count Basie's band.

Lawrence Brown was one of the first trombonists of the swing era to play with a very smooth, large, consistent sound. His tone added a great deal of body to the Ellington trombone section. Brown had an aggressive sound and excellent intonation. Ellington wrote "Blue Cellophane" (*The Indispensable Duke Ellington*), and "Golden Cress" (*The World of Duke Ellington*) as features for Brown's style.

Ellington had several outstanding bassists including Wellman Braud, Junior Raglin, Oscar Pettiford, and **Jimmy Blanton** who, during his two years with Ellington, shattered traditional conceptions of jazz bass playing with his impressive instrumental proficiency and imagination. His driving facility and melodic solos demonstrated that, in the hands of a virtuoso, the string bass can contribute exciting solo lines and ensemble interplay instead of being assigned exclusively to time-keeping. Ellington took full advantage of Blanton's potential, sometimes using Blanton's bass as though it were a horn. And Blanton's bass was also a powerful component of the rhythm section in Ellington's band. Blanton played melody on Ellington's 1940 "Jack the Bear" (*At His Very Best—Duke Ellington and His Orchestra*) and the 1940 "Concerto for Cootie" (*Smithsonian Collection*). He also solos on the 1940 "Sepia Panorama" (*In a Mellotone*). Ellington and Blanton made several duet recordings, which were actually two-way musical conversations: their 1940 "Pitter Panther Patter" and "Mr. J. B. Blues" (*The*

Indispensable Duke Ellington). Blanton died in 1942 at the age of twenty-one.

Not all of Ellington's recordings represent entirely his own musical ideas. Numerous tunes were written by his sidemen or in collaboration with them. Bubber Miley was involved in composing "Black and Tan Fantasy" and "East St. Louis Toodle-Oo" (*The Ellington Era Vol. 1*). Barney Bigard worked on "Mood Indigo" (*This Is Duke Ellington*); Otto Hardwicke collaborated on "Sophisticated Lady" (*This Is Duke Ellington*); and baritone saxophonist Harry Carney coauthored "Rockin' in Rhythm" (*The Ellington Era Vol. 1*). Valve trombonist **Juan Tizol** wrote several exotic pieces, including "Caravan" (*The Ellington Era Vol. 1*), "Bakiff," and "Conga Brava." Tizol also wrote "Perdido" (*This Is Duke Ellington*), a melody often mistakenly credited to Ellington.

From 1939 until 1967, Ellington worked closely with another very creative pianist-composer-arranger, **Billy Strayhorn.** The two men collaborated on countless pieces, and their styles were so similar that most listeners never knew which of them contributed the larger portion of any particular arrangement. There are, however, several pieces usually credited just to Strayhorn. The most famous is "Take the 'A' Train" (*This Is Duke Ellington*), a classic which Ellington used as his band's theme. Ballads were Strayhorn's real forte. "Chelsea Bridge" (*The Indispensable Duke Ellington*), and "Lush Life" are gorgeous examples. ("Lush Life" was recorded by numerous groups, including Nat King Cole and John Coltrane. Coltrane made two separate versions, one with singer Johnny Hartman.)

Strayhorn's arrangements, though often indistinguishable from Ellington's contained a few non-Ellington surprises. For example, in his 1941 "Take the 'A' Train" (*This Is Duke Ellington*), there is a four-measure interlude in meter of three. The rest of the piece is in meter of four. The basic melody fits a thirty-two bar AABA form. Listen to this famous work, and examine the following guide:

Four-measure piano introduction.

First Chorus

AA Saxes state the melody (key of C) in unison and are answered alternately by muted trumpets in harmony and trombones in harmony. Rhythm section accompanies. Drummer is using wire brushes on snare drum.

B Saxes continue with the melody and are answered by trombones only.

A Saxes finish the melody and are answered by a new figure played by muted trumpets and trombones together. Piano comments near the end of the section.

Second Chorus

AABA   Rex Stewart improvises a solo on muted trumpet while harmonized saxes are talking underneath. It sounds like the saxes are having an entire conversation filled with original, nonrepetitious lines. Rhythm section continues as before.

Four-Measure Interlude

This interlude is in meter of three. Trumpets play a question and saxes answer in each measure. Bass plays only on the first beat of each measure. Guitar is silent. Drummer makes syncopated cymbal splashes. By the time this waltz section is over, the band has changed from the key of C to the key of E-flat.

One-Bar Insert

A big chord, and timekeeping resumes in meter of four.

Third Chorus

A   First four measures: Saxes enter for a harmonized melody statement answered by unmuted trumpeter Ray Nance improvising. Second four measures: Nance continues his solo while saxes accompany with sustained chords. Drummer Sonny Greer now using sticks on snare drum.

A   First four measures: Saxes pose the same harmonized question again, but Nance improvises a new answer for them. Second four measures: Nance continues while saxes return to sustained chords underneath.

B   First four measures: Nance continues while saxes state a theme independently and trombones carry an additional theme in harmony of their own. Saxes comment briefly.
Two measures: Nance continues while trombones accompany him with chords.
Two measures: A fanfare, each note drawn from instruments in a different section of the band. Rhythm section does not play timekeeping patterns but cymbal crashes punctuate the fanfare.

A   Rhythm section returns to timekeeping. Original A section is played by saxes in unison but this time in key of E-flat instead of C. Brass punctuates the sax statements by alternating open horn notes in harmony with muted horn notes in harmony.

A   Same as previous eight measures, but softer.

A   Same again, softer still, but piano answers sax figures, and finally saxes add a "tie-it-up" figure to end the piece.

Diversity of the Ellington Band

The Ellington band repertory displayed far more variety than that of any other big band. There were more themes within a single arrangement, and the different rhythmic figures in those themes, the back-up figures, and the combinations of instruments were all greater than usual. The lack of repetition within pieces is striking. The pieces themselves also fit into a larger variety of types than was common for big bands. One might describe the Ellington repertory as a number of separate books, each of which was both large and distinctive. Here are six categories which come to mind, most of which occasionally overlap each other:

1) An impressionistic book with arrangements that place more emphasis on orchestral colors and shading than on swinging: from his pre-LP work: "Transbluency" (*At His Very Best—Duke Ellington and His Orchestra*), "On a Turquoise Cloud" (*The World of Duke Ellington*), etc. From his LP work there are portions of *Anatomy of a Murder* and *Paris Blues*.

2) A book of romantic ballads: from his pre-LP work: "Daydream," "Prelude to a Kiss" (*Ellington Indigos, The Ellington Era Vol. 1*), "Sophisticated Lady" (*The Ellington Era Vol. 1, The Indispensable Duke Ellington*), etc. From his LP work: recordings *Ellington Indigos, At the Bal Masque*, etc.

3) An exotic book: "Caravan" (*The Ellington Era Vol. 1*), "Flaming Sword," "Bakiff," etc. from pre-LP work; and entire LPs such as *Latin American Suite* and *Togo Brava Suite*, etc.

4) A concert book, each piece a long work with much less improvisation than his usual repertory contained. "Reminiscing in Tempo," "Black, Brown, and Beige" (*At His Very Best—Duke Ellington and His Orchestra*), "Deep South Suite," etc. for his pre-LP work and *Such Sweet Thunder, Suite Thursday, A Drum Is a Woman*, etc. for his LP work.

5) A book of concertos, each piece framing the style of an Ellington sideman. "Clarinet Lament" (Barney Bigard), "Echoes of Harlem" (Cootie Williams), "Boy Meets Horn" (Rex Stewart) (all from *The Ellington Era Vol. 1*), etc. for his pre-LP work and "Cop-Out" (Paul Gonsalves), "Lonesome Lullaby" (Ray Nance) (*Duke Ellington—The Bethlehem Years Vol. 1*), etc. for his LP work.

6) A book of three-minute masterpieces. Ellington could pack more music into a three-minute piece than anyone else. The amount of orchestration plus the development of written and improvised themes was very large compared to three-minute recordings by other swing bands. He was not as involved in three minute pieces after the advent of the LP, but his pre-LP

work is filled with them. A treasury of music can be found in old Ellington 78 rpm recordings, most of which are available today in LP reissue packages.

Among the hundreds of Ellington recordings there are numerous masterpieces which have not been extensively described. A few outstanding examples include the 1940 "Harlem Air Shaft," the 1941 "Raincheck" by Strayhorn, the 1939 "The Sergeant Was Shy," and the 1941 "I Don't Know What Kind of Blues I've Got." The vastness of Ellington's contribution becomes evident when you explore a few hundred different selections. In addition to all that material, Ellington also composed several operas, a couple of ballets, and about ten shows, most of which were never performed.

Many listeners believe that Ellington's peak of creativity was in the years 1939–41 when his band members included Ben Webster, Johnny Hodges, Barney Bigard, Jimmy Blanton, Tricky Sam Nanton, Harry Carney, Cootie Williams, and Rex Stewart. His 1956–59 band was also exceptional, featuring Clark Terry, Jimmy Hamilton, Paul Gonsalves, Harry Carney, and Johnny Hodges. When the band's personnel changed, the band's sound changed correspondingly. Every five to ten years there was a difference in the band sound.

The Ellington band never really fell into any fixed category—early jazz, swing, or modern. It was always unique. Ellington created a jazz classification which was practically his own. Not only did the Duke Ellington band present a very colorful and more varied sound than is usually heard, but it maintained a consistent level of creative energy for more than four decades.

TABLE 7.1. Count Basie Band Alumni—A Partial Listing

Trumpet	Saxophone	Composer-Arranger
Carl Smith	Lester Young	Eddie Durham
Hot Lips Page	Herschel Evans	Don Redman
Buck Clayton	Jack Washington	Jimmy Mundy
Harry "Sweets" Edison	Tab Smith	Don Kirkpatrick
Shad Collins	Earle Warren	Ernie Wilkins
Emmett Berry	Buddy Tate	Thad Jones
Clark Terry	Jack Washington	Frank Foster
Thad Jones	Wardell Gray	Frank Wess
Joe Newman	Lucky Thompson	Neal Hefti
Al Aarons	Don Byas	Quincy Jones
Sonny Cohn	Illinois Jacquet	Benny Carter
Snooky Young	Serge Chaloff	Billy Byers
Wendell Culley	Paul Gonsalves	Chico O'Farrill
	Eddie "Lockjaw" Davis	Sammy Nestico
Trombone	Frank Foster	Al Grey
	Eric Dixon	
Dickie Wells	Jimmy Forrest	**Drums**
Benny Morton	Billy Mitchell	
Vic Dickenson	Frank Wess	Jo Jones
Al Grey	Marshall Royal	Shadow Wilson
Henry Coker	Charlie Fowlkes	Gus Johnson
Curtis Fuller	Bobby Plater	Sonny Payne
Benny Powell	Paul Quinichette	Louis Bellson
		Harold Jones
	Bass	Butch Miles
		Rufus Jones
	Walter Page	
	Eddie Jones	
	Buddy Catlett	

chapter 7
THE COUNT BASIE BANDS

Although the general public thinks of Benny Goodman as the "King of Swing," most jazz musicians agree that the title should be applied to Count Basie. Even compared with the swinging bands of Fletcher Henderson, Duke Ellington, Jimmie Lunceford, and Woody Herman, the Basie band, never out of breath or the least bit frantic, always seems to swing more.

With the exception of the years 1950–51, when he had to reduce the size of his group to a combo, Basie has led a big band continuously from 1937. Nearly every edition of the band had one or two players who made important contributions to jazz history, and some editions have had four or five.

Basie the Pianist

Basie was originally a Fats Waller–influenced stride pianist and a prominent soloist with some of his own bands. During the 1950s, 60s, and 70s, however, he often played through an entire selection without the audience's hearing more than his piano introduction and a few characteristic "plink plink" interjections during dramatic silences. Succinct and compact statements are hallmarks of Basie's style. When he does solo, he artfully uses silence to pace his lines while guitarist Freddie Green strums his supple four strokes to the measure over quiet bass and drums. Basie's touch is unique among jazz pianists. It is very light yet extremely precise. His choice of notes is near perfect, as is his timing. Basie's piano usually sets the mood and tempo for his band's performances.

Basie's Rhythm Section during the Late 1930s and Early 40s

Basie led the first rhythm section in jazz history that consistently swung in a smooth, relaxed way. That famous rhythm section consisted of Basie himself (piano), Freddie Green (rhythm guitar), Walter Page (string bass), and Jo Jones (drums).

The special qualities of the Basie rhythm section were:

1) An excellent sense of tempo.
2) The ability to keep time without using a hard-driving, pressured approach.
3) Quiet, relaxed playing, which conveyed a feeling of ease.
4) A fairly even beat with very subtle emphasis on the second and fourth beats.
5) Emphasis on buoyancy rather than intensity.

Bassist **Walter Page** contributed:

1) A supple walking bass.
2) A strong tone, an articulated sound with life in it, not the dead thud common to many premodern bassists.
3) A walking style which led the beat instead of dragging it, as had the playing of many premodern bassists.

Guitarist **Freddie Green** was noted for:

1) His crisp four strokes to the measure on unamplified guitar.
2) His close coordination with drums.

The style of drummer **Jo Jones** consisted of:

1) Precise playing, but not stiff precision. Jones displayed precision within a loose, assured manner.
2) Quieter bass drum playing than was common in the swing era, much softer, for example, than Gene Krupa's. Jones sometimes omitted bass drum entirely.
3) Quiet use of wire brushes on high-hat, ride rhythms played on high-hat while opening and closing.
4) Very discreet fills.

In Basie's interjections, jazz piano had the bounce, syncopation, and flexibility that characterized what became known as *comping*, a very important element in modern jazz. Listen very carefully to the faint piano sound during Carl Smith's trumpet solo on the 1936 "Shoe Shine Boy" (*The Lester Young Story Vol. 1*). You will hear Basie comping in the manner adopted by modern jazz pianists years later. Throughout his career, Basie also mixed Fats Waller stride style with "plink plink" interjections, but his accompaniment for Smith is one of the earliest recorded examples of modern jazz comping. Even during the 1940s, many excellent jazz pianists had not learned to comp. They continued in the accompaniment styles of the 1920s and 30s, including stride style, playing a chord on each beat in the manner of a rhythm guitarist, or playing flowery countermelodies and embellishments.

An isolated example of comping from an earlier period can be heard on a version of "The Mooch" recorded by Duke Ellington on November 30, 1928 (*Duke Ellington—Mood Indigo*). If you listen carefully, you can detect Ellington comping under the first chorus of an alto sax solo by Johnny Hodges. This was very unusual for the 1920s because most pianists, including Ellington, usually played a chord on each beat instead of employing irregular, syncopated bursts of brief chords.

Arrangements   The Basie band of the late 1930s often used arrangements which were based on simple repeated musical phrases. Such riffs were played over the twelve-bar blues progression and progressions of such pop tunes as "Honeysuckle Rose," "I Got Rhythm," "Shoe Shine Boy," "Lady Be Good" etc. (*The Lester Young Story Vol. 1*). Riffs served both as ensemble statements and backgrounds for improvised solos. Some of the riffs were written down, but many were created spontaneously during a performance ("off the top of someone's head"), learned by ear and kept in the heads of the players. Arrangements of that kind were called **head arrangements** and were part of the riff band style common in Kansas City bands of the 1930s (Jay McShann, Bennie Moten, etc.). Many riff tunes which band members at first identified only by number were later given names and composer credits. Basie himself is credited with "One O'Clock Jump" and "Jumpin' at the Woodside" (*The Best of Count Basie*).

Count Basie's band has always placed more emphasis on swing and simplicity than on complexity and colorful sounds. Even during the 1950s and 60s when composers and arrangers such as Ernie Wilkins, Quincy Jones, Neal Hefti, and Benny Carter were writing for Basie, simple, catchy riffs were the rule. The band was really just an oversized combo during the late 1930s and early 40s. Basie placed much more emphasis on swinging solo improvisations than on fancy arrangements. His approach provided a contrast to the highly polished, well-arranged Jimmie Lunceford band and the elaborate embroidery of written music and improvisation in Ellington's band. Basie's was primarily a soloist's band, and Lunceford's was more an arranger's band.

Basie's emphasis on a combo style decreased during the 1950s (and especially during the 60s and 70s) when the band performed slick, swinging arrangements in which solos were sometimes rare, short, and occasionally constituted inconsequential portions of a recording. Basie's band achieved a very high level of polish and assumed a position Lunceford had held twenty years earlier. The band was a showcase for ensemble sound. But in spite of an increased emphasis on ensemble playing, the band continued to carry excellent soloists.

Many of the best jazz trumpeters and saxophonists of the late 1930s and 40s played with Count Basie at one time or another—the list of notables is incredible. In that respect, his band was similar to Fletcher Henderson's in that Henderson had employed most of the best soloists available during the 1920s and early 30s (see Table 7.1).

The most notable soloist Basie had during the 1930s and 40s was tenor saxophonist **Lester Young.** He was so good that he was nicknamed "Pres" (or "Prez"), short for president of tenor saxophone players. Young played lines which were fresher, longer, more concise and smoothly swinging than those of any previous improvisers. He paved the way for modern saxophone tone color, vibrato, rhythmic conception, and phrasing. Young offered a clear alternative to the heavy tone, fast vibrato, and richly ornamented style of Coleman Hawkins.

Young's light tone, slow vibrato, and loping, buoyant phrases became the model for an entire generation of tenor saxophonists, including Stan Getz, Zoot Sims, Brew Moore, Herbie Steward, and Allen Eager. Young influenced the playing of the 1950s West Coast tenor saxophonists, including Dave Pell, Richie Kamuca, Bob Cooper, Bill Perkins, etc. Young's was not the only influence absorbed by these players, but his ideas were quite significant for them. These saxophonists often copied Young solos note for note. Complete choruses of famous Lester Young improvisations can occasionally be heard in their playing.

Young also influenced a school of saxophonists who favored darker tone colors: Wardell Gray, Dexter Gordon, Gene Ammons, Sonny Stitt, etc. In addition to influencing tenor saxophonists, Young also inspired alto saxophonist Charlie Parker, who, more than any other single player, was responsible for the development of modern jazz.

Although his playing did not match the complexity of Hawkins, Young's melodic ideas were at least as advanced. Listen to his 1939 "Taxi War Dance" (*The Smithsonian Collection of Classic Jazz*) solo where he seems to play against Basie's rolling piano figure, or his improvisation on Basie's 1939 "Jive at Five" (*The Best of Count Basie*), which anticipates the fluffy tone and melodic approach Stan Getz was to display eight years later with the Woody Herman band.

Whereas Hawkins was bound up in complex chord changes and busy ornamentation, Young implied new and additional chords in standard pop tune progressions and treated them with a cool, extremely concise approach. But he did have moments of many notes, too. Listen to his famous 1939 "Lester Leaps In" solo recorded with a combo of Basie sideman (*The Smithsonian Collection of Classic Jazz*). It is nearly all eighth notes, but the sequences are clear in spite of the number of notes and surprises they contain.

Instead of incorporating afterthoughts into every other phrase, as

Hawkins was prone to do, Young concerned himself with only a core of melodic material. He possessed the virtue of deliberate restraint. He could pace a solo so well that it seemed an integral part of the written arrangement. Young seems to have possessed a musical storytelling talent which surfaced in nearly every solo. His clarinet solos on the 1938 "I Want a Little Girl" and "Pagin' the Devil" are good examples of this restraint (*The Commodore Years—Lester Young, Ben Webster, Chu Berry*). Young's light, dry clarinet tone was unique in the 1930s. His big band tenor sax solos on the 1939 "Pound Cake" and "Ham 'n' Eggs" (both on *Lester Young Memorial Album*) also typify his melodic gift and sensible pacing. (On "Ham 'n' Eggs" his is the *second* tenor solo; Buddy Tate takes the first, a solo whose style is distinctly different from Young's.)

The advanced level of Young's conception was evident in his easy swing and in his placement of phrases that seemed unhindered by turnarounds and bridges within chord progressions. Young tran- scended the phrasing of many premodern players who had organized lines around the two- and four-bar sequences of chord progressions. He improvised long lines which had a fresh, expansive feeling. It would be difficult to derive a crowded feeling from a Young solo. An- other aspect of Young's advanced conception was his ability to play against the chord changes instead of playing directly through their tones. The internal logic of his lines took precedence over strict ad- herence to the underlying harmonies, a characteristic of the approach taken by hundreds of good improvisers later in jazz history.

Young's playing was strongest during the late 1930s, and his very first recordings were probably the best of his entire career. When he left Basie in 1940, his tone began to darken, his vibrato quickened, and his rhythmic precision decreased. This process began well before 1944, the year most fans cite as the beginning of a serious decline for him. His playing seemed to lose energy steadily until his death in 1959. Yet Young's work remained intelligent and swinging all those years, and he never played badly. In fact, his loyalty to storytelling type improvisa- tions increased. But after 1940, he seemed unable (or unwilling) to jump into his solos with the animation and freshness of his early work.

A representative of one major branch of the Coleman Hawkins school of tenor saxophone style was **Herschel Evans.** A smoother, more graceful player than Hawkins, he rejected the intricate approach to improvisation favored by Hawkins. Evans played with a fast vibrato and about as deep and dark a tone as any swing tenor, even darker than Hawkins. One reason for his dark tone color was his preference for the saxophone's low register. His lines were neither as long nor as ornamented as Hawkins. Yet neither were they as concise as Lester Young's. Like Ben Webster and Hawkins, he excelled in ballad work. His 1938 recording of "Blue and Sentimental" with Basie was widely imitated (*The Best of Count Basie*). He influenced Buddy Tate, Illinois Jacquet, Ike Quebec, Arnett Cobb, and others. Evans was with Basie from 1936 until he died in 1939.

Trumpeter **Oran "Hot Lips" Page** was a strong player who had a dramatic and melodic solo conception as well as a solid sense of pacing. He had a big, thick tone and good high range. Page could produce a brassy, open-horn sound and muted growl style with equal ease. Initially influenced by Louis Armstrong, he played longer lines than Armstrong, but he was not rhythmically or melodically as advanced as Roy Eldridge. He played with two Kansas City bands, Walter Page's Blue Devils and the Bennie Moten band, members of which eventually appeared in the Count Basie band. Page was with Basie from 1935 until 1936.

Page was replaced by **Buck Clayton** who stayed with Basie until 1943. Clayton was one of the greatest swing era trumpeters and the best Basie had until the 1950s. He seems to have played the most intelligent lines of any early Basie trumpeters. His clear, warm tone and relaxed, graceful command of the trumpet's full range was almost as inspiring as the work of Louis Armstrong, one of Clayton's major influences (he had memorized Armstrong solos during the early 1930s). He often played with a cup mute, yet for a muted sound, his tone was unusually full. Listen to his sensitive cup-muted playing at the beginning, and gorgeous open-horn sound at the end of the 1938 "I Want a Little Girl"; also note his muted work on the 1938 "Good Mornin' Blues" (*The Commodore Years*). Clayton was a very consistent player. He maintained an excellent technique and remained active as a trumpet player during the 1970s.

Another distinctive trumpeter who was with the Basie band during its first decade was **Harry Edison** (nicknamed "Sweets"). Not the powerhouse trumpeter that Eldridge was, Edison developed a more economical style. He preferred short, sweet-sounding phrases, and his playing was almost entirely legato. Edison liked to milk a single note over and over, building tension by using various kinds of attacks. He bent the note, wiggled it, dropped it, squeezed it, pounced on it, opened it, closed it, and shook it, even when his trumpet was muted (he preferred metal mutes to cup mutes). Sweets was with Basie from 1937 until 1950. He updated his style, maintained his chops and remained a solid jazz trumpeter in the 1970s.

Probably the most colorful trombonist with Basie in the late 1930s was **Dickie Wells**. Always strikingly melodic, Wells played with a clear, humorous conception that was amusing without being corny.

Kansas City Five; Jones-Smith, Inc.

Several records were made by combos composed of Basie band members. Variously called the Kansas City Five, Six, or Seven, depending on how many musicians were used, these combos often included the entire Basie rhythm section plus Lester Young, Buck Clayton, and

Dickie Wells. Their 1939 recordings, such as "Dickie's Dream" and "Lester Leaps In" (*Smithsonian Collection*), are combo classics which in jazz history rank alongside Louis Armstrong's Hot Five and Hot Seven recordings and the Miles Davis album series *Steamin'*, *Cookin'*, *Workin,* and *Relaxin'*.

One of the first of these combos included drummer Jo Jones and trumpeter Carl Smith, and was given the group name Jones-Smith, Inc. The 1936 recordings made by Jones-Smith, Inc., which include "Shoe Shine Boy" and "Lady Be Good," are masterpieces in jazz history (*The Lester Young Story Vol. 1*). Lester Young, Smith, and Basie outdo themselves on these wonderful records.

Sidemen of the 50s, 60s, and 70s

In later years, Basie retained his swing style rhythm section (guitarist Freddie Green was still with him, playing in the same style as when he joined Basie in 1937), but most of his soloists during the 1950s, 60s, and 70s were modern.

Probably the most original trumpeters in Basie's band during the 1950s and 60s were **Thad Jones** and Joe Newman. Each had a distinctive modern style. In fact, Jones is considered by many to be one of the most original trumpeters to come along since Dizzy Gillespie. His early 1950s work with the Charlie Mingus group was astounding, both instrumentally and melodically. His lines are composed of very unusual intervals; they are unpredictable and full of surprises. Furthermore, they are not at all natural to the trumpet, and consequently, they are very difficult as well as unique (Count Basie—*Chairman of the Board*). His command of the trumpet is impressive. Since 1966 he has been co-leading the Thad Jones–Mel Lewis big band and not playing very much himself. He had written for Basie, and with his own band, he has concentrated even more on composing and arranging (*Central Park North,* Count Basie—*Chairman of the Board, New Life, Presenting Thad Jones–Mel Lewis and the Jazz Orchestra, Thad Jones–Mel Lewis*).

The sax section has probably had greater players than any other section of Basie's band. During the 1950s and 60s, the tradition was maintained by such strong modern players as Wardell Gray, **Frank Foster,** Eddie "Lockjaw" Davis, Billy Mitchell, and Eric Dixon.

During the 1950s and 60s, two of Basie's saxophonists, **Frank Wess** and **Eric Dixon,** doubled on flute. They became two of the leading flutists in jazz. Dixon and Wess were clearly superior to their non-Basie contemporaries, Sam Most, Bud Shank, and Herbie Mann.

A trademark of the 1950s and 60s sax section was the lead alto sax style of **Marshall Royal.** Primarily an ensemble player rather than an improvising soloist, Royal produced a sweet conception with glowing tone which set the pace for the mellow yet precise sound of the entire band. His style influenced arrangers when they wrote for the Basie saxophone section. Royal's lead alto work for Basie was as much a big band sax section model as Maynard Ferguson's lead trumpet work with Stan Kenton. It was interesting to note that the same year Duke Ellington's lead alto, Johnny Hodges, died, Marshall Royal left Basie. Both men were cornerstones for the styles of their respective bands.

For twenty years the Basie band has had the unusual distinction of being practically the only big band that swings *while* playing softly. The band maintains precision and balance without losing the subtle drive that is expected of jazz performances. And the band is precise without sounding mechanical. Much of the book that Neal Hefti (*Basie Plays Hefti, Fantail, On My Way and Shoutin' Again*), Benny Carter (*Kansas City Suite/Easin' It, The Legend*), and Quincy Jones (*Basie, One More Time, Li'l Ol' Groovemaker*) wrote for Basie during the late 1950s and early 60s capitalizes on the band's skill with dynamic contrasts: loud passages which instantaneously get soft; soft passages interrupted momentarily by very loud chords; passages which rise and fall in volume so gradually that one wonders how it is possible.

The Count Basie bands of the 1970s sound much like those of the 50s and 60s with many new arrangements done in the old style. However, Basie's soloists have not been as strong as those of the 50s.

PART III

modern jazz: the early 1940s to the early 1960s

Jazz historians tend to date the beginning of modern jazz in the 1940s ("early jazz" is sometimes referred to as the "classic period"). Styles which have emerged since 1940, except those that are revivals of previous styles, are classified as modern jazz. The first modern jazz musicians were alto saxophonist Charlie Parker, pianist Thelonious Monk, and trumpeter Dizzy Gillespie. By the middle 1940s, they had inspired a legion of other creative musicians including trumpeter Miles Davis and pianist Bud Powell. By the late 1940s Parker and Gillespie had also influenced the big bands of Billy Eckstine, Claude Thornhill and Woody Herman.

Modern jazz did not burst upon the jazz scene as a revolution. It developed gradually through the work of swing era tenor saxophonists Lester Young and Don Byas, pianists Art Tatum and Nat Cole, trumpeter Roy Eldridge, guitarist Charlie Christian, the Count Basie rhythm section, bassist Jimmy Blanton, and others. Parker and Gillespie themselves began their careers playing improvisations in a swing era style. They expanded on this music and gradually incorporated new techniques; their work eventually became recognized as a different style, which, though departing appreciably from swing era approaches, was still linked to the swing era.

The new music was primarily a combo style. But modern jazz and its combo format did not emerge solely because young improvisers disliked swing era big band playing. The big bands and written arrangements certainly imposed restrictions on the amount of solo time and on the spontaneous musical interaction between soloist and accompanist. But both combo and big band formats have existed in most eras. Apparently both have been useful. In fact, Parker developed part of his advanced improvisatory style while playing with the big band of Jay McShann. He later recorded with Machito's Latin American big band and sat in with the big bands of Gillespie and Woody Herman. Gillespie played in Cab Calloway's big band, and both Parker and Gillespie worked with the 1940s big bands of Earl Hines and Billy Eckstine. If modern jazz represented a rejection of big bands, why would such leading modern jazz musicians like Gillespie, Thad Jones, Clark Terry, Miles Davis, Gil Evans, Gerry Mulligan, and others endure great hardships to lead their own? The scarcity of big bands in modern jazz compared to their proliferation during the swing era could be due to a number of factors, a small one being the possible distaste some jazz musicians had for big bands. But we should take care to avoid overrating the influence of that factor. Eventually combos became the standard band size for popular music. Jazz was not the only type of music which moved away from large ensemble format. Rather than a reaction *against* swing styles, modern jazz developed smoothly *from* swing styles.

Modern jazz improvisers were also inspired by contemporary classical music. The work of Béla Bartók and Igor Stravinsky was favored by many musicians of the 1940s, just as the music of Claude Debussy and Maurice Ravel influenced Bix Beiderbecke during the 1920s. The music of Edgard Varese, Charles Ives, and the Polish composer Krystof Penderecki has influenced some jazz styles of the 1960s and 70s.

It is important to realize that previous styles do not die just because new styles arise. And jazz history is so short that styles from every phase in its development coexist. Today in fact, during the last quarter of the twentieth century, fourth-generation Dixieland players are appearing.

chapter 8

BOP:
THE EARLY 1940s
TO THE MIDDLE 1950s

The most advanced swing era players (Lester Young, Coleman Hawkins, Teddy Wilson, Charlie Christian, Art Tatum, Roy Eldridge) had a pronounced effect on the new jazz style called bop, or bebop, which appeared during the early 1940s.

How the names bop and bebop originated is uncertain. But they might have come from the vocabulary of nonsense syllables which jazz musicians use to sing jazz phrases. Instead of singing "la, la, la" or "da, da, da," they might sing "dwee li du be bop oolya koo" or a similar sequence. It is also possible that the style's name was derived from the title of a Gillespie tune: "Bebop."

Bop made its first appearances in the playing of alto saxophonist Charlie Parker, pianist Thelonious Monk, and trumpeter Dizzy Gillespie, whose approaches were developed independently but were compatible and mutually inspiring. Parker, Gillespie, and Monk played together and refined a very complex kind of music. Their improvisations were composed mostly of eighth-note and sixteenth-note figures which seemed jumpy, full of twists and turns. The contours of the melodic lines were jagged; there were often large intervals between the notes and abrupt changes of direction. The rhythms in those lines were quick and unpredictable, with more syncopation than any music previously common in Europe or America.

For the basis of their lines, bop musicians did more than embellish the melody. They usually departed from the melodies and retained only the chord progressions. Often they enriched a progression by adding new chords. Swing players and early jazz players might have employed fewer than five or ten chord changes in a twelve-bar blues, but

TABLE 8.1. Bop Style Musicians—A Partial Listing

Trumpet

Dizzy Gillespie
Fats Navarro
Howard McGhee
Miles Davis
Kenny Dorham
Red Rodney
Benny Harris
Sonny Berman
Freddie Webster
Conte Candoli
Clark Terry
Idrees Sulieman
Benny Bailey

Trombone

J.J. Johnson
Kai Winding
Bennie Green
Frank Rosolino

Bass

Oscar Pettiford
Ray Brown
Tommy Potter
Curly Russell
Nelson Boyd
Al McKibbon
Gene Ramey
Red Callender
Teddy Kotick
Chubby Jackson
Eddie Safranski

Saxophone

Charlie Parker
Dexter Gordon
Lucky Thompson
Stan Getz
Wardell Gray
Allen Eager
Herbie Steward
Brew Moore
Gene Ammons
Sonny Stitt
Flip Phillips

James Moody
Charlie Ventura
Zoot Sims
Al Cohn
Ernie Henry
Leo Parker
Sonny Criss
Serge Chaloff
Don Lamphere
Charlie Rouse
Sonny Rollins
Phil Urso
Boots Mussulli

Vibraharp

Milt Jackson
Teddy Charles
Terry Gibbs

Drums

Kenny Clarke
Max Roach
Joe Harris
Tiny Kahn
Don Lamond
Roy Haynes
Osie Johnson
Denzil Best

Piano

Bud Powell
Thelonious Monk
Al Haig
Dodo Marmarosa
Joe Albany
Walter Bishop, Jr.
Duke Jordan
George Shearing
Oscar Peterson
Billy Taylor
Hank Jones

Argonne Thornton
 (Sadik Hakim)
Hampton Hawes
John Lewis
Tadd Dameron
Ahmad Jamal

Guitar

Arv Garrison
Tal Farlow
Bill DeArango
Jimmy Raney
Johnny Collins
Barry Galbraith
Chuck Wayne
Barney Kessel
Billy Bauer
Johnny Smith

Composer-Arranger

Gil Fuller
George Russell
Neal Hefti
Dizzy Gillespie
Charlie Parker
Thelonious Monk
Tadd Dameron
John Lewis
Shorty Rogers
Ralph Burns
Gil Evans
Gerry Mulligan

a bop player might want ten or twenty chord changes (see third example under "Chord Progressions for the Twelve-Bar Blues" in Chapter 18). Art Tatum had previously explored reharmonization of melodies and had added chords to existing progressions. Lester Young and Coleman Hawkins had been so fluent in devouring every existing chord change, that they and Tatum had set the stage for addition of chords and the related melodic complexity of Parker and Gillespie. Addition of chords is often called substitution because, in place of a single chord or a common chord sequence, new chords are substituted. Some bop lines implied chords which were not originally in a tune; these lines were sometimes played against a tune's original harmonies to achieve purposely clashing effects. In other cases, the rhythm section would instantaneously change chords and chord progressions to fit the new harmonic directions implied by an improvised line. Bop rhythm sections learned to be quite sensitive and resourceful.

Bop players also altered existing chords. The lowered or flatted fifth was one of the alterations common in bop (the raised eleventh and the tritone are alternate labels for that interval). It became distinctive as a jazz interval much as the lowered third and lowered seventh had been in early jazz (see Chapter 17). Bop players made all three intervals basic to modern jazz flavor.

Because bop musicians liked to improvise on difficult chord progressions, they sometimes wrote original progressions themselves; Dizzy Gillespie's "Con Alma" is an example. But more often the bop players improvised on pop tune progressions which were more challenging than average, like "Cherokee" and "All the Things You Are." Charlie Parker based his tune "Ko Ko" on the chord progression of "Cherokee." (This means that improvisations based on the chord changes of "Ko Ko" are also compatible with the chord changes of "Cherokee.")

Bop players often wrote original tunes based on standard pop tune progressions, and many of these new tunes went without names. The leader just called out the key and the name of the pop tune which had originally provided the chord progression. In that way, members of the rhythm section could immediately play a tune they might have never previously heard. This technique had also been employed during the swing era, and the twelve-bar blues progression had been used in that way for decades. The chord progression of George Gershwin's "I Got Rhythm" was used so much that musicians just called the chord changes "rhythm changes" ("I Got Rhythm chord changes" was probably abbreviated as "I Got Rhythm changes" which in turn was abbreviated as "rhythm changes" or just "rhythm"). The pop tunes "Indiana," "What Is This Thing Called Love," "Whispering," and "How High the Moon" respectively provided chord progressions for the bop compositions "Donna Lee," "Hot House," "Groovin' High," and "Ornithology."

Modern jazz performers overcame the tendency of premodern improvisers to stop phrases at or before turnarounds (see Chapter 17 for explanation of turnarounds). Bop players took a cue from Lester Young and often began phrases in the middle of eight-bar sections, continuing them through the turnarounds, past the traditional barriers of the eighth bar (twelfth bar in the blues). They planned ahead further and mastered the improvisation of extended lines which reflected a tune's underlying chord progression less and less.

Popular Appeal   Bop was not nearly as popular as swing had been. When Charlie Parker died in 1955 he was an obscure figure compared to Benny Goodman, whose name was a household word. And yet Parker was musically a more significant force in jazz than Goodman. Some people have tried to explain bop's lack of popularity by contrasting it with jazz of the swing era. Bop was primarily a combo music and swing a big band music. It is reasonable to believe that people can grasp the simple, repeated figures which normally characterize big band arrangements more readily than they can the complex and unpredictable phrasing which characterizes improvised jazz lines. The reproduceability and polish possible with written arrangements also eases the listener's task. Big band listeners can hear much of the same music at a live performance that they have heard on broadcasts and recordings by the same band. Because it is familiar, it is easier to follow than if it were improvised anew at each performance. In combo jazz, improvisation provides far more of the music than written arrangements, thus creating greater variety and less repetition, thereby leading to increased difficulty for the listener and consequently, less popularity.

Another possible argument to explain bop's lack of popularity is a lack of singers. Traditionally, singers have been more popular with the listening public than instrumentalists. Perhaps people relate more easily to music with lyrics than music without. Bop had far fewer singers than the swing era although the bop era did produce two great singers: Billy Eckstine and Sarah Vaughan.

Another explanation often posed for bop's lack of popularity is that bop was not danced to and swing was. That is, with exceptions, quite true. Yet people could have danced to bop if they had wanted to. Bop had a steady beat and great rhythmic vitality.

Another argument attributes bop's lack of popularity to the fact that the relationship between the improvised line and the original tune was almost impossible to detect. This may have confused the listener, leaving him without a reference point. Louis Armstrong, Sidney Bechet, Coleman Hawkins and others had already departed from the original tune and used only the tune's chord progression as basis for their improvisations, but Parker, Gillespie and Monk severely stretched the connection between tune and improvisation. This argument can also be tied to the notion that jazz improvistion is too abstract for most listeners to enjoy. The increased complexity of bop was no help to that category of listeners who already had trouble following an improvised line. Perhaps when jazz improvisation was interspersed throughout simple, repeated ensemble figures, as it had been in the Count Basie and Benny Goodman bands, it was easier to appreciate than when it appeared in the concentrated bop form of solo after improvised solo.

With the advent of bop, the status of jazz began to resemble that of classical chamber music more than that of American popular music. It became an art music in the sense that its performance required highly sophisticated skills and its popular appeal was limited. Jazz had always required special skills, and, as far as American popular music went, it had long been in the elite because of its demand for so much spontaneous creativity. Yet bop seemed to crystallize those tendencies and remove jazz further from the mainstream of American popular music. It is important to note, however, that like all jazz styles, bop had fans who could not follow every note and chord, but loved it anyway. Most jazz appeals to thousands of fans who like its sound but who may not have a sophisticated understanding of its structure or historical significance. The fans of jazz proportionally include far more musicians than the fans of pop, rock and country music, but even musician-fans do not technically understand what every improviser does. Musicians do have a greater appreciation for the underlying complexities of music, but that appreciation must be coupled with an attraction to the sound before they will spend time and money to hear it. (I do not believe any understanding is necessary for a listener to enjoy jazz—modern jazz or any other style. But it is reasonable to assume that knowledge of musical techniques will increase a listener's appreciation.)

Modern jazz continued the jazz tradition of influencing American popular music and symphonic music, but it seemed to carve its own sturdy path for musicians and a small segment of the listening public. Bop became parent for a series of styles (discussed in the next several chapters) which were also less popular than swing. Jazz did not regain its popularity until the 1970s when a jazz-rock fusion brought millions of new fans.

Charlie Parker By the mid-1930s, tenor saxophonist Coleman Hawkins had taken chord-based improvisation far beyond the level of early jazz clarinetists and trumpeters. By 1940 Lester Young had contributed a light-toned swinging alternative to the ornamented and heavy-toned style of Hawkins. Bop alto saxophonist Charlie Parker (nicknamed Bird) assimilated the work of these two predecessors and created a very original style that swung gracefully and went beyond Hawkins and Young in the complexity of its melodic, harmonic, and rhythmic concepts. Compare Parker's 1940 Jay McShann recording of "Lady Be Good" (*First Recordings*) with Lester Young's 1936 Count Basie recording of the same tune. Then compare Parker's 1940 McShann version of "Body and Soul" (*First Recordings*) with the 1939 Coleman Hawkins version. The ways in which Parker was influenced by Young and Hawkins become clear.*

Bird's innovations were embodied in his lightning fast innovative alto saxophone solos. His playing was quite different from that of swing era alto giants Johnny Hodges and Benny Carter. Hodges and Carter produced lush, deep tones and quick vibrato, whereas Bird played with a dry, bittersweet tone and slower vibrato. His tone was clear and had depth, but was more biting than Carter's and Hodges's. Parker's playing was that of a high-speed modern composer rather than that of a romantic.

His improvisations were inspired by many sources. He quoted Lester Young solos (listen to Parker's 1940 recordings with Jay Mc-Shann: "Moten Swing," "Coquette," and "Lady Be Good" on *First Recordings*), traditional melodies ("Reuben, Reuben I've Been Think-ing," "Humoresque," "In a Country Garden," for example), opera (Bizet's "Carmen" was a favorite of both Parker and Gillespie), twen-tieth-century classical music (Stravinsky's prelude to "The Fairy's Kiss"), as well as hundreds of melodic fragments and inflections that were traditional in the music of black America (blues singers and early jazz hornmen). Parker ingeniously incorporated fragments from all those diverse sources into his improvisations.

Bird played with exuberance and incredible energy. He was able to breathe inspiration into his horn regardless of the musical circum-stances. When playing pop tunes such as "I'll Remember You," "The Song Is You," "April in Paris" or "Autumn in New York," he brought new life to the melodies because his interpretations were so full of warmth and confidence (*The Verve Years*). Parker was a remarkable improviser in that he maintained a high level of creativity, and the flow of his ideas seemed like an endless fountain. Bird's overall level of drive and creativity made him one of the most consistent improvisers in jazz history. For sheer number of ideas per solo, he remains un-equalled (see Figure 8.1).

After co-leading a combo with trumpeter Dizzy Gillespie (*In the Beginning—Dizzy Gillespie*), Parker led a series of his own groups, using several of the best players in bop—trumpeters Miles Davis, Red Rodney, Fats Navarro, Howard McGhee, and Kenny Dorham; pianist Al Haig; drummer Max Roach; and others (*Charles Christopher Parker, Jr. Bird/The Savoy Recordings, Charlie Parker on Dial Vols.*

---

* Alto saxophonist Buster Smith, a key figure in the 1930s jazz scene of Kansas City (Bird's hometown), was an important early influence on Parker.

Figure 8.1. Charlie Parker (alto sax) and Miles Davis (trumpet), 1949. Parker was 29 and Davis 23 years old. *Duncan Schiedt*

1–6). Not only was Parker heard with his own combos, but also with Dizzy Gillespie's big band, Woody Herman's big band, Machito's Latin band, all-star jam sessions organized by Norman Granz, and groups employing violin, viola, cello, oboe, and rhythm section. Each recording sounded as though Parker were just sitting in and so happy to be playing that he was practically blowing the roof off.

Bird also composed new material: fresh, logical melodies which had great melodic appeal and unity. They were not melody-like in the pop tune sense, but they were catchy lines in a jazz vein. Parker's phrases, both improvised and written, were memorized and analyzed by hundreds of jazz soloists. Not just alto saxophonists, but players of all instruments learned Bird's lines. Bird probably contributed more to jazz than any other bop musician.

A large number of Parker's compositions are in the twelve-bar blues form ("Billie's Bounce," "Cheryl," "Barbados," "Au Private," "Bloom-dido," "Bird Feathers," "Cool Blues," "Now's the Time," "Air Conditioning," and others). These were Parker improvisations that had been memorized and written down. They had the same style as his sponta-neous lines, but were now available for two horns to play in unison as a jumping off point for improvisation. Some of Parker's tunes were based on original chord progressions, but most were based on pop tune progressions. "Confirmation," "Billie's Bounce" and "Now's the Time" became jazz standards.

Bird directly influenced the alto saxophone styles of Phil Woods, Charlie Mariano, Sahib Shihab, Ernie Henry, Sonny Criss, Charlie McPherson, Frank Strozier, Jimmy Heath, Lou Donaldson, Davey Schildkraut, Sonny Stitt, James Moody, Jackie McLean, Cannonball Adderly, Eric Dolphy, and countless others. Bop trumpeter Dizzy Gillespie also cites Parker as a primary influence on his own style. Bop pianist Bud Powell modelled lines after those of Bird. John Coltrane, the leading saxophonist (tenor and soprano) of the 1960s, is said to have played alto in the style of Bird before he became an original and influential force himself. Parker's tunes, and occasionally his favorite phrases, could even be heard in the first recordings of saxophonists Ornette Coleman and Albert Ayler, two of the leading innovators of the 1960s. Bird, of course, was not the only musician to influence their styles, but his ideas were quite significant for them.

Parker's impact on jazz was immense. Jazz clubs were named for him: Birdland in New York and Birdhouse in Chicago. Bop singer Eddie Jefferson performed Parker's "Billie's Bounce" and "Parker's Mood" with lyrics which had been written for both the melodies of the tunes and Bird's improvisations on them. (When you hear Parker's work set to lyrics, Parker's melodic skills become all the more evident.) During the 1970s, bassist Buddy Clark and alto saxophonist Med Flory started a group called Supersax which consisted of five saxes and rhythm section playing harmonized transcriptions of Parker solos. Supersax treats Parker's improvisations as written compositions. On their recordings, the saxes are often augmented by brass or strings, but no one improvises except trumpet, trombone, and piano. Their in-person performances do contain saxophone improvisations, however.

Dizzy Gillespie   Louis Armstrong was the jazz trumpet virtuoso of the late 1920s and early 30s. Roy Eldridge held a similar position in the late 30s. But the innovative melodic concepts, high-register playing, and overall instrumental proficiency achieved by Dizzy Gillespie were not only phenomenal for the 1940s, but have rarely been matched since. Great instrumental proficiency seems to have been a necessary prerequisite for bop improvisation, and Gillespie's awe-inspiring command of the trumpet accounts for only part of his impact. His stirring musical ideas and the blazing force with which they were delivered account for much of his influence.

In addition to absorbing the saxophone-style lines and excitement of Roy Eldridge's approach, Diz contributed what was probably the most rhythmically varied style in jazz. He invented intricate syncopations which, though extremely complex, sounded both natural and vital (*Charlie Parker on Dial Vols. 1–6, The Verve Years, The Sonny Rollins/Sonny Stitt Sessions, First Recordings, The Greatest of Dizzy Gillespie, In the Beginning—Dizzy Gillespie, The Newport Years Vol. 5*).

Gillespie's phrases were full of surprises and playful changes of direction. His harmonic skills were startling, and he flaunted them. Diz could precariously go in and out of keys within a single phrase, always managing to resolve the unexpected at the next chord. He often zoomed up abruptly to the trumpet's high register in the middle of a phrase and still managed to connect the melodic ideas logically. Gillespie's lines made sense even when he played rapid cascades of notes.

Diz enjoyed playing quotes from non-jazz pieces. Bizet's opera "Carmen" was a favorite of his as it also was for Parker. Like Harry "Sweets" Edison, Gillespie could toy with a single note, playing it again and again, each time in a different way, creating different rhythmic patterns. Like Roy Eldridge, Diz made use of changes in loudness and tone color for a variety of effects. One of these was to make his tone brittle and then crack it resoundingly in a burst of high notes. Also, like Eldridge, he could channel all his terrific energy into a ballad, using his exceptional skill with harmony, his fertile imagination, and virtuoso technique to mold a unique, personal creation. A masterpiece of this kind was his 1945 "I Can't Get Started" solo (*Smithsonian Collection*).

Gillespie's pet phrases became stock clichés for two generations of jazz trumpeters; these phrases can also be heard in the playing of pianists, guitarists, saxophonists, and trombonists. During the 1940s, he influenced countless trumpeters including Howard McGhee, Red Rodney, Benny Harris, Conte Candoli, Kenny Dorham, Fats Navarro, Miles Davis, Thad Jones, and Clark Terry. Some of these players had originally derived their styles from premodern sources, but they incorporated Gillespie devices after hearing him. Though only a year or two older than several of them, Gillespie exerted the influence of a classic model rather than a mere contemporary (see Figure 8.2). During the 1970s, trumpeter Jon Faddis appeared, often quoting Gillespie recordings of the 1940s note for note.

As a composer, Gillespie also made lasting contributions to modern jazz ("Birks Works," "Emanon," "Groovin' High," "Blue 'n' Boogie," "Salt Peanuts," "Woody 'n' You," "Con Alma," "A Night in Tunisia," and others). "Con Alma," "Groovin' High" and "A Night in Tunisia" became jazz standards and have been played for decades.

After co-leading a combo with Charlie Parker and leading a few small bands of his own, Gillespie began a series of modern jazz big bands. He did some of the writing himself and assigned some to such excellent composer-arrangers as Gil Fuller, Tadd Dameron, and John Lewis. One of Gillespie's special interests, Afro-Cuban music, was explored in the big band numbers "Manteca" and the two-tune combina-

Figure 8.2. Dizzy Gillespie (wearing glasses and playing bent trumpet), age 56, and Joe Newman, age 51. *Bill Smith,* Coda

tion "Cubano Be" and "Cubano Bop." These pieces, for which Gillespie employed conga drummer Chano Pozo, are among the earliest appearances of Latin American music in modern jazz.

Gillespie kept his big bands going through most of the late 1940s and then formed another during the mid-50s for a foreign tour sponsored by the U.S. State Department. The Gillespie combos and big bands saw a powerful flow of strong players, many of whom went on to lead their own groups (see Table 8.2).

Gillespie sporadically led big bands after the State Department tour, but usually remained in a small combo format. He did not drastically alter his trumpet style after 1947, but he has remained an active performer into the 1970s.

Thelonious Monk

Though the emphasis of bop was on improvisation, there were a few outstanding bop composers. The work of pianist-composer Thelonious Monk contributed distinctively to the bop repertory. Monk wrote what were undoubtedly the most original and difficult chord changes of his era.

Monk's tunes bore a logic and symmetry all their own. Monk was expert at placing accents in irregular order. He was especially skilled

TABLE 8.2. Dizzy Gillespie Band Alumni—A Partial Listing

Saxophone

George "Big Nick" Nicholas
Don Byas
Dexter Gordon
Lucky Thompson
Sonny Stitt
James Moody
Cecil Payne
Ernie Henry
John Coltrane
Budd Johnson
Jimmy Heath
Hank Mobley
Paul Gonsalves
Yusef Lateef
Sahib Shihab
Gigi Gryce
Ernie Wilkins
Jerome Richardson
Phil Woods
Billy Mitchell
Benny Golson
Charlie Rouse

Drums

Specs Wright
Chano Pozo
Shelly Manne
Cozy Cole
Zutty Singleton
J. C. Heard
Sid Catlett
Stan Levey
Kenny Clarke
Max Roach
Joe Harris
Roy Haynes
Charlie Persip
Rudy Collins
Mickey Roker

Guitar

Kenny Burrell
George Davis
Mike Howell
Al Gafa

Trumpet

Lamar Wright
Dave Burns
Willie Cook
Gerald Wilson
Benny Harris
Kenny Dorham
Benny Bailey
Quincy Jones
Ernie Royal
Idrees Sulieman
Lee Morgan

Piano

Al Haig
John Lewis
Bud Powell
Wynton Kelly
Lalo Schifrin
Mike Longo
Billy Taylor
Junior Mance
Ray Bryant
Kenny Barron

Bass

Percy Heath
Al McKibbon
Ray Brown
Nelson Boyd
Paul West
Chris White
Tommy Bryant
Earl May
Andrew Gonzales

Trombone

J.J. Johnson
Jimmy Cleveland
Jimmy Wilkins
Billy Byers
Frank Rehak
Al Grey
Melba Liston
Sam Hurt
Curtis Fuller
Trummy Young

Vibes

Milt Jackson

Figure 8.3. Thelonious Monk (piano), age 47, Percy Heath (bass), Dizzy Gillespie. *Bill Smith,* Coda

in ending phrases on the least expected notes, yet making the piece sound as though those phrase endings had been expected all along. His "Off Minor" is a good example (*Complete Genius*).

Monk employed simple compositional devices with very original results. His "Straight, No Chaser" (*Complete Genius*) employs a single phrase played over and over again, each time in a different part of the measure. It has a few connecting passages, but it consists basically of a series of rhythmic variations on a single phrase. The shifting accents reflect a craftsmanship which can produce depth in simplicity. "Straight, No Chaser" is an ingenious invention based on the twelve-bar blues progression. Find a recording of it; no words can describe it well.

Monk's "Misterioso" (*Smithsonian Collection*) is another masterpiece of simplicity. A twelve-measure sequence of almost unending eighth notes, it has no rests, no sustained tones, just legato eighth notes. These eighth notes are not arranged in the bop manner, either. They are smooth alternations of low and high notes. Pairs of notes gradually move up and down a scale, never stopping to rest, constantly moving in stepwise fashion. "Misterioso" has exquisite simplicity.

A large portion of Monk's compositions are in thirty-two-bar AABA form: "Epistrophy" (*Complete Genius*) and "'Round Midnight" are two examples. "Epistrophy" is one of those Monk tunes which is simultaneously simple and quite original. It is usually played in medium tempo. "'Round Midnight" is one of the most frequently played ballads of the bop era. Although it is one of Monk's prettiest melodies, it is not at all conventional. Some measures contain four different chords. The tune does not even start on the first beat of the chord progression. It begins on the second beat with four notes on that single beat. Again, you must hear the tune to understand that description.

As a composer, Thelonious Monk ranks with the best in jazz history. His "Straight, No Chaser," "Well, You Needn't," "52nd Street Theme," and "'Round Midnight" are jazz standards. Bop pianist Bud Powell recorded an album called *Portrait of Thelonious*. Soprano saxophonist Steve Lacy led a band whose repertory consisted exclusively of Monk compositions.

As a pianist, Monk is a curious mixture. His use of stride piano techniques suggests Fats Waller. Some of his horn-like lines are reminiscent of Earl Hines. In some voicings, Monk's playing suggests Ellington's. Monk's style also resembles Ellington's in the percussive way both men strike the piano keys, and especially in their allowing notes to ring long after the keys are struck. Monk also likes the lower register, another Ellington preference. Monk's lines are jagged yet, at times, seem quite playful. For example, he loves to insert a whole tone scale abruptly (see Figure 8.4).

Like Basie and some examples of Ellington, Monk is extremely economical. Silence is as important as sound in his piano improvisations. He uses notes sparingly. His marked deliberation seems to preclude the long, bouncing, horn-like improvisations typical of most other modern jazz pianists. Monk's work sounds very calculated.

Monk does not swing in the easy, relaxed manner of Teddy Wilson or Nat Cole. In fact, some people feel that Monk does not swing at all,

Figure 8.4. Piano keyboard illustration of a whole tone sequence.

although his groups often swing because of his swinging bassists and drummers. Monk simply plays as a composer who is always concentrating on choosing notes and chords. Some of his rhythmic conception is anti-swing. He often builds tension with little attempt at subsequent relaxation of that tension. Monk's approach is very intense and percussive. He often strikes a note or chord several times in sequence as though knocking on a door.

Monk has influenced the compositional and improvisational flavor of much modern jazz. His style has had a direct influence on pianists Randy Weston, Herbie Nichols, Cecil Taylor, Mal Waldron, Andrew Hill, Misja Mengelberg, and Dollar Brand, and an indirect influence on many others.

Monk rarely recorded with Parker or Gillespie. He usually led his own groups, one of which almost attained the status of a jazz institution. This was the group he led between 1959 and 1970 with tenor saxophonist **Charlie Rouse.** Together with bass and drums, they made several outstanding records for Columbia (*It's Monk's Time*) and a few for other companies. Rouse, though rooted in bop tenor style, often sounded like Monk playing sax. Instead of the long, eighth-note lines of bop, Rouse often used a Monk-like approach to phrasing. Rouse was biting and percussive like Monk and often engaged in the insistent, staccato hammering of notes characteristic of Monk. He had very little vibrato and rarely sustained his tones. Rouse's style was dark, dry, and blunt.

Monk often stopped comping for considerable lengths of time. Rouse was consequently left to improvise with just bass and drums. When Monk did comp, it was not at all like conventional comping. He was neither as flexible nor as tender as many modern pianists. Monk seemed to be setting up spaces framed by resounding punches. His comping was more like a drummer's snare drum than a guitarist's chording. The Monk quartet with Rouse created a sound quite different from other modern jazz groups.

Trumpet Dizzy Gillespie was the leading jazz trumpeter at the beginning of the bop era, but by the end of the 1940s Miles Davis was also exerting an influence. And by the early 50s, Fats Navarro had influenced Clifford Brown, the most frequently imitated trumpeter of the 50s.

Gillespie's use of a very slow, almost unnoticeable vibrato soon appeared in bop trumpet styles and was not appreciably altered until Clifford Brown emerged during the early 50s with a pronounced, even vibrato.

When Charlie Parker and Gillespie separated, **Miles Davis** became Parker's new trumpeter. Davis and Parker recorded together from 1945 to 1948, but only sporadically thereafter. Counting alternate takes and recordings for both Savoy and Dial record companies, Davis recorded more than one hundred selections with Parker (*Charles Christopher Parker, Jr. Bird/The Savoy Recordings, Charlie Parker on Dial Vols. 1–6*). In these recordings, Miles displayed elements of both Gillespie's and Parker's styles, though he used a lighter, softer tone and played less in the high register than Gillespie. Other players also seem to have influenced Davis. Trumpeters Freddie Webster and Clark Terry had previously played in styles not unlike that of Davis in the Parker sessions, although it is difficult to be certain of the extent to which Davis drew on the styles of these performers. Even in 1945 Davis was an original and gifted improviser. Both his Parker combo work and his influence on trumpeters Shorty Rogers, Chet Baker, and Jack Sheldon attest to that.

The trumpeter most often mentioned as a match for Gillespie was **Fats Navarro**. The tremendous high range, speed, and instrumental proficiency of Gillespie were equalled by Navarro. In addition to that, he had a fuller, brassier tone which he used more smoothly than Gillespie. His tone was a bit clearer and more even: Navarro was not prone to alter his tone size or color as did Gillespie and Roy Eldridge. However, Navarro did not have the rhythmic imagination and daring of Gillespie. There is no question that Gillespie developed the style in which Navarro played, but Navarro offered Gillespie competition (*Prime Source*).

Rhythm Section   Concepts of rhythm section playing did not advance as rapidly as those of solo playing. On some pre-1947 recordings by Gillespie and Parker, melodies and improvisations are in a characteristic bop style, yet the rhythm sections are playing in an advanced swing era style. Some of Gillespie's rhythm sections consisted of swing style players. Like Louis Armstrong, Bird and Diz were more advanced than their accompanists.

It is difficult to find records which document the early achievements of modern jazz rhythm sections. Recordings of night club engagements and on-location radio broadcasts are more likely to feature bop playing in the rhythm section than are records of studio sessions. Drummers like Max Roach, Kenny Clarke, and Joe Harris often played conservatively in recording studios, but played innovatively during night club performances, although pianists Al Haig, Dodo Marmarosa, and Joe Albany sounded modern in both live and recorded contexts.

It is difficult to hear clearly recorded bass playing on either live or studio recordings. **Oscar Pettiford** was a bop bassist who recorded with Duke Ellington (*The World of Duke Ellington*) in the late 1940s, and although this work was not in a bop context, it was better recorded than most bop bass playing (Lucky Thompson—*Dancing Sunbeam*). Ellington's bassist Jimmy Blanton inspired most bop bassists, including Pettiford. Though many bop bassists began playing in the swing era style of Basie's Walter Page, most tried to learn some of Blanton's techniques. Few, however, could match Blanton's tone or agility, and fewer had his drive. But over the twenty years following his death, Blanton's ideas became a standard part of modern jazz bass playing. Oscar Pettiford was Blanton's strongest disciple, though Ray Brown, Tommy Potter, Al McKibbon, and Curley Russell were also favored by bop bandleaders. Pettiford explored the solo potential of the bass and led the way for such strong 1950s bass soloists as Paul Chambers, Doug Watkins, and Sam Jones. Charles Mingus, though possibly more important as a composer and bandleader, was also an inventive bassist who emerged during the bop era.

Jo Jones and Sid Catlett were the swing drummers who contributed to the development of bop drumming styles. Jones virtually eliminated bass drum playing in some contexts and had played fills which constituted some of the earliest examples of flexible interaction between soloist and drummer. Catlett kept time with a more swinging feel than was common to drummers in the 1930s. He was one of the few who was able to play with bands from both the swing and bop eras. Their advances became crystallized in the work of **Kenny Clarke** and **Max Roach**. Clarke is generally credited with influencing the adoption of ride rhythms played on a cymbal suspended up over the drum set (see Chapter 3). Those rhythms (see Chapter 18 for notations) had previously been played on the snare drum and the high-hat.

Tempo had traditionally been stated by striking the bass drum on every beat. Clarke added to that pattern by placing syncopated accents on the bass drum and snare drum (sometimes called "dropping bombs") and by keeping time on the bass drum more softly than most swing drummers. He and Max Roach also developed ways of accenting and coloring horn lines by striking their snare drums. The "fills" they played were a kind of communication between them and the improvisers. Bop drummers were not mere timekeepers.

Bop drummers, especially Max Roach, had better instrumental proficiency than the average swing drummer. Increased instrumental command was a common trait for bop players in general, but in the rhythm section, its effects were to lighten the group sound and propel it with greater momentum. Many bop tunes were taken very fast, the average tempo being greater than in swing. Bop drummers had to have more technique so that they could handle those tempos with ease.

Composer-Arrangers

One of bop's favorite composers was pianist **Tadd Dameron** (*Capitol Jazz Classics Vol. 13 Strictly Bebop, Fats Navarro—Prime Source, John Coltrane—Mating Call*). His work covered a broad range—from a bop melody based on a pop tune chord progression ("Hot House," based on "What Is This Thing Called Love") to a simple, catchy line with interesting chord changes ("Good Bait") to a pretty song scored for wordless vocal in the manner of Duke Ellington ("Casbah"). Much of his work consisted of arrangements for medium-sized bands. Dameron was good at getting a big band sound from a small band. His arrangements had voicings with the thick textures and the rhythmic style of bop piano. He would use a strong, clear-toned lead trumpet like Fats Navarro, and then assign melody notes in a block chord-fashion to alto sax, tenor sax, trombone, and baritone sax. The range of the voicing might encompass three octaves. Dameron's arranging concepts turned up in later work by Benny Golson, Gigi Gryce, and Sun Ra.

Dameron's "Hot House," "Our Delight," "Good Bait," and "Lady Bird" were quite popular with bop musicians. In 1956, tenor saxophonist John Coltrane recorded an entire album of Dameron's tunes including Dameron's attractive ballads "On a Misty Night" and "Soultrane" (*Mating Call*). Dameron was an exceptional song writer. His "If You Could See Me Now" was set to lyrics and eventually recorded by Sarah Vaughan.

The Dizzy Gillespie big band had several good writers: Gil Fuller, George Russell, Gillespie himself, and pianist **John Lewis.** For Lewis, contributing to the Gillespie library and being the band pianist was only the beginning of a productive career which had as its cornerstone more than twenty years membership in one of the most popular jazz combos in history, the **Modern Jazz Quartet** (*European Concert, The Modern Jazz Quartet*). Two of Lewis's best compositions for Gillespie were "Two Bass Hit" (also known as "La Ronde") and "Toccata for Trumpet and Orchestra." He is probably better known for works featured by the Modern Jazz Quartet such as "Django," "20°E–3°W," and his waltz "Skating in Central Park." He has written hundreds of tunes and composed for a variety of instrumentations. His ballet music, "Original Sin," was scored for symphony orchestra. "Music for Brass," on *The Golden Striker* LP, was scored for four French horns, four trumpets, two trombones, tuba, string bass, and drums. His *European Windows* LP was arranged for seventeen strings, two flutes, baritone sax, oboe, clarinet, bassoon, two French horns, three trumpets, two trombones, harp, tuba, string bass, tympani, and drums. He has also composed scores for several movies, including "A Milanese Story," "Odds against Tomorrow," "No Sun in Venice," and "One Never Knows."

One of Lewis's special interests is combining classical music and jazz. This style is called Third Stream and usually consists of mixing the instrumentation and forms characteristic of classical music with jazz improvisation and jazz feeling. The Modern Jazz Quartet often played Third Stream pieces. Another composer interested in Third Stream is Gunther Schuller, whose compositions include "Concertino for Jazz Quartet and Orchestra," written especially for the Modern Jazz Quartet. The idea of combining jazz and classical music has influenced bandleaders and composers in every era of jazz: Paul Whiteman in the 1920s; Artie Shaw in the 30s; Duke Ellington and John Lewis beginning in the 40s; and Charles Mingus, Gunther Schuller, Stan Kenton, John Lewis, George Russell, Jimmy Giuffre, Miles Davis, and Gil Evans beginning in the 1950s. The Don Ellis big bands of the 60s and 70s also explored Third Stream techniques.

In 1952 Lewis and three other former Gillespie sidemen formed what was originally called The Milt Jackson Quartet but soon became the Modern Jazz Quartet (*European Concert, The Modern Jazz Quartet*). Vibraharpist Milt Jackson, pianist John Lewis, bassist Percy Heath, and drummer Kenny Clarke created a subdued, cool sound in a bop context. Kenny Clarke left in 1955, and Connie Kay took his place. Jackson, Lewis, Heath, and Kay remained intact as a quartet until the fall of 1974 when they disbanded, but they have occasionally regrouped for tours. Over the years the Modern Jazz Quartet won many popularity polls sponsored by jazz magazines. Because of their good management and large following, they were one of the first jazz groups to play concert halls almost exclusively. The group had a delicate, chamber music sound which was polished and dignified.

Vibraharpist **Milt Jackson** (nicknamed "Bags"), who had been prominently featured in several Dizzy Gillespie groups, became recognized in the 1950s as the leading vibraharpist in modern jazz (see Figure 8.5). Not until the 1960s, when vibraharpists Gary Burton and Bobby Hutcherson began performing, was his pre-eminence seriously challenged. But Jackson, Burton, and Hutcherson do not really compete with one another because each has chosen a distinctly different area within modern jazz. Jackson is a bop player, whereas Burton and Hutcherson developed styles which reflected the significant changes that occurred in jazz of the late 1950s and early 60s.

In spite of the mechanical and percussive nature of the vibraharp, Jackson manages to extract a warm sound and project remarkable presence by a careful regulation of the vibraharp's tremolo speed (he uses especially low rates of tremolo) together with bluesy melodic figures. He often adjusts the tremolo rate while playing just as a saxophonist alters his vibrato and blowing pressure for expressive purposes. His lines are richly ornamented in a graceful, relaxed way. He ties up each phrase neatly. Jackson paces the notes within his phrases and the phrases within his choruses. Catchy melodic figures fill his lines and seem to swing effortlessly. Subtlety is a prime characteristic of Jackson's approach (see Figure 8.6).

Jackson's style is not exclusively idiomatic to the vibraharp. His lines would also sound good played by a jazz trumpeter or flutist. The

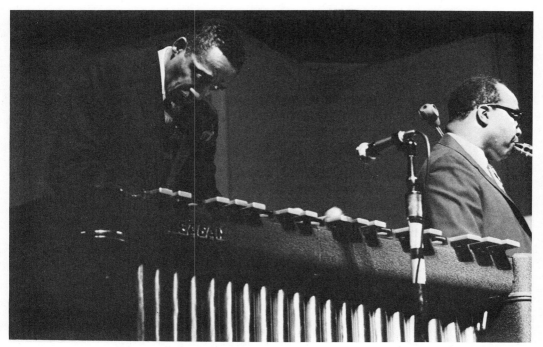

Figure 8.5. Milt Jackson (vibraharp) and James Moody (sax). *Bill Smith,* Coda

unhurried, but simmering feeling conveyed by his lines would enhance any number of styles. Jackson is a very fluid, clear-thinking improviser able to articulate his ideas beautifully through the vibraharp. His refinement of bop phrasing is a solid contribution which should not be viewed solely as the product of jazz vibraharp.

Pianist Lewis and vibraharpist Jackson occasionally improvised different lines at the same time (counterpoint). Sometimes the result was balanced and provocative, but often the two lines got in each other's way. Lewis sometimes accompanied Jackson's improvisations with piano comments which seemed almost pre-written and did not flexibly relate to directions in Jackson's lines. It might seem that because of this situation, Jackson's work with less rigid pianists should be superior to that with Lewis. But, paradoxically, Jackson's work with the Modern Jazz Quartet is better than most recordings he had made outside of its context. Jackson has also played brilliantly with Thelonious Monk (*Complete Genius*), another pianist who presents difficulties to the soloist because of his style as an accompanist. Jackson probably works well with Lewis and Monk because, in spite of their occasional lack of flexibility, they are two of the most freshly inventive pianists in jazz. Their figures probably inspired Jackson more than they hindered him.

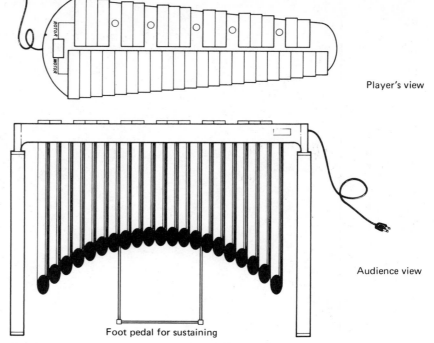

Player's view

Audience view

Foot pedal for sustaining

Figure 8.6. Vibraharp. To most people, the vibraharp (also called the vibraphone or vibes) looks like a marimba or a big xylophone with tubes hanging under its keys. The vibraharp is played similarly to the marimba and xylophone, but it is constructed differently. Its keys are metal; those of the xylophone and marimba are wooden. The vibraharp's resonating tubes are like those of the marimba, but each tube contains a disc that twirls by means of an electric motor. The twirling discs enable the sound of ringing keys to project and sustain. The discs also give the vibraharp sound a wavering character, an even pulsation called a tremolo. The sound reaches our ears in alternating pulses (wuh . . . wuh . . . wuh . . .). Tremolo is not to be confused with vibrato. Tremolo is an alternation of loudness, whereas vibrato is an alternation of pitch. Some vibraharps allow the player to control the rate of tremolo by means of a dial attached to the rotor motor. All vibraharps allow the player to start and stop sustaining the sound by means of a foot pedal.

Piano As bop styles developed, jazz piano arrived at the level of jazz trumpet and saxophone in improvisational conception, and developed from the point of just "playing with a band" to the level of sophisticated skill required for comping. By the standards of early jazz and swing, all good bop pianists were very exceptional musicians. They took up where Earl Hines and Teddy Wilson left off. Swing piano styles began to take advantage of the widening use of string bass. Pianists placed less emphasis on the left hand for supplying chorded or single note bass lines. By the time bop was under way, pianists had almost entirely abandoned the left hand's bass functions so common in stride, boogie woogie and swing piano; a new left-hand style evolved which was to characterize jazz piano for several decades. Bud Powell reduced the function of the left hand to playing syncopated bursts of chords which were rarely sustained. The left hand often jabbed two-note chords instead of three- and four-note chords. The two notes were chosen to indicate the bare essentials of chord progressions (musicians note that these jabs were often composed of a chord's root and seventh).

Bop pianists had to be musically well-rounded and very quick-witted. Bop hornmen were breaking records for speed and complexity, and the bop pianists had to do more than just solo effectively; they had to keep up with and anticipate the hornmen. They had to understand all the harmonic and rhythmic innovations of Bird and Diz, and anticipate the soloists in order to comp for them. Bop pianists had to use chords imaginatively, rhythmically set up and underscore both solo and ensemble figures, and inspire the entire group.

Bud Powell was as inspiring to pianists as Bird was to saxophonists and Diz to trumpeters (*Charles Christopher Parker, Jr. Bird/The Savoy Recordings,* Fats Navarro—*Prime Source,* Dexter Gordon—*The Dial Sessions, The Genius of Bud Powell 1949–51, Gordon/Long Tall Dexter, Smithsonian Collection*). Powell drew from Art Tatum and Nat Cole as well as from Bird and Diz. He was a driving improviser with a jabbing left hand and a harmonic imagination that possibly surpassed Tatum's. In his prime (prior to the mid-1950s), Powell had the speed and dexterity to create piano solos that matched the high-powered inventions of Bird and Diz. He mastered the erratically syncopated rhythms of bop and charged through his solos with terrific force. He employed the octave-voiced horn lines of Earl Hines and the complex runs of Art Tatum. Powell was the model for hundreds of pianists during the 1940s and 50s, as James P. Johnson had been during the 1920's and Earl Hines had been after Johnson.

Though Powell lived until 1966, he was only sporadically active throughout most of his career. He did not appear on nearly the number of recording sessions that pianist **Al Haig** played (*The Greatest of Dizzy Gillespie, In the Beginning—Dizzy Gillespie, Stan Getz—Greatest Hits*). Haig was the most in-demand bop pianist. He traveled with many of the top groups, including Parker's and Stan Getz's, and made hundreds of recordings. His flowing solos and tasteful comping made him a figure on the bop scene who paralleled Tommy Flanagan's position during the middle 1950s and early 60s and Herbie Hancock's position throughout the 60s.

Though still a developing bop pianist when he recorded with Diz in 1947, Haig was a very solid craftsman by the time he began recording with Stan Getz in 1949. He never seemed at a loss for ideas. His touch was light and clean. In some ways he resembled Teddy Wilson. Haig could play hard, driving pieces or slow, pretty ballads. On occasion he could be quite flowery, but usually he was a very direct, swinging player.

Two bop pianists who found much larger popular audiences than

Haig or Powell were **George Shearing** and **Oscar Peterson.** Shearing became known primarily for the group sound he perfected: soft, polished ensemble statements voiced for piano, guitar, vibraharp, bass, and drums. Peterson's reputation was established in a trio format (piano, guitar, and bass; and later, piano, bass, and drums).

Shearing has what is probably the cleanest, lightest piano sound in bop. His music is so refined that it has been called polite bop. In addition to playing single note lines and octave-voiced lines, he helped popularize the locked-hands style first heard in Milt Buckner's playing of the mid-1940s. Shearing's voicings contrast markedly with those of Buckner, however. Shearing brought a very sophisticated harmonic conception to jazz piano (*The Best of George Shearing, Touch of Genius, You're Hearing George Shearing*). Shearing often voiced melodies so that chording was achieved by ensemble playing of a line in harmony or in octaves. Piano, guitar, and vibes might play a melody in unison or in harmony while bass and drums underscored critical figures and kept time. Individual solos followed, framed by ensemble fills and endings, all well rehearsed and precisely performed. Everything swung and was well controlled.

Shearing also achieved a successful integration of Latin American elements and bop. Armando Peraza played auxiliary percussion in Shearing's group from 1954 until 1964. Shearing's bassist Al McKibbon had developed Latin American bass figures while playing Afro-Cuban music in Dizzy Gillespie's big band with Cuban drummer Chano Pozo. McKibbon brought Peraza to Shearing's attention and then collaborated with Peraza to integrate Latin rhythms with Shearing's techniques.

Peraza was not the only exciting player Shearing employed. Guitarists Chuck Wayne and Joe Pass, vibraharpists Cal Tjader and Gary Burton, and many other excellent modern jazz musicians worked in Shearing's groups.

Shearing also wrote many interesting jazz tunes. His "Conception," with its difficult chord changes, was recorded by Miles Davis twice, though the name was changed to "Deception." "Local 802 Blues" was popular with late 1940s and early 50s musicians. Shearing's "Lullaby of Birdland," a theme song for the New York jazz club, Birdland, became a very popular jazz standard.

Oscar Peterson is one of the most widely envied pianists in jazz history. His extraordinary pianistic facility and endurance enable him to take incredibly fast tempos which bassists and drummers can barely maintain. Peterson has a distinctive style stemming from the approaches of Nat Cole, Bud Powell, and Art Tatum. He has the combined drive of Powell and Tatum yet lacks the originality they brought to jazz. He also has incorporated the funky, gospel-flavored figures popularized by Horace Silver during the 1950s. Peterson's ballad style is full and orchestral. He sweeps the entire keyboard with astounding command. Since the late 1940s, Peterson has been a solid force on the modern jazz scene whose surging power and vitality never seemed the least bit diminished (*The Modern Jazz Quartet and the Oscar Peterson Trio at the Opera House, Return Engagement, Tenderly*).

Clarinet   The clarinet has not been an important instrument in modern jazz. One of the most popular instruments during the swing era, it became one of the least popular during the bop era. Clarinet has almost disappeared as a jazz instrument. It is easy to name ten to twenty bop saxophonists and at least ten good bop trumpeters. Few people can name more than two bop clarinetists. Tony Scott, Stan Hasselgard, and Buddy DeFranco made valiant attempts to adopt bop to the clarinet, but their efforts did not catch on.

Guitar   Guitar disappeared as a member of the rhythm section during the bop era, but it returned as a solo instrument. Bop was a style pioneered by Bird and Diz which was soon assimilated by players of other instruments. Guitarists were among the last to play in a bop style, and when they did, they still were not improvising with the originality of Parker and Gillespie. The strongest bop guitarists were more active during the late 1940s and early 50s than during the developmental period of the mid-40s. Jimmy Raney and Tal Farlow were outstanding bop guitarists. Raney made several very impressive records with Stan Getz (*Best of Stan Getz*), and Farlow recorded with Red Norvo. Both men also worked with Buddy DeFranco's sextet.

Trombone   The bop style was so instrumentally demanding, that it is surprising that it could be adapted to so difficult an instrument as the slide trombone. And it is a paradox that the two major bop trombonists, J.J. Johnson and Kai Winding, did not use the easier valve trombone, and that Bob Brookmeyer, a performer who specialized in valve trombone, actually preferred a conception that was slower and more easygoing than the high-speed style mastered by Johnson and Winding. Brookmeyer occasionally played fast but always sounded laid back.

J.J. Johnson developed a dense, clean, full sound, which was darker than Winding's. He concentrated on simple, swinging lines and used very little vibrato (*The Eminent Jay Jay Johnson Vols. 1 and 2, Stan Getz and J.J. Johnson at the Opera House*). Johnson attacked each note cleanly and maintained consistent size and quality throughout its duration.

As a trombonist, leader, and composer-arranger, Johnson was prominent in modern jazz of the 1950s and 60s. But by the early 70s, he was primarily involved in composing and arranging music for movies and television instead of improvising jazz. His style was imitated by most trombonists during the 50s and 60s. There were several other modern jazz trombone styles (Bob Brookmeyer's, Frank Rosolino's, Roswell Rudd's, Jimmy Knepper's), but none had the impact of J.J.'s.

Tenor Saxophone

Bop tenor saxophonists drew their styles from two primary sources: Lester Young and Charlie Parker, and several secondary sources including Coleman Hawkins, Herschel Evans, Illinois Jacquet, and Don Byas. Some preferred to play the phrases of Lester Young almost unmodified, while others simply adopted the phrases of alto saxophonist Charlie Parker and played them on tenor sax. The most original players mixed several sources with a quantity of their own ideas. None were of Parker's stature, but several helped lay the groundwork for the styles of Sonny Rollins and John Coltrane.

It is possible to classify bop tenor saxophonists in several ways, but the most direct approach lies in the dimension of tone. Bop tenor saxophonists preferred either light-weight, light-colored tones or heavy-weight, dark-colored tones. There are gradations within these categories, of course, but it might be helpful to first describe players in terms of the two extremes, and then form your own descriptions to increase and refine your perceptions. The light-toned players include Stan Getz, Herbie Steward, Allen Eager, Brew Moore, and several players of a somewhat later style (West Coast): Buddy Collette, Bill Perkins, Bob Cooper, Richie Kamuca, and others. The heavy-toned players include Dexter Gordon, Gene Ammons, Lucky Thompson, Wardell Gray, Sonny Stitt, and others.

Dexter Gordon was one of the least stereotyped bop tenor saxophonists. He used a large variety of melodic devices to create his lines. His phrase lengths and rhythms were varied, and he combined bop clichés with his own inventions. Gordon loved to quote from pop tunes and bugle calls. His tone was deep, dark, and full. Although his style was quite aggressive, his work conveyed great ease. He used the entire range of the tenor but had a special love for its low register (*The Dial Sessions, Long Tall Dexter*). Gordon was a favorite player for many saxophonists who were later called hard bop tenors. Among them was John Coltrane, whose early 1950s recordings with Johnny Hodges and Dizzy Gillespie sound a bit like Gordon. Gordon has had a strong recording career from the 1940s to the present, and his playing has displayed depth and swing for over three decades. Since 1962, he has been based in Denmark.

Wardell Gray was often compared with Gordon because the two men occasionally played together and, for many people, represented the best of bop tenor (*Central Avenue*). Gray's approach was different from Gordon's, however. Gray was cooler and melodically less adventurous. He also had a lighter tone and slower vibrato, and his playing bore smoother, more predictable contours than Gordon's. Gray's debt to Lester Young was obvious in almost every chorus. He mixed some

Parker with his Young and produced a style characterized by uniformity of swing, note duration, attacks, and tone quality. Whereas Gordon was quite aggressive, Gray was graceful.

Lucky Thompson was significantly different from both Gordon and Gray. Instead of using Lester Young, Thompson used Don Byas as a model. He swung more easily than Byas, and had more consistent facility, and used a slower vibrato. Thompson's lines were very long and harmonically rich. He seemed to be using as many chords as he could imagine fitting in a chord progression. Though not as melodic as Gordon, he constructed solos which displayed a lot of continuity (*Dancing Sunbeam*). Like Gordon, Thompson has remained active into the 1970s and spent considerable time in Europe.

For flowing, powerfully swinging solos, very few modern saxophonists can compete with **Sonny Stitt.** His instrumental speed and precision are awesome. During the late 1940s and early 50s, Stitt was second only to Charlie Parker as the leading bop alto saxophonist, and his recordings with Bud Powell placed him in the highest rank of bop tenor saxophonists. Stitt's playing has a consistently logical construction and rarely lacks continuity. Though not the original idea man that either Don Byas or Dexter Gordon was, Stitt still managed to influence young saxophonists of the 1950s with a style which owed much to Lester Young and Charlie Parker. Some of Stitt's best work can be found in recordings made with Dizzy Gillespie ("Eternal Triangle," *The Sonny Rollins/Sonny Stitt Sessions*), Bud Powell ("All God's Chillun," *Bud's Blues*), and fellow tenor saxophonist Gene Ammons ("Blues Up and Down"). Frank Foster, George Coleman, and Joe Henderson are among the saxophonists who have cited Stitt as an influence.

Stan Getz was the most popular tenor saxophonist to emerge during the 1940s (see Figure 8.7). Unlike most bop tenors, he used few of Parker's and Gillespie's pet phrases. He developed an original melodic and rhythmic vocabulary. His phrasing and accenting were less varied and less syncopated than Parker's or Gillespie's. At times, pre-twentieth century classical music seems to have influenced him more than bop (*Best of Stan Getz, Stan Getz—Focus, Greatest Hits, Stan Getz and J.J. Johnson at the Opera House*). His main influences were Lester Young and Herbie Steward. (Getz and Steward played together in the sax section of Woody Herman's band. Steward had an original approach inspired by Lester Young.) Some 1949–50 Getz recordings also sound a bit like Lee Konitz, a modern jazz alto saxophonist not influenced by Parker (see Chapter 9).

Like Wardell Gray, Getz played in a style rhythmically more like that of Lester Young than like Bird. Getz did not usually sound as relaxed as Gray or Gordon, but he was just as melodic as Gordon, perhaps more melodic. His improvisations were less like bop melodies

Figure 8.7. Stan Getz, age 47. *Bill Smith,* Coda

than like melodies in classical music. Some were quite pretty. That aspect of his style fit well with his light, fluffy tone and graceful approach to the sax.

One of the prettiest pieces the Woody Herman big band ever recorded was "Summer Sequence" by Ralph Burns. It was rearranged several times during the late 1940's. One segment often lifted out was "Early Autumn," a feature for the inventions of Stan Getz. That piece became a thirty-two-bar AABA pop tune and brought Getz to national attention. With that recording, Getz proved that he was one of the most sensitive and resourceful ballad players in jazz history.

His other hits also took the form of slow, pretty pieces. His 1952 "Moonlight in Vermont" with guitarist Johnny Smith was quite popular. His 1962 "Desafinado" with guitarist Charlie Byrd was a major event in the popularization of bossa nova, a cross between Brazilian music and jazz.

Getz has led several excellent groups, some of which had the best rhythm sections in jazz. For a while in the early 1950s, Getz played with pianist Al Haig, bassist Teddy Kotick, and drummer Tiny Kahn. He had another outstanding rhythm section for a short time during the early 1970s: pianist Chick Corea, bassist Stanley Clarke, drummer Tony Williams, and auxiliary percussionist Airto Moreira.

Bop did not have the large popular following of swing, but a few bop bandleaders were financially successful. At times, both Gillespie and Parker made good salaries, and pianists George Shearing and Oscar Peterson saw continued success in the 1950s and 60s. One band in particular was acclaimed by a broader audience than that which usually greeted modern jazz. That band was led by tenor saxophonist **Charlie Ventura** (*In Concert, It's All Bop to Me*). Ventura was a solid bop tenor player with a very large, deep, dark tone. He was not a notable innovator, but he played with a lot of power. Ventura's group included trumpeter Conte Candoli, trombonist Bennie Green, and alto saxophonist Boots Mussulli. All three men were, like Ventura, very strong players, but not outstanding originators. The band also featured a team of very musical singers: Jackie Cain and Roy Kral. Both singers were almost as good as bop hornmen. They had full, clear tones and sang with excellent intonation and diction. Many of their parts were wordless, so they were actually functioning as instruments. They played an important role in the polished, tightly arranged pieces performed by Ventura's group.

TABLE 9.1. West Coast Style Musicians—A Partial Listing

Trumpet

Chet Baker
Conte Candoli
Jack Sheldon
Shorty Rogers
Stu Williamson

Trombone

Bob Brookmeyer
Frank Rosolino
Bob Enevoldsen
Milt Bernhart

Tenor Sax

Bill Perkins
Richie Kamuca
Bob Cooper
Jack Montrose
Buddy Collette
Dave Pell
Bill Holman
Jimmy Giuffre
Zoot Sims

Alto Sax

Art Pepper
Bud Shank
Herb Geller
Lennie Niehaus
Paul Desmond

Baritone Sax

Gerry Mulligan
Bob Gordon

Guitar

Howard Roberts
Barney Kessel

Piano

Hampton Hawes
Claude Williamson
Russ Freeman
Pete Jolly
Vince Guaraldi
Carl Perkins
Andre Previn
Dave Brubeck

Bass

Red Mitchell
Red Callender
Leroy Vinnegar
Buddy Clark
Carson Smith
Howard Rumsey
Curtis Counce
Joe Mondragon
Monte Budwig

Drums

Shelley Manne
Mel Lewis
Stan Levey
Larry Bunker
Chico Hamilton

Composer-Arrangers

Gerry Mulligan
Dave Brubeck
Shorty Rogers
Dave Pell
John Graas
Jimmy Giuffre
Bill Holman
Marty Paich
Dave Brubeck

chapter 9
JAZZ IN THE 1950s

TRANSITIONAL
FIGURES OF
THE 40s:
Lennie
Tristano
and Lee
Konitz

Lennie Tristano is a pianist, composer and bandleader who created a modern jazz alternative to bop during the late 1940s. At that time, it was the strongest alternative available. Although rarely a performer since then, he impressed his students enough to inspire them to carry on his style (see Figure 9.1).

Tristano was a pianist so skilled he could play impressive Art Tatum runs. (Tatum and tenor saxophonist Lester Young were both important influences for him.) Another technique he perfected was improvising in the locked-hands style of Milt Buckner, though his work was more varied and daring than Buckner's.

Tristano's long lines were less jumpy than Charlie Parker's and Dizzy Gillespie's, with smoother, more straight-line contours than bop improvisation. They often seemed not to stem directly from the chords, either. Tristano's lines often seemed a step or a half step away, creating an unresolved feeling. His lines were not melodic in the pop tune sense or in the bop sense.

Like bop, Tristano's music was harmonically complex, often employing several chord changes in a single measure. Yet the pet phrases of Charlie Parker and Dizzy Gillespie did not find their way into his improvisations. Tristano's playing seemed full of precisely calculated complexity. Bop had moments of calculated complexity also, yet seemed to generally flow naturally and warmly from Parker's and Gillespie's horns.

Tristano's most talented students during the late 1940s were alto saxophonist Lee Konitz, tenor saxophonist Warne Marsh, and guitarist Billy Bauer. Together with bass and drums, these musicians made

Figure 9.1. Lee Konitz (alto sax), Warne Marsh (tenor sax), Lennie Tristano (piano). *Duncan Schiedt*

recordings displaying technical feats which still dazzled other musicians decades later.

As in the subsequent West Coast style, bass and drums played a very conservative role in Tristano's music. In fact on several recordings they can hardly be heard. Timekeeping seemed to be their only function. But keeping time for the Tristano groups was no easy job: some tunes were played at furious tempos.

Alto saxophonist Konitz played lines very similar to those Tristano used, and his instrumental technique was as impressive as Tristano's. Konitz's tone color was quite unlike the lush sound of his predecessors Benny Carter and Johnny Hodges, or the bittersweet style of his contemporary, Charlie Parker. Konitz played with a dry, light tone and slow vibrato reminiscent of Lester Young.

It is quite important to realize that Konitz was developing and maintaining his own Tristano-inspired, modern jazz alto style at a time when nearly every young alto saxophonist was imitating Charlie Parker, not only in tone, but in bop rhythmic and melodic conception. Konitz was almost totally unrelated to Parker. He was much more a product of Tristano's piano style. That piano style was, in turn, unlike most of bop piano. Bop pianist Al Haig was influenced by swing pianist Teddy Wilson, and Bud Powell was influenced by swing pianists Art Tatum, Billy Kyle, and Nat Cole. But Tristano was as much a product of twentieth-century classical music as of swing styles. In fact, Tristano did not swing in the customary bop manner. He tended instead to be tight, very much on top of the beat rather than laid back of the beat, with less pronounced syncopation than Parker and Gillespie used. Tristano's playing lacked the rhythmic variety of bop; his improvisations were characterized by long strings of uninterrupted eighth notes. His style swung, but in a much tighter way than bop.

Lee Konitz went on to influence many alto saxophonists during the 1950s. Although Konitz was based in New York, his influence was strongest in California. West Coast alto players Bud Shank and Lennie Niehaus absorbed portions of both Konitz and Parker to create their own styles. Art Pepper developed the strongest West Coast alto style by combining the influences of Konitz, tenor saxophonist Zoot Sims, and Charlie Parker.

During the middle 1950s, especially after 1954, Konitz initiated a gradual change in style which continued through the 1970s. It resembled a dilution of his previously full, meaty lines inspired by Tristano; Konitz apparently lost some of his speed and tone as well. Silences became more common in his playing, which was more varied rhythmically than it was with Tristano. His music was also a bit bluesy on occasion.

Some of Konitz's best work, apart from his playing with Tristano, can be found in the 1949–50 Miles Davis *Birth of the Cool* recordings, the 1953 Lee Konitz–Gerry Mulligan–Chet Baker recording *Konitz Meets Mulligan*, and his 1947 recordings with Claude Thornhill (*The Memorable Claude Thornill*).

Tenor saxophonist **Warne Marsh** had a tone and vibrato similar to Lester Young's. And Marsh, like Konitz, played lines constructed much like Tristano's. Marsh and Konitz often played unison melody statements written in the distinctive Tristano manner (*Subconscious-Lee with Lennie Tristano*). Their performances were so precise that it often seemed that only a single horn was playing. Their instrumental skill and familiarity with the Tristano sound was so remarkable that, especially at furious tempos, it was sometimes difficult to determine which lines were prewritten and which were improvised. Some Marsh and Konitz playing resembled Bach fugue style. This was no coincidence; they actually rehearsed and practiced improvising fugues.

Warne Marsh was heard during the 1970s in a group called Supersax, which consisted of five saxes, one or two brass soloists, and a rhythm section. Supersax played harmonized transcriptions of Charlie Parker solos. Marsh was rhythmically looser and more daring during the 1970s than in the 1940s and remained a thoroughly inventive improviser with a style unlike that of any other tenor saxophonist.

Guitarist **Billy Bauer** possessed that awesome instrumental speed typical of bop guitarists Bill DeArango and Tal Farlow. Bauer's technique was equal to the complex lines and feverish tempos of Tristano, Konitz, and Marsh. Of the three major Tristano alumni (Konitz, Marsh, and Bauer), Bauer reflects Tristano's style the least, displaying the additional influences of bop and Charlie Christian.

In addition to adapting melodic concepts unusual in jazz playing, Tristano was also one of the first to record collective improvisation free of preset melody and preset chord progressions ("Intuition" and "Digression," *Crosscurrents*). The music was not totally free of form in that large portions of it approximated constant tempo and key feeling, but it was quite free compared to most jazz of the 1940s. (During the 1960s and 70s, Ornette Coleman, Cecil Taylor, and others commonly improvised without preset chord progressions.)

Lennie Tristano has recorded very little in his career—the equivalent of approximately four albums. Since his work does not sell at all well, his recordings are collectors' items. The only work in the catalogs when this book went to press was half of an album on Capitol (the other half is Buddy DeFranco) called *Crosscurrents*. Tristano remains active as a teacher, and in fact, teaching has been his primary occupation since 1951.

Through Konitz, Tristano has influenced Bill Evans, a pianist who became very important during the 1960s. Although very much his own man by 1959, Evans displayed Tristano-like phrases in his work with George Russell and Tony Scott during the late 1950s. Tristano's piano style has directly influenced two strong jazz pianists, Sal Mosca and Ronnie Ball. Mosca has appeared on several albums with Konitz and Marsh.

Birth of the Cool

After leaving Charlie Parker's group, Miles Davis rarely appeared as a sideman. In 1949 and 1950, he recorded for Capitol record company with a nine-piece band of his own.° That work has become known as *The Birth of the Cool,* and it was to have an important influence on jazz in the 1950s (*The Complete Birth of the Cool*). Its sound stemmed partly from concepts pioneered during the 1940s by pianist-composer-arranger-bandleader Claude Thornhill and arranger Gil Evans (*The Memorable Claude Thornhill*). But there were other ingredients as well. Lee Konitz's lines, inspired by Lennie Tristano, and his light, dry, almost vibratoless tone were fundamental to the *Birth of the Cool* sound. In addition to Konitz on alto sax and Davis on trumpet, the session included Gerry Mulligan, a baritone saxophonist who also had

---

° The selections, which were eventually grouped on a 33 r.p.m. long-playing album entitled *The Birth of the Cool,* had originally been issued as 78 r.p.m. records with two tunes on each.

a light, dry tone and had played and arranged for Thornhill. A departure from convention was made in that neither tenor saxophone nor guitar was used, and the instrumentation was filled out by French horn, tuba, trombone, and rhythm section.

The subdued feeling that Davis, Konitz, and Mulligan brought to their solos and the dry, mellow textures achieved by the nonet's unique instrumentation created a truly delicate, cool sound. The band was not loud, brassy, or massive sounding. The music was light, sophisticated and, at times, resembled classical chamber music. Recordings by Lennie Tristano-led groups of the same period also achieved that effect. The influence of Claude Thornhill, Gil Evans, and Lennie Tristano was strongly felt by young jazz arrangers during the late 1940s (*The Memorable Claude Thornhill*). It was the freshest sound in the air during that period.

The Thornhill band had an unorthodox instrumentation, sometimes including six clarinets, two French horns, and tuba in addition to the usual trumpets, trombones, and rhythm section. (In fact, for all *Birth of the Cool* recording sessions, Davis employed Thornhill's tuba player Bill Barber, his alto saxophonist Lee Konitz, and, for one session each, bassist Joe Shulman and French hornist Sandy Siegelstein.) This combination of instruments and the characteristic Thornhill voicings stemming from his love for the music of Claude Debussy were the basis of an original sound. For example, French horn sometimes had the lead. Clarinet sometimes doubled the melody with French horn. Saxophones were voiced below French horn and clarinet. The lowest sounds (tenor sax, baritone sax, or tuba) often doubled the melody. It was Gil Evans's idea to assign tuba the melody, but Thornhill was already using French horn and clarinet at the time Evans joined him. The saxophones and clarinets sometimes played softly, in very low registers, with little or no vibrato. Compared to conventional big band arranging which employed much internal movement and brassy excitement, Thornhill's work created a stillness and replaced bright, loud, conventional big band colors with pastels.

Miles Davis consolidated the influences of Thornhill, Evans, and Tristano in his high-quality *Birth of the Cool* sessions. Of all the late 1940s recordings made by groups employing these concepts, the Davis nonet recordings are remembered and cited the most. This was the first of many instances in which Davis was closely involved with major innovations in jazz.

The tunes played by the Davis nonet, however, were more within the bop idiom than within the Tristano idiom or the swing idiom. But emphasis on arrangements was not frequent in bop, and the nonet's arrangements gave bop tunes distinctive twists. Most bop groups assigned the melody to the horns, playing in unison before and after a series of long, improvised solos with the rhythm section, but the Davis nonet replaced that with a scheme which wove short, improvised solos into written arrangements much as Duke Ellington had done. Some arrangements also placed attractive melodic figures underneath some of the solos. Orchestral textures were occasionally altered within a single arrangement, also. The alterations were always made gracefully. Davis, Gil Evans, Gerry Mulligan, John Lewis, and Johnny Carisi wrote for the nonet. Mulligan wrote the largest number of arrangements: a total of five.

As early as 1946, pianist Dave Brubeck had recorded work similar to the *Birth of the Cool*. During the 1950s, baritone saxophonist Gerry Mulligan, French hornist-composer John Graas (also a veteran of the Thornhill band), composer-trumpeter Shorty Rogers and others composed for, arranged for, and led bands similar to the Miles Davis nonet. Davis himself abandoned the nonet approach not long after beginning it. Except for his late 1950s big band collaborations with Gil Evans, Davis subsequently remained with small groups and concentrated almost exclusively on improvisation instead of arranging.

WEST COAST STYLE OF THE 1950s   The Birth of the Cool was an important influence in the development of the so-called West Coast style. During the 1950s, the style of jazz which seemed to dominate the playing of California musicians employed light-weight, light-colored tones which had soft, dry textures. Although incorporating the melodic and harmonic advances of bop, the West Coast style had a smoother, more tune-like sound than bop improvisation. The music often projected a relaxed feeling, in contrast to the intensity of bop. It was a restrained, understated approach labeled cool by many listeners (see Table 9.1).

Lester Young, Miles Davis, and Lee Konitz were important in influencing the West Coast style. West Coast trumpeters mixed larger portions of Davis in their styles and smaller portions of Gillespie. Tenor saxophonists seemed more inspired by Lester Young than by Dexter Gordon or Lucky Thompson. Alto saxophonists mixed large portions of Lee Konitz with the ideas of Charlie Parker. (Different proportions surfaced in the playing of each musician.) Arrangers adopted the approaches of Claude Thornhill and Gil Evans. Several bands were modeled after the 1949–50 Miles Davis nonet.

The style of jazz known as West Coast was played far more by white than by black musicians. A number of these musicians had been members of the predominantly white big bands of Woody Herman and Stan Kenton (see Table 9.2).

West Coast was not the only style of jazz being played in California during the 1950s. Charlie Parker and Dizzy Gillespie both performed there, and tenor saxophonists Wardell Gray and Dexter Gordon spent more time there than Bird and Diz. Dixieland was also

TABLE 9.2. West Coast Style Players Who Were Alumni of the Woody Herman and Stan Kenton Big Bands

Kenton	Herman
Lee Konitz	Bill Perkins
Art Pepper	Richie Kamuca
Bud Shank	Shorty Rogers
Lennie Niehaus	Jimmy Giuffre
Bill Holman	Conte Candoli
Richie Kamuca	Stan Levey
Conte Candoli	Shelly Manne
Jack Sheldon	Red Mitchell
Mel Lewis	Stu Williamson
Stan Levey	
Shelly Manne	
Bob Cooper	
Frank Rosolino	
Stu Williamson	
Milt Bernhart	

popular. The light, dry melodic playing characteristic of West Coast players could also be heard on the East Coast in the Basie-derived approaches of saxophonist Al Cohn, pianist Nat Pierce and others, as well as several Konitz-influenced players.

Gerry Mulligan was the baritone saxophonist and the primary composer-arranger in the 1949–50 Miles Davis nonet sessions. He also wrote for the Claude Thornhill and Stan Kenton big bands. Mulligan had a dry, light-weight, light-colored tone and an unhurried and sub-dued approach to improvisation. In 1952, Mulligan moved to California and began a series of piano-less quartets consisting of himself on baritone sax, another horn, bass, and drums (*Timeless, Two of a Mind—Paul Desmond, Gerry Mulligan; What Is There to Say?*). The Mulligan quartets became popularly identified with West Coast style jazz. It is interesting to note that although much attention was gained by Mulligan's abandoning the use of piano, several later groups also omitted piano and created far more radical sounds (Ornette Coleman, Albert Ayler, Archie Shepp, The Art Ensemble of Chicago, and others).

Mulligan's compositions were neither as complex as Lennie Tristano's, nor full of the twists and turns which typified bop writing. A few were quite song-like. They had the same soft, calm character that was projected by Mulligan's improvisations.

Compared to East Coast contemporaries Art Blakey and Philly Joe Jones, Mulligan's drummers Chico Hamilton and Larry Bunker played conservatively. One of Mulligan's trumpeters, **Chet Baker,** also had a soft, mellow approach. Baker's cool, relaxed style is often considered a parallel to those of Bix Beiderbecke and early Miles Davis.

Mulligan considers his best recordings to include some 1953 material produced by a ten-piece band employing tuba and French horn, an instrumentation similar to that of the 1949–50 Miles Davis nonet. Mulligan's writing also played a significant role in his East Coast-based big band called The Concert Jazz Band, which employed simple, relaxed playing with a light, dry sound. It was one of the most unusual bands to emerge in the early 1960s. Mulligan shared the band's composing and arranging assignments with Bob Brookmeyer, Gary McFarland, Johnny Carisi, and others.

Valve trombonist **Bob Brookmeyer** was a frequent member of Mulligan's piano-less quartets and The Concert Jazz Band. His melodic, often humorous lines and relaxed, laid-back style were quite compatible with Mulligan. Brookmeyer is one of the few modern players whose work strongly suggests early jazz and swing. He loves bending notes and altering tone color. Brookmeyer's arranging is clear and intelligent, sometimes reminiscent of Gil Evans (see Chapter 10). Brookmeyer and Mulligan were The Concert Jazz Band's primary soloists, although trumpeter Clark Terry, tenor saxophonist Zoot Sims, and others were sometimes featured. Brookmeyer later wrote for and played with the Thad Jones–Mel Lewis big band of the 1960s and 70s.

One of the most novel West Coast combos was led by former Mulligan quartet drummer **Chico Hamilton**. Like the Mulligan quartet, Hamilton's quintet had no piano. It consisted of guitar, cello, bass, drums, and a hornman who played saxophones, flute, and clarinet. With tightly arranged pieces and excellent musicianship, Hamilton's quintet created a jazz style which resembled classical chamber music. Its textures were light and pretty, and the arrangements displayed variety, too (*Spectacular! The Chico Hamilton Quintet*). Several melodies were sometimes played at the same time. That technique is called counterpoint, and it characterized early jazz improvisation. (Mulligan and his hornmen had also shown interest in reviving counterpoint as a jazz device.)

The Hamilton quintet employed cellist Fred Katz, guitarist Jim Hall, bassist Carson Smith, and reedman Buddy Collette—all careful, understated improvisers who were attuned to the general feeling of West Coast style. Eventually Chico altered the character of his group and employed such outgoing saxophonists as Eric Dolphy and Charles Lloyd. But while Buddy Collette was with him, things were rather calm.

California pianist-composer-arranger **Dave Brubeck** (see Figure 9.2) led a series of small bands during the late 1940s which employed approaches similar to the 1949–50 Miles Davis nonet (*The Dave Brubeck Octet*). From 1951 to 1967, he maintained a quartet with alto

Figure 9.2. Dave Brubeck (piano), Paul Desmond (alto sax), Joe Morello (drums). *Duncan Schiedt*

saxophonist **Paul Desmond** and occasionally regrouped thereafter. Except for a few LPs recorded for Fantasy, most of Brubeck's albums were made for Columbia (*The Fantasy Years, Gone With the Wind/ Time Out*).

Desmond's light, dry tone resembled that of Lee Konitz, but Desmond's approach to improvisation was his own. He was extremely economical, very cool, and quite melodic. Desmond was one of the first jazz alto players to explore the instrument's extreme high register, the altissimo range. Some of Desmond's solos contained notes far higher than the normal high range of the alto saxophone. He composed "Take Five," the Brubeck quartet's biggest hit.

Brubeck himself is a prolific composer. The melodic quality of his tunes and improvisations is outstanding. Trumpeter Miles Davis has recorded Brubeck's "In Your Own Sweet Way" and "The Duke," the latter arranged by Gil Evans. Brubeck's work has much in common with classical music. In fact, a lot of his piano playing has a distinctly classical rhythmic feeling. Though a competent pianist, he does not play with the ease, speed, or precision of his West Coast contemporaries, Claude Williamson and Hampton Hawes.

Brubeck's drummer for many years, Joe Morello, has amazing

speed and precision. He became known to thousands of young musicians during the 1960s because of the Brubeck quartet's immense popularity and Morello's drum company-sponsored clinics. It is ironic that he received more notice than such innovative drummers as Max Roach, Art Blakey, Philly Joe Jones, Tony Williams, and Elvin Jones. Like another very popular drummer, Buddy Rich, Morello has impressive facility, but is conservative as a rhythm section member. It is also ironic that Morello and Rich both gained great response for soloing, an aspect of modern jazz drumming which was secondary to the advances being made at that time in emancipating concepts of rhythm section playing. Morello was quite successful in mastering unusual meters, however.

An interest of Brubeck's which brought him a large amount of publicity was the use of meters unusual to jazz, such as three, five and seven.* His albums *Time Out* and *Time Further Out*, which explored those meters, were very popular. His recording of Desmond's "Take Five," in a meter of five, was also issued as a single, an unusual occurrence for jazz of the late 1950s and early 60s. Brubeck was one of the most popular jazz musicians of the 50s, and "Take Five" carried his commercial success well into the 60s.

The composer-arranger for the Woody Herman big band's famous sax feature, "Four Brothers," was **Jimmy Giuffre.** One of the most versatile and original exponents of the cool style, Giuffre composes and performs in a multitude of contexts, including unaccompanied clarinet ("So Low"); clarinet and string orchestra ("Mobiles"); clarinet, trombone, and guitar (*Western Suite* and *Travelin' Light*); clarinet and celeste (with Jimmy Rowles, "Deep Purple"); clarinet, alto clarinet, and bass clarinet ("The Sheepherder"); clarinet, piano, and bass (*Fusion* and *Free Fall*); flute, bass, and drums (*Music for People,*

---

* The use of meters other than four had received only isolated interest before the success of Brubeck's *Time Out*. Early jazz pianist Fats Waller had written the "Jitterbug Waltz" in three, and Benny Carter recorded his composition "Waltzin' the Blues" in the 1930s. Billy Strayhorn's 1941 "Take the 'A' Train" arrangement for Ellington's band contained a four-measure interlude in three. Gerry Mulligan's "Jeru," for the 1949 Miles Davis nonet, used a meter of three for the bridge, although the improvisations were all in four. Brubeck recorded his tune "The Waltz" in 1955, and Sonny Rollins's "Valse Hot," was recorded in 1956 by the Clifford Brown–Max Roach group. Brubeck's "Watusi Drums," in six, was recorded in 1957, and in 1958, Charles Mingus recorded his "Better Git It In Your Soul," also in six. The 1959 Miles Davis *Kind of Blue* LP contained a piece in six, alternately labeled "All Blues" and "Flamenco Sketches" (see Chapter 10). A California-based band of the 1970s, the Don Ellis big band, explored unusual meters extensively. Ellis learned about meters common in the music of India, and played in a group called the Hindustani Jazz Sextet which fused jazz and Indian music. Like Brubeck, Ellis received a large amount of interest in his odd-metered music.

Birds, Butterflies, and Mosquitoes); tenor sax, bass, and drums (*Music for People, Birds, Butterflies, and Mosquitoes*).

As a composer and improviser, Giuffre has created work in the swinging bop style, the cool West Coast style, twentieth-century classical music styles, big band, small band, and solo styles. Giuffre plays flute, clarinet, and all the saxophones with an unconventional sound. The tone colors he prefers are even lighter and softer than those of other West Coast musicians.

Giuffre is one of the most thoughtful improvisers in jazz. In fact, he plays like the composer he is. Most of his work has a fresh, melodic character. Some of it strongly resembles folk music. Like Count Basie, Thelonious Monk, and Miles Davis, Giuffre places melody at the center of his musical conception, and the use of silence and careful pacing is essential to that.

Trumpeter-composer-arranger **Shorty Rogers,** like Giuffre, also wrote for Woody Herman (*Early Autumn, Shelly Manne: "The Three" and "The Two," Shorty Rogers and His Giants, Teddy Charles–Shorty Rogers Collaboration: West*). He led jazz quintets and produced music (with his Giants) which was.similar to that of the 1949–50 Miles Davis nine-piece and the 1953 Mulligan ten-piece bands. Some of the most adventurous products of the West Coast style were recordings made by Rogers, Giuffre, and vibraharpist Teddy Charles, apparently the first after Lennie Tristano's "Intuition" and "Digression" to display improvisation which had no prearranged chord progressions. Their 1954 work predated the Ornette Coleman recordings of 1958 and 1959 which launched an entire style centered around the "free jazz" concept. Rogers also recorded pieces in which improvisation was based on modes instead of frequent chord changes. These predated the 1958 Miles Davis "Milestones," which launched the popular mode-based improvisatory styles of the 1960s and 70s. That is interesting in light of the fact that Rogers derived his trumpet style primarily from the late 1940s approach of Miles Davis.

HARD BOP: THE EARLY 1950s THROUGH THE LATE 1960s

The 1950s was dominated by two jazz styles: West Coast and hard bop (also called bop or bebop). Hard bop began somewhat later than West Coast style and lasted proportionately longer (see Table 9.3). It differed from West Coast style in several respects:

1) West Coast style was characterized by light-colored, light-weight, soft-textured tone colors; hard bop employed dark-colored, heavy-weight, raw-textured tone colors.

2) In contrast to the light, cool, melodically simple improvisation of West Coast style, hard bop employed hard-driving, fiery, melodically complex improvisation.

TABLE 9.3. Hard Bop Style Musicians—A Partial Listing

Trumpet

Clifford Brown
Kenny Dorham
Miles Davis
Blue Mitchell
Donald Byrd
Thad Jones
Art Farmer
Bill Hardman
Joe Gordon
Carmell Jones
Lee Morgan
Freddie Hubbard
Wilbur Hardman
Tommy Turrentine
Benny Bailey
Booker Little
Nat Adderley

Baritone Sax

Pepper Adams
Cecil Payne

Tenor Sax

Sonny Rollins
John Coltrane
Jimmy Heath
Frank Foster
Clifford Jordan
Teddy Edwards
Benny Golson
Billy Mitchell
George Coleman
John Gilmore
Oliver Nelson
Stanley Turrentine
Junior Cook
Booker Ervin
Joe Henderson
Wayne Shorter
Hank Mobley
Harold Land
J.R. Monterose
Tina Brooks
Yusef Lateef

Trombone

J.J. Johnson
Curtis Fuller
Jimmy Knepper
Jimmy Cleveland
Frank Rehak
Tom McIntosh

Piano

Tommy Flanagan
Barry Harris
Cedar Walton
Duke Pearson
Bobby Timmons
Red Garland
Wynton Kelly
Joe Zawinul
Junior Mance
Kenny Drew
Horace Parlan
Les McCann
Gene Harris
Ramsey Lewis
Horace Silver

Alto Sax

Cannonball Adderley
Jackie McLean
Lou Donaldson
Gigi Gryce
Frank Strozier
Phil Woods

Bass

Paul Chambers
Sam Jones
Doug Watkins
Wilbur Ware
Bob Cranshaw
Gene Taylor
Reggie Workman
Percy Heath
Jymie Merritt
Butch Warren

Drums

Philly Joe Jones
Roy Brooks
Louis Hayes
Art Taylor
Roy Brooks
Roy Haynes
Roger Humphries
Elvin Jones
Lex Humphries
Max Roach
Art Blakey
Mickey Roker
Al Heath
Ben Riley
Jimmy Cobb
Frankie Dunlop

Composer-Arrangers

Horace Silver
Benny Golson
Gigi Gryce
Oliver Nelson
Cannonball Adderley
Nat Adderley
Wayne Shorter
Bobby Timmons
J.J. Johnson
Jackie McLean
Tom McIntosh

Organ

Jimmy Smith
Jack McDuff
Richard "Groove"
  Holmes
Don Patterson
Jimmy McGriff
Shirley Scott

Guitar

Wes Montgomery
Kenny Burrell
Grant Green

3) The West Coast style evolved from the tone and mood of Lester Young, Count Basie, Lennie Tristano, Lee Konitz, and the Miles Davis *Birth of the Cool* sessions; hard bop evolved directly from bop.

4) Though played all over America, hard bop gathered its strongest proponents from Detroit, Philadelphia, and New York instead of Los Angeles and San Francisco.

5) Although hard bop was played by both black and white musicians, there was as much a black dominance in hard bop as white dominance in the West Coast style.

6) In contrast to the polite, chamber music feeling projected by much of West Coast style, some hard bop projected a funky, earthy feeling with elements similar to black gospel music.

West Coast alto saxophonists had developed styles primarily from those of Lee Konitz and Charlie Parker, but hard bop altoists were not influenced by Konitz. West Coast tenor saxophonists modeled their styles on the playing of Parker and Lester Young. Hard bop tenor saxophonists, on the other hand, drew their inspiration from Parker, Don Byas, Dexter Gordon, and Sonny Stitt. Miles Davis also influenced hard bop trumpeters, but not as much as he influenced West Coast trumpeters. Hard bop trumpeters preferred Dizzy Gillespie, Fats Navarro, and Navarro's best disciple, Clifford Brown (Davis was probably an additional influence on Brown, but not as strong an influence as Navarro).

Hard bop evolved smoothly from bop. Trombonist J.J. Johnson, trumpeter Kenny Dorham, tenor saxophonist Sonny Rollins, and drummer Max Roach were among the musicians who earned reputations in bop and maintained them in hard bop, adding to their styles and changing various aspects. One of the prominent features of hard bop styles was the use of funky, earthy phrases and harmonies derived from gospel music. Not all hard bop players used these devices, but a sizeable portion did.

Pianist **Horace Silver** (see Figure 9.3), initially a Bud Powell disciple, was a strong influence in pioneering funky melodic figures and gospel-like harmonies in modern jazz (*A Night at Birdland, Art Blakey with the Original Jazz Messengers, Finger Poppin', In Pursuit of the 27th Man*). As a young player, Silver had learned, note for note, the Avery Parrish piano solo on the 1940 Erskine Hawkins recording of "After Hours." This was one of the first funky piano solos adapted to modern jazz. Silver's incorporation of its devices influenced jazz pianists and hornmen alike. Pianists Gene Harris (of the Three Sounds), Ramsey Lewis, Les McCann, organists Jimmy Smith, Groove Holmes, Jack McDuff, and others based entire styles on the funky melodic figures and gospel-like harmonies pioneered by Silver. 1950s bop pianists whose styles had not originally been funky also absorbed

Figure 9.3. Horace Silver, age 44. *Bill Smith*

elements of Silver's style. Pianists of the 1960s, including Bill Evans, Herbie Hancock, McCoy Tyner, and Chick Corea occasionally employed Silver's figures, too. Corea has cited Silver as an early influence on his style. Hundreds of small-time pianists and organists who played in taverns and hotel cocktail lounges incorporated these bluesy devices into their styles, and big band arrangers also added them to their repertory.

The few hard bop recordings that became popular with the general public were simple, funky pieces. Several hits originated in a combo led by alto saxophonist Cannonball Adderley: his "Sack o' Woe"; his brother Nat's "Jive Samba" and "Work Song" (subsequently recorded by Herb Alpert and the Tia Juana Brass); his pianist Bobby Timmons's "Dat Dere" and "Dis Here" (*Them Dirty Blues*). In the 1960s, several funky hard bop tunes were on juke boxes, rare places to find jazz: "Mercy, Mercy, Mercy" (*Mercy, Mercy, Mercy*), written by Adderley's pianist Joe Zawinul, "Song for My Father," written by Horace Silver; "Sidewinder," written by trumpeter Lee Morgan (recorded both by his own group and a studio group led by arranger

Quincy Jones); and "Comin' Home, Baby," written by flutist Herbie Mann's bassist, Ben Tucker (see Figure 9.4).

Trumpet   The model for numerous hard bop trumpeters was **Clifford Brown** who molded a style which combined the influences of Fats Navarro and Miles Davis. Brown had superior speed and incredible stamina. His lines were rich and bouncing. Brown's tone was supple and warm, with a wider, more deliberate vibrato than Gillespie or Davis used. He was so consistent that nearly every record he made is representative Brown material. Many listeners feel that his recordings surpass those of the best trumpeters playing in the 1950s, 60s, and 70s. Brown rivalled Gillespie and Parker in the mastery with which he created solo lines over unusual chord progressions (Clifford Brown—*The Quintet Vol. 1 and 2*, Sonny Rollins—*Saxophone Colossus and More*).

Clifford Brown died in 1956, having been an active influence for no more than four years. The following players were probably influenced directly by Brown: Donald Byrd, Bill Hardman, Louis Smith, Carmell Jones, and Lee Morgan (although it is also possible that they sounded like Brown because they, like Brown, were influenced by the same sources). Freddie Hubbard's trumpet playing also resembled Brown's

Figure 9.4. Cannonball Adderley (soprano sax) and Nat Adderley. *Bill Smith, Coda*

at times, but Hubbard produced such an original style that his early debt to Brown may be difficult to detect in his later playing.

Thad Jones is possibly the most original post-Gillespie trumpeter, but he has had far less influence than Brown or Hubbard (see Chapters 7 and 13 for additional discussion of Jones). His lack of influence is not due to any deficiency, but, on the contrary, to the very demanding nature of his style—his unique ideas and skill together are almost impossible to duplicate (*Detroit–N.Y. Junction, The Magnificent Thad Jones*).

Art Farmer is another of the more original hard bop trumpeters. Compared to Clifford Brown and Thad Jones, Farmer could easily be called a soft rather than hard bop player because his tone is neither brassy nor full-bodied. It resembles the soft, light tone of early Miles Davis. Farmer, like Brown, is also an improviser of consistent quality.

From 1959 to 1962, Art Farmer co-led one of the most well-organized, high-quality combos in hard bop: the Jazztet (*The Jazztet at Birdhouse, Meet the Jazztet*). Tenor saxophonist Benny Golson was his partner. During the 1970s, Farmer has played more in Europe than in the United States.

Though most hard bop trumpeters sounded like variations of Clifford Brown, **Freddie Hubbard** managed to develop a distinctly original style. Hubbard's tone is quite brassy and his lines are always spirited. During the middle 1960s, his solos often contained almost endless sequences of original phrases (*Maiden Voyage, Olé Coltrane*). His exceptional command of the trumpet was rarely held in reserve; it became instead a fundamental part of his conception. For example, the frequent use of shakes is a technically demanding Hubbard trademark.

Though he is primarily a performer in the hard bop idiom, Hubbard has participated in free form jazz recordings and other non-bop approaches. His creative peak was probably attained in his work as a sideman on recordings led by Art Blakey, Herbie Hancock, Eric Dolphy, Oliver Nelson and others prior to the late 1960s. Hubbard's influence began to appear in prominent trumpeters of the 1970s. Woody Shaw, Mike Lawrence, Kenny Wheeler, Charles Sullivan, Randy Brecker, Marvin Peterson, Oscar Brashear, and others have shown discernible Hubbard influence in their playing.

Tenor Saxophone

Hard bop produced a large number of excellent tenor saxophonists. Tenor sax was a key instrument in the hard bop style, as trumpet had been in early jazz, and drums were to become during the 1970s. Though there were at least twenty important tenor saxophonists, there is little dispute that Sonny Rollins and John Coltrane were the two most outstanding performers. Coltrane's hard bop approaches are discussed at length in the chapter devoted to him.

Sonny Rollins would undoubtedly have been an exceptional jazz musician no matter what instrument he had chosen (see Figure 9.5). Many of his virtues are not exclusive to tenor saxophone playing. The Rollins solos have a well-reasoned quality. His clarity of mind, even at furious tempos, enables him to transcend the cliché figures and technically accessible melodic patterns most saxophonists must employ when high speeds press their skills (*The Amazing Bud Powell, Collector's Items, Dig, The Genius of Bud Powell, Saxophone Colossus, Smithsonian Collection, Sonny Rollins—More from the Vanguard, The Sonny Rollins/Sonny Stitt Sessions, Tallest Trees*).

Rollins's compositions, like those of Monk, are deceptively simple. Their architecture embodies odd placement of accents and many other surprises. Yet, his unusual compositions sound so logical that the most remarkable features of their construction may not immediately be obvious. "Valse Hot" is an example of Rollins's cleverness in this regard. The piece is syncopated in the most basic sense of the term: accents fall on beats or portions of beats expected to be weak. The phrases in "Valse Hot" start and stop in unusual places.

Figure 9.5. Sonny Rollins, age 37. *Bill Smith*

Rollins's attraction to calypso is manifested in "St. Thomas," one of the simplest jazz tunes written in the 1950s. In spite of a tendency to be predictable, "St. Thomas" is unified and reveals a playfulness characteristic of Rollins.

Miles Davis recorded several Rollins tunes, all of which have become jazz standards: "Airegin" (Nigeria spelled backwards), which has an unusual construction; "Doxy," a sixteen-bar AABA tune with a common chord progression; and "Oleo," a very syncopated line with no melody in its bridge, based on the chord progression of "I Got Rhythm." Miles recorded these tunes with Rollins and recorded "Oleo" and "Airegin" again with Coltrane. (See Chapter 10 for discussion of Davis–Rollins recordings.) "Oleo" was later recorded twice by Davis with tenor saxophonist Hank Mobley.

In addition to his recordings with Davis and others, Rollins made several outstanding records as a member of the Clifford Brown–Max Roach quintet. The Brown–Rollins "Kiss and Run," "Pent Up House," and "Valse Hot" recordings were among the best trumpet–tenor sessions to come out of the 1950s. Both Brown and Rollins played with wonderful ease and great imagination.

Rollins was one of the ultimate masters of jazz improvisation. He had exquisite command of the tenor saxophone, and his solos easily incorporated every chord, even in the fastest progressions. And, what is most important, he transcended the chord progressions and spontaneously set new melodies to them. The improvisations of Rollins abounded in melodies and were possibly as inventive as those of any saxophonist to appear since Charlie Parker.

Rollins mastered the rhythmic devices necessary to swing, and he swung when he wished, but he played against or apart from the tempo at other times. He could go in and out of tempo with amazing skill. He seems to have gotten inside the beat one moment and ignored it the next. But he always treated a piece as though it, its tempo, chord changes, and melody were but a small toy to be quickly and effortlessly redesigned from moment to moment.

Rollins differed from the majority of bop tenormen in that he often used staccato phrasing instead of an exclusively legato style. He could manage a blunt, brittle attack, move to legato and back again to staccato. His vibrato was slow and very deliberate. The Rollins tone is rough but not as deep or richly textured as Coltrane's. It is brittle and quite unique among tenor saxophonists.

Rollins could deliver bursts of rich, swinging phrases or short spurts within long pauses. His use of silence was an important aspect of his skill in pacing. Rollins used silence to set off short phrases, some of which were repeated in varied form. Sometimes he repeated a single note, attacking it with different rhythms and tone colors. Like West Coast baritone saxophonist Gerry Mulligan, Rollins played so clearly that it was as though you could hear him thinking. There was a logical development within each solo. It was especially obvious when he played a figure and then, using the same rhythm but different notes, played it again. He also repeated figures using the same notes but varying the rhythm in their repetition. Rollins began recording actively in 1949 and had considerable impact on tenor saxophonists of the 1950s. His influence is difficult to pinpoint in the playing of others, however, because some of his virtues were also possessed by Charlie Parker, whose influence was also strong at that time. The Rollins name often appears next to those of Charlie Parker, Sonny Stitt and John Coltrane in lists of saxophonists favored by saxophonists themselves. For example, such prominent saxophonists of the 1970s as Pat La Barbera, John Klemmer, and Billy Harper have all cited Rollins as a favorite.

A man whose playing is sometimes reminiscent of Rollins, sometimes suggests Coltrane, but usually exemplifies his own personal style, is **Joe Henderson** (*Power to the People, Tetragon*). Along with Wayne Shorter (see Wayne Shorter section of Chapter 15), Henderson is probably the most original tenor saxophonist produced by hard bop after Rollins and Coltrane. He has a hard, shiny tone with a razor-sharp edge. The biting effect of his playing is enhanced by his ability to subdivide each beat very precisely. This, combined with a high level instrumental proficiency enables him to play extremely quick figures with uncanny accuracy. The sharpness of his attacks and releases also contributes to the biting effect.

Like Rollins, Henderson can play intense, provocative lines. Some contain syncopated staccato figures alternating with churning legato lines. Henderson can swing conventionally, playing perfectly within tempo, or he can play against the tempo, over the beat, as though free of it. He alternates swing eighth note figures with straight eighth notes, sometimes interjecting bursts of sixteenth notes. Dramatic use of shakes and trills is also characteristic of Henderson and is consistent with his love of variety. Sometimes he employs shrieks which sound like animal cries. He varies the speed of his vibrato, also.

Henderson began his career in the mainstream of hard bop, but blended well with newer styles introduced during the 1960s by Ornette Coleman, Albert Ayler, and John Coltrane (see Chapters 11 and 14). He has led an assortment of groups, appeared on numerous albums with other leaders, and written tunes which are quite distinctive. His influence could be heard during the 1970s in both the style of tunes being written and in the playing of young tenor saxophonists who had chosen not to base their approaches entirely on Coltrane's.

Alto Saxophone

Cannonball Adderley was one of the best improvisers to play alto saxophone after Charlie Parker died. In fact, Adderley's style was initially derived from Parker's. Though he led several good hard bop combos, some of the most popular of that era, Cannonball's most outstanding recorded solos were made as a member of the Miles Davis group (see Chapter 10). When Adderley was playing with Davis, tenor saxophonist John Coltrane was also in the group. The fact that Adderley could keep up with Coltrane and sometimes surpass him is a measure of Adderley's improvisational prowess (*Cannonball and Coltrane*).

Cannonball had an inventive mind combined with the high-level instrumental proficiency of Parker and Coltrane. His tone was so deep and full that it sometimes sounded like a tenor sax. He had an earthy, legato style and amazing energy. Adderley's style displayed the influence of Parker (as early as 1955), some Coltrane devices (after 1958), and his own unique, bouncing rhythmic conception. A trait which served to distinguish him from Coltrane and Lee Konitz, and to a certain extent from Parker, too, was his use of funky melodic figures. Cannonball bent his huge, flowing tone with blue notes and wails. Bits of pop tunes crept into his lines. Humor was also part of his outgoing style.

Jackie McLean was another highly respected alto saxophonist. Originally a Parker protégé, McLean developed his own style and eventually incorporated elements of new styles which became prominent during the 1960s. He had a dry, biting tone and very insistent delivery. His style was unusually intense (*Dig, Right Now*). Also a solid hard bop composer, McLean wrote numerous tunes for his own albums, some of which were also recorded by other leaders. Miles Davis recorded McLean's "Donna" (also known as "Dig"), "Little Melonae," "Minor March," and "Dr. Jackle" (also known as "Dr. Jekyll").

Drums   In addition to leading a series of hard-driving quintets and sextets containing a stream of outstanding hard bop players, drummer **Art Blakey** paved the way for conceptions of jazz drumming which called for active interaction with soloists. Blakey's drumming was often as much in the forefront of his combo sound as were trumpet and sax. His rhythm section playing was so vital and dynamic that for him to solo was almost anticlimactic (see Figure 9.6). His 1954 work with trumpeter Clifford Brown and pianist Horace Silver (*A Night at Birdland*) shows him engaged in volatile rhythm section drumming years before such activity was common practice.

A partial list of Blakey trumpeters includes Clifford Brown, Donald Byrd, Bill Hardman, Lee Morgan, Freddie Hubbard, and Woody Shaw. A partial list of Blakey saxophonists includes Jackie McLean, Hank Mobley, Wayne Shorter, Benny Golson, and Johnny Griffin. His pianists have included Horace Silver, Keith Jarrett, Cedar Walton, and other topnotch players. The compositions of Blakey's sidemen helped determine the character of his group sound. Some of the best tunes were contributed by Horace Silver, Benny Golson, and Wayne Shorter

Figure 9.6. Art Blakey. *Henry Kahanek,* Coda

(see Table 15.1, Chapter 15, listing Shorter's compositions recorded by Blakey).

Philly Joe Jones was as active as Blakey in his rhythm section playing. His imagination was always at work, and his crisp fills were a vital part of the 1955–58 Miles Davis combos (see Chapter 10 for further discussion of Philly Joe).

Max Roach was an important figure in the later days of bop, and he continued as a leader in hard bop. His drumming was quick, cleanly executed, and rarely flashy. As a rhythm section player, he was conservative compared to Art Blakey and Philly Joe Jones.

Roach's exceptional technique did not overshadow his overall musical sense. He, unlike many drummers, did not flaunt his proficiency. As a soloist he stood above most others, with solos which were carefully developed, and often quite melody-like.

Roach co-led one of the very best groups in hard bop: The Clifford Brown–Max Roach Quintet (*Clifford Brown—The Quintet Vols. 1 and 2*). With bassist George Morrow, pianist Richie Powell, and either tenor saxophonist Sonny Rollins or Harold Land, the quintet turned out high-quality performances and made several excellent recordings. After Brown died in 1956, Roach continued to lead good groups with trumpeters Kenny Dorham, Tommy Turrentine, and Booker Little; and tenor saxophonists Rollins, Stanley Turrentine, Clifford Jordan, and George Coleman (see Chapter 15 for a discussion of Coleman).

Piano

Hard bop pianists drew liberally from Bud Powell. **Tommy Flanagan** (*Giant Steps, Sax Colossus, Tallest Trees, While We're Young*), probably the best hard bop pianist, drew from Powell, Tatum, and Teddy Wilson. He was also influenced by Hank Jones, an excellent bop pianist whose own influences included Wilson. (See Chapter 10 for further discussion of Flanagan.) **Red Garland** combined the influences of Powell and others to create his own style (see Chapter 10). Throughout the 1960s, **Barry Harris** probably appeared as a sideman on more hard bop dates than any other pianist, with the possible exception of Flanagan. He did not have the exquisite command of the piano possessed by Flanagan, but he was a reliable and hard-working accompanist and soloist in the Bud Powell style.

Horace Silver had also used Powell as a starting point. Like John Lewis, Horace Silver used his piano more to set up figures which sounded prewritten than to comp. The style of accompaniment which Silver developed resembled big band arrangements in that the soloist was heard over a predictable, but interesting background. Silver led a long string of quality quintets containing solid hard bop players such as trumpeters Blue Mitchell, Art Farmer, Tom Harrell, Woody Shaw, and Randy Brecker; saxophonists Hank Mobley, Bob Berg, Junior Cook, Joe Henderson, and Michael Brecker; drummers Roy Brooks, Louis Hayes, Al Foster, and Billy Cobham. Silver is probably the most prolific composer in hard bop. His better known tunes include "Doodlin'," "Sister Sadie," "Senōr Blues," "Filthy McNasty," "Song For My Father," and "The Preacher." His many albums are loaded with originals he has penned.

Composer-Arrangers

In hard bop, improvisers were less dependent on chord progressions of pop tunes than bop players had been. They wrote many of their own tunes and original chord progressions. Some tunes departed from standard thirty-two-bar and twelve-bar forms. **Clifford Brown**'s "Joy Spring" (*Jordu*) is an ABCA form in which B and C are basically A in different keys. Gigi Gryce's "Minority" is sixteen bars long and all A. **Horace Silver**'s "Nica's Dream" is an AABBA form in which A is sixteen bars long and B is eight bars long. Tenor saxophonist **Benny Golson**'s "I Remember Clifford" (named for trumpeter Clifford Brown) is a ballad with interesting chord changes and an unusual form: six-bar section, eight-bar repeated A section, eight-bar bridge, A section and a return to the six-bar section (*Meet the Jazztet*). Golson's "Along Came Betty" may be divided into 8+8+8+10. "Stablemates" is 14+8+14.

Golson was responsible for many arrangements played by the Art Farmer–Benny Golson Jazztet. His popular "Whisper Not" is a thirty-two-bar AABA tune, and his "Blues March" (*Meet the Jazztet*) is a twelve-bar blues. Golson's "Killer Joe" became popular when Quincy

Jones recorded it. The Jazztet had outstanding sidemen and was a polished and imaginative group. At various times it included trombonist Curtis Fuller, pianist McCoy Tyner (see Chapter 14), pianist Cedar Walton, and trombonist Tom McIntosh, who was also a good composer-arranger.

Bass

Hard bop produced a number of very solid bassists, some of whom were remarkably melodic soloists. **Paul Chambers** was the first choice for many hard bop record dates. His large, dark sound and horn-like bop solos, both pizzicato and arco, impressed many leaders (see Chapter 10). Chambers expanded the solo potential of jazz bass with his instrumental proficiency and unique bop horn approach to bass solos. Though active for approximately eight years in Miles Davis's groups, Chambers also appeared on numerous records with other leaders.

Sam Jones was another skillful hard bop bassist. Together with drummer Louis Hayes, he gave the Cannonball Adderley Quintet a buoyant yet driving foundation. Like Paul Chambers, Jones and Hayes were in constant demand at jazz recording sessions. Jones continued to be in demand during the 1970s.

Trombone

In hard bop, **J.J. Johnson** continued to retain the good reputation he established during the end of the 1940s (*The Eminent Jay Jay Johnson Vol. 1 and 2, Stan Getz and J.J. Johnson at the Opera House*). In addition to his swinging trombone style, he wrote many hard bop tunes, such as "Shutterbug" and "Sidewinder" (not the same "Sidewinder" written by Lee Morgan during the 1960s), and led tight, well-rehearsed combos. Johnson's groups employed drummer Elvin Jones, trumpeters Nat Adderley and Freddie Hubbard, pianists Tommy Flanagan and Cedar Walton, tenor saxophonists Bobby Jasper and Clifford Jordan, as well as other exceptional players. Several recordings were made with the excellent team of bassist Paul Chambers and drummer Max Roach.

Trombonist **Curtis Fuller** became, along with Johnson, the leading trombonist in hard bop. Though sounding a lot like J.J., Fuller uses a softer, more diffuse tone and prefers lines which are constructed more subtly. He was a bit more adventurous than J.J., and not quite as economical. He sometimes plays as fast as J.J., but his attacks and releases are not as clipped as J.J.'s. Fuller was known more as a sideman than J.J. Fuller is featured on records made by the Art Farmer–Benny Golson Jazztet, and Art Blakey, as well as numerous Blue Note records for a variety of leaders.

Guitar

The peak creative period of hard bop's leading guitarists, **Kenny Burrell** and **Wes Montgomery,** was in the late 1950s and early 60s. Burrell blended characteristics of Charlie Christian, Django Reinhardt, and

Oscar Moore with bop horn lines. The funky melodic figures of Horace Silver slipped into Burrell's work often, but Burrell was also capable of nonfunky solos which contained meat and depth (*Detroit–N.Y. Junction, Kenny Burrell/John Coltrane*).

Wes Montgomery was probably the best hard bop guitarist (*While We're Young*). It is ironic, though, that his reputation with non-musicians was earned by recordings for Verve and A & M which did not reflect much of his great talent. He played tastefully on these records, but his work of the late 1950s and early 60s is a far richer jazz vein.

Montgomery created a relaxed, melodic style derived from Charlie Christian. His tone was round and full, cleanly articulated, and not edgy or excessively percussive. He had a well-paced style where everything swung comfortably. Voicing lines in octaves was not new to jazz guitar, but Montgomery's use of this device did much to popularize the approach.

chapter 10

MILES DAVIS, HIS GROUPS & SIDEMEN

Although Miles Davis is known to many people primarily as a trumpet player, he has probably had more influence as an innovative bandleader and composer. A large portion of modern jazz history is documented in Davis-led recording sessions. In fact, Miles was bandleader at several major landmark recording sessions: the 1949 *Birth of the Cool,* which influenced West Coast jazz styles; the 1959 *Kind of Blue,* which was important in the development of improvisation techniques using modes instead of chord changes; and the 1969 *In a Silent Way* and *Bitches Brew,* which were influential in the fusion of jazz with rock. After the recording of *In a Silent Way* and *Bitches Brew,* many jazz-rock groups were formed, including Joe Zawinul's and Wayne Shorter's Weather Report, Tony Williams's Lifetime, John McLaughlin's Mahavishnu Orchestra, Herbie Hancock's Headhunters, and Chick Corea's Return to Forever.

Miles was not personally responsible for all the ideas at these recording sessions, but he was the overseer, and much in the progression of modern jazz styles has occurred within Davis–led groups. Because Miles has been innovative for so long, many fans are not familiar with every phase of his career. Music from one of his stylistic periods often sounds quite different from that of another period. The *Birth of the Cool* was the first of a series of Davis recordings which helped bring about new styles in jazz. Davis has kept his ears open so that, at crucial times, he has chosen leading innovators as composers, arrangers, and players for his bands.

Miles Davis has composed tunes which have become standard repertory of jazz musicians, including "Four," "Milestones," and "So

TABLE 10.1. Men Who Have Made Significant Contributions to the Music of Miles Davis

Saxophone
Sonny Rollins (1951–56)
John Coltrane (1955–61)
Hank Mobley (1960–62)
George Coleman (1963–64)
Wayne Shorter (1964–69)

Piano
Horace Silver (1954)
Red Garland (1955–58)
Bill Evans (1958)
Wynton Kelly (1959–63)
Herbie Hancock (1963–69)
Chick Corea–Keith Jarrett (1969–71)

Bass
Percy Heath (early 1950s)
Paul Chambers (1955–63)
Ron Carter (1963–68)
Dave Holland (1969–71)
Michael Henderson (1970s)

Drums
Max Roach (late 1940s)
Art Blakey (early 1950s)
Kenny Clarke (early 1950s)
Philly Joe Jones (1950s)
Jimmy Cobb (1959–63)
Tony Williams (1963–69)
Jack DeJohnette (1969–72)
Al Foster (1970s)

Guitar
John McLaughlin (1969)
Reggie Lucas (1970s)
Pete Cosey (1970s)

Composer-Arranger

Gil Evans–Gerry Mulligan–
John Lewis
Birth of the Cool

Al Cohn
"For Adults Only"
"Tasty Pudding"
"Floppy"
"Willie the Wailer"

Thelonious Monk
"Bemsha Swing"
"Well You Needn't"
"'Round Midnight"
"Straight, No Chaser"

Ahmad Jamal
"Ahmad's Blues"
"New Rhumba"

Johnny Carisi
"Israel"
"Springsville"

Gil Evans
Miles Ahead
Porgy and Bess
Sketches of Spain
Quiet Nights

Bill Evans
Kind of Blue

Victor Feldman
"Joshua"
"Seven Steps to Heaven"

Sonny Rollins
"Airegin"
"Oleo"
"Doxy"

Jackie McLean
"Donna" (also known as "Dig")
"Minor March"
"Doctor Jackle" (also known as "Dr. Jekyll")
"Little Melonae"

Dave Brubeck
"The Duke"
"In Your Own Sweet Way"

George Gershwin
"But Not for Me"
"The Man I Love"
"Porgy and Bess"

Richard Rodgers
"My Funny Valentine"
"It Never Entered My Mind"
"Surry with the Fringe on Top"
"I Could Write a Book"
"Blue Room"
"Spring Is Here"
"Wait Till You See Her"

Jimmy Van Heusen
"It Could Happen to You"
"I Thought About You"
"Darn That Dream"

J.J. Johnson
"Kelo"
"Enigma"
"Lament"
"Poem for Brass"

Dizzy Gillespie
"Woody 'n' You"
"Blue 'n' Boogie"
"Salt Peanuts"
"A Night in Tunisia"

Bud Powell
"Budo"
"Tempus Fugit"

Ron Carter
"R.J."
"Eighty-One"
"Mood"

Tony Williams
"Pee Wee"
"Hand Jive"
"Black Comedy"

Joe Zawinul
"Pharoah's Dance"
"Double Image"
"In a Silent Way"
"Orange Lady" ("Great Expectations")
"Directions" ("Black Beauty")

Herbie Hancock
"Little One"
"The Sorcerer"
"Riot"
"Madness"

Wayne Shorter
"E.S.P."
"Iris"
"Limbo"
"Vonetta"
"Prince of Darkness"
"Masqualero"
"Dolores"
"Orbits"
"Footprints"
"Nefertiti"
"Fall"
"Pinocchio"
"Paraphernalia"
"Sanctuary"
"Water Babies"
"Capricorn"
"Sweet Pea"
"Two Faced"

What." His treatment, on records, of popular tunes such as "Bye Bye, Blackbird" and "On Green Dolphin Street" has made them into jazz standards. Several jazz tunes also became jazz standards after he recorded them (Richard Carpenter's "Walkin'," Jimmy Heath's "Gingerbread Boy," Eddie Harris's "Freedom Jazz Dance," etc.).

The quality of Davis's recordings usually reflects his collaboration with great sidemen, some of whom were directly responsible for many of the innovations of his groups; but since he chose them and provided an excellent working environment, he gets and deserves much of the credit. He has an uncanny knack for choosing the best sidemen. The saxophonists employed by Miles (whether or not they recorded with him) comprise a Who's Who of modern jazz sax men: Lee Konitz, Sonny Rollins, Jackie McLean, Sonny Stitt, Jimmy Heath, Cannonball Adderley, John Coltrane, Hank Mobley, Joe Henderson, Sam Rivers, George Coleman, Wayne Shorter, Steve Grossman, Gary Bartz, Bennie Maupin, David Liebman, Carlos Garnett, Sonny Fortune, etc. (see Table 10.1).

Almost the entire evolution of modern jazz rhythm sections can be traced through Miles Davis recordings:

1950: Pianist John Lewis, bassist Al McKibbon, drummer Max Roach on *Birth of the Cool.*

1951: Pianist Walter Bishop, Jr., bassist Tommy Potter, drummer Art Blakey on "Conception"; "Denial"; "Paper Moon."

1956: Pianist Tommy Flanagan, bassist Paul Chambers, drummer Art Taylor on "No Line"; "Vierd Blues"; "In Your Own Sweet Way."

1955–58: Pianist Red Garland, bassist Paul Chambers, drummer Philly Joe Jones on *The New Miles Davis Quintet; Steamin'; Cookin'; Workin'; Relaxin'; 'Round About Midnight; Milestones.*

1959–63: Pianist Wynton Kelly, bassist Paul Chambers, drummer Jimmy Cobb on *Someday My Prince Will Come; In Person at the Blackhawk; Miles Davis at Carnegie Hall.*

1963–68: Pianist Herbie Hancock, bassist Ron Carter, drummer Tony Williams on many albums, including *My Funny Valentine; Sorcerer; Miles in the Sky; Nefertiti.*

1971: Pianist Keith Jarrett, bassist Mike Henderson, drummer Jack DeJohnette, percussionist Airto Moreira on "Sivad" from *Live-Evil.*

1969–72: Groups whose rhythm sections sometimes included two or three keyboards (Miles drew from a pool of pianists which included Joe Zawinul, Chick Corea, Keith Jarrett, Herbie Hancock, Larry Young, Harold Williams, Hermeto Pascoal, Lonnie Liston Smith, and Cedric Lawson); bass (Dave

Holland, Ron Carter, or Mike Henderson); drummers (Jack DeJohnette and Billy Cobham and percussionist Airto Moreira).

1970s: Groups whose rhythm sections sometimes included two or three guitars (Miles drew from a pool of guitarists which included Reggie Lucas, Pete Cosey, David Creamer, Dominique Gaumont, and Cornell Dupree); bassist Michael Henderson, drummer Al Foster, and percussionist M'Tume Heath. Occasionally in his post-1968 groups Davis also employed Khalil Balakrishna or Colin Walcott on sitar and Badal Roy on tabla. Use of instruments native to India, such as the sitar (a stringed instrument) and tabla (drums), was possibly as unusual in jazz as use of three keyboards at once.

With only a few exceptions, recordings led by Miles Davis are full of sensitivity and stand out above most other jazz records made during the same years. There is a feeling of intelligent, well-measured musical creation throughout the Davis recording career. His musical presence prevails even in performances for which he did not write the tunes and in which he is only one of several soloists. A feeling of balance and concentration pervades Davis–led sessions, even when he does not solo at all ("Two Bass Hit" on *Milestones*, and "Pee Wee" on *Sorcerer*).

Miles Davis as a Trumpet Player   Miles is generally a very melodic soloist. Much of his work is characterized by unusually skillful timing and dramatic construction of melodic figures. Listen to his solos on the 1954 session with Milt Jackson and Thelonious Monk ("The Man I Love," "Bags Groove," etc., *Miles Davis and the Modern Jazz Giants, Tallest Trees*), the 1959 *Kind of Blue* LP, his "Eighty-One" solo on the 1965 *E.S.P.* LP, side one on the 1970 *Jack Johnson* LP, and his "Sivad" solo on the 1971 *Live-Evil* LP. Davis, like pianists Count Basie and Thelonious Monk, is a master of self-restraint in construction of improvised lines. He seems to be editing at all times.

By his placement of silence as well as his choice of notes, Davis has created logical and dramatic solos. During his solos, Miles often lets several beats pass without playing. During that time, the sound of bass and drums comes clearly to the listener. This is an especially dramatic technique employed by few other improvisers. (One musician who does is pianist Ahmad Jamal, whose light touch and use of silence enhanced his well-known 1958 recording of "Poincianna" on *Ahmad Jamal at the Pershing*, Argo or Cadet LP 628. The amount of variety and contrast in Jamal's solo work provides another point of similarity with Davis.)

Few improvisers invent phrases as well thought out as those of Miles. He rarely plays an obvious phrase or cliché. Subtlety is central to the Miles Davis style. To say "his solos make sense" is to sum up much of it.

During the 1940s and 50s, and on many albums of the 60s (*Seven Steps to Heaven, E.S.P., Sorcerer, Miles Smiles, Nefertiti*), Miles played with a lighter, softer, less brassy tone than was common for bop and hard bop trumpeters. He used almost no vibrato and favored the trumpet's middle register over its flashier and more popular high register. Double-timing was rare in his playing. The Miles Davis trumpet style of the 1940s and 50s was gentle.

During the 1950s, Miles was one of the few modern trumpeters to employ colorful alterations of pitch and tone color reminiscent of pre-modern trumpeters. His ways of varying the pitch, color, and size of his tone constituted critical dramatic devices in his playing on *Porgy and Bess* (especially "Fishermen, Strawberry and Devil Crab") and *Sketches of Spain* (especially "Saeta").

Miles created a personal sound by playing through a Harmon mute without its shank (or stem). These muted solos were amplified by placing the mute very close to the microphone. The result was a wispy quality, delicate and quite intimate, as on the down-tempo pieces in the 1963 *Seven Steps to Heaven* and the 1959 *Kind of Blue*.

During the 1960s, Miles began to reach into the high register more often. Listen to the 1963 *Miles in Europe* and the 1964 *Four and More*. During the 1970s, he developed a more explosive and violent style which, like his 1960s developments, also emphasized the trumpet's high register. This style also employed long bursts of notes, splattered tones, electronically produced echo, and electronic "wah wah" alterations of the trumpet tone. Listen to *Bitches Brew, Live-Evil,* and side one of *Jack Johnson*.

In spite of his strikingly original phrases and his unusually skillful pacing, Miles Davis does not possess the awesome instrumental proficiency of trumpeters Dizzy Gillespie, Clifford Brown, and Maynard Ferguson. He does not play as fast, as high, or as clearly as these performers. Davis occasionally cracks his tone or misses a note he intended to reach. He often attempts trumpet lines which are faster than he is able to play, as on *Miles in Europe, Miles in Berlin, Miles in Tokyo,* and *Four and More*. He does, however, maintain the momentum of even the fastest tempos, whether or not he succeeds in sounding every single note he attempts. Miles is seldom unable to express his ideas because of technical limitations.

Many listeners are so obsessed with the limitations of Davis's trumpet technique that they fail to recognize his assets. They ignore not only his tremendous skills as an improviser but also his talents as a composer and bandleader. The fact that Davis occasionally fluffs notes should not be allowed to obscure the fact that he improvises lines which are possibly more varied and original than those of any other trumpeter. He has a great melodic gift, and he is one of the few jazz musicians who can improvise swinging figures in constant tempo ("Freddie the Freeloader" on *Kind of Blue,* "Sid's Ahead" on *Milestones,* "Devil May Care" on *Basic Miles*) as well as figures which imply freedom from strict tempo and swing feeling (second selection of second side of *Kind of Blue,* "Fishermen, Strawberry, and Devil Crab" on *Porgy and Bess,* the first few measures of "My Funny Valentine" and "Stella by Starlight" on *My Funny Valentine*). When Miles plays a tune he makes it completely his own, but at the same time he expresses its essential character (his 1956 recording of "It Never Entered My Mind," his 1963 recording of "I Fall in Love Too Easily," and his 1964 recordings of "My Funny Valentine" and "Stella By Starlight" on *My Funny Valentine*). These musical strengths outweigh any specific technical limitations Davis displays in his trumpet playing.

The Miles Davis trumpet style partially influenced many trumpeters, including Clifford Brown (whose other primary influence was Fats Navarro). Miles was a direct influence, perhaps the primary one, on West Coast-style trumpeters Chet Baker, Shorty Rogers, Jack Sheldon, and on hard bop trumpeters Nat Adderley, Charles Moore, Johnny Coles, and Eddie Henderson.

Recordings

During the early 1950s, Miles recorded with a large variety of modern jazz players. The results were interesting, especially a 1951 session with tenor saxophonist Sonny Rollins, alto saxophonist Jackie McLean, pianist Walter Bishop, Jr., bassist Tommy Potter, and drummer Art Blakey. This group recorded "Dig" and "Conception" (*Dig*).

Another session which stood out is the 1954 recording with vibraharpist Milt Jackson, pianist Thelonious Monk, bassist Percy Heath, and drummer Kenny Clarke. The combination of Jackson, Heath, and Clarke was the Modern Jazz Quartet minus pianist John Lewis. Often called the "Man I Love" session, it included two versions of George Gershwin's "The Man I Love," two versions of Milt Jackson's "Bags' Groove" (Jackson's nickname is Bags), and one version each of "Swing Spring," composed by Davis, and "Bemsha Swing," composed by Monk (*Miles Davis and the Modern Jazz Giants, Tallest Trees*).

Davis–Rollins– Flanagan

Another outstanding recording was made at a 1956 session with tenor saxophonist Sonny Rollins, pianist **Tommy Flanagan,** bassist Paul Chambers, and drummer Art Taylor. Only three selections were recorded—"No Line," "Vierd Blues," and "In Your Own Sweet Way"— but the solos contributed by Davis, Rollins, and Flanagan rank with their best (*Collector's Items*). The peak reached by the collective creative powers of Davis and Rollins here surpasses even that of a 1954 session the two made with pianist Horace Silver ("Oleo," "But Not For Me," "Doxy," and "Airegin" on *Tallest Trees*).

The Flanagan–Chambers–Taylor rhythm section was probably the lightest, most discreet rhythm section modern jazz had had up to that time. Paul Chambers brought a large, dark, buoyant sound to the group. His walking swung propulsively yet blended smoothly into the rhythm section sound. Drummer Art Taylor extended the easy, cooking feel of Kenny Clarke's style. Not as explosive as Art Blakey or Max Roach, Taylor was one of the last drummers to be happy just keeping time and making sure everything swung.

Flanagan had better instrumental proficiency than almost any other hard bop pianist. He was influenced by Teddy Wilson, Bud Powell, Art Tatum, and Hank Jones. His touch was very clean, and his lines were well-conceived and effortlessly played. In spite of a meticulous attention to technique, Flanagan managed to extract a very warm, clear tone from the piano. Neither Red Garland, who played with Miles from 1955 to 1958, nor Wynton Kelly, who was Miles's pianist from 1959 to 1963, could comp as lightly and discreetly as Tommy Flanagan. Flanagan's tasteful comping, flowing solos, and polite touch provided an exquisite complement to the relaxed yet provocative solos of Davis and Rollins. Herbie Hancock, who did not join Davis until 1963, was the first pianist to challenge Flanagan's position as hard bop's most sensitive and most in-demand accompanist.

**Coltrane–
Garland–
Chambers–
Jones**

Both the "Man I Love" session and the 1956 "Vierd Blues" session were recorded for Prestige record company. Before his contract with Prestige expired, Miles recorded five albums with one of the most exciting combos in jazz history. Those albums were *The New Miles Davis Quintet*, recorded in 1955, and *Steamin'*, *Cookin'*, *Workin'*, *Relaxin'*, all recorded in 1956. Davis put together a rhythm section consisting of pianist Red Garland, bassist Paul Chambers, and drummer Philly Joe Jones; he chose tenor saxophonist John Coltrane as his front line partner (see Chapter 14).

After leaving Prestige, Davis signed with Columbia records and has remained with them as of this writing. With Columbia, the Coltrane-Garland-Jones quintet made *'Round About Midnight* in 1956 and, with the addition of alto saxophonist Cannonball Adderley, *Milestones* in 1958. The period of Adderley's association with Davis and Coltrane marked his creative peak. His solos on the 1958 *Milestones* album and those on a 1959 quintet LP (*Cannonball and Coltrane*) recorded with the Davis group minus Davis ("Limehouse Blues," "Grand Central," "The Sleeper," etc.) are rich in melodic material and infused with astonishing energy.

Most of the tunes Davis recorded before 1958 were written by either pop song composers or bop-oriented writers. Many are in twelve-bar blues form or thirty-two-bar AABA form. They were the basis for bop-style improvisation guided by chord progressions. But with the "Milestones" selection, for which the *Milestones* album was named,

Davis broke away from the tradition of improvisation guided by chord progressions. Davis was one of the first and most important musicians to move away from jazz improvisation based on chords. Instead of using chord changes, "Milestones" used two different modes, the first lasting sixteen measures, the second for another sixteen measures, followed by a return to the first for a final eight measures. The use of modes in "Milestones" was a prelude to Davis's *Kind of Blue* album, which contained several modal pieces (see chapters 17 and 18 for explanations of modes).

Red Garland played in a style derived partly from Bud Powell and other bop pianists and partly from the locked-hands style typical of Milt Buckner. His playing of "Billy Boy" on the *Milestones* LP contains passages identical to Ahmad Jamal's 1951 Epic recording of the same tune, which also employs the locked-hands style. Garland's comping was not as sensitive or imaginative as that of Tommy Flanagan or of subsequent Davis pianists, yet his solos were quite creative within the bop context. He sometimes improvised his solo lines in the lower register of the piano, a very unusual practice (the 1956 Davis recording of "Oleo" on *Miles Davis*). Garland also recorded solos in which he did not comp for himself. His horn-like lines were supported only by string bass and drums. This device had previously been used by Lennie Tristano ("Line-Up" on a 1955 Atlantic record). It was subsequently used by Herbie Hancock with Miles Davis on "Orbits," "Dolores," and "Gingerbread Boy" (*Miles Smiles*, 1966) and "Hand Jive" (*Nefertiti*, 1967).

Bassist **Paul Chambers** was a driving and buoyant force in the Davis group. Much of the momentum generated by the group can be attributed to Chambers, who remained with Davis through many changes in quintet personnel. He was the last original Miles Davis Quintet sideman when Davis disbanded in 1963.

Philly Joe Jones was possibly the most adventurous rhythm section drummer of the 1950s. His crisp snare drum fills, bass drum accents, and cymbal splashes were so well-conceived that he became far more than a mere timekeeper. Philly Joe's playing conveyed a constant excitement. He helped emancipate drummers by showing how active they could be without disturbing the pulse. His playing interacted intelligently with the solos of Davis, Coltrane, and Garland. His solos and solo-like fills retained the character of a piece; they did not seem isolated from what the rest of the group was doing, as did the drum solos in much pre-1960 jazz. His fills on "Two Bass Hit" (*Milestones*) and "Budo" (*Basic Miles*) are models of originality and assured execution. His fills could be unusually melodic, as in "Billy Boy" (*Milestones*), on which he employs brushes instead of sticks.

Collaborations with Gil Evans

In 1957, Miles renewed his association with former *Birth of the Cool* arranger Gil Evans (see Figure 10.1). Together they produced several Columbia albums on which Miles was the only soloist playing with a large band. Evans conducted his own arrangements for groups of brass, woodwinds, string bass, drums, and occasionally, harp. The brass section included French horn and tuba in addition to trumpets and trombones. The woodwind section consisted of flutes and clarinets in addition to saxophones; bassoon was added for *Sketches of Spain*. The arrangements reflected the prolific imagination and high-level workmanship of Gil Evans and produced some of the freshest, most well-balanced recordings in jazz history: *Miles Ahead, Porgy and Bess,* and *Sketches of Spain.*

Miles Ahead was recorded in 1957 with Davis playing fluegelhorn throughout. Although trumpeters Clark Terry and Shorty Rogers had played fluegelhorn prior to 1957, Miles's use of the instrument probably provided the impetus for its ensuing popularity. By the 1970s, many jazz trumpeters doubled on fluegelhorn, and arrangers who

Figure 10.1. Gil Evans conducting from the piano, age 58. *Bill Smith,* Coda

worked for popular singers and put together night club acts frequently included fluegelhorn parts in their scores. The Davis stimulus in the popularization of the fluegelhorn paralleled the influence of his *Birth of the Cool* on the subsequent use of French horn and tuba. (Similarly, there was a widespread use of the soprano saxophone following the release of John Coltrane's 1960 *My Favorite Things.*)

The program of *Miles Ahead* includes both popular tunes and jazz tunes. The pieces are connected by brief interludes which Evans composed specially to bridge the gaps between selections. *Miles Ahead* contains writing which ranges from the subtle, unforced swinging of the *Birth of the Cool*, to lush pastels in slow tempo, to moments of brassy excitement. Compared to other big band writing of the 1950s and 60s, it was far more reflective. Here Evans mastered the effective use of shading and contrast of both rhythmic and tonal dimensions. Probably the only arranging style of similar character and quality was Ellington's. Like Ellington, Evans also freed himself of the formula writing which pitted brasses against saxes. He freely voiced across sections and assigned different parts of a melody to different instruments. Like Ellington's writing and his own work on *Birth of the Cool*, Evans's arrangements for *Miles Ahead* managed to weave improvisation into the framework of a piece without sounding contrived or awkward. There were brief passages in which Davis interpreted pop tune themes, or in which he improvised on the chord progressions in the arrangements. In either case, the scoring was perfectly conceived to match the mood and color of Davis's style.

Porgy and Bess, recorded in 1958, is a lush scoring of music from George Gershwin's opera, "Porgy and Bess." Evans created sweeping colors and breathtaking drama. Miles plays some numbers on trumpet and others on fluegelhorn, reworking the frequently played Gershwin melodies so that they acquire a new, fresh quality. That flavor of sweet sadness so characteristic of Davis's style is especially noticeable in his work on "Summertime," "Fishermen, Strawberry and Devil Crab," and "My Man's Gone Now."

Sketches of Spain, recorded in November, 1959, and March, 1960, is nearly a classical album. Except for "Solea," in which Miles develops a long modal improvisation, the music on this recording was almost exclusively prewritten. The "Concierto de Aranjuez" for guitar and symphony orchestra by Joaquin Rodrigo was rescored by Evans for trumpet and wind orchestra; there are no strings. "Pan Piper," "Saeta," and "Solea" are developments of Spanish folk themes. Evans embroidered the melodies in a delicately beautiful way, and then he placed the haunting sound of the Miles Davis trumpet on top.

Sketches of Spain is a truly unique album. It easily qualifies as Third Stream because it combines jazz improvisation with the forms and instrumentation of classical music. Yet it has a more soulful punch than do most Third Stream efforts. The subtleties of the Evans arrangements—the voicings of tuba, harp, bass clarinet, snare drum, trumpets, and French horns—combine with the understated approach of Miles Davis to create very unusual music.

Kind of Blue   During the time between the *Porgy and Bess* sessions and the *Sketches of Spain* sessions, the Miles Davis sextet recorded *Kind of Blue*. Davis, alto saxophonist Cannonball Adderley, tenor saxophonist John Coltrane, pianist Bill Evans, bassist Paul Chambers, and drummer Jimmy Cobb comprised the group. On one track, "Freddie the Freeloader," Wynton Kelly replaced Evans, thus forming the Kelly-Chambers-Cobb rhythm section that Miles retained until 1963.

Each player on *Kind of Blue* had already made or would soon contribute approaches which dominated jazz of the 1960s. Miles Davis and Bill Evans collaborated on all the pieces, with the exception of "Freddie the Freeloader," composed by Davis, and "Blue in Green" (also called "Blues in Green"), which was written by Evans (it was mistakenly credited to Davis).

Davis, Adderley, Coltrane, Evans, Chambers, and Cobb had played together on another quiet record date ("Stella by Starlight," "Put Your Little Foot Out," "On Green Dolphin Street," *Basic Miles*, 1958), but *Kind of Blue* surpassed even the high quality of this earlier recording. Things were just right for the *Kind of Blue* session.

Bill Evans had been with Miles for an eight-month period after Red Garland left. Evans was replaced by Wynton Kelly and had been gone for a few months but returned for this record date. Philly Joe Jones and Jimmy Cobb had alternated as Miles's drummer until the *Kind of Blue* session, when Cobb became the permanent drummer until Davis disbanded in 1963.

It rarely happens that so many soloists are all playing in excellent form at the same time. Nearly every selection on the album represents a "first take." This means that the musicians themselves were so pleased with their first improvisations that they decided to release them instead of trying again for better ones. The music is a model of pacing and spontaneous balance. The mood of the album is one of calm, consistent thoughtfulness.

The construction of pieces on *Kind of Blue* marked a departure from pre-1959 jazz albums. The first selection on the second side, entitled either "All Blues" or "Flamenco Sketches" depending on what album copy you have, is basically a twelve-bar blues in meter of six. Unlike most modern jazz blues, this piece did not have a variety of chord changes in the first four measures. Instead, the first four measures were dominated by a single mode centered on the I chord of the piece. The absence of harmonic movement helped create a calm feeling. The entire blues progression was treated in this manner, with the exception of an interesting chord progression in the ninth and tenth measures: the V chord moves up one half-step then back down again.

The reduced number of chord progressions together with the swaying feeling created by meter of six, gave the piece a calm, almost hypnotic quality. Vamps sandwiched between theme statements and solos helped maintain the effect.

At the beginning, the rhythm section played a figure one two THREE four five SIX one two THREE four five SIX for four measures. The saxes then joined them for an additional four measures prior to Miles's solo entrance. This vamp was employed frequently throughout the performance. It provided time for things to air out. It accompanied the first four bars of Davis's melody statement, and it was inserted as a four-measure breathing space between the first and second choruses of the theme. It was played for an additional four bars after the theme statement and before Miles began his improvised solo. The vamp was always inserted between soloists thereafter. It was a calming device typical of Miles Davis's skill in pacing. It also provided a graceful transition, setting the stage for a new voice instead of making the awkwardly quick shift in style which occurs in many jazz performances when several soloists improvise choruses back to back.

Evans was the final soloist. His improvisation was followed by the four-bar vamp. Then Miles returned with the theme statement, accompanied by the saxes and rhythm section playing the vamp. Finally the performance faded out on the beginning of a new improvisation by Miles. A year earlier Miles had also used a fade-out to conclude his "Milestones" performance, but the device was uncommon until the 1960s. Here it adds further to the calm achieved by the vamps, the slow tempo, the meter of six, and the modal approach to harmony.

The harmonic form of the pieces and the dominant flavor of the album was modal. This approach was a continuation of the modal interest Davis had shown on the title track of *Milestones* and an interest he was to display in "Solea" on the *Sketches of Spain* LP. Modal forms also interested his pianist, Bill Evans. Evans's "Peace Piece," which he recorded under his own name (*Peace Piece and Other Pieces*) is modal, based exclusively on a repeating two-chord pattern. Its beginning is identical to the beginning of the second selection on *Kind of Blue*'s second side. "Peace Piece" was recorded by Bill Evans in December of 1958, four months before *Kind of Blue*'s second side. The primary difference between the two performances, aside from personnel and instrumentation, is that "Peace Piece" is based on a single mode, whereas its counterpart employs four additional modes. The role Bill Evans played in working out the style of the 1959 *Kind of Blue* was similar to that Gil Evans played in the 1949 *Birth of the Cool* and that of Joe Zawinul in the 1969 *In a Silent Way* and *Bitches Brew*.

"So What" began with a slow, written introduction played by pianist Evans and bassist Paul Chambers (*Smithsonian Collection*). It was not in strict tempo but was played rubato. The introduction conveyed a mood of quiet anticipation. The theme, a new melodic figure in strict tempo, was then stated by the bass played pizzicato. It was a thirty-two-bar AABA form with a question and answer pattern: the bass asked a question and the answer was stated by piano and drums during the first eight bars, and then by horns and piano together through most of the remaining question-answer segments. The bridge of the tune is identical to the A section, but it is played a half step higher.

Instead of using a variety of chord changes within each few measures, "So What" employed a single chord or mode for eight or sixteen consecutive measures.

One mode is the basis for the first sixteen bars, the A section and its repetition. The same mode is raised a half step for the eight-measure bridge, then lowered again to the original mode for the final eight-bar A section.

"So What" popularized a relatively new style for jazz pieces because it was modal. It was also unusual because it had an out-of-tempo, prewritten introduction followed by a theme statement in the form of a call by pizzicato bass and a response by horns and piano. Duke Ellington had used bassist Jimmy Blanton in a similar capacity for his 1940 "Jack the Bear" and other recordings. The Davis recording of "So What," however, caught on more with the mainstream of jazz bassists.

The Bill Evans composition "Blue in Green" was also on *Kind of Blue*. It is ten measures long, an unusual form for jazz. The improvisational technique used on it was even more unusual. Each soloist was free to halve or double the duration of the chord progression and use that alteration as the harmonic basis of his improvisation.

The second selection on the second side of *Kind Of Blue* is known by two different titles because many records were released with the second side's tune titles interchanged. The name that seems to have stuck for the *second* selection is "Flamenco Sketches." Bill Evans's album jacket notes indicate that the piece was supposed to be called "All Blues." But several subsequent Davis versions of the second side's *first* selection have been released using the "All Blues" title. Other groups have also recorded the tune, a blues in meter of six, with that title. The title "All Blues" seems to have stuck as the name of the *first* selection, leaving "Flamenco Sketches" as the title for the *second*.

The second selection on *Kind of Blue*'s second side was created by an interesting improvisational technique. No melody or chord progressions were written. Instead of playing a melody and improvising on its chord changes, the sextet followed a preset sequence of five modes.

Each mode served as the harmonic guide for improvisation as long as a soloist wanted to use it. Then, whenever he wanted a change, he moved to the next mode. Although there were no restrictions on the duration of any mode, the soloists tended to use each mode for an even number of measures. In fact, most soloists used each mode for four measures and then moved to the next. So, in spite of the increased freedom allowed by this technique, the players usually chose duration patterns which typically occur in conventional jazz improvisation.

Davis, Ornette Coleman, and Free Jazz

In bop and bop-influenced styles, the chords were basically prescribed before improvisation. Each chord also lasted a specific number of beats before moving to the next. Constant tempo was also maintained, and rarely was a meter other than four employed. In bop, the chords changed quickly and often moved in directions less predictable than most pop tune progressions. The chord progressions of Dizzy Gillespie's "Con Alma," George Shearings' "Deception," Clifford Brown's "Joy Spring," and John Coltrane's "Giant Steps" are quite difficult.

When a jazz musician improvises at a constant tempo but does *not rely on preset chord progressions* which have *preset durations,* at least four alternatives are available to him:

1) He can invent his own chord progressions while he improvises. The progressions need not repeat nor fall into four- or eight-measure phrases.

2) He can follow a preset sequence of chords or modes whose durations are not fixed, employing each chord or mode only as long as he wishes and moving to the next at his own discretion.

3) He can follow a preset sequence of modes in which each mode has fixed duration.

4) He can base his entire improvisation on a single chord or mode.

For more conventional jazz forms, in which chords change frequently and have preset durations, Miles Davis substituted forms in which a single chord might last four or more measures. He then preset the durations ("Milestones," "So What"), left the durations up to the spontaneous discretion of the soloist (second selection on second side of *Kind of Blue*), or produced music with a preset chord progression whose total duration might be altered during improvisation ("Blue in Green").

Interestingly, at the same time that Miles Davis was altering the bop approach (1958–59), Ornette Coleman, a saxophonist known for improvising without preset chord changes, was making his first recordings. Their techniques had similarities. Both Davis and Coleman maintained constant tempo during most improvisations, for example (although Coleman occasionally changed meters spontaneously). Instead of setting certain chord progressions in advance, Coleman preferred to invent them while improvising. Miles Davis used this technique to a limited extent in "Dolores" (1966 *Miles Smiles*), "Hand Jive" and "Madness" (1967 *Nefertiti*), and in his post-1969 work. Ornette Coleman occasionally avoided improvising in four- and eight-measure phrases. For example, he might switch keys after the first twenty-nine measures of a piece instead of switching after the first thirty-two measures ("Dee Dee," *At the Golden Circle*). His improvisations moved freely from key to key, following only the logic of the line or the impulse of the moment rather than adhering to a single key or changing keys at predetermined times.

Much post-1959 improvisational music employed the alternatives demonstrated by Davis and Coleman. During the late 1960s and 70s, numerous players rejected the bop convention of frequent chord changes which bore preset durations. Entire performances were sometimes based on a single chord instead of an involved progression of different chords. Some performances contained spontaneous chord changes and spontaneous key changes. But in spite of these new aspects, much free-form music retained the sound and feeling of bop-influenced performances. Bop phrases and melodic devices continued to appear.

Lennie Tristano, Lee Konitz, et al. ("Intuition" and "Digression"), and Jimmy Giuffre, Shorty Rogers, et al. ("Abstract #1," "Etudiez Le Cahier") had employed the techniques of free jazz years earlier. But with the work of Miles Davis and Ornette Coleman the approach caught on in the mainstream of jazz. During the late 1960s and 70s, more than half of all jazz and jazz-derived performances contained either modal or free-form improvisations. During the 1970s, fewer than twenty prominent modern jazz combos played selections which fit neither modal nor free-form styles.

1959–63   The rhythm section employed by Davis from 1959 to 1963 consisted of pianist **Wynton Kelly**, bassist Paul Chambers, and drummer Jimmy Cobb. This was the rhythm section that played on *At Carnegie Hall, In Person at the Blackhawk*, and *Someday My Prince Will Come*. Wynton Kelly derived his style primarily from Bud Powell, but there was also a funky, bluesy quality which might be attributed to the influence of Horace Silver. Kelly's playing on *Someday My Prince Will Come* also displays some of the voicings, sustained, ringing tones, and feeling of Bill Evans.

Drummer **Jimmy Cobb** was more conservative than Philly Joe Jones but contributed a significant characteristic to modern jazz drumming. His ride rhythms were placed toward the front edge of the beat, so that they seemed to be pulling it. Philly Joe Jones, Art Taylor, and Art Blakey had tended to play more toward the center of the beat.

Cobb took that tendency a bit further. This aspect of timekeeping is subtle but quite significant. Tony Williams, who replaced Cobb, played consistently on the leading edge of the beat. That technique, coupled with its counterpart in walking bass, became a prime characteristic of the Davis Quintet sound.

Tenor saxophonist **Hank Mobley** was with Davis in the very early 1960s. His style was characteristic of hard bop tenor except that his tone had a soft, muffled quality. Mobley attacked his notes bluntly instead of using the sharp attack of Rollins. Like nearly all Davis sidemen, Mobley was a solid jazz improviser. He was not, however, an improviser of the Rollins or Coltrane level.

modern jazz: the early 1960s to the late 1970s

The 1960s was an especially fertile period for changes in the sound of jazz. During these years, a number of innovators whose first records had appeared in the 1950s reached their creative peaks, and their influence was discernible in recordings of both new and established players by the late 1960s. There was a proliferation of new approaches to the creation of jazz. Collective improvisation (which had been a central feature of Dixieland jazz) was used by Ornette Coleman, John Coltrane, Sun Ra, Cecil Taylor, and a group called Weather Report. Other changes were influenced partly by non-jazz styles. For example, Don Ellis created jazz pieces using unusual meters common to the native music of India. John Coltrane explored improvisatory methods inspired partly by the modal music of India. Bill Evans and Chick Corea have been affected by the twentieth-century composer Erik Satie. During the 1970s an enormous number of jazz groups adopted the instruments and rhythms of rock music.

The spectrum of tone colors was broadened by increased use of numerous instruments previously uncommon in jazz and several which had only limited use in earlier jazz styles. Added to the standard collection of trumpet, trombone, saxophone, piano, bass, and drums was frequent inclusion of fluegelhorn, flute, soprano saxophone, and auxiliary percussion. Some trumpeters actually adopted fluegelhorn as their primary instrument. Most saxophonists were now playing soprano saxophone and flute as commonly as their 1930s and 40s counterparts had played clarinet. The use of electronic instruments, amplification, and electronic devices to alter the sound of conventional instruments became widespread during the 1970s. Pianists explored electronic keyboard instruments which offered countless new sounds. Many pianists also learned how to use synthesizers which had no keyboard attached to them. Amplification of the string bass enabled the audience to actually hear each note instead of detecting only the vague, low-pitched presence which had reached them prior to the use of new bass amplification devices. In the 1970s the string bass was replaced by the electric bass guitar (Fender bass) in the majority of bands. It required different playing techniques and produced a different sound. Both of those factors contributed to a significant alteration of the character associated with jazz bass playing.

Drummers incorporated a wider variety of percussion instruments than ever before. Some instruments were native to India, South America, and Africa. Drummers further augmented their arsenal with homemade instruments constructed of tin cans, pebbles, surgical tape, scrap iron, sheet metal, etc. The development of special microphones for amplifying drums and the extensive interest in better recording techniques were also applied to the instruments of the jazz drummer.

In addition to using new instruments, jazz musicians were playing old instruments in new ways. For example, the high range of the average late 1960s–early 1970s hornman was greater than that of his counterpart in the 1930s and 40s. Trumpeters Cat Anderson and Maynard Ferguson had the status of freaks during the late 1940s and the 50s. Yet, during the 1970s many trumpeters played as high. Similarly Tommy Dorsey's smooth technique and high range on trombone which was unusual for the 1940s was surpassed by many trombonists during the 1960s and 70s. The high notes of saxophonists Illinois Jacquet and Earl Bostic which were unusual even for the 1950s became common by the late 1960s. Saxophonists cultivated more techniques to radically "bend" their pitch and tone color, sometimes playing several notes at the same time and producing a huge assortment of shrieks, squawks, and wails. Instrumental proficiency increased during the 1960s and 70s. Guitarists, pianists, bassists, and drummers generally played faster and more precisely.

The sound of jazz was altered not only by way of different instruments and different techniques but also by new settings for old instruments. For example, piano was absent from many recordings by Ornette Coleman, Archie Shepp, Albert Ayler, The Art Ensemble of Chicago, Elvin Jones, Sam Rivers, and others. In addition a number of duet albums appeared. This was a striking departure from the traditional practice of building a combo by starting with bass and drums, then adding instruments. (Interesting duet approaches were recorded by saxophonist John Coltrane and drummer Rashied Ali, pianist Bill Evans and guitarist Jim Hall, saxophonists Anthony Braxton and Joseph Jarman, pianist Chick Corea and vibraharpist Gary Burton, saxophonist David Liebman and pianist Richard Beirach.) Starting in

1970, a very large number of pianists recorded solo albums without the usual accompaniment of bass and drums. (Keith Jarrett recorded five LPs full of unaccompanied piano improvisation.) In a period when tremendous importance was placed on electronic instruments, such acoustic solo piano performances offered a strong contrast.

The 1960s saw significant transformations of the rhythm section which gave its members far greater stylistic freedom than they had ever known before.

To appreciate the innovations of the 1960s, let us examine a few events and attitudes of the previous two decades. The idea that the bassist and drummer were present primarily to keep time and make the band swing was firmly entrenched during the 1940s and 50s. But the bassist began to discover his melodic potential in the early 1940s bowed work of Slam Stewart and the plucked work of Jimmy Blanton. Similarly, Benny Goodman's drummer, Gene Krupa, had popularized drum solos. Then, during the late 1940s, bop drummers Kenny Clarke and Max Roach expanded the amount of communication between drummers and soloists.

Despite improved solo capability of bassists and drummers, a smooth, musical integration of their work into the overall concept of a piece was unusual. Rarely was an overall musical purpose served by inserting a bass or drum solo in the sequence of improvised choruses. In fact, it usually broke the rhythmic and tonal texture of the piece.

During the 1950s drummers Art Blakey and Philly Joe Jones began playing more actively, sometimes to the point of enveloping an improvising soloist. The drummers of the 1960s, especially Elvin Jones and Tony Williams, took up where Art Blakey and Philly Joe Jones had left off. The musical personality of the combo drummer moved more and more into the forefront of the group sound. He was no longer thought of as simply a timekeeper but now became responsible for imaginatively decorating the combo sound and engaging in musical conversation with fellow group members.

During the early 1960s, beginning with the trio of pianist Bill Evans, bassist Scott LaFaro, and drummer Paul Motian, some rhythm sections succeeded in maintaining three-way musical conversations which displayed sensitive and imaginative interplay.

The new role of bass and drums included accompaniment as only one aspect of their job. Much of the time they came to the forefront in ways previously assigned to soloists. This new style of rhythm section embellished the work of improvising soloists with diverse musical comments, yet still managed to provide swing feeling and the chord changes expected of bop style rhythm sections. These new rhythm sections kept time with an unprecedented assortment of changing rhythmic figures. In some pieces, ride rhythms and walking bass were barely suggested. This was exemplified by the brilliant work Scott

LaFaro contributed. His Evans trio playing included walking, soloing, spontaneously contributing melodic figures, mimicking, and underscoring piano and drum statements. Beginning with Jimmy Blanton and Kenny Clarke, running through Art Blakey and Philly Joe Jones, and culminating with Scott LaFaro, Elvin Jones, and Tony Williams, jazz experienced an emancipation of the rhythm section. In several groups of the 1960s and 70s, the distinction between soloists and accompanists became quite loose.

The 1970s group, Weather Report, provided a context for breaking down traditional ideas regarding the separation of solo roles and rhythm section roles. Their bassist, Miroslav Vitous, combined the melodic conception of a modern jazz hornman plus good rhythm section bass playing. He was very flexible and interacted with great imagination and sensitivity. In Weather Report, spurts of melody might come from any member, not just from the saxophonist or pianist. Rhythmic figures and fills could also be produced by any member, not solely by the bassist or the drummer. The kinds of interaction between members were so varied that in some passages of Weather Report's music there was little or no distinction between soloist and accompanist. One player's sound might stand out momentarily, but it soon blended into the overall musical texture again. For the first time, a jazz combo molded nonformula improvisations into well-balanced musical textures. Weather Report was able to collectively improvise extended performances which had the color, pacing, and unity of prewritten pieces by such impressionist orchestral composers as Claude Debussy and Maurice Ravel.

Much of the emancipation and electrification of the modern jazz rhythm section is well-chronicled by Miles Davis recordings of the 1960s and 70s. The influence of the innovative 1960–61 Bill Evans trio is evident in the playing of pianist Herbie Hancock and bassist Ron Carter on 1963–68 Davis quintet recordings. The active, imaginative approaches developed by Max Roach, Philly Joe Jones, and Louis Hayes are evident as the jumping off points for development of Tony Williams's style in those same recordings. Radical alterations of jazz rhythm section concepts and the adoption of rock feeling are documented in 1969–75 Davis recordings in which several electronic keyboard instruments were used simultaneously, several electric guitarists played at the same time, Indian instruments were used, auxiliary percussionists were employed, and a rock style Fender bassist is used. The rhythm section innovations in the Davis recordings of 1969–72 were so influencial that the 1970s bands of Herbie Hancock, Chick Corea, Tony Williams, John McLaughlin and others could easily be conceived as being Miles Davis rhythm sections.

The ways in which jazz musicians approached basic elements of music became the scene of marked variation during the 1960s. Some performances by Cecil Taylor, Ornette Coleman, The Art Ensemble of Chicago, and Sun Ra rejected the maintenance of strict meter. A few performances completely dispensed with constant tempo. Many drummers and bassists who did not go that far nevertheless preferred to state the beat in less obvious and more interesting ways than their predecessors. Changes in the use of swing eighth notes and the rising-falling style of improvised lines were partly responsible for a difference in what was meant by jazz swing feeling. Some performances did not swing at all in the sense traditionally meant by the term jazz swing feeling. Some were not meant to swing, either. New jazz styles of the late 1960s and 70s did not swing in the manner of previous periods. Some performances swung only in the way in which a rhythmically successful rock performance swings.

Much improvisation of the 1960s and 70s was based on progressions which employed far fewer chords than had typified bop progressions. Many pieces actually had very few chord changes at all. Entire pieces were based on a single chord.

For many performances the player invented his own harmonies while improvising instead of presetting them beforehand. Some of this music was called free jazz because it was free of preset chord progressions.

Melodic styles in written tunes were unlike those of bop. Some composers, especially John Coltrane, McCoy Tyner, Wayne Shorter and Joe Zawinul, often used less pronounced syncopation and fewer notes than bop composers had. Sustained tones and silences became just as important to the styles of Shorter and Zawinul as rapid-fire eighth notes had once been. The interval of a fourth also became very characteristic of 1960s and 70s composition. It lent an open feeling to the music.

Compositional forms changed as well. A large portion of the new tunes were written without bridges or turnarounds (and where turnarounds existed, they were far simpler than those of bop). Many employed silence as an essential aspect of their construction. Few fit traditional twelve-bar blues and thirty-two-bar AABA chord progressions. These tunes projected a more expansive, free, floating feeling than melodies with frequent chord changes, bridges, and turnarounds. But at the same time that tunes were becoming simpler and smoother, rhythm section activity was becoming more complex and turbulent. Many of these changes in style are well documented by 1960s records of the Miles Davis Quintet and the John Coltrane Quartet.

To many listeners, some jazz of the 1960s and 70s seemed to be motivated by musical goals which differed sharply from those which had previously guided jazz. Some performances by Cecil Taylor, Sun Ra, John Coltrane, and others seemed to be the result of inventing sound for sound's sake rather than for the sake of melody, harmony, or jazz swing feeling. Some pieces generated moods and textures instead of making sounds which fit traditional patterns of melody and accompaniment. Some performances seemed to make rhythm for rhythm's sake in place of rhythm as an accompaniment to melody or as a component of melody. The 1960s and 70s saw an emphasis on amassing colorful sounds and provocative rhythms which rivalled the emphasis which modern jazz of the 1940s had placed on amassing complex chord progressions and elaborately syncopated melodies. Drummers had always been particularly interested in colorful sounds and provocative rhythms. During the 1970s it was as though hornmen and bandleaders were taking a cue from them.

chapter 11
ORNETTE COLEMAN

One of the most influential forces in jazz of the 1960s and 70s was Ornette Coleman. Some consider him to have been as historically significant as Charlie Parker and John Coltrane (see Figure 11.1).

Though he also plays trumpet and violin, Coleman is primarily an alto saxophonist. On his 1958–59 recordings, he displayed a soft, pure tone and moved from note to note in legato fashion, as if smoothly sliding along small subdivisions of pitch. His tone did not have the edge of Charlie Parker's or the body of Cannonball Adderley's. Coleman began his notes more bluntly and used a slow vibrato. Later he made his tone somewhat brighter and gave it an edge. Though he seems able to play almost everything he attempts, he lacks the instrumental proficiency of such virtuosos as Parker, Adderley and Lee Konitz.

Coleman is one of the freshest, most prolific post-bop composers; he has written every tune on each of more than twenty albums. His style is quite original, and he has an exceptional gift for melody. Some of his tunes are quite catchy, and, like those of Thelonius Monk, sound simple, in spite of their unusual rhythmic and harmonic qualities. The playfulness of Coleman's tunes is also reminiscent of Monk's work. The Coleman style has surfaced noticeably in the work of pianist-composer Keith Jarrett, who acknowledged Coleman in his "Piece for Ornette." Fellow saxophonist Roscoe Mitchell wrote a piece simply entitled "Ornette."

Other musicians have also shown interest in Coleman's compositions. Ran Blake, Denny Zeitlin, and the Modern Jazz Quartet have all recorded his "Lonely Woman," not to be confused with another tune of the same name by Benny Carter (Ornette Coleman—*The Shape of*

Figure 11.1. Ornette Coleman (alto sax), Charlie Haden (bass), Eddie Blackwell (drums), 1972. *Bill Smith,* Coda

Jazz to Come). The New York Contemporary Five recorded his "Emotions." Bobby Hutcherson recorded his "Una Muy Bonita." Both Paul Motian and Charlie Haden have made albums which included his "War Orphans." Fellow alto saxophonist Jackie McLean recorded Coleman's "Old Gospel" and "Strange As It Seems." John Coltrane made an album using Coleman sidemen and playing Coleman's tunes, including "The Invisible," "The Blessing," and "Focus on Sanity." Pianist Paul Bley has used Coleman's "Crossroads," "The Blessing," "Free," "Blues," "Ramblin'," and "When Will the Blues Leave?". Saxophonist Archie Shepp has also recorded "When Will the Blues Leave?," "O.C.," and "Peace."

Though many of Coleman's pieces are simply springboards for improvisation, some have been arranged for ensembles. His "Forms and Sounds" was scored for flute, oboe, clarinet, bassoon, and French horn. Coleman's "Saints and Soldiers" and "Space Flight" were arranged for two violins, viola, and cello (*The Music of Ornette Coleman*). "Skies of America," which he considers one of his best works, was scored for symphony orchestra (*Skies of America*).

On some pieces in his first album (*Something Else*), Coleman used a pianist and improvised to preset chord changes. Except for that work, however, and a recorded concert with pianist Paul Bley (*Paul Bley at the Hillcrest Club*), Coleman generally stayed away from using preset chord changes for his improvisation, and he omitted chording instruments (piano, organ, guitar, etc.). Because his improvisations were free of preset chord changes, Coleman's music became known as *free jazz*.

With neither a chording instrument nor preset chord progressions, Coleman has few harmonic restrictions, quite an open and uncluttered harmonic base. But Coleman's work not only casts off the restraints of preset harmonies; it also freely adjusts tempo and meter. The format for most Coleman performances is simple and unrestricting. He begins by playing a pre-written tune, then, retaining its tempo and mood, he improvises. Finally, after all solos are over, he plays the tune for an ending.

To the nonmusician who imagines that chord changes create difficulties for the improviser, the absence of preset chord changes might seem to make improvisation easier. To a certain extent, that is true. But complications arise. The central problem is simply that, along with constant tempo, chord progressions provide coherence, direction, and momentum for the improviser. They can add interest to an otherwise uninspired solo. An effective rhythm section can support a poor soloist or complement a good one if chord changes are used. Even during the improvisations of a good soloist there may be moments when the activity of changing chords prevents a loss of continuity. Chord changes probably help more than they hinder.

Coleman attempts a difficult task when he rejects the use of preset chord changes. Without the rise and fall of musical tension indicated by chord changes, Coleman still has the rise and fall of tension generated by his bassist and drummer. But that is all he has to musically support and inspire his creations. Outside of that, every measure is taxing his imagination, requesting that it be filled with interesting and meaningful lines. Yet none of those measures is supplying any organizational ideas in the form of chord changes. Coleman has chosen a situation in which his improvising cannot fall back on the underlying musical motion of chord changes or on the supportive sound of a pianist's comping. With the absence of preset chord changes, and the regular chorus lengths, turnarounds, and bridges indicated by them, Coleman has brought us an especially abstract form of musical experience.

Despite the freedom of his improvisational approach, Coleman improvised lines which often resembled chord progression-based lines. For Coleman, melody is primary and harmony secondary. So it may sound as though he is inventing chord progressions as he improvises lines, but this is only because the harmonic logic of those lines resembles that of chord progression-based lines which we have previously heard in non-Coleman performances. The construction of his lines is ruled by his musical past in the way that our perception as listeners is ruled by our past listening experiences. Coleman plays freely, but in his lines we can hear organization resembling that which characterizes improvisation based on preset harmonies. The feeling of a definite key is present in each portion of his solos, though he changes keys at will. (For example, he used nine different keys in improvising on "Dee Dee," *At the Golden Circle*.) And part of the chord progression feeling in Coleman's music stems from the approach taken by his bassists, especially Charlie Haden. Though Coleman's bassists follow the harmonic directions indicated by his improvisations, at times they also take the lead. Coleman's line may suggest a chord progression which the bassist will complete, or the bassist's line may suggest a chord progression which Coleman picks up. Coleman and his bassist remain alert to each other's patterns of harmony.

It is important to note that Ornette Coleman was not the first soloist to suggest new chord progressions during improvisation. Lester Young and Coleman Hawkins had done it as early as the 1930s, and added chords are also implied by Louis Armstrong's lines of the 1920s. During the 1940s Art Tatum, Don Byas, Charlie Parker, Dizzy Gillespie, and their disciples also invented and substituted chord progressions while they improvised. The difference between their approach and Coleman's is in the starting point. Tatum, Parker, et al. began with preset chord progressions and then added to those progressions. Coleman starts with only a key, a tempo, and the mood of the tune. Nevertheless, if Charlie Parker had returned to life during the 1960s and walked into a free-form jam session of Coleman or his disciples, he probably would have fit in quite well. Parker would have been able to retain his own style because he had been an extremely versatile and imaginative improviser, and because he would have had no trouble inventing original lines regardless of the session's lack of preset chord progressions. He had invented his own chord progressions during the bop era; he could do so again within the free jazz style of the 1960s.

It is also important to note that Coleman is neither the first nor the only person to improvise jazz without the use of preset chord progressions. Many musicians quite unself-consciously improvise without giving thought to a preset melody, key, or chord progression. Little of this has been commercially recorded. But it has gone on for decades, continues to occur, and it is not revolutionary at all. Many people played free jazz long before they discovered Ornette Coleman, and many of them undoubtedly remain unaware of his work.

It is interesting to compare Parker and Coleman. Both played alto saxophone. Both were energetic improvisers. Both had a gift for melody. On his first few recordings, Coleman's tonal inflections and their timing resemble Parker's. Much of Coleman's early alto work contains tonal inflections derived from black vocal styles, and his playing is quite bluesy, more so than Parker's. Coleman's tone was unique, but it resembled Parker's more than it resembled that of Johnny Hodges, Benny Carter, or Lee Konitz. Coleman also used a few bop phrases in his improvisation and recorded Parker's tune, "Klactoveedsedstene" (*Paul Bley at the Hillcrest Club*). His playing had the soulfulness of Bird's and the explosions of slippery notes which can be found in some Bird improvisations. Like Bird, Coleman also liked to quote pop tunes briefly. Themes from "If I Loved You," "Hawaiian War Chant," "Cherokee," and "Blues in the Night" ("My Mama Done Told Me") have all been interjected in his improvisations at various times.

Although I disagree with the statement, I have heard Coleman called "just another bebop alto player." For me, the rhythmic complexity of bop makes Coleman's less complex music easily differentiable. But I understand how the bop tonal inflections, bop phrasing, steady tempo, and bluesy melodic figures in Coleman's playing might lead a listener to call him a bebop player. A striking aspect of this perception is that it coexists with a completely different response to Ornette Coleman's style: many people, after all, consider him a revolutionary figure. There are valid reasons for both reactions. Coleman was genuinely innovative, but he built on a bop foundation; he did not step out of thin air. Coleman drew from Bird just as Bird drew from Hawkins and Young. Coleman is innovative, but has not shown the genius of Bird.

Coleman's tunes are original and his saxophone style is unique, but it is with his approach to improvisation that he has had the most impact on modern jazz. Coleman's decision to discard chord changes, and the style he developed without them, influenced the playing of numerous improvisers during the 1960s and 70s—not only saxophonists but also trumpeters, trombonists, and composers. Although Coleman was not the only influence they absorbed, the following players have all displayed varying proportions of Coleman characteristics: John Tchicai, Marion Brown, Dewey Redman, Jimmy Lyons, Sonny Simmons, Prince Lasha, Henry Threadgill, Carlos Ward, Archie Shepp, Oliver Lake, Roscoe Mitchell, Jan Garbarek, Anthony Ortega, Albert Ayler, and John Coltrane (see Chapter 14 for extended discussion of possible Coleman influence on various directions in Coltrane's work).

Though it is not his best album, Coleman's 1960 *Free Jazz* paralleled Miles Davis's *Kind of Blue* in its effect on improvisational approaches. *Kind of Blue* popularized modal approaches, and *Free Jazz* might have contributed to more frequent use of free-form collective approaches. Coleman used two pianoless quartets. The personnel of the first included himself, trumpeter Don Cherry, bassist Charlie Haden, and drummer Eddie Blackwell. The second was made up of alto saxophonist-bass clarinetist Eric Dolphy, trumpeter Freddie Hubbard, bassist Scott LaFaro, and drummer Billy Higgins. The eight musicians played together, sometimes improvising all at once. There was no preset arrangement of themes, chord changes, or chorus lengths. Tonal centers were used, though they were not agreed upon in advance.

Despite the album title, the music on *Free Jazz* is not haphazard, random, uncontrolled, without pulse, or atonal. There are prearranged ensemble passages, solos with rhythm section accompaniment, as well as a string bass duet. Some of the solos, especially Freddie Hubbard's, sound as though they were based on a preset chord progression, but the progression is actually being composed spontaneously during the solo. Brief themes recur in the improvisation and are passed back and forth among group members. Rarely are all eight men improvising at the same time. Both bassists and both drummers play throughout most of it, but usually a single horn (Coleman, Dolphy, Hubbard or Cherry) surfaces while the others lay out. Occasionally all the horns return to embellish the prominent voice.

Other jazz groups had recorded collectively improvised free pieces at about the same time and prior to Coleman's first recordings. But they were isolated efforts, and the approach did not catch on in the jazz mainstream. After Coleman's *Free Jazz,* however, a number of other musicians also recorded collective improvisations without prewritten melodies, chord changes, or chorus lengths (see following discussions of Sun Ra, Cecil Taylor, and John Coltrane). Members of the Chicago-based Association for the Advancement of Creative Musicians (AACM) have recorded free-form collective improvisations which sound similar to Coleman's *Free Jazz.* Although they may have come up with these approaches on their own, it is likely that, having appeared after Coleman's work, the AACM members were at least influenced in part by *Free Jazz.*

FREE JAZZ Although often called "free jazz," Coleman's music actually has quite a bit of self-imposed structure. Constant tempo is usually employed. Written and memorized tunes are usually used during some portion of his performances. And, of course, there is nothing haphazard about the freedom with which he and his sidemen play. They are limited by their own decision to listen to each other carefully and plan their music while they improvise.

In addition to the discipline of prewritten melodies, constant tempo, key feeling, conscious self-editing, and sensitivity to fellow group members, Coleman's "free jazz" also uses instruments in conventional solo and accompaniment roles. In his trio, Coleman usually seems to be soloing while his bassist and drummer accompany. Of course there is interaction, give-and-take, and mutual stimulation, but there is little doubt that Coleman is the soloist.

If a performance were truly free of role conventions, the three instruments would be undifferentiated in that respect. The absence of solo voices would occur as often as the presence of a single voice. Why should the horn necessarily be a solo instrument and the bass and drums accompanying instruments? In a truly free situation the drums would be accompanied by sax and bass just as often as the sax was accompanied by bass and drums.

Why should there be any solos at all? For me, free means the absence of prescribed roles or prescribed forms. The concepts of solo and accompaniment are roles, just as the use of constant tempo, meter, key, chord changes (and their chorus lengths) and so forth constitute forms.

Free can also mean not having to play within an expected style. Freedom hinges on the ability to play whatever is in your head regardless of its relation to (a) intonation, (b) key, (c) expectations of melodic continuity, (d) chord changes, (e) tempo, (f) instrumental proficiency, (g) the playing of other group members or (h) the expectations of the audience. That sounds like a superhuman task, and it is! That kind of freedom is not humanly possible. Our musical conditioning prevents so great an independence from rules, skills, and habits.

If "free jazz" means only that a musician is allowed total freedom of choice, and Coleman's freedom simply led to his choice of constant tempo, key, solo roles, and accompanying roles, then his music qualifies as free. But if "free jazz" means music devoid of all rules, roles, and expectations, as it does for some people, then Coleman's music is far from free. Rarely does any kind of music qualify as free by that strict definition. To fit such a description, the music would have to simultaneously assign (a) instruments at random, (b) notes at random, (c) durations at random and (d) note combinations at random. There are computer programs which rely on a random number function to generate just such a musical situation. But it is almost impossible for improvisers to achieve that degree of freedom.

In short, Coleman's music is free in some respects: it is free of preset chord progressions and their chorus lengths. Some of his work is also free of meter and constant tempo, though that is not characteristic for most of his recordings. Coleman freely changes keys, but he usually stays in each one long enough for us to hear that he is, indeed, in a particular key. And his key changes are logical and obvious; they reflect harmonic planning. The music does not lack key feeling, it is not atonal, and it is certainly not random (see Chapter 17 for discussion of scales, modality, tonality, and atonality).

DON CHERRY Ornette Coleman employed trumpeter Don Cherry on twelve albums (Ornette Coleman—*The Shape of Jazz to Come, Smithsonian Collection, Something Else!*). Cherry has a soft tone and plays with an understated quality reminiscent of pre-1960 Miles Davis. Though

Cherry's improvisations are rooted in bop, as is evident in his earliest recordings, they are quite different from conventional bop trumpet lines. Occasionally they resemble the lines of Ornette Coleman or Miles Davis, but they are generally quite original. They contain more variety in rhythm and phrasing than the long eighth-note sequences of bop. Together with Freddie Hubbard, Cherry is often considered to be among the few original trumpeters prominent during the 1960s and 70s (*Complete Communion*).

During the 1970s Cherry spent a considerable amount of time in Europe, where he was active as a composer and bandleader. Much of his music is available only through French and Swedish record companies.

ARCHIE SHEPP

Several unconventional saxophone styles arose soon after Coleman's first recordings. One of them was created by tenor saxophonist Archie Shepp. A primary characteristic of Shepp's style, as well as other post-Coleman styles, was a departure from bop phrasing and rhythmic conception. Although the early recordings by most post-Coleman players bear some resemblance to bop, these musicians usually lost that resemblance within a few years. The vocabulary of phrases and chord changes used in bop was almost, but not completely, discarded.

The tone color range of the new styles was broader than bop's. At the beginning of his career, Shepp's tone was similar to Ben Webster's in texture, attacks, and releases. Shepp, like many post-Coleman players, cultivated an assortment of squawks, wails, and shrieks, often in abrasive combination. The Coleman-Shepp conception of melody resulted in a loosening of bop pitch and rhythmic conventions; it signalled an end to the long, precisely executed streams of eighth-note figures with the twists and turns and stereotyped syncopations of bop. Coleman's and Shepp's phrasing was fragmented: sustained notes, screeches, and moans were more common in their music than in bop. Some of the screeches and moans sounded like animal cries. A great range of tone colors was vigorously explored. Hoarseness alternated with smoothness. Guttural sounds were interspersed with pretty sounds. Bop tone colors were mixed with gurgles.

Archie Shepp's varied attacks and rhythmic playfulness are reminiscent of Sonny Rollins. Like Rollins, both Shepp and Coleman project humor in their playing.

In many ways Shepp combines the characteristics of Ben Webster and Ornette Coleman. Neither Webster nor Coleman could be called a bop stylist. Webster was a swing era player with a husky, rough-textured tone, and Coleman had improvised without preset chord changes (see Chapter 6 for a discussion of Webster). These elements are combined in Shepp, who does, however, employ chord changes and modes on some of his records. Shepp's interest in Webster and Ellington is also indicated by his use of many Ellington ballads.

Though he often led his own groups, Shepp produced some of his best work under the leadership of pianist Cecil Taylor (*Air*). The LPs Taylor and Shepp made together show aspects of Shepp's talent not evident in the work he recorded as leader on a string of sessions for Impulse (*Four for Trane*).

ALBERT AYLER   One of the most original saxophone styles to emerge after Parker, Rollins, Coltrane, and Coleman was that of tenor saxophonist Albert Ayler (see Figure 11.2). Some listeners heralded his music as revolutionary and more important than John Coltrane's. It is interesting to note that, like Coleman, Ayler also used a Parker tune, "Billie's Bounce," on one of his first recordings (*Introducing Albert Ayler, My Name Is Albert Ayler*). And, like Coleman, he followed its harmonies only loosely. In other words, he acknowledged bop but did not actually play in the bop style. Ayler's rhythmic conception was unlike bop rhythmic conceptions and perhaps unlike any swinging jazz style. His melodic and rhythmic approaches had more in common with classical music and folk music than with jazz.

Figure 11.2. Albert Ayler. *Bill Smith, Coda*

Coleman and Shepp swung in a manner which only approximated conventional jazz swing feeling. Much of their work did not swing at all. The lack of swing feeling was often caused by a continuously high level of tension, in place of the constant alternation of tension and relaxation characteristic of bop. Ayler definitely swung in the general sense of the term but not in the conventional jazz sense typified by swing era, bop, West Coast, or hard bop styles.

Like Coleman, Ayler followed preset harmonic and rhythmic structures only loosely, and he preferred groups with no chording instrument. His bassists were some of the same gifted men employed by Bill Evans and Ornette Coleman. His drummers were of the "free" school, little concerned with simple timekeeping, and very interested in group interaction and the creation of varied tone colors.

Ayler was one of the most unusual tenor saxophonists jazz has ever known. He perfected an approach to improvisation that was so technically demanding that even if an imitator could figure out Ayler's lines, he probably would not be able to play them. Ayler's lines ran the entire range of the tenor saxophone and through at least one additional octave of pitches beyond the conventional "highest note." He played throughout that range with swooping, swirling legato figures, and a light, slippery tone, at times reminiscent of the C-melody saxophone. Like Shepp, and to a certain extent Coleman, Ayler made moans and wails an essential part of his musical vocabulary. Much of his music was strikingly voice-like (Albert Ayler Trio—*Spiritual Unity*). His vibrato was sometimes slow, at other times moderately fast, but always very natural in a driven sort of way. There was never anything mechanical or academic about Ayler's playing.

In his extended high-register, Ayler played with the ease good players have in the conventional mid-range of the tenor saxophone. His playing often sounded like rapid, legato violin-playing. These elements contributed to an overall feeling which had an otherworldly quality to it. Whether listeners enjoyed his music or not, it provided an intensely emotional experience for them.

Like those of many innovative jazz figures, Ayler's career was very short. His first American recording came out in 1964, and he died in 1970 at the age of 34. And like many other great American musicians, he was more popular in Europe than at home.

chapter 12

BILL EVANS, SUN RA, & CECIL TAYLOR

BILL EVANS Pianist Bill Evans played with Miles Davis for only about nine months, but that tenure brought his style the recognition of both jazz musicians and fans (see Figure 12.1). His work on *Kind of Blue* is jazz piano at its elegant best! His tone and conception were delicate without being fragile.

By May of 1958, when he first recorded with Davis ("Stella by Starlight," "Put Your Little Foot Out," "On Green Dolphin Street," *Basic Miles*), he had already impressed the jazz community with his "All About Rosie" solo (*Modern Jazz Concert,* George Russell's work for a 1957 Brandeis University commission) and made a trio record with bassist Teddy Kotick and drummer Paul Motian (*New Jazz Conceptions,* Riverside, 1956). Before making *Kind of Blue,* he had recorded another trio LP, *Everybody Digs Bill Evans,* which, as late as the mid-1970s, he still considered one of his very best recordings. One of the selections on that album, "Peace Piece," is the all-time favorite Evans performance for many listeners.

Kind of Blue and *Everybody Digs Bill Evans* are classic examples of his style. He strikes single tones and lets them ring, as though to savor each vibration before proceeding to the next. The effect is harp-like. Listen to his work on "Blue in Green" (*Kind of Blue*); "Young and Foolish" (*Everybody Digs*); second selection on *Kind of Blue,* second side; "Peace Piece"; and "What Is There to Say" (*Everybody Digs*). That way of playing was later picked up by pianists Herbie Hancock and Chick Corea (as in Hancock's "Pee Wee" solo on the 1967 Miles Davis *Sorcerer* and Corea's playing on his own *Piano Improvisations Vol. I.*).

Figure 12.1. Bill Evans, age 45, 1974. *Henry Kahanek*

Prior to 1959, Evans displayed considerable dexterity, and his style included elements from several sources. His long, fast, smoothly contoured eighth-note lines were reminiscent of alto saxophonist Lee Konitz, one of his early favorites. Because Konitz derived his style from pianist Lennie Tristano, the Evans approach exhibits recognizable Tristano influence. Evans's piano solos also contain elements borrowed from bop pianist Bud Powell, another Evans favorite. Occasionally, Evans used some bluesy figures which might be traced to pianist-composer Horace Silver, a far-reaching force during the 1950s.

After *Kind of Blue*, Evans made the first of four LPs with bassist Scott LaFaro. Evans developed a very personal style during that time. He began ridding himself of typical bop clichés and common jazz piano devices. His left hand gained importance and was soon sustaining chords in almost every measure instead of merely punctuating right-hand lines. He worked out a style of voicing his chorded lines in terms of modes and used tight clusters of notes.

Most of Evans's lines were composed of smoothly connected notes. Rarely after 1959 did he play lines with disconnected or staccato notes. He tended instead to favor a legato style. The melodies he improvised were frequently chorded, note for note, in the locked-hands style.

During 1960 and 61, **Scott LaFaro,** Evans's bassist, effectively did for modern jazz bass styles what Jimmy Blanton had done for swing era bass playing: he reminded us that, in the hands of a virtuoso, the bass can contribute exciting solo lines and ensemble interplay that provide a feeling of grace and freedom for the underpinnings of a group sound.

The idea of pianists and bassists engaging in active musical conversation had been explored by Duke Ellington and Jimmy Blanton in their 1940 duets, "Mr. J.B. Blues" and "Pitter Panther Patter." Evans and LaFaro refined this idea, together with drummer Paul Motian. LaFaro sometimes walked and soloed, but more often he vigorously interacted with piano and drums. While Evans was playing melody or improvising, LaFaro contributed a great diversity of musical ideas. He would throw in melodic figures, mimic Evans or answer Evans, and underscore the figures which Evans and Motian played. In addition, LaFaro often fed ideas to Evans. LaFaro was not merely a timekeeper or even a timekeeper capable, on occasion, of impressive solos. He was a melodic instrument at least as important to the Evans trio as a hornman was to the standard jazz quintet.

Some Evans trio passages, instead of treating all four beats of each measure, tend to concentrate on the first and third ("All of You," *The Village Vanguard Sessions*). La Faro's playing often seemed to decorate the first and third beats and let the second and fourth beats pass. A rhythm section which pronounces primarily the first and third beats is playing what is called a two-beat style. Even though four beats are present, only two are emphasized; musicians would say the music is "in two." What LaFaro frequently did is called a "decorative two feel."

When he died in 1961 at the age of 25, LaFaro had been an active influence for less than three years. In this short period of time he set the pace for a whole school of modern jazz bassists, including Gary Peacock, Eddie Gomez, Richard Davis, Stanley Clarke, Michael Moore, George Mraz, Miroslav Vitous, Arild Andersen, and Palle Danielsson. Most of these men were directly influenced by LaFaro, but even those who were not created similar styles, characterized by the enormous instrumental facility typical of LaFaro. And like LaFaro, they interacted with pianists and drummers in an imaginative and highly active manner.

Drummer **Paul Motian** contributed an approach of great imagination and discretion. He colored the combo sound and produced accents which complemented the rhythms of LaFaro and Evans. Motian masterfully employed wire brushes to obtain light, crisp sounds from his snare drum and cymbals. He controlled the degree to which his high-hat cymbals opened, so that they would swish and zing, chick and splash. He interacted as sensitively and inventively as any previous drummer in jazz history. His style of interactive coloring in the intimate trio context became a model for drummers playing in similar settings and contributed to the emancipation of the rhythm section.

The 1961 recordings Evans made with LaFaro and Motian are usually considered his best trio performances, yet Evans continued to record throughout the 1970s with similar groups of remarkably high quality. A particularly creative combination was achieved with bassist Eddie Gomez and drummer Marty Morrell. Gomez began recording with Evans in 1966, Morrell in 1969, and the trio played together throughout the early 1970s. Listening to the LaFaro-Motian LPs and the Gomez-Morrell LPs back to back, I am unable to decide which combination is more successful in the delicate brand of collective improvisation that Evans pioneered.

To sum up, the post-1959 Bill Evans trios are a great deal more than a piano accompanied by a walking bass and a timekeeping drummer. Instead, there are three constantly shifting parts which sway together. Constant tempo is usually employed but not manifested by explicit statement of each separate beat. The trio members often seem to be carrying on three-way musical conversations in tempo ("Solar," *The Village Vanguard Sessions*). The musical words and phrases are both long and short, fluid and abrupt; they are not necessarily made up of the intricate eighth-note figures typical of bop or the long, smoothly contoured, eighth-note lines typical of Tristano and Konitz. In other words, much rhythmic and melodic variety is present. If the music swings, it is because that is what happened at the moment, not because swinging is the prime goal. Music is the goal. Jazz swing feeling is one of a number of rhythmic possibilities, and it is a means to a musical end rather than being an end in itself.

The Evans trios occasionally played in conventional bop style as well (walking bass, drummer playing ride rhythms and closing his sock cymbal on second and fourth beats, etc.). But their major contribution was toward loosening the bop formula patterns which had become standard during the 1940s and 50s. Evans, LaFaro, and Motian played an important role in the emancipation of the rhythm section. A vivid illustration of their influence is provided by comparing the rhythm section style of pre-1963 Miles Davis records (*Milestones* or *Miles Davis at Carnegie Hall*) with that on "Circle" (*Miles Smiles*), "Pee Wee" (*Sorcerer*), or "All of You" (*My Funny Valentine*). It was the Evans trio of *The Village Vanguard Sessions* which made the crucial difference.

Evans often chose pretty melodies which were economical in their construction yet provided interesting chord progressions for the improviser. His best-known composition, "Waltz for Debby," embodies the essence of his style. He liked waltzes, an unusual preference for a jazz musician. Among the waltzes to which he gave his tender treatment were "Someday My Prince Will Come" (recorded two years before the Miles Davis version), "Alice in Wonderland," "Tenderly," "Skating in Central Park," and "I'm All Smiles."

Two recordings which almost attain the perfection and uniqueness of the Evans–LaFaro–Motian trio work are *Undercurrent* and *Intermodulation*. These albums were made by Evans and guitarist Jim Hall without string bass or drums. The music is very pretty and lacks neither continuity nor originality. The austere and extremely thoughtful musical conceptions of these two musicians are about as free from redundancy and cliché as any jazz recorded.

Bill Evans may have been almost as significant an influence on pianists of the 1960s as Bud Powell was on pianists of the 50s. Evans's influence is evident at various stages in the careers of Clare Fischer, Denny Zeitlin, Jan Hammer (*The First Seven Days, Piano Jazz in Czechoslovakia*), and Cees Slinger. Chick Corea learned Evans solos while developing his own style (he also wrote a piece called "Waltz for Bill Evans"). Corea's "Song for Lee Lee" (*Piano Improvisations Vol. II*) bears a distinct resemblance to "Peace Piece." There is also much Evans-like playing in Corea's work on the Stan Getz LP *Sweet Rain*. Evans's influence on Herbie Hancock was very strong, as is apparent on "Pee Wee" (*Sorcerer*), "My Funny Valentine" (*My Funny Valentine*), and "He Who Lives in Fear" (*The Prisoner*). Obvious Evans characteristics are employed by Wynton Kelly on "Drad Dog" (*Someday My Prince Will Come*) and by Keith Jarrett on "Pretty Ballad" (*Somewhere Before*). Evans's influence on four successive Davis pianists (Wynton Kelly, Herbie Hancock, Chick Corea, and Keith Jarrett) is interesting because the history of the modern jazz rhythm sections is well documented by Davis recordings and provides strong evidence for the significance of Evans.

The overall conception of Evans's trio was influential also, possibly more influential than the Evans piano style. The Evans–LaFaro–Motian trio approach is especially evident in 1960s and 70s trio recordings by Jan Hammer, Chick Corea, Denny Zeitlin, Clare Fisher, Paul Bley, Steve Kuhn, Don Friedman, Keith Jarrett, and in the rhythm section playing on such Miles Davis LPs as *Sorcerer* and *Nefertiti*. The calm thoughtfulness, subtlety, and delicate interaction among the members of the Evans trio provided a solid alternative to the incessantly hard-driving, straight-ahead style of the Oscar Peterson trios or the simple, gospel-like orientation of such groups as The Ramsey Lewis Trio and The Three Sounds.

SUN RA   Sun Ra is a very creative pianist, composer, arranger, and bandleader. He has written and performed in a kaleidoscopic range of musical styles (see Figure 12.2). But in spite of the unusual breadth and depth of his music, he is relatively unknown. His recordings probably number over one hundred, but, because most were made on his own poorly distributed Saturn record label, few have received any attention. Even

Figure 12.2. Sun Ra at electric piano. Tenor saxophonist John Gilmore is drummer on far left, Marshall Allen and Pat Patrick are the saxophonists at the back, others unidentified. *Bill Smith,* Coda

during the 1970s when the well-distributed Impulse label bought and reissued many Saturn LPs, Sun Ra remained an obscure name.

Active as a professional musician since the 1930s, Sun Ra formed his own big band during the mid-50s. Like Duke Ellington, many of Ra's principal sidemen stayed with him for more than twenty years at a stretch. Actually, it might be more accurate to refer to his personnel as the Sun Ra bands, because the size and instrumentation vary from one player (his solo piano) to over fifty musicians. He draws from a pool of musicians who have rehearsed with him over the years. Although all jazz musicians have been known to play for very small amounts of money, often playing for free in order to perform at all, Sun Ra's band has been known to play regularly for extremely low fees. His sidemen are unusually dedicated and especially loyal to him. Even for a profession in which extraordinary dedication is commonplace, Sun Ra's players stand out.

Most of the music performed by the Sun Ra groups is original material put together by Sun Ra himself. But, as is true of Duke Ellington, another prolific composer-arranger, Sun Ra occasionally performs the compositions of others, also. He has performed Ellington's "Lightning," Jelly Roll Morton's "King Porter Stomp," Henry Mancini's "The Days of Wine and Roses," and pop standards such as "Just in

Time" (*Bad and Beautiful*). Whenever he performs a piece composed by someone else, however, the arrangement bears his own distinctively original style.

Some Sun Ra performances resemble the chant music of Africa. Some suggest exotic mode-based improvisations of the 1960s John Coltrane and Pharoah Sanders groups (*Nubians of Plutonia*). Some of Sun Ra's mid-1950s work resembled a modern jazz version of 1940 Ellington big band music (*Sun Song, Super-Sonic Sounds*). In the mid-60s, Sun Ra's music had much in common with contemporary classical composers who use electronically altered and synthesized sounds. The orchestrations of Sun Ra transcend the stock arranging practices developed by Fletcher Henderson and Don Redmen. In their originality, they go beyond the work of popular arrangers who have written for the Stan Kenton, Woody Herman, and Maynard Ferguson big bands. Sun Ra's work capitalizes on most of the diversity that is possible with big band instrumentation. In addition to creating many different combinations of instruments using trumpets, trombones, saxophones, piano, bass, and drums, he has substantially extended the range of available tone colors by the addition of electronic instruments and a wide variety of exotic percussion instruments. Sun Ra employed electric piano and synthesizers long before rock groups made their use common. Tympani, or kettle drums (see Figure 12.3), celeste, xylophone, bass marimba, bells, and chimes have been imaginatively employed on many Sun Ra recordings. Nearly all Sun Ra's sidemen doubled on percussion instruments long before this became a common practice in jazz groups. Another element contributing to the diversity of sounds produced by Sun Ra's bands is the ability of his saxophonists to play instruments unusual in jazz, such as oboe, piccolo, and bass clarinet (see Figures 12.4 and 12.5).

Figure 12.3. Kettledrum. Two or more kettledrums are called tympani.

Figure 12.4. Left to right: Piccolo, flute, clarinet, bass clarinet is lying in front. *Barry Perlus*

Figure 12.5. English horn, oboe, bassoon. *Barry Perlus*

As a pianist, Sun Ra resembles Ellington in his rich imagination and unpredictability. Both Ellington and Sun Ra are often underrated as pianists because the work of their bands overshadows their piano playing. But careful listening reveals not only the importance that their keyboard techniques have in the band sound, but also the uniquely creative approaches they have devised for the piano.

Sun Ra's use of synthesizers and the overall conception for many of his 1960s albums, especially *Heliocentric Worlds of Sun Ra Vol. I and II* suggest the work of twentieth-century classical composers Edgard Varèse and Krzysztof Penderecki. Central to the conception of such work is the notion that music can consist of sound by itself instead of sound in the conventional form of melody and harmony. Chunks of sound are sequenced in place of the standard ideas of melody and chord progression. When Sun Ra and his improvisers address themselves to this style the result has a more natural and flowing character than similar music performed by symphony orchestra musicians.

Sun Ra has also been active in the "free jazz" approach. Portions of his performances are collectively improvised with little apparent pre-arrangement (*Astro Black, Magic City, Heliocentric Worlds of Sun Ra Vol. 2*). His free jazz passages differ from those of Ornette Coleman and John Coltrane in that, in spite of the leadership qualities of Coleman and Coltrane, Sun Ra exerts a stronger, more pervasive artistic control over the proceedings. The music has a continuity and compositional organization superior to most free jazz of other groups. It is important to note that Sun Ra has succeeded with free-form collective improvisation in large ensemble contexts, a situation which poses great difficulty because of the problems musicians must overcome, listening to a large number of simultaneous lines while constructing their own improvisations to be compatible with those lines. Problems are considerably augmented as the size of the group increases. Dixieland combos rarely numbered more than seven men. Coltrane's *Ascension* used eleven musicians, and Ornette Coleman's *Free Jazz* used eight musicians. Sun Ra's works within free jazz are not all great successes, but most outshine similar attempts by other leaders.

At first, Sun Ra's groups were based in Chicago; later they were active in New York and Philadelphia as well. During the 1970s, Sun Ra received wider exposure than he had previously been accustomed to. Jazz festivals invited the band, and he toured Egypt. His music was heard in night clubs and on college campuses where he had not previously performed. But as far as the mainstream of jazz fans were concerned, his work remained in the peripheral avant-garde.

Sun Ra's live performances are accompanied by singing, dancing, costumes, and unusual lighting. Attending a Sun Ra concert is a multimedia experience. It is not always easy to concentrate on the music. Perhaps many people have failed to recognize the variety and depth of

Sun Ra's music because they were paying more attention to the visual aspects than the musical aspects. Perhaps some listeners fail to take Sun Ra's music seriously partly because it is mixed with theater and partly because he attaches a strong emphasis on philosophy, astrology, space travel, and astronomy. Another factor explaining his lack of widespread audience appeal is Sun Ra's diversity. People who hear a single performance and do not enjoy it fail to realize that what they have heard represents only a small portion of what Sun Ra has to offer. It is possible to hear five different Sun Ra approaches and still not be acquainted with all of his facets. Sun Ra's musical world is vast, and it is unfair to judge him on the basis of just a few performances or a few albums.

Members of the Chicago-based Association for the Advancement of Creative Musicians have presented concerts which resembled those of Sun Ra in that theatrical aspects were stressed, sound was often employed simply for sound's sake, free-form passages were employed, conventional jazz swing feeling was often missing, and unusual wind and percussion instruments were liberally employed. The fact that Sun Ra was based in Chicago for many years prior to the emergence of the AACM suggests that he may have influenced the musical directions which the AACM followed (see Table 12.1).

A few musicians who have worked with Sun Ra have also played with better known groups. Trombonist Julian Priester worked with

TABLE 12.1. Sun Ra Band Alumni—A Partial Listing

Trumpet	James Scales	Lex Humphries
	James Spaulding	Art Jenkins
Dave Young	Pat Patrick	William Cochran
Art Hoyle	Charles Davis	Robert Barry
Hobart Dotson	Danny Davis	Roger Blank
Walter Miller	Robert Cummings	John Gilmore
Ahk Tal Ebah		Edward Skinner
Phil Corhan		
Chris Capers	**Trombone**	
		Piano and
	Julian Priester	**Synthesizers**
Bass	Teddy Nance	
	Bernard Pettaway	Sun Ra
Richard Evans	Nate Pryor	
Ronnie Boykins	Ali Hassan	
Victor Sproles		
Alan Silva		
John Gilmore	**Drums**	
	Jim Hearndon	
Saxophone	Clifford Jarvis	
	Jimhi Johnson	
Marshall Allen		

drummer Max Roach and, during the 1970s, he was part of an innovative septet led by pianist Herbie Hancock. Interestingly, Hancock's group, like Sun Ra's, used synthesizer, varied percussion sounds, piccolo, and bass clarinet, and often produced music resembling that of Edgard Varèse. That Varèse-like style, as practiced by Hancock and Sun Ra, resembled background music for science fiction and space travel films and it was popularly labeled "space music."

One of Sun Ra's drummers, Clifford Jarvis, has also traveled with the band led by saxophonist Pharoah Sanders. Drummer Roger Blank has also played with Sanders. Bassist Victor Sproles and alto saxophonist James Spaulding were present on several Blue Note records by better known groups during the 1960s.

Saxophonists **Marshall Allen** and **John Gilmore** are probably the band's strongest improvisers, and both have remained with Sun Ra for more than twenty years. Marshall Allen plays all the woodwind instruments and has contributed extremely imaginative oboe and piccolo solos to Sun Ra's recordings. Gilmore has recorded with the bands of drummer Art Blakey and pianist Andrew Hill, among others. John Coltrane took an interest in Gilmore's 1960 style; he later recorded solos in which some of the melodic figures bear a discernible resemblance to a few favorite Gilmore melodic devices. Gilmore stands out among late 1950s–early 60s tenor men. Like Marshall Allen, he is an intelligent, imaginative improviser, and also a good flutist.

In many ways, Sun Ra is like Ellington. His fascination with widely diverse tonal textures and his unconventional arranging methods strongly suggest the work of Ellington. Sun Ra has the rare skill, also possessed by Ellington, of being able to oversee combinations of improvisation and composition and blend them in a unified form. Sun Ra and Ellington both bring out the best in their sidemen. And those players, in turn, adapt their improvisatory styles to the varying moods within each of their leader's compositions. Respect for Sun Ra's musical conception and artistic control is evident in his sidemen's sensitive ensemble improvising.

THE ART ENSEMBLE OF CHICAGO: ROSCOE MITCHELL, JOSEPH JARMAN, LESTER BOWIE, MALACHI FAVORS

During the late 1960s an interesting group emerged in Chicago (*People in Sorrow*). It had much in common with Sun Ra's ensemble, which had been based in the same city. The group performed in a broad range of styles, some of which, like those of Sun Ra, were not squarely within the jazz tradition:

1) They mimicked street bands of foreign countries,
2) performed light-hearted dramatic sketches,
3) made sounds for sound's sake (as opposed to traditional concepts of melody and harmony),
4) recited poetry,

5) improvised without preset harmonies, in addition to

6) applying conventional jazz approaches.

Some of their work is similar to that of Ornette Coleman, Don Cherry, Albert Ayler, and Archie Shepp. Their jazz solo conceptions owe much to Coleman. No piano is used, and, although all group members play percussion instruments, many of the Art Ensemble's recordings dispense with the conventional jazz drum set. Timekeeping and a harmonic background are provided by bassist Malachi Favors, who has outstanding technique and distinctive improvisational flexibility. Without his strength and imagination much of the Art Ensemble's music would be weak.

Although the Art Ensemble members seem to play almost every instrument, Lester Bowie is primarily a trumpeter, Malachi Favors concentrates on bass, and Joseph Jarman and Roscoe Mitchell are primarily saxophonists. In addition to percussion instruments, Mitchell plays soprano, alto, tenor, and bass saxophones, clarinet and flute. In addition to percussion instruments, Joseph Jarman plays soprano, alto, tenor and bass saxophones, clarinet, bassoon, flute, oboe, and vibraharp. Since 1970, drummer Don Moye has also been recording with the Art Ensemble (see Figure 12.6).

Like Sun Ra, the Art Ensemble has played in a great variety of styles, and it is a mistake to form an opinion of their music after hearing only a small number of performances. Much of it is not intended to be taken seriously, and this can be deceptive. For example, you might mistakenly think that the sloppiness on some pieces is unintentional when in fact it is deliberately employed to create musical effects. Art Ensemble members are all skilled instrumentalists, capable of bop-style improvisation. Some of their more conventional pieces resemble both bop and Ornette Coleman–Archie Shepp approaches.

The Art Ensemble of Chicago makes music which does not follow any strict set of rules. They choose styles freely, and they refuse to base their music on the expectations set up by a particular idiom or a particular audience. The Art Ensemble embraces the music of the whole world as its repertory. In that way, their musical viewpoint is similar to Sun Ra's. But despite all the similarities the Art Ensemble has its own identity, separate from that of Sun Ra. To appreciate and distinguish these two identities, you must become familiar with a large portion of the various styles and techniques which make up the music of Sun Ra and the Art Ensemble of Chicago.

Sun Ra's lack of public exposure has been partly due to his recording for small, poorly distributed record labels, including Saturn, Shandar, Blue Thumb, Transition, and Delmark. The Art Ensemble has had similar difficulties. Most of their best work is available only on imported labels such as French BYG, the British Alan Bates–Freedom

Figure 12.6. Art Ensemble of Chicago. Left to right: Roscoe Mitchell, Lester Bowie and Joseph Jarman, 1973 (the large sax in foreground is a bass sax). *Bill Smith,* Coda

label, the German MPS, and other small labels such as Nessa, America, Sackville, Trio, Saravah, Pathe, and Delmark.

CECIL TAYLOR Cecil Taylor is a pianist, composer, and bandleader who developed a unique and specialized style of modern jazz during the late 1950s and early 60s. His style is not simply different, innovative, or unconventional; it is, rather, a major alternative to the mainstream of modern jazz styles (see Figure 12.7).

Taylor does not play with modern jazz swing feeling, and he emphasizes musical textures rather than musical lines. Although quite syncopated, his rhythms tend to be played ever so slightly ahead or on top of the beat and lack the lilt and buoyancy of conventional jazz rhythmic style. Taylor does not try to swing. His notes seem to be generated in layered groups, designed to create textures of sound rather than singable phrases. The textures are rich in internal movement; they seem to shimmer and explode. In fact, much of Taylor's music is very percussive and quite violent. There is little serenity. Many of his performances seem to draw on a continuous source of high energy; they maintain a feverish intensity which seems to never let up.

Figure 12.7. Cecil Taylor, age 41. *Bill Smith*, Coda

During the late 1950s, Taylor based his improvisations on tunes and chord changes and employed conventional hard bop bassists and drummers (*In Transition*). Then, during the 1960s, he began playing with neither preset chord progressions nor constant tempo, and frequently he did not use a bassist. He played free of the harmonic restrictions imposed by preset chord changes. Brief portions of some Taylor improvisations are genuinely atonal. This is unusual in jazz, and in Taylor's work as well, because even the most adventuresome, free-form improvisations are usually organized around tone centers, keys, modes, or shifting tone centers. But Taylor followed only his inspiration, thus producing harmonies which were truly spur-of-the-moment (*Silent Tongues*). He employed several excellent drummers, including **Sunny Murray** and **Andrew Cyrille,** who perfected a style of playing which often did not imply meter or tempo. Those drummers concentrated almost entirely on color and shading, constantly interacting in original and unpredictable ways with the other group members.

When Taylor plays horn-like lines, they sound unlike any other style in jazz. They may have some hint of Thelonious Monk or Duke Ellington, but actually seem more like mid-twentieth-century composers Stockhausen, Ives, and Berio. Taylor's style is orchestral rather than horn-like. Taylor's comping, even in conventional jazz settings, is jagged and dense, and does not provide the springboard for soloists that hard bop comping usually does. When Taylor plays at the same time as the soloist in his group, his work is more like a separate and contrasting activity, which increases the density of the group sound because it does not parallel the soloist.

Some of Taylor's performances begin with a theme loosely stated by horns and accompanied by his orchestral piano improvising. Then a collective improvisation begins, in which nearly everyone participates. The emphasis is on creating textures. The style is not melodic in the pop tune sense, the swing era sense, or the bop sense. Some textures change gradually, others abruptly. Occasionally a preorganized ensemble portion erupts. Usually the group creates a whirlpool of sound and maintains a frantic pace (*Smithsonian Collection, Unit Structures*).

Three of Taylor's saxophonists have been especially important in creating his group sound. **Archie Shepp, Jimmy Lyons,** and **Sam Rivers** all have quite individual styles themselves, but have also been compatible with Taylor's concepts. All three have led their own groups and made their own albums. Rivers toured and recorded with Miles Davis in 1964. Both Taylor and Shepp have recorded with John Coltrane. By the 1970s, Taylor, Sunny Murray, Andrew Cyrille, Archie Shepp, and Sam Rivers had become accepted as leading figures in free-form jazz styles.

chapter 13
CHARLES MINGUS

Though one of the more adventuresome string bass soloists in modern jazz, Charles Mingus is best known as a composer and bandleader (see Figure 13.1). This chapter is devoted to music which is separate from the mainstream of modern jazz. For the 1950s, 60s, and 70s, this music could be identified by pronouncing just one word, Mingus (*Charlie Mingus, Mingus Revisited, Stormy Weather—The Charlie Mingus Jazz Workshop, Tia Juana Moods, Trio and Sextet*). The jazz mainstream during this period included the groups and sidemen of Art Blakey, Horace Silver, Miles Davis, and John Coltrane. Though there is some overlap in personnel and style, Mingus created a whole stream of approaches apart from that mainstream. Like Ellington, he represents an idiom which though rooted in idioms which span large periods, is uniquely his own. His music is described here because it represents a variety of original sounds widely respected by musicians and because it has included the work of many exceptionally creative sidemen. Whether his music influenced other bandleaders or composers is not our chief interest in this chapter.

Mingus has written more than one hundred and fifty pieces, many of which have been re-arranged and recorded several times. The Mingus career has explored styles as diverse as:

1) program music ("Pithecanthropus Erectus," the story of man)
2) funky, bluesy, gospel-oriented music, with shouting and hand clapping ("Better Git It in Your Soul" and "Eat That Chicken")
3) Third Stream music (Columbia recording of "Revelations," commissioned by Brandeis University Festival of the Arts,

Figure 13.1. Charles Mingus, age 50.
Bill Smith, Coda

Bethlehem recordings made with cellist Jackson Wiley and tenor saxophonist Teo Macero)

4) hard bop (recordings with pianist Don Pullen and tenor saxophonist George Adams)

5) jam sessions (Massey Hall concert with Charlie Parker, Dizzy Gillespie, Bud Powell, and Max Roach; Carnegie Hall concert with Roland Kirk, Jon Faddis, George Adams, John Handy, Charlie McPherson, Don Pullen, and Dannie Richmond)

6) free jazz (portions of "What Love," *Stormy Weather*)

7) music for film ("Shadows")

Mingus has employed diverse instrumentations:

1) his own solo piano (*Mingus Plays Piano*)

2) jazz quintets of trumpet, tenor saxophone, piano, bass and drums (*Mingus Moves*)

3) pianoless quartet (with Dannie Richmond, Dolphy, and Curson, available on Candid and Barnaby LPs)

4) five trumpets, four trombones, tuba, cello, oboe, flute, six saxophones, piano, bass and three drummers ("Half Mast Inhibition" and "Bemoanable Lady," *Pre-Bird*)

5) two trumpets, trombone, French horn, flute, bassoon, two saxophones, harp, piano, guitar, vibraharp, two basses and drums ("Revelations," *Modern Jazz Concert*).

Some Mingus works contain no improvisation. They are much like twentieth-century classical music, but contain the tone colors, varied rhythms and characteristic vitality of jazz. And some of his jazz works have odd construction. For example, in one piece, Mingus juxtaposed the pop tune "Exactly Like You" on the A section of Billy Strayhorn's "Take the 'A' Train." In another piece, he juxtaposed the A section of Duke Ellington's "Do Nothin' 'Til You Hear from Me" on the A section of Ellington's "I'm Beginning to See the Light."

The music of Mingus has much in common with that of Duke Ellington and Sun Ra. The music of all three men shows (1) compositional quality, originality, and diversity, (2) a careful blend of improvisation and composition, and (3) an ability to bring out the creative best in sidemen. But the relationship between Ellington and Mingus reflects more than similarity. Ellington has had direct influence on Mingus. Albums by Mingus contain tunes associated with Ellington such as "Do Nothin' 'Til You Hear from Me," "Sophisticated Lady," "Mood Indigo," "Take the 'A' Train," "Perdido," "Things Ain't What They Used to Be," "Flamingo," and "Stormy Weather." Mingus has also composed and recorded pieces dedicated to Ellington: "Duke's Choice" and "An Open Letter to Duke." Ellington-like use of plunger-muted brass has appeared in many Mingus works. The Johnny Hodges alto saxophone style has, at the request of Mingus, been incorporated into the playing of such otherwise non-Hodges alto saxophonists as Charlie Mariano, Jackie McLean and John Handy.

Mingus has recorded pop standards, including "Body and Soul," "A Foggy Day," "Laura," "I Can't Get Started," "I'll Remember April," "I'm Getting Sentimental Over You," and others. To each, Mingus brings his personal style. Like Ellington, Mingus arranges and performs the work of other composers in ways that sound as though he had written it all.

A successful integration between the improvised and composed portions is achieved in a number of Mingus performances. This is partly due to shifting accompaniment patterns during improvised solos. His 1958 Columbia recording "Fables of Faubus" employs varied accompanying devices which change the mood of solos in midstream and provide more contrast than was common to the long improvised solos of 1940s and 50s jazz (*Better Git It in Your Soul*). The Mingus techniques of shifting accompaniments were employed in addition to the more subtle changes in piano comping, bass lines and drum fills which occur in all post-bop combo improvisations. The compositions of Mingus furnish mood and loose structures for solos. The improvisations of his sidemen are so thoughtfully appropriate that very cohesive blends result. Collective improvisation on his 1957 "Ysabel's Table Dance" and his 1958 "Bird Calls" (*Better Git It in Your Soul*) is so well managed that listeners are often unable to determine what elements are improvised and what elements composed.

From 1960 until 1964, flutist-clarinetist-saxophonist **Eric Dolphy** recorded with Mingus. He had previously played with the Chico Hamilton quintet and others. In 1961 and 1962, Dolphy toured and recorded with John Coltrane. The arrangements for Coltrane's *Africa/Brass* album were written by Dolphy. Solos on Coltrane's "India" (*Impressions*) and "Spiritual" (*"Live" at the Village Vanguard*) are by Dolphy. Coltrane's *Olé* album uses Dolphy, but lists him as "George Lane" on the album jacket. Before his death in 1964 he also made a

TABLE 13.1. Charles Mingus Band Alumni*

Trumpet	George Barrow
	Roland Kirk
Thad Jones	Clifford Jordan
Ted Curson	George Adams
Lonnie Hillyer	
Clarence Shaw (Gene Shaw)	
Richard Williams	**Piano**
	Mal Waldron
Alto Sax	Horace Parlan
	Wade Legge
John LaPorta	Don Pullen
John Handy	Jaki Byard
Shafti Hadi (Curtis Porter)	Roland Hanna
Charlie Mariano	
Jackie McLean	
Eric Dolphy	**Drums**
Charles McPherson	
	Dannie Richmond
Tenor Sax	**Trombone**
Teo Macero	Jimmy Knepper
Booker Ervin	Willie Dennis
Yusef Lateef	Eddie Bert
J.R. Monterose	Britt Woodman

* The quantity of exceptional musicians who have performed with Mingus is as large as that of this book's lists of bop and hard bop musicians combined; therefore, only his most prominent sidemen are listed here.

number of albums himself, but some of his best work was documented in Mingus recordings.

Modern jazz has known countless virtuoso reedmen: alto saxophonists Charlie Parker, Sonny Stitt, Lee Konitz, Cannonball Adderly; tenor saxophonists Sonny Rollins, John Coltrane, Albert Ayler, and others. But few could be called virtuoso on three different instruments: flute, alto saxophone, and bass clarinet. Eric Dolphy mastered the complete range of every instrument he played, and then he capitalized on almost every sound it could produce. He even studied bird calls and mimicked them in his solos. Slides and smears connected Dolphy's notes. He sounded like a frantic version of Johnny Hodges—bouncing and twittering exuberantly, animal cries interspersed with bop licks.

Dolphy's 1958–59 work with Chico Hamilton's group was rooted in bop phrasing and swing feeling. Some of his alto saxophone playing of that period sounds like Charlie Parker and Cannonball Adderly. His later work, however, is characterized by explosive torrents of notes, bearing neither conventional melodic development nor bop phrasing. Though much of his work had quite irregular contours, he could play with swing era lushness, approximating the romantic feeling projected by alto saxophonists Benny Carter and Johnny Hodges. Dolphy's unaccompanied alto saxophone solo on "Tenderly" (*Far Cry*) is reminiscent of Benny Carter. The long duet between flute and bowed bass on "You Don't Know What Love Is" (*Last Date*) is so richly tonal, it is as though Dolphy savors the vibrations of each note before proceeding to the next.

In the 1960 pianoless quartet of Mingus, Dolphy, trumpeter Ted Curson and drummer Dannie Richmond, an exceptional level of empathy existed between Mingus and Dolphy. There is an extended dialog between the two of them on "What Love" which is filled with humor and flexible interaction, free jazz at its best (*Stormy Weather*). The conversation between Mingus's pizzicato bass and Dolphy's bass clarinet is so human that it almost makes you think words are being exchanged. It is very coherent and skillful—without the haphazardness which a dependence on luck brings to much free jazz.

An invaluable asset to many of Mingus's groups was drummer **Dannie Richmond.** He was employed by Mingus more frequently than any other drummer. Richmond is one of the most sensitive and tasteful of all post-bop drummers, supplying the varied rhythms and textures demanded by Mingus's unusual music. A marvelously loose and imaginative drummer, his drums provide a crisp, happy sound.

During 1954, 55 and 56, Mingus collaborated with trumpeter **Thad Jones.** Together, they made several albums, some with Mingus as leader and some with Jones (*Charlie Mingus, Trio and Sextet*). Mingus and other musicians consider Jones's creative ability to be at the genius level. If you listen to his work with Mingus, you will probably agree that few trumpeters can match his melodic ingenuity, unpredictability, and command of the instrument. He even rivals Dizzy Gillespie, one of his influences. Jones is often listed along with Miles Davis, Clifford Brown, Art Farmer, and Freddie Hubbard as the best post-Gillespie trumpeter. He went on to co-lead the Thad Jones–Mel Lewis big band, thus nurturing an interest kindled by playing in Count Basie's big band from 1954 until 1963. Interestingly, a few key members of the Jones–Lewis band were also with Mingus: pianist Roland Hanna, saxophonist Jerome Richardson, baritone saxophonist Pepper Adams, and trombonist Jimmy Knepper.

During 1961 and again in 1974, saxophonist **Roland Kirk** recorded with Mingus. Kirk has led several popular combos with strong, but relatively unknown sidemen. He is a very outgoing player, quite aware of showmanship and maintaining excitement. Besides flute, clarinet, and all the saxophones (sometimes two or three at a time!), Kirk plays nose flute, siren, and numerous unusual wind and percussion instruments. His music is as varied as that of Mingus: running from simple pop tunes and funky, gospelish twelve-bar blues to freer forms with techniques similar to these of Coltrane, Dolphy, and Ornette Coleman (*The Best of Rahsaan Roland Kirk*).

chapter 14
JOHN COLTRANE

If you had to make a list of the greatest musicians in jazz history, you would undoubtedly include those whose playing directly influenced generations of improvisers, those who possessed extremely creative talents, and those who played with such awesome power that people sometimes looked upon them as almost superhuman.

The 1950s and 60s produced a man who fits all three classifications: John Coltrane. As a saxophonist, composer and bandleader, he has had profound influence on jazz of the 1960s and 1970s. The improvisational concepts he introduced were absorbed by pianists, trumpeters and guitarists in addition to saxophonists.

ORIGINS OF THE COLTRANE SAX STYLE
Because recordings of Coltrane's pre-1950s work have yet to be discovered or distributed, there remains some mystery about his primary influences. We do know, however, that he probably absorbed much from Lester Young and Charlie Parker. Interviews with him and with people who heard his pre-1950 playing seem to indicate an attraction to Parker and Young and also to Coleman Hawkins. Parker phrases were evident in his late 1950s recordings although you might have difficulty detecting them because they are played so fast, they are played within Coltrane's own unique approach, and, of course, they are on tenor instead of on alto saxophone. Coltrane's preference for intricate, ornamented playing has much in common with the Hawkins style. Alto saxophonist Johnny Hodges has also been mentioned as an early idol. Coltrane played alto before concentrating on tenor, and might well have learned some of the Hodges approach. Whether or not

he learned it as a young man, he definitely had an extended opportunity to study it later, because he was a Hodges sideman during a portion of the early 1950s when Hodges was separated from Ellington (Dizzy Gillespie/*Dee Gee Days, Great Moments in Jazz Vol. 2: Alto Masters*).

Regardless of Coltrane's initial influences, the phrasing, tone, and general feeling of Lester Young and Dexter Gordon are apparent in samples of early Coltrane—with Dizzy Gillespie's and Johnny Hodges's combos—which can be found embedded in a few, rare, early 1950s records (*Dee Gee Days, Alto Masters*). Early Coltrane resembled Dexter Gordon in his deep, dark, full-bodied tone, as well as his legato style and his phrasing. Both men linked long strings of notes together without a break, almost devoid of staccato playing. Coltrane has further indicated a debt to Gordon by citing him as a favorite. But what "favorite" means, in terms of influence, is an open question. Coltrane has also cited Sonny Rollins, Sonny Stitt, and Stan Getz as favorites. A frequent problem in determining a style's origins is that what we like is not necessarily what we absorb or copy. So even if we know a player's likes, we never know for sure whether a player sounds like another player because he has copied the other, he has absorbed the same influences used by the other, or he has coincidentally arrived at a similar approach. Accordingly, Coltrane might have copied Dexter Gordon, or he might have arrived by chance at a style which resembled Gordon's. The third possibility is that he absorbed the same influences used by Gordon (the deep, dark-colored, heavy-weight tone of Coleman Hawkins, Herschel Evans, and Chu Berry, and the phrases of Lester Young and Charlie Parker). This idea is not too far-fetched because Coltrane was only three and a half years younger than Gordon, and likely to have been developing at the same time. Keep in mind, however, that Coltrane had a slower vibrato and a darker, rougher, more cutting tone than Gordon's.

Coltrane was infrequently recorded during his pre-Miles Davis years, yet his strongest contemporary, tenor saxophonist Sonny Rollins, had already made his mark on the record scene. By the time Coltrane began to record, Rollins was a major figure, even though Rollins was three years younger than Coltrane. This may partly explain the widespread feeling that Rollins came first. The fact is that Coltrane was an outstanding, but underrecorded, player at the same time that Rollins was a heralded soloist on recordings with Miles Davis and others. Then, when Coltrane came along—with a style drawn from some of the same sources that had influenced Rollins—people thought of Coltrane as being directly influenced by Rollins. If you listen carefully to early Coltrane and early Rollins, you can easily tell them apart. Both had unique styles.

To many people, it is not important whether Coltrane's early style came from Lester Young, Coleman Hawkins, Charlie Parker, Dexter Gordon, or Sonny Rollins. What is most important is that he had developed his own powerful style by the time he first recorded with Miles Davis in 1955, and he continued to develop it until his death in 1967. The product of that incessant activity was a stream of recordings in which can be distinguished at least two, perhaps three or four, robust styles of saxophone playing and several styles of composing.

SAXOPHONE STYLE

By the early 1950s, Coltrane already had an unusually vigorous style. Although he had been a sideman in several big-name jazz groups, including those of Dizzy Gillespie and Johnny Hodges (*Dee Gee Days, Alto Masters*), he did not record lengthy solos until he joined the Miles Davis Quintet in 1955 (*Kind of Blue, Miles Davis, Milestones, 'Round About Midnight, Tallest Trees, Workin'* and *Steamin'*). His tone was rough textured and biting, huge and dark. Coltrane gave it a massive core and a searing intensity. Some saxophonists lose the body of their tone when they play in the high register, and lose definition and agility in the low register. Coltrane's tone was full and penetrating in every register. He improvised with such proficiency that his work even impressed listeners accustomed to the phenomenal speed and accuracy of saxophonists like Lee Konitz, Charlie Parker, and Sonny Rollins. Coltrane was more than mere tone and speed, however. He played with an urgency which reflected a severely critical craftsman; his music was very serious, almost devoid of humor. Throughout his career, Coltrane's recordings displayed a consistency of strength and inspiration, quite rare even among jazz greats. He and Charlie Parker were two of the most consistent and intense soloists jazz has known.

Throughout the late 1950s, Coltrane recorded with Miles Davis. He was a member of the Davis group on and off for almost six years. During 1957, he worked with pianist-composer Thelonious Monk. Coltrane's Davis recording (*Milestones*) which followed his stint with Monk shows a bit more assurance and increased instrumental proficiency over his pre-Monk Davis recordings (*Steamin', Cookin', Workin', Relaxin'*). This change may or may not have been a result of his experience with Monk. Coltrane undoubtedly learned from nearly all the music he heard and the musicians with whom he performed, Monk included.

During the early 1960s Coltrane was interested in the music of Sun Ra and Sun Ra's powerful tenor saxophonist, John Gilmore. Coltrane's influence seems to have surfaced in Gilmore's work during 1960. But now it was Gilmore's turn to contribute to Coltrane's own work. If you listen to Coltrane's solos on "Impressions" (*Impressions*), and "Chasin' the Trane" (*Live at the Village Vanguard*), you will hear melodic figures which bear a discernible resemblance to a few favorite Gilmore melodic devices used in his own solos on Sun Ra's *The Futur-*

istic Sounds of Sun Ra. (These are different devices than those of Coltrane's which Gilmore employed.) Again, as with Dexter Gordon, it is possible that the strains of influence traveled full circle.

Coltrane cultivated several expressive techniques. On a 1954 Johnny Hodges recording, for example, he sounds like Illinois Jacquet or Earl Bostic—milking high notes in a very emotional way (*Alto Masters*). This style of wailing into the high register became a Coltrane signature during the 1960s. He eventually employed notes far above the saxophone's conventional upper limit. He may well have learned these techniques as a member of Bostic's band. Bostic himself had an exceptional command of the saxophone and explored techniques of high-register playing (*Changing Face of Harlem*). These, along with several favorite phrases, are strikingly similar to some Coltrane work of the 1960s. Coltrane also used shrieks and squawks, which were composed of several frequencies sounding simultaneously. These multiphonics (to give them their technical name) occasionally sound like chords.

During the early 1960s, Coltrane's tone became smoother. It retained the edge and bite of his pre-1960s sound, but the texture was not as rough and the color was brighter. The confidence projected by his sound increased to awesome proportions. Perhaps it was the terrific presence projected by this tone and its delivery that led some listeners to feel a spiritual force in Coltrane's music. His sound was so overwhelming and his solos maintained high energy for such long periods it was sometimes difficult to believe a mere mortal capable of such power.

Coltrane's pre-1960s playing showed an infatuation with chord changes matching the earlier interest in harmonic complexity which had characterized bop pianists (*Kind of Blue, Miles Davis, Milestones, 'Round About Midnight, Soul Trane, Tallest Trees, Workin'* and *Steamin'*). He loved to add chords to a tune's existing chord progressions, much as Art Tatum, Lennie Tristano, and Don Byas had done. Coltrane devoured the tune's chord changes, trying to acknowledge every note in every chord and every scale which might be compatible with it. He played so fast that he frequently succeeded in that demanding task. Notes seemed to cascade from his horn in an unending stream. They were not thrown casually at the listener, either. There was no emotional detachment in their selection or in their speed. Each note was carefully chosen to fit a melodic idea or to become an essential element of a sweeping run.

His work was often so technical that some listeners felt they were hearing practice exercises and said Coltrane's playing was "just scales." But transcriptions of those scale-like lines show that his fast runs deviate significantly from the sequence of notes that constitute most scales. And when you listen carefully, you discover that even Coltrane's most scale-like and exercise-like moments have an elusive construction that distinguishes them from practice room routines. Even his most elementary phrases were delivered with a surging power which set his music apart from its construction, making his phrases solidly musical expressions.

The culmination of Coltrane's infatuation with chord progressions came with his *Giant Steps*. This was near the end of the period in which his playing contained furiously paced streams of notes and dense textures with little open space. The title of the album comes from a tune which Coltrane had originally written as an exercise to master the navigation of giant steps between chords. In the progression, few notes are held in common from one chord to another. The chords move frequently, giving the improviser almost no time to develop an idea on a single chord. In that way, "Giant Steps" was like the tunes with which earlier improvisers enjoyed testing themselves, such as "All the Things You Are" and "Con Alma." "Giant Steps," too, eventually became that kind of tune in the jazz world.

With the exception of work on his tune "Naima," Coltrane's playing throughout the *Giant Steps* album demonstrated dense improvisation over frequent chord changes. "Naima" was recorded seven months after the other tunes. The construction of "Naima" forecast one of Coltrane's next interests, the *absence* of frequent chord changes. "Naima" was a slow piece which employed a drone (also called a pedal point). One note, the drone note, was sustained in the accompaniment for the first eight measures. Then another note served that same purpose throughout the second eight measures. The utter simplicity of the melody and almost total lack of abrupt chord changes marked the beginning of a new phase in Coltrane's career, the *modal* style.

COLTRANE RECORDS By the time he left Miles for good, Coltrane had appeared on several Davis albums for Prestige and a few more for Columbia. During the late 1950s, he had also recorded for Prestige under his own name. Most of those recordings represent combos put together solely for the recording studio. Coltrane used Davis quintet sidemen for a large percentage of them, particularly pianist Red Garland and bassist Paul Chambers. Both Garland and Chambers reciprocated when running their own record dates, too.

I have tried to sort his busy recording career so that you can see where your own records fit and what records are available for periods which you might wish to sample. More than eighty albums have been released under his name, so you should understand that the accompanying table only begins to accommodate his output. It does represent the major trends, however (see Table 14.1).

TABLE 14.1. John Coltrane Records—A Partial Listing

Red Garland—Paul Chambers—
Louis Hayes (Prestige Records)

The Believer (1958)
The Last Trane (1958)
Lush Life (1958)

Red Garland—Paul Chambers—
Art Taylor (Prestige Records)

Tenor Conclave (1956)
Traneing In (1957)
Soultrane (1958)
Trane's Reign (1958)
Black Pearls (1958)

Red Garland—Paul Chambers—
Jimmy Cobb (Prestige Records)

Stardust (1958)
Standard Coltrane (1958)
The Master (1958)
(same as *Standard Coltrane*)
Bahia (1958)

Tommy Flanagan—Paul
Chambers—Art Taylor

Kenny Burrell—John Coltrane
(1958) (Prestige record)
Giant Steps (1959)
(Atlantic record)

Thelonious Monk—Leader

*Thelonious Monk with John
Coltrane* (1957) (Jazz-
land record)
Monk's Music (1957)
(Riverside record)

McCoy Tyner—Steve Davis—
Elvin Jones (Atlantic Records)

My Favorite Things (1960)
Coltrane's Sound (1960)

Coltrane Plays the Blues
(1960)

Miles Davis—Leader (Prestige
Records)

*The New Miles Davis Quin-
tet* (1955)
*Steamin', Cookin', Workin',
Relaxin'* (1956)
*Miles Davis Plays Jazz
Classics* (1956)
*Miles Davis and John Col-
trane Play Richard Rogers*
(1956)

Miles Davis—Leader (Columbia
Records)

'Round About Midnight
(1955–56)
Milestones (1958)
Jazz Track (1958)
Miles and Monk at Newport
(1958)
Kind of Blue (1959)
*Someday My Prince Will
Come* (1961)

McCoy Tyner—Elvin Jones—
Jimmy Garrison (Impulse
Records)

Impressions (1961, 2, 3)
Live at the Village Vanguard
(1961)
Coltrane (1962)
Ballads (1961–62)
*John Coltrane with Johnny
Hartman* (1963)
Selflessness (1963)
Live at Birdland (1963)
Crescent (1964)
A Love Supreme (1964)
*The John Coltrane Quartet
Plays* (1965)

Kulu Sé Mama (1965)
Transition (1965)
Sun Ship (1965)
Infinity (1965–66)

Pharoah Sanders—Tyner—
Garrison—Jones (Impulse
records)

Ascension (1965)
Live in Seattle (1965)
OM (1965)
Meditations (1965)

Pharoah Sanders—Alice Coltrane—Garrison—Rashied Ali
(Impulse Records)

Cosmic Music (1966)
*Live at the Village Vanguard
Again* (1966)
Concert in Japan (1966)
Expression (1967)

Before totally immersing himself in a modal approach, Coltrane first examined several alternatives. Having decided to leave the complex base of frequent chord changes, he spotted an avenue already being investigated by Ornette Coleman. In 1960, Coltrane recorded an album, *The Avant-Garde*. Here, he was trying improvisation in the loose harmonic format Coleman had explored, with few prearranged chord progressions (or even none). This was somewhat less restricting than the modal format to which Coltrane had already been exposed in his work with Miles Davis. The 1960 album uses Coleman's group (trumpeter Don Cherry, bassist Charlie Haden, drummer Eddie Blackwell) minus Coleman. And three Coleman compositions are included ("Focus on Sanity," "The Blessing," and "The Invisible").

It must be remembered, in discussing the modal pieces of Coltrane and Pharoah Sanders, that by strictly legitimate musical terminology, the Coltrane-Sanders playing was not entirely modal. It was only loosely based on the critical intervals characteristic of certain modes. A mode is a scale containing a limited number of notes. If notes other than those defined by the mode are used, the resulting music is not strictly modal. Coltrane adhered to the general harmonic orientation and flavor of certain modes, but also employed notes outside of the mode. For that reason, his playing was not modal in the strictest sense of the word; only modal in the loose sense which jazz musicians and jazz journalists use. It is therefore not inaccurate to speak of the Coltrane and Sanders work as based on the repetition of one or two chords. Strictly speaking, you need not bring in the word modal at all.

In 1960, he recorded "My Favorite Things," improvising at length, using primarily a single scale or mode (*My Favorite Things*). In 1961, he recorded "Olé" and "Impressions," both based on one or two modes. In 1962, he recorded "Tunji," "Miles Mode," and "Out Of This World," improvisations which were also mode-based.

What was the source of Coltrane's interest in these formats? First of all, he might have become interested in them entirely on his own. Secondly, his interest might have arisen from his work with Miles Davis on the 1958 *Milestones* and 1959 *Kind of Blue*. And thirdly, it might have resulted from his studying the native music of Africa, India, and other cultures. (He was known to have spent considerable time researching the use of modes in music outside of jazz.) We find support for the idea that Davis influenced Coltrane in the fact that Coltrane's "Impressions" is based on the same modes (Dorian) as Davis's "So What." The relative duration of modes in the two tunes is also the same: the first lasts sixteen bars, the second for eight, and then the first returns for a final eight (see notations in Chapter 18).

In 1965, Coleman's influence seemed once more to have asserted itself. Coltrane recorded *Ascension,* an album which employed high-intensity collective improvisation with four other saxophonists, two trumpeters, and a rhythm section, and with a less restricting prearranged form than either Coltrane or Davis had previously used. Its approach and sound strongly resembled Ornette's 1960 *Free Jazz* album.

During the 1960s and 70s the use of collective improvisation, as well as the use of harmonic bases freer than chord progressions or modes, became generally popular. This could be attributed to the influence of Ornette Coleman, Miles Davis, Sun Ra, John Coltrane, or any combination of those leaders. But since Coltrane was the most prominent bandleader engaging in that new style, it is likely that some of it caught on because of his 1965 *Ascension,* his 1965 *Meditation,* and other albums using similar approaches.

Ascension was not totally collective improvisation nor totally free of prearrangement. Nor was it atonal. (See Chapter 17 for scales, tone center, and atonality.) Careful listening will reveal a few changes of chord or tone center. (Coltrane preset four scales for the musicians to use.) The changes do not occur often, but they do occur. So it is not totally free of form. Brief, loosely stated ensemble passages separate the solos. Those solos, in turn, receive rhythm section accompaniment. Collectively improvised sections are balanced in duration and texture. Coltrane preset the order for the solos so that no two similar instruments played back to back. That procedure, for example, allowed a trumpet solo to follow a sax solo instead of following another trumpet.

Ornette Coleman and John Coltrane each recorded large ensemble, collective improvisation only once. They preferred to limit such techniques to quartets and quintets instead of the eight and eleven men groups of *Free Jazz* and *Ascension,* respectively (*Free Jazz, Smithsonian Collection*).

SOPRANO SAXOPHONE   About the time he formed his own groups (1960–61), Coltrane began playing soprano saxophone in addition to tenor. (Coltrane plays soprano on the title track of *My Favorite Things,* "India" on *Impressions,* and "Afro-Blue" on *Live at Birdland.*) Soprano saxophone had been previously used on recordings by Sidney Bechet, Johnny Hodges, Charlie Barnet, and Steve Lacy, but it had yet to catch on as a standard jazz instrument. But a few years after Coltrane first used it, the soprano saxophone had become quite popular with jazz saxophonists and by 1970, most tenor saxophonists were performing on it. By the early 1970s, even players who were not necessarily followers of Coltrane also used soprano. Such men as alto saxophonist Cannonball Adderly and tenor saxophonist Sonny Rollins, who had established unique, well-known styles on their chosen saxes, also began recording with soprano sax. Some players adopted it almost to the exclusion of their tenors. On their post-1968 Miles Davis recordings, Coltrane disciples Steve Grossman and Dave Liebman played more soprano than tenor. Saxophonist Joe Farrell, another player who absorbed portions of the Coltrane style, recorded an entire album, *Moon Germs* (CTI), without using his tenor. The range and tone quality of the soprano sax helped saxophonists cut through the sound created by increasing numbers of drums and amplified instruments which comprised groups of the 1970s.

BALLADS A large number of listeners know only the hard-driving Coltrane reflected in medium- and up-tempo pieces. But Coltrane was also one of the strongest ballad players that jazz tenor has known. When Coltrane played slow melodies, he was usually more economical than when involved in full-blown improvisation. It seemed as though he harnessed all the energy customarily released in dense, multinoted passages, and channeled it into a few deep, full-bodied tones. He breathed through long tones, and flawlessly slid from one interval to another. There was special warmth and tenderness in his ballads which was less obvious in his nonballad performances. Like alto saxophonist Johnny Hodges and tenor saxophonist Ben Webster, Coltrane could bring a glowing fullness to the phrases of a slow song.

Coltrane's Prestige albums usually contained a ballad or two. His 1956 *Mating Call* has several lush ballads. And his *Soul Trane* featured "Theme for Ernie" and "I Want to Talk About You."

Some of Coltrane's best compositions took the form of ballads. There is the haunting beauty of his "Naima" (*Giant Steps*), his "After the Rain" (*Impressions*), his 1964 "Wise One" and "Lonnie's Lament" (*Crescent*), his "Dear Lord" (*Transition*), and his "Ogunde" (*Expression*).

SIMPLE HARMONIC BASES AND COLTRANE'S MODAL WORK Much as Coltrane had influenced the adoption of soprano saxophone, he and his 1965–67 associate, tenor saxophonist Pharoah Sanders, also influenced the adoption of modal approaches to improvisation. Although Miles Davis had been one of the first to introduce modal methods, he emphasized them far less during the early 1960s than Coltrane did.

One of Coltrane's most popular records was his 1960 *My Favorite Things*. The improvised portions of the title track were based primarily on the repetition of a few chords with which a single scale or mode was compatible. Toward the end of the improvisation, the chord and its corresponding scale was changed (the first part was minor tonality, the last part major tonality). The piece was a waltz, a fact which, coupled with the extensive repetition of those few chords, gave the piece a swaying, hypnotic quality. It provided an easy basis for improvisation because its construction was as undemanding as "Giant Steps" had been demanding.

Even when the compositional forms Coltrane employed were relatively simple, he managed to create complexity. On much of his early 1960s work, there was a lessening of the pre-"My Favorite Things" style characterized by its barrage of notes. Some of his lines resembled the elementary phrases and simple melodic development characteristic of pre-1960s Ornette Coleman recordings. But those were only hints of a change in style. The infatuation Coltrane had with harmonic complexity touched most of his playing, even when the primary basis of improvisation was a single mode or a repeating bass figure. It was as though Coltrane determined how many chords could fit the mode or bass figure, then improvised on all of them as if they were chord progressions. He stacked chords on top of other chords. Coltrane was, in effect, spontaneously inventing additional chord changes whenever the musical situation did not already provide a large quantity. His improvisations were harmonically rich in pieces whose harmonic bases were not nearly as rich.

Coltrane sought uncluttered harmonic bases which provided exotic colors and moods—those of Spain and India were favorites of his— and which allowed him great freedom in adding and altering harmonies within his improvisation. Widely imitated examples of Coltrane's uncluttered bases can be found in his 1965 duet with drummer Elvin Jones, "Vigil" (*Kulu Sé Mama*) and his 1967 duets with drummer Rashied Ali (*Interstellar Space*).

Not all of Coltrane's 1960s playing was based on modal approaches to improvisation. He continued to play pop tunes and continued to write his own melodies for sixteen-bar progressions and the twelve-bar blues progression. In fact, he recorded an entire album of blues (*Coltrane Plays the Blues*). "Pursuance" (*Love Supreme*) and "Bessie's Blues" (*Crescent*) are also twelve-bar blues pieces.

WAS COLTRANE A MELODIC IMPROVISER?

Despite the melodic gift demonstrated in his tune writing, Coltrane was only sporadically melodic when improvising. In the pop tune sense of melody, Coltrane's improvisations were rarely melody-like. Compared with bop melody style as conceived by Charlie Parker, Dizzy Gillespie, and Thelonious Monk, Coltrane's improvisations were sporadically melodic before 1960 and rarely melodic after that.* In his work both before and after 1960, there was a tendency to alternate between technical complexity and the lyricism which is characteristic of his compositions. If you slow down his most complex improvisations (or speed up your hearing so that every phrase is very clear to you), you will find that his work is often melodic in the bop sense but only

* Lester Young was melodic most of the time. Coleman Hawkins placed great emphasis on technical complexity and was possibly less melodic than Young. In those respects, Coltrane was closer to Hawkins.

sporadically melodic in the simple, singable melody sense. It takes an exceptionally quick ear to keep up with Coltrane, but once you have attained the necessary listening pace, you will notice more melodic tendencies than were apparent at first. However, I do not feel that Coltrane's lines possessed the songlike quality or bop lyricism typical of Charlie Parker and Sonny Rollins. Harmonic development received a higher priority than melodic development.

THE COLTRANE QUARTET   After leaving Miles in 1960, Coltrane formed his own group with pianist McCoy Tyner, bassist Steve Davis and drummer Elvin Jones (see Figure 14.1). He had tried several different musicians but finally stuck with Tyner and Jones. During the 1960s, he used bassists Art Davis, Steve Davis, Reggie Workman, Donald Garrett, and Jimmy Garrison. Garrison was with Coltrane for most of the 1960s recordings and remained even after McCoy Tyner and Elvin Jones had left. The quartet had wide influence during the 1960s and continued to exert an influence more than ten years after it disbanded. Its effect is especially notable in records by Pharoah Sanders, the Bobby Hutcherson–Harold

Figure 14.1. Left to right: McCoy Tyner (piano), John Coltrane (tenor sax), Jimmy Garrison (bass), Elvin Jones (drums), 1962. *Duncan Schiedt*

Land groups, and those of David Leibman, McCoy Tyner, Charles Lloyd (1966–69), John Handy (mid-1960s only), and Gato Barbieri.

Elvin Jones As far as some listeners are concerned, Elvin Jones has proven himself to be the most overwhelming drummer in jazz history. He has established a position on the drums that equals the power and innovation established by Charlie Parker and John Coltrane on the saxophone. Like Parker and Coltrane, Jones is a remarkably consistent performer. He seems to play every tune as though it is his last chance. An almost superhuman energy and endurance is associated with Elvin. And his imagination seems to match his energy.

Elvin avoids the relative simplicity and repetition of most pre-1960 drummers. He rarely plays the obvious. In fact, in his most adventuresome work, he even avoids directly stating the first beat of each measure. He plays around the beat instead of precisely subdividing it. His conception of the beat is a wider unit in time than had been usual with previous drummers. Elvin's timekeeping is steady, but loose, filled with rhythmic subtleties. He roams through his drums and cymbals distributing portions of triplets. He tends to divide measures into three equal parts instead of two or four. He often begins his triplex division of time at the middle or end of a beat, and continues to juxtapose a staggered waltz feeling across the duration of several measures (for explanation of triplets, waltz meter, etc., see Chapter 17). During all that time he would still be maintaining a basic meter of four.

With Coltrane's group, Jones was able to play many rhythms at once and have the entire sound swell and heave like an ocean of activity under Coltrane's playing. Elvin was one of the first drummers to play polyrhythmically and still swing hard in a loose, flowing way (for definition and explanation of polyrhythm, see Chapter 17). Earlier drummers who attempted to use polyrhythms sounded stiff, self-consciously calculating while doing it.

While listening to Elvin, you might get the impression that he is juggling. Things seem forever in the air, never sharply defined in exact, predictable proportions. But the different rhythms Elvin played simultaneously were not just randomly different. Like those in an African drum ensemble, they were constructed to complement each other. And, in a broad sense, they fit together. It might not be obvious unless you listen carefully to four and eight measure sequences in their entirety. Some of his figures purposely omit a stroke or two but let you feel the missing stroke in the overall pattern. Elvin distributes the parts of his triplets so that perhaps the first third is silent and next two are sounded on snare drum. Or perhaps the middle member is omitted. Sometimes the first two members of a triplet will sound on the snare drum and the third on the high hat or the bass drum. It might be because of his complexity and lack of predictability that few drummers in the 1970s manage to sound like him. A greater number, it seems, sound like more basic drummers such as Tony Williams (Miles Davis Quintet, 1963–69) and Billy Cobham (John McLaughlin's Mahavishnu Orchestra). In place of Elvin's broadness, Williams gives the impression that the beat is sharply defined. He seems to divide rhythmic figures into two's, four's, and eight's instead of Elvin's three's. Elvin is clearly more difficult to imitate than Williams, even though both styles are intricate and varied.

What bassist Scott LaFaro was doing with Evans, drummer Elvin Jones was doing with John Coltrane's quartet. Jones interacted in as important a way as any front-line hornman at a Dixieland jam session, exemplified by his work on "Sun Ship" (*Sun Ship*) and "My Lady" (*Live at Birdland*). The whole character of the Coltrane quartet reflected the highly interactive style of Elvin Jones. Jones played with the surging power and imagination of two or three drummers combined, and his force was absorbed quite musically into the quartet concept. In fact, the style of Elvin Jones was possibly the most indispensable part of that ensemble concept. Can you imagine any other drummer with the 1961–65 Coltrane quartet? Even as dynamic and versatile a modern drummer as Roy Haynes was unable to supply the texture that Elvin created ("My Favorite Things" in *Selflessness* album uses Haynes in place of Jones).

When drummer Rashied Ali joined Coltrane, Elvin left. There apparently was not room for both of these drummers, though Coltrane had imagined a new ensemble concept in which there was. But it is very difficult to find two drummers, each with a complete drum set, who can comfortably improvise together in a group with sax, piano, and bass.

Elvin proceeded to form a sequence of high quality groups which, during the late 1960s and throughout the 1970s, offered some of the rare jazz neither significantly influenced by rock or electric instruments nor predominantly modal in orientation. He usually employed two tenor saxophonists and a bassist, but no piano. He employed some of the best saxophonists playing at that time (most of his tenor men were influenced by Coltrane): Joe Farrell, George Coleman, Frank Foster, Steve Grossman, David Liebman, and others. His groups almost achieved the solemn urgency possessed by the Coltrane quintet.

McCoy Tyner   Coltrane's pianist from 1960 to the end of 1965 was McCoy Tyner. Creating an original approach from the linear style of Bud Powell, the block chording of Red Garland, and the voicings of Bill Evans and Horace Silver, he achieved a fresh approach to jazz piano. He had been a distinctive and aggressive stylist in the Art Farmer–Benny Golson Jazztet (*Meet the Jazztet*), but carved a very personal style for himself within the Coltrane quartet. Along with Bill Evans and Herbie Hancock, he was a prime force in 1960s and 70s jazz piano styles. In fact, he was possibly as influential as Evans. Tyner's extensive use of chords voiced in fourths was widely adopted (see Figure 14.2).

McCoy provided a pivot point in the Coltrane quartet. His clear, ringing, open-voiced chords stood in between the passionate bashing and crashing of Elvin Jones and the soaring of Coltrane, as on "The Promise" and "Afro-Blue" (*Live at Birdland*). Along with his preference for fourths, his comping style became a model for pianists of the late 1960s and the 1970s, especially those pianists playing in Coltrane-inspired groups. His fast solo lines also inspired numerous pianists, though few could match his imagination and freshness. Among the many pianists he influenced were Chick Corea, Alice McLeod Coltrane, Kenny Gill, Bobo Stinson, Joe Bonner, Bill Henderson, Lonnie Liston Smith and Onaje Allan Gumbs.

After leaving Coltrane, Tyner led a series of his own combos. He continued to play in the style he had employed with Coltrane and remained an exceptionally forceful player. But he often seemed out of place when not in the equally inspired context provided by Coltrane and Elvin Jones. Much of his work continued the modal tradition extended by Coltrane. Tyner also continued to write compelling tunes in a style which was frequently imitated.

It is interesting to note that, by the mid-1970s, neither Tyner nor pianist Keith Jarrett had adopted the electric piano. Though nearly every jazz pianist was using it, both these leading figures on the piano scene remained with the conventional piano.

Jimmy Garrison   Jimmy Garrison was an imaginative bass player, one who held his own within the fiercely active Coltrane quartet. He invented rhythms which countered and complemented those of Tyner and Jones. Occasionally, Garrison took to strumming his bass as though it were a guitar. His use of double stops (two strings sounding together) and his strumming

Figure 14.2. Piano keyboard illustration of fifths in left hand and fourths in right hand.

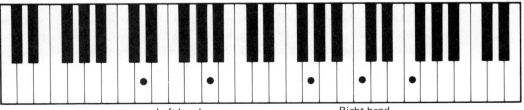

Left hand
(5th)

Right hand
(4ths)

have been widely imitated. He was not the first to use such techniques, but his particular handling of them might have been the stimulus behind their popularity with jazz bassists of the 1960s and 70s.

Some of Garrison's double stopping may have had its source in Coltrane's interest in drones and in music employing two tones sustained together, a fifth apart. In the modal music of their native cultures, bagpipes, sitars, and tamboura achieve exactly that effect. Coltrane's use of two bassists on "Olé" (*Olé Coltrane*) and "India" (*Impressions*) might also have stemmed from that interest.

INFLUENCE ON SAXOPHONISTS

Coltrane had a marked impact on saxophonists of the 1960s. In addition to his influence on young, developing saxophonists, we should also note that several older players incorporated his techniques in midcareer. During the 1960s, such established players as Frank Foster, Harold Land, and Teddy Edwards all demonstrated the acquisition of Coltrane techniques. While with Coltrane in the late 1950s groups of Miles Davis, Cannonball Adderly also absorbed Coltrane techniques, some of which were especially evident in later work. Adderly's "Fun" solo (*Mercy, Mercy, Mercy*) is like Coltrane, and is less bouncy than the typical Parker-influenced Adderly lines.

Along with Ornette Coleman, Coltrane was the primary model for new saxophonists to study. Among the younger saxophonists showing Coltrane influence were Pharoah Sanders, Charles Lloyd, Joe Farrell, Wayne Shorter, Gato Barbieri, John Klemmer, Nathan Davis, Lew Tabackin, Robin Kenyatta, Steve Grossman, Billy Harper, David Liebman, John Surman, Benny Maupin, Carlos Garnett, Steve Marcus, Pat Labarbera, Bob Berg, Sonny Fortune, Jan Garbarek, Michael Brecker, Andrew White, and countless others. Andrew White was so inspired by the craft of John Coltrane that he transcribed over two hundred Coltrane solos, note for note. Coltrane was not the only influence on those styles (though his ideas were quite significant for them). Joe Farrell, for example, also cites Charlie Parker as a primary influence. Bob Berg also shows the influence of Joe Henderson. Jan Garbarek has Ornette Coleman-like devices in his style plus European classical saxophone characteristics.

Many Coltrane-influenced saxophonists have led their own unique groups. One of the best saxophonists to emerge during the 1970s was David Liebman. After appearing with both Elvin Jones and Miles Davis, Liebman toured and recorded with his own bands. His name is occasionally mentioned at the same time as Steve Grossman's because the two saxophonists worked together with Jones and followed each other through stints with Miles Davis. Both men play Coltrane's phrases, have his inflection and much of his phenomenal speed and energy. But their tones are not as large or coarsely textured as Coltrane's. Nor are their lines as varied rhythmically. Once you have learned to distinguish their sounds from Coltrane's, you might enjoy trying to differentiate them from each other. I find Grossman's tone edgier than Liebman's. The overall feeling of Liebman's approach is more tender than Grossman's. In fact, of all the players listed above, Liebman and Charles Lloyd stand out as having brought the Coltrane approach a tenderness which many Coltrane disciples never had. Lloyd has a light-colored, light-weight, soft-textured tone quite unlike the tone of most Coltrane disciples.

Coltrane's influence has also shown up in a big band saxophone section which had previously been quite loyal to the sounds of Lester Young and Stan Getz. Such Woody Herman saxophonists as Gregory Herbert, Steve Lederer, and Frank Tiberi, have all displayed Coltrane characteristics. The Herman band, in fact, has even recorded arrangements of Coltrane's "Giant Steps" and "Naima."

chapter 15

THE MILES DAVIS GROUPS & SIDEMEN OF THE 1960s & 1970s

In 1963, Davis formed a new quintet consisting of tenor saxophonist George Coleman, pianist **Herbie Hancock,** bassist **Ron Carter,** and drummer Tony Williams. The members of Davis's new band were as young as the *Birth of the Cool* musicians had been; Williams was only seventeen years old. By the summer of 1964, the quintet had made one-half of a studio album, *Seven Steps to Heaven,* and three live concert albums: *Miles in Europe, My Funny Valentine,* and *Four and More.*

The Hancock–Carter–Williams rhythm section was superb. It had the excitement of the Garland-Chambers-Jones rhythm section and the sensitivity and delicate interaction which typified the Bill Evans-Scott LaFaro-Paul Motian unit. The Davis rhythm section remained intact, at least on records, from 1963 until 1968. It was probably the smoothest rhythm section sound jazz had experienced. Along with the 1961–65 John Coltrane rhythm section (pianist McCoy Tyner, bassist Jimmy Garrison, drummer Elvin Jones), the Davis rhythm section was a leader during the 1960s. Both the Davis and the Coltrane rhythm sections consolidated the innovations of modern jazz and became far more than simply accompanying units.

Hancock, Carter, and Williams maintained excellent rapport. They were able to play cohesively at breakneck tempos ("Walkin'" on *Four and More*), or, in the context of a slow piece, they could avoid stating tempo, and sounding as though someone were conducting them through gradual accelerations and decelerations ("My Funny Valentine" on *My Funny Valentine,* "Madness" on *Nefertiti,* and "Masqualero" on *Sorcerer*). Their rapport and high level of musicianship allowed them to change rhythms, textures, and moods spontaneously at any moment of a performance, at any tempo, and on any chord progression. Their versatility and lightening quick responsiveness were extraordinary.

Hancock, Carter, and Williams were all exceptionally skilled on their respective instruments. Hancock seemed to combine all the best qualities of an improviser: a clear conception, fertile imagination, a sense of continuity, and excellent instrumental proficiency. He had a quick, precise touch and comped briskly. These qualities put him in great demand as a recording pianist. Hancock appeared on more record dates than any other jazz pianist of the 1960s.

Carter had a slick, round tone with excellent intonation. He walked with uncanny perfection and buoyancy. Both his tone and his sense of timing exhibited a uniformly high level of quality. Carter played more toward the front of the beat than Chambers did. He provided a sturdy, yet responsive foundation for the quintet. Miles was not the only leader who appreciated Ron Carter's skill and reliability. By the mid-1970s, Carter had been employed on more than four hundred records.

Tony Williams represented the very highest level of drum technique, and he was possibly the most influential jazz drummer of the 1960s. He was very fast and his cymbal tones were separated with crystal clarity. Williams provided a model of light, sharp sounds. His ride cymbal sound was very crisp and distinctive, and, because he used a smaller bass drum than most pre-1960s drummers, the low register component of his sound was well articulated.

Drummer Tony Williams was an extremely sophisticated rhythm section player, looser and more daring than Paul Motian. Williams did more than kick and prod the hornmen. By the time *Filles de Kilimanjaro* was recorded, he had assumed a role so prominent that he often overshadowed the other sounds in the group. His was a very assertive style, quite the opposite of Kenny Clarke's and the conservative mid-1950s West Coast style drummers. Compare Clarke's performance on the records Miles Davis made during the early 1950s (*Miles Davis and the Modern Jazz Giants, Tallest Trees*) with Williams's playing on *Filles de Kilimanjaro* or *Miles Smiles*. You will hear a drastic difference between the two.

The 1963–68 Davis rhythm section style was heard later in recordings by Joe Henderson (*Power to the People; Tetragon; In Pursuit of Blackness; The Kicker; If You're Not Part of the Solution, You're Part of the Problem*) and Joe Farrell (*Joe Farrell Quartet*). The rhythm section style of *Miles In Europe* and *Four* and *More* was later heard in records by Freddie Hubbard, Jackie McLean (*Right Now*), and others. The Davis quintet approaches on *Miles Smiles, Miles in the Sky,* and *Nefertiti* influenced Kenny Cox and the Contemporary Jazz Quintet (*Multidirection*), as well as Art Lande (*Rubisa Patrol*).

Tenor saxophonist **George Coleman** had already distinguished himself in the combos of Max Roach, but his best recordings were made with Davis. Coleman had a light-textured, dark-colored tone, a bit softer than that of most hard bop tenor men. His attacks were very clean, sharper than the blunt beginnings of Hank Mobley's notes, and sharper than those of Wayne Shorter and Sonny Rollins. Before 1963, Coleman had sounded somewhat like Sonny Stitt and Sonny Rollins, but with Davis he displayed more Coltrane influence. Coleman, however, did not closely imitate Coltrane. He was an original player who played with unusual evenness and precision. He swung gracefully, handling very quick tempos and flawlessly executing long, sharply defined musical statements. His overall approach projected a gentler feeling than that of Coltrane.

In 1964 Coleman left, and tenor saxophonist **Wayne Shorter** joined Davis, Hancock, Carter, and Williams. This group remained together until the late 1960s and recorded *E.S.P., Sorcerer, Miles Smiles, Nefertiti, Miles in the Sky,* and one-half of *Filles de Kilimanjaro.* Shorter's influence on the group was possibly as great as that of its remarkable rhythm section. Shorter was a superb saxophonist and his composing style was an original and fresh contribution to the Davis library. That quintet, their compositions, and improvisations brought the Miles Davis name to a new plateau of creativity.

Compositional Style

Most tunes Davis played during the 1950s fit conventional song forms. An examination of the tunes on his 1961 *Someday My Prince Will Come* and *In Person at the Blackhawk,* his 1963 *Seven Steps to Heaven* and *Miles in Europe,* and his 1964 *Four and More* and *My Funny Valentine* reveals that, after the departure of Bill Evans and prior to his work with Shorter, Davis had not explored much new territory in the area of song forms. After Shorter joined him, however, Davis recorded very few conventionally constructed pieces. After 1964, Davis favored tunes which did not have bridges, complex turnarounds, or any section demarcations which can easily act as barriers to an unencumbered, free-flowing sound. Most of his recordings were made up of tunes which had fewer chord changes than the pop standards of Richard Rodgers or George Gershwin, or the jazz standards by Charlie Parker, Dizzy Gillespie, Tadd Dameron, John Lewis, or Thelonious Monk. In fact, some tunes recorded by Davis from 1965 to 68 have no preset chord changes. Their function is only to set tempo, key, and mood. The choice of chord changes is left to the inspiration of the improviser.

A large number of post–1964 compositions are all A instead of AABA, ABAB or ABAC. Shorter's "Iris" is a sixteen-bar waltz, all A (*E.S.P.*). His "Prince of Darkness" is sixteen bars long with very few prearranged harmonies (*Sorcerer*). Shorter's "E.S.P." is sixteen bars long, all A, with important and frequent chord changes. It is played twice, as:

twelve bars + four-bar turnaround

twelve bars + four-bar conclusion.

The four-bar sections differ, but the twelve-bar sections are identical. "E.S.P." displays what became a characteristic sound in much late 1960s and 70s music, the fourth (see Figure 15.1 and Chapter 17).

Figure 15.1. Piano keyboard illustration of "E.S.P." The first nine notes of "E.S.P." are separated by the interval of a fourth.

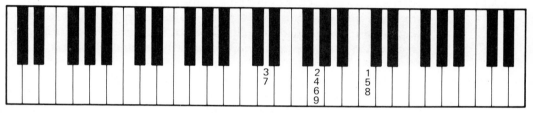

Another trait which lent the 1965–68 recordings their distinctive flavor was the use of space in tune construction. Several measures of the melody were filled with silence. Quite often, trumpet and tenor would lay out while the rhythm section continued to play and generate a mood. For example, Shorter's "Dolores" is thirty-eight bars long, divided into phrases of two, two and one-half, three, and three and one-half measures (*Miles Smiles*). These phrases are separated by spaces in which the horns do not play. Only the rhythm section is heard, continuing and developing patterns they played underneath the horns.

Another important aspect of the group's compositional style was the small number of rapid, jumpy eighth-note figures and highly syncopated lines which had been typical of bop. Of course they still used eighth notes and syncopation, but many of the post-1964 tunes were constructed of smoothly contoured lines of connected, sustained tones. The tunes had fewer changes of direction than bop melodies, with their many twists and turns. Shorter's "Nefertiti" (*Nefertiti*) is a good example. It is a sixteen-bar tune, all A. There is a new chord in nearly every measure, but the motion always has a slow, floating quality. Nothing abrupt or jumpy happens in either the melody or the chord changes. This style places the burden of complexity on the rhythm section, quite the reverse of bop tendencies. In fact, with no improvised solos by anyone else, the 1967 version of "Nefertiti" is practically a feature for Tony Williams. The melody is repeated again and again, a device later employed extensively by post-1968 Davis groups and spin-offs from those bands. The lazy, expansive feeling evoked by the performance of "Nefertiti" suggests the impressionistic classical music of Claude Debussy ("La Mer," "Prelude to the Afternoon of a Fawn") and Ravel ("Daphnis and Chloe"). The melody's silences and sustained tones produce an effect quite the opposite of that created by typical bop melodies such as Charlie Parker's "Confirmation" or Tadd Dameron's "Hot House." The melody's accompaniment, a loose but highly active rhythm section improvisation, contrasts sharply with the bop accompaniment style of walking bass and ride rhythms. The post-1964 Davis quintet discarded the bop formula of quick, jumpy melodic figures on top and stable, metronomic pulse patterns on the bottom. Shorter's writing brought stable simplicity to the top, and Williams's drumming brought super-charged rhythmic complexity to the bottom. This reversal of roles became especially common in later jazz-rock groups, especially Weather Report.

Rhythm Section Style

The members of Davis's rhythm section employed many unusual devices. As early as the 1964 *Four and More*, Tony Williams had played pieces without consistently closing his high-hat on the second and fourth beats of each measure. He kept time with the ride cymbal and used the high-hat only for bursts of color. Then on the 1966 "Freedom Jazz Dance" (*Miles Smiles*), he closed his high-hat on every beat, a time-keeping device later adopted by hundreds of jazz-rock drummers. He also colored the group sound with an endless variety of cymbal splashes, snare drum fills, and imaginative rhythmic patterns played on all of his drums and cymbals, extending the techniques which had been employed by Philly Joe Jones, Art Blakey, Louis Hayes, and Paul Motian. These are just a few of the numerous devices which Williams employed. Only by listening to the recordings can you appreciate his tremendous inventiveness and understand how his creations fit with those of Hancock, Carter, Davis, and Shorter.

Bassist Ron Carter did not always restrict himself to walking. He incorporated figures similar to those used by Scott LaFaro and other inventive bassists. Carter embellished walking sequences and set up new rhythmic patterns. He constantly thought of new ways to both underpin the group sound and enrich the musical events that occurred around him. Listen to his playing on "Pee Wee" and "Masqualero"

Figure 15.2. Miles Davis group of the middle 1960s. Personnel: Davis playing Harmon-muted trumpet; tenor saxophonist Wayne Shorter with bassist Ron Carter; drummer Tony Williams (this photo was taken after the middle 60s); Herbie Hancock playing electric piano (this photo was also taken later). *Bill Smith,* Coda

(*Sorcerer*), "Freedom Jazz Dance" (*Miles Smiles*), and "Riot," "Fall," and "Nefertiti" (all on *Nefertiti*).

Pianist Hancock comped with calculated intensity, politely but firmly. He also layed out for long stretches, especially on *Miles Smiles*. In his own solos, he sometimes omitted all comping, thus treating his piano strictly as a melody instrument.

Varied Approaches

The variety of moods and rhythmic styles employed by the 1963–68 quintet was huge. They recorded:

1) waltzes, including Davis's "Circle," Hancock's "Little One," Shorter's "Iris," Carter's "Mood," Williams's "Pee Wee";
2) fast pieces, including Jimmy Heath's "Gingerbread Boy," Shorter's "Dolores" and "Orbits," Williams's "Hand Jive," Hancock's "The Sorcerer," Carter's "R.J.," Shorter's "E.S.P.";
3) slow, reflective pieces (Shorter's "Fall," "Masqualero," and "Vonetta");
4) pieces in which they created a sequence of different rhythmic styles ("Country Son," *Miles in the Sky*).

Rhythmic styles other than bouncy, swinging jazz patterns appear throughout their records. Straight, repeating eighth-notes played by Williams on the ride cymbal, and occasionally the statement of all four beats on the sock cymbal, are sometimes coupled with simple, repeated bass figures by Carter, figures which do not fit traditional walking bass rhythms. All of this bears a marked similarity to the rhythmic feeling of rock. Hints of these rock-like patterns can be heard in portions of "Eighty One," "Freedom Jazz Dance," "Masqualero," "Frelun Brun," "Tout de Suite," "Filles de Kilimanjaro," and other pieces. The latter three tunes appeared on the 1968 *Filles de Kilimanjaro*, an LP which strongly indicated a trend away from conventional, buoyant, modern jazz swing feeling and the beginning of a fusion with the rhythmic feel of rock. On "Stuff" in *Miles in the Sky*, Davis asked Hancock to play electric piano, thus creating a tone color associated with rock. This marked the first use of that instrument on a Davis recording.

1968–75

The next two LPs that Davis recorded became significant in directing modern jazz of the 1970s. For these sessions, Miles drew from a pool of drummers which included Tony Williams, Jack DeJohnette, Lenny White, Charles Alias, and Jim Riley. His pool of keyboard players included Herbie Hancock, Chick Corea, Joe Zawinul, and Larry Young. Wayne Shorter played tenor and soprano saxophones, Bennie Maupin played bass clarinet, John McLaughlin played guitar, and the bassists included Dave Holland and Harvey Brooks. The records were

In a Silent Way and *Bitches Brew*, both made in 1969. They contained a variety of musical approaches, but the dominant style was a combination of jazz and rock. Many melodies were reminiscent of the floating, almost motionless feeling of Shorter's "Nefertiti." In fact, a Shorter tune, "Sanctuary," was included on *Bitches Brew*.

In a Silent Way was the beginning of Davis's partnership with pianist-composer Joe Zawinul, who had been with the Cannonball Adderly quintet during the 1960s. Davis's relationship with Zawinul was similar to those he had with Gil Evans in the late 1940s and late 50s, with Bill Evans on *Kind of Blue*, and with Shorter from 1964 to 1969. Davis recorded Zawinul pieces of the "Nefertiti" style: "In a Silent Way" (*In a Silent Way*) and "Pharoah's Dance" (*Bitches Brew*). Miles continued to employ Zawinul's work on later LPs but did not always credit Zawinul on the album labels. (Most Davis recordings made after 1969 list Davis as sole composer in spite of the fact that he was sometimes performing the compositions of others. Zawinul's "Double Image" is properly credited on the Davis *Live-Evil* LP, but his "Orange Lady" which is the last third of "Great Expectations" on the *Big Fun* LP, is credited to Davis.)

The post-1968 music of Davis differed in several respects from his 1963–68 style. **Instrumentation** was altered.

1) Electric piano and organ replaced conventional piano. And Davis often employed two or more electric keyboard instruments at once.

2) Fender electric bass guitar replaced acoustic string bass violin.

3) Except for George Benson's work on one tune ("Paraphernalia," in the 1968 *Miles in the Sky*), Miles had not previously used guitar. It was an important change when guitarist John McLaughlin appeared on *In a Silent Way*, *Bitches Brew*, and *Live-Evil*. After that, Davis used quite a few guitarists; at one time, he had three in a single band.

4) The Davis saxophonists of this period spent more time on soprano sax than on any other instrument. The soprano had the potential for penetrating and carrying its sound out over drums and electric instruments, where a tenor might not be able to cut through.

5) Davis usually employed two or more drummers. By the early 1970s, he had settled into the pattern of using one man on conventional drum set and another man on auxiliary percussion such as conga drums, shakers, rattles, gongs, whistles, and a large quantity of instruments native to Africa, South America, and India. On several LPs he used Indian musicians playing the sitar (a stringed instrument) and tabla (drums) (see Figure 15.3).

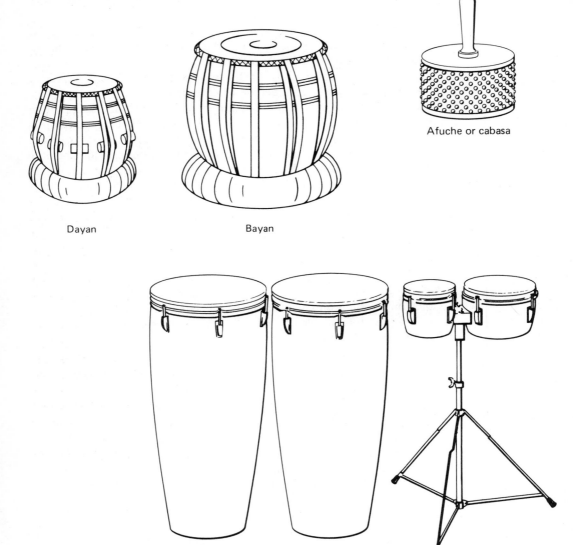

Dayan

Bayan

Afuche or cabasa

Figure 15.3. Auxiliary percussion. Tabla is the name for a set of two drums used in Indian music: the dayan, a small, high-pitched drum, and the bayan, a larger, low-pitched drum. Tabla are the most popular drums in the music of India. The afuche or cabasa is common in Latin American music. It consists of many strings of beads wound around a spool or gourd which is rotated clockwise and counterclockwise by one hand while the other hand is held against the beads to keep them in contact with the surface. The conga drum is another common Latin American instrument. It is played alone or in combination with other congas. A single drummer may play a set of congas, or there may be several drummers. Bongo drums usually come in sets of two. Bongos are like small, high-pitched versions of conga drums.

The **rhythm section concept** was another way in which Davis's post-1968 groups differed from his 1963–68 groups. The post-1968 groups featured elaborate configurations of colors and textures, and rhythm section members played with a very high level of activity. The beat was easily detectable, but it was surrounded by a mass of constantly changing sounds, sometimes delicate and gentle, sometimes turbulent. Textures often seemed to be created for their own sake rather than as accompaniments. The textures on *In a Silent Way* and *Bitches Brew* were as much in the forefront as the written melodies and improvised solo lines. The textures were generated by several electric keyboard instruments (pianos and organ), guitar, basses, several drummers, and, on *Bitches Brew,* partly by Bennie Maupin's bass clarinet playing. Bass lines were composed of a blend of rock formulas, the freely improvised nonwalking style of Scott LaFaro, and figures borrowed from Latin American music (see notated rock and Latin bass figures in Chapter 18).

Most post-1968 Davis music was centered around a few repeated chords, a repeating bass figure, or a mode, rather than a sequence of frequently changing chords. The tunes reflected Shorter's composing style and the departures he had made from bop. Complexity was now centered in the rhythm section figures, rather than in the melodies. Performance format differed as well. Instead of improvising on a single tune for five to ten minutes, everyone taking his turn soloing, and then stopping before going on to the next tune, the post-1968 format accented medleys. Davis conducted the transitions between tunes, and his bassists led the way by changing the patterns of their repeating figures. The bass was the pivot in this music; bass figures were as essential to the 1970s style as complex chord changes had been to bop and hard bop.

In spite of the marked simplification occurring in rhythm section harmonies, improvising soloists tended to retain the harmonic complexity of chord progression-based styles. The more thoroughly grounded in chord progression-based styles an improviser was, the more variety he could bring to a solo whose accompaniment was extremely repetitive. John Coltrane had perfected techniques for spontaneously inventing chord progressions while improvising on mode-based forms and repeating bass figures (see Chapter 14). The Davis saxophonists and guitarists used these same techniques. They had also abandoned bop concepts of phrasing; none of Parker's or Gillespie's pet phrases could be heard, although many of Coltrane's were evident. Improvisers seemed more intent on creating moods than melodic lines.

Davis's sidemen of this period were highly skilled players. (If they lacked the innovative gifts of such former Davis associates as Gil Evans, Sonny Rollins, John Coltrane, Bill Evans, and Wayne Shorter, they lacked none of the training necessary for keeping up with the demands of this intense music.)

After 1968, Miles led groups whose personnel were not as stable as his late 1950s and 1960s bands. During the 1968–73 period, each new LP had new personnel, and the musicians on tour were not always the same as those used in the studio. Coltrane had been with Davis on and off for five years. Shorter had also stayed approximately five years. But after Shorter left, Miles employed more than five different saxophonists in five years (Steve Grossman, Gary Bartz, Carlos Garnett, David Liebman, Sonny Fortune, Sam Morrison, and others) (see Figure 15.4).

His rhythm sections were more stable, however. After various combinations of pianists (Joe Zawinul, Herbie Hancock, Chick Corea, Keith Jarrett, and others), bassists (Ron Carter, Dave Holland, Harvey Brooks, Mike Henderson, and others) and drummers (Tony Williams, Lenny White, Jack DeJohnette, Billy Cobham, Airto Moreira, and others), he settled for several years with bassist Michael Henderson and drummers Al Foster (conventional set) and M'Tume Heath (conga drums and auxiliary percussion). After pianist Keith Jarrett left, Miles rarely used a keyboard instrument. He occasionally played organ himself to set harmonies and moods, but usually depended on guitarists Reggie Lucas and Pete Cosey to supply chords.

Fender bassist **Michael Henderson** was on the road with Davis longer than Ron Carter had been. Although he made recordings with Davis as late as 1968 and 1971, Carter was not a full-time touring member of the group after 1966. Henderson was approaching the length of employment seen by Paul Chambers (1955–63). He was well versed in rock bass playing, having worked with several well-known rock bands before joining Davis. His musicianship was solid and provided a reliable foundation for the Miles Davis sound of the 1970s.

From 1968 to 1975, Davis recorded *In a Silent Way, Bitches Brew, Live at the Fillmore, Jack Johnson, Live-Evil, On the Corner, In Concert, Big Fun, Get Up with It,* and *Agharta.* Some of these LPs were drawn from the recordings of different bands. In other words, some LPs are simply collections of Davis tapes rather than consistent samples of a single group.

For the new jazz-rock idiom, Davis altered his trumpet style. He often played fast, sweeping runs in and out of his extreme high register. He wired his instrument to an amplifier and connected electronic attachments which simulated echo (by means of a tape loop device called Echoplex) or created alterations of tone color previously achieved by rubber plunger mutes (by means of the wah wah pedal). He could be quite violent and sound much like a rock guitarist, or he could play in the tender, mournful manner he had displayed on *Porgy and Bess* and *Sketches of Spain.* Sometimes most of the band would become silent while he quietly played with only one other musician, but that was rare. Usually the mood was very outgoing and full of

Figure 15.4. Miles Davis group of the 1970s. Personnel: Carlos Garnett (soprano sax), Al Foster (drums), Davis (wearing sun glasses), Badal Roy (percussionist). *Bill Smith,* Coda

unrelenting tension. The level of musicianship was very high, and the complexity of the music set it apart from rock, but its effect was often quite similar to that of the loud turbulence generated by rock bands of the late 1960s and 70s. Admiration for such rock musicians as Jimi Hendrix and Billy Preston was evident in Miles's music. The post-1968 Davis recordings displayed a blend of the jazz tradition, 1960s and 70s rock, and the music of India and South America. It was infused with the spirit of Charlie Parker and John Coltrane, but the tone colors were those of rock.

Popular Appeal of the 1968–70 Davis Concepts

The 1968–75 Davis records and concerts drew a larger audience than Davis had previously enjoyed. *Bitches Brew* sold more copies than any other Miles Davis record. This new-found popularity was not restricted only to Davis. The styles which began at the same time as the Davis jazz-rock approach and those which were spawned by it gained the largest audience jazz had known since the swing era. Herbie Hancock's 1973 *Head Hunters* and Weather Report's *Sweetnighter* broke numerous sales records as did other jazz-rock albums.

There are several possible explanations for this new popularity. Rock had been popular for more than fifteen years by the time *Head Hunters* was released. So perhaps when jazz adopted the electric instruments associated with rock in addition to a number of typical rock rhythm section patterns, jazz was enabling non-jazz audiences to enjoy it. The prominence of drums and frequently repeating rhythmic figures of rock also helped bring a wide popular audience to the jazz-rock styles of the 1970s. Solo improvisation retained the harmonic complexity of bop and John Coltrane. But those solos were accompanied by harmonically simple forms (drones and repeating bass figures which, together, gave a modal flavor). The simple harmonic nature of the accompaniments, mixed with the prominence of rock tone colors and rock drumming, could explain the appeal of jazz-rock fusion for non-jazz audiences.

Both swing era riff bands and 1970s jazz-rock groups mixed improvisation with simple, repeated riffs and striking rhythmic vitality. The fact that both forms drew larger popular audiences than other jazz styles, leads me to think a prime attraction was the combination of simplicity, repetition, and rhythmic vitality. (People seem to especially enjoy percussion, catchy, repeated rhythmic figures, and bluesy, funky melodic figures. Jazz-rock is characterized by more of these traits than bop, and displays all of them in quite obvious ways.)

Influence of 1968–70 Davis Concepts

The instrumentation and rhythmic style introduced by *In a Silent Way* and *Bitches Brew* inspired a number of creative jazz-rock combos, including several led by former Davis sidemen. (Weather Report's ideas stemmed directly from concepts employed in those two LPs. The group also contained three men who had recorded with Davis—saxophonist Wayne Shorter, pianist Joe Zawinul, percussionist Airto Moreira—and one who had performed with Davis but not recorded with him, bassist Miroslav Vitous.)

Herbie Hancock's groups reflected some characteristics of the 1960s Davis style in that:

1) the Davis style had depended partly on Hancock himself;
2) Hancock employed trumpeters who displayed Davis influence (Johnny Coles and Eddie Henderson);
3) Hancock used Bennie Maupin, who had recorded with Davis on *Bitches Brew* and *Big Fun;*
4) Hancock fused rock with jazz techniques; and
5) Hancock made the exploration of new tone colors an essential part of his music.

One of the groups led by Tony Williams extended some of the concepts explored in *Filles de Kilimanjaro, Miles Smiles,* and *Miles in the Sky.* The unique drumming concepts of Williams had been central to the Davis sound of the 1960s, and in his own group the Williams identity was continued. John McLaughlin, an important musician on the Davis LP's *In a Silent Way, Bitches Brew, Big Fun, Jack Johnson,* and *Live-Evil* was employed by Williams, as was organist Larry Young who also appeared on *Bitches Brew.*

The groups of Chick Corea, another former sideman of Davis, reflected jazz-rock tendencies pioneered by both Davis and Williams. Corea employed Brazilian percussionist Airto Moreira and drummer Lenny White, both of whom had recorded with Davis.

HERBIE HANCOCK

Herbie Hancock became the most sought-after jazz pianist of the 1960s. His work suggests the light, brisk comping of Tommy Flanagan and the chord voicings of Bill Evans. His gentle, even touch resembles George Shearing's. Hancock apparently absorbed several influences while he was developing during the late 1950s and early 60s. Some of his playing has the funky, bluesy figures and the rhythmic bounce which typified Horace Silver and Wynton Kelly. But Bill Evans probable had the greatest influence on Hancock. Evans's harp-like, ringing tones surrounded by silence, his chord voicings, smooth legato lines, and locked hands style—all of these can be heard in Hancock's playing on the Miles Davis albums *Four and More* and *My Funny Valentine.* And, at times, the Tristano-like approach to constructing lines is also evident in Hancock's work, as on his solos in "The Sorcerer" (*Sorcerer*), "Agitation" (*E.S.P.*), and "Orbits" (*Miles Smiles*). The flexible and intelligent interaction between Hancock, Ron Carter, and Tony Williams on "Pee Wee" (*Sorcerer*) and between Hancock, Buster Williams, and Al Heath on "He Who Lives in Fear" (*The Prisoner*) is reminiscent of the sensitive interactions which typified the 1961 recordings of Bill Evans, Scott LaFaro, and Paul Motian (*Village Vanguard Sessions*).

Hancock's playing nearly always has a meticulousness and finished quality. His execution is firm and swinging without being violent or insistent. Both his solo work and his accompanying project a politeness and sensitivity. Hancock has shown broad scope and versatility: his style is compatible with several different streams of modern jazz. He has contributed immeasurably to hundreds of records—not only those of the Miles Davis Quintet, but also those of Joe Henderson, Joe Farrell, Freddie Hubbard, Paul Desmond, Milt Jackson, and others.

Hancock was not as innovative as Bill Evans or McCoy Tyner. His special achievement was the creation of a very convincing synthesis of pre-1960 jazz piano styles. Many good pianists, including Larry Willis, George Cables, and others, sounded like Hancock but this may have been that, rather than drawing directly from his style, they drew from the same sources as he did: Bill Evans, Wynton Kelly, and so forth. What distinguished Hancock was that he created consistently stimulating, swinging, and polished piano improvisations, something that cannot always be said even for the most innovative of his contemporaries.

There is no doubt about Hancock's creativity as a composer and arranger. By the early 1970s, he had written every tune on eight of his own albums, and written or coauthored many of the tunes on seven more of his own. His funky, bluesy piece called "Watermelon Man" (*The Best of Herbie Hancock*) became very popular, especially in Mongo Santamaria's version, during the mid-1960s. The big bands of Woody Herman, Si Zentner, and Maynard Ferguson all played their own arrangements of it. Hancock's "The Sorcerer," "Little One," "Riot," and "Madness" were all recorded by the Miles Davis Quintet.

Among the many idioms which Hancock has employed as a composer are:

1) the lush, classical music style of "Suite Revenge" on *Death Wish*,

2) the rock-influenced *Fat Albert Rotunda, Head Hunters*, and *Thrust*,

3) the funky, hard bop approach of *Taking Off*,

4) Gil Evans-like work on *The Prisoner*,

5) writing like that of Sun Ra on *Sextant* and *Crossings*,

6) the style of the 1960s Miles Davis Quintet on *Maiden Voyage* and *Empyrean Isles*.

Hancock did much of his creative writing after he left Miles and began leading his own groups. (Hancock had led groups in recording studios before and during his years with Davis, but they were not usually working bands. Most were put together solely for the recordings.) The music produced by Hancock's first post-Davis group capitalized on some of the advances made in the Miles Davis groups of the 1960s. In *The Prisoner,* Hancock wrote lines for trumpeter Johnny Coles, trombonist Garnett Brown, and tenor saxophonist Joe Henderson which had few eighth-note figures or jumpy syncopations and were full of legato passages employing sustained tones. Hancock, bassist Buster Williams, and drummer Al Heath generated considerable stimulating accompanying activity in the manner that Hancock, Carter, and Williams had done in the Miles Davis quintet.

Hancock's second band recorded *Mwandishi, Crossings,* and *Sextant,* albums which employed concepts similar to those used on the Davis LPs *Nefertiti, In a Silent Way,* and *Bitches Brew.* The presence of synthesizer, the extensive use of other electronic instruments, and exotic percussion effects also suggests the early 1960s work of Sun Ra. Each of Hancock's group members was responsible for creating a larger assortment of sounds than were traditionally required of most jazz musicians. Eddie Henderson doubled on fluegelhorn and percussion. Julian Priester played tenor trombone, baritone trombone, bass trombone, and percussion. Bennie Maupin played alto flute, soprano saxophone, piccolo, bass clarinet, and percussion. And Hancock often electronically altered the sound of his piano, creating echo and fuzz. The group was rounded out with Buster Williams (bass), Patrick Gleeson (synthesizer), and Billy Hart (drums). Sometimes every member of the band was playing percussion, and there was no instrument which suggested harmonies. Because of the electronically synthesized sounds, the legato lines of sustained tones, and the exotic percussion sounds, Hancock's style on *Sextant, Mwandishi,* and *Crossings* was often referred to as "space music."

Hancock's next band was a quintet with saxophonist Benny Maupin, bassist Paul Jackson, drummer Harvey Mason, and auxiliary percussionist Bill Summers (*Thrust*). The style of this group was much like the rock styles of Sly Stone and Curtis Mayfield. Hancock retained a high level of musicianship, but spent more time constructing rock style rhythmic effects, with their repeated piano and bass figures, than he spent inventing long jazz piano solos. The music was tightly organized and hard driving. Syncopated rhythms were laid layer upon layer, and there were colorful, electronically produced sounds and percussion effects. Hancock's first album in this style, his 1973 *Head Hunters,* sold far more copies than most previous best-selling jazz records. The group which recorded *Head Hunters* disbanded during the winter of 1976.

WAYNE SHORTER   Between 1964 and 1969, Miles Davis employed Wayne Shorter, one of the most outstanding tenor saxophonists in jazz (*Bitches Brew, E.S.P., Filles de Kilimanjaro, In a Silent Way, Miles in the Sky, Miles Smiles, Nefertiti, Sorcerer*). Shorter was also a composer whose work dramatically changed the sound of the Davis Quintet. His writing and playing later became central to the work of Weather Report, a creative jazz-rock group of the 1970s.

Shorter had a gray tone with a broad, textured surface and soft edges. It was a hard sound, but he could temper that hardness according to the mood of the music. His tone had no vibrato except in rare circumstances. Though most saxophonists depend partly on vibrato as an expressive device, Shorter cultivated so many other expressive devices, you did not miss the vibrato. He made masterful use of various attacks and releases. He could slide up into the pitch of a note or strike it head on. He could release a note by carefully tapering it or by bending its pitch up or down. The note might trail off and disappear or it might fall and then slide up to another note. He could flit from note to note like a bird going from branch to branch. Though his technique was primarily legato, he sometimes gave out stark announcements consisting of brief tones.

Wayne Shorter brought a gift for melody to his solos. Listening to him improvise is like looking over the shoulder of a composer as he invents and develops themes. Shorter was a very intelligent improviser who brought a strong sense of continuity to his lines. He played unusual intervals in a manner which was somehow graceful and ferocious at the same time. Almost every chorus was a coherent and concise melodic statement.

By the early 1960s, Shorter had abandoned the bop approach to melody. The pet phrases of Parker and Gillespie were absent from his playing. The intricate bop eighth note figures with their never-ending twists and turns were disappearing from his work. Shorter played lines of smoother contours. His melodic approach often recalled the concise floating themes of turn-of-the-century French composers Maurice Ravel, Claude Debussy, and Erik Satie.

His early playing had shown a Coltrane influence, but his tone color and texture were unlike Coltrane's. And Shorter's rhythmic conception was looser than Coltrane's; he seemed to be floating around the beat rather than precisely subdividing it. He also played fewer notes in his lines.

By 1964, Shorter had become an extremely fresh improviser. He had eliminated most of the bop influence in his lines and reworked so much of Coltrane's style that he presented a sound which was almost entirely his own. His playing was almost free of clichés. He could handle hard, raw playing, and yet his ballad work was as tender as that of Stan Getz. His best improvisations are to be found in the 1965 Miles Davis LP *E.S.P.* Listen to his solo on "Eighty-One." Note the middle section which is so melodic that it could be taken out of context and used as a tune. Yet in spite of its very deliberate construction, it carries an emotional impact of searing depth. Listen to his improvisation on "Pee Wee" on Davis's *Sorcerer*. It is haunting in its otherworldly beauty.

Shorter began playing soprano saxophone on his last two Davis LPs, *In a Silent Way* and *Bitches Brew*. He continued to play both soprano and tenor saxophones with Weather Report.

Shorter changed his style drastically when he joined Weather Report. Instead of long, melodic phrases, he often played short bursts of notes alternating with long silences and sustained tones. This new style meshed well with the unusual percussion sounds, conversational bass figures, and crackling keyboard ideas which characterized the group. Often Shorter would go several measures without playing. Then, after playing only a note or two, he would become silent again. His was a very difficult role. Instead of creating melodic improvisations, he participated in a collective effort to create textures. The delicate balance achieved in the collective improvisations of Weather Report is due in part to Wayne Shorter's tasteful and very disciplined sense of musical discretion. He artfully made the difficult transition from jazz soloist in the conventional sense to ensemble improviser in the new context created by Weather Report. Listen to "Umbrellas" and "Seventh Arrow" on *Weather Report* and "Surucucu" on *I Sing the Body Electric*.

Shorter was one of the most original and prolific composers of the 1960s and 70s. He wrote extensively for albums of his own and contributed substantially to the repertories of three important groups: Art Blakey's Jazz Messengers, the Miles Davis Quintet, and Weather Report. He wrote every tune on two albums under his own name (*Ju Ju* and *Speak No Evil*), and all but one tune on each of an additional six more of his LPs. While with Blakey's group, from 1959 to 1963, he wrote much of the material they recorded (see Table 15.1).

Shorter and Joe Zawinul were the principal composers for Weather Report (see Table 15.2). The most important aspect of the Shorter–

TABLE 15.1. Wayne Shorter Compositions Recorded by Art Blakey

"Contemplation"	"Backstage Sally"
"Mr. Jin"	"The Summit"
"Free for All"	"Ping Pong"
"Hammerhead"	"Roots and Herbs"
"Sleeping Dancer Sleep On"	"The Back Sliders"
"Noise in the Attic"	"United"
"Giantis"	"Look at the Birdie"
"Children of the Night"	"Master Mind"
"Sincerely Diana"	

TABLE 15.2. Composer Credits for Weather Report Compositions

Zawinul	Shorter
"Orange Lady"	"Tears"
"Waterfall"	"Eurydice"
"Boogie Woogie Waltz"	"Manolete"
"Adios"	"Non-Stop Home"
"125th Street Congress"	"The Moors"
"Unknown Soldier"	"Surucucu"
"Second Sunday in August"	"Mysterious Traveller"
"Directions"	"Blackthorn Rose"
"Nubian Sundance"	"Lusitanos"
"Jungle Book"	"Freezing Fire"
"Man in the Green Shirt"	"Lost"
"Between the Thighs"	"Elegant People"
"Badia"	"Three Clowns"
"Five Short Stories"	"Harlequin"
"Early Minor"	"Palladium"
"Black Market"	
"Cannonball"	**Zawinul–Shorter–Vitous**
"Gibraltar"	
"Birdland"	"Umbrellas"
"A Remark You Made"	"T.H."
"The Juggler"	
	Alphonso Johnson
Vitous	
	"Herandnu"
"Seventh Arrow"	
"Morning Lake"	**A. Johnson–Shorter–**
"Will"	**Zawinul**
"Crystal"	
	"Scarlet Woman"
Zawinul–Shorter	
	Zawinul–A. Johnson
"Milky Way"	
	"Cucumber Slumber"
Zawinul–Vitous	
	Jaco Pastorius
"Vertical Invader"	
"American Tango"	"Barbary Coast"
	"Teen Town"
	"Havona"

Weather Report relationship was one of the styles in which Shorter composed. Zawinul had been attracted to it when he heard Shorter's "Nefertiti" on the 1967 Miles Davis LP of the same name. Zawinul wrote a few tunes in a similar vein, with sustained tones, active rhythm section, and floating lines which had a pastoral feeling. The conception of Shorter's "Nefertiti," and Zawinul's "Dr. Honoris Causa" and "In a Silent Way" became essential for much of Weather Report's sound.

When pianist-composer Joe Zawinul left Cannonball Adderley's quintet and saxophonist-composer Wayne Shorter left the Miles Davis quintet, they joined bassist Miroslav Vitous to form an unusual group called Weather Report (see Figure 15.5). The ideas developed by Weather Report had first appeared in the late 1960s and were especially evident in the Miles Davis albums *Nefertiti, In a Silent Way,* and *Bitches Brew.* Shorter, Zawinul, and Vitous came together and consolidated their ideas in 1970 and 1971. They were joined by two drummers, Alphonse Mouzon, on conventional drum set, and Airto Moreira, on auxiliary percussion. Shorter had written many tunes for Davis, including "Nefertiti." And his own LP, *Super Nova,* had used concepts similar to those used by Weather Report. Zawinul had written "Mercy, Mercy, Mercy" for Cannonball Adderley and "In a Silent Way," "Pharoah's Dance," and other pieces for Miles Davis. Vitous's album *Infinite Search* (later reissued as *Mountain in the Clouds*) had employed adventurous concepts of jazz bass playing and broken away from conventional rhythm section roles. Airto Moreira had played with Davis and recorded several Davis albums which had set the pace for a fusion of jazz, rock, and elements of Indian and Latin American music.

Figure 15.5. Wayne Shorter (soprano sax), Miroslav Vitous (bass), Joe Zawinul (electric piano), in the early 1970s. *Bill Smith,* Coda

Alphonse Mouzon had been with a jazz-rock group led by vibraharpist Roy Ayers.

The collective improvisation of musical textures and the emancipation of rhythm section instruments from conventional roles were significant aspects of the Weather Report approach. **Miroslav Vitous** was a bassist uniquely able to improvise melodies as well as or better than the average hornman. He had abandoned the bass timekeeping role in several selections on his *Infinite Search* LP. Vitous had a sophisticated melodic sense; he was in a class with such outstanding bass soloists as Paul Chambers and Scott LaFaro. He was also very capable with bowed bass. Vitous had a keen sense of what to play for the sake of creating interesting rhythmic textures and how to keep his instrument's voice in sensitive musical conversations with other group members. Vitous did not simply break up walking bass lines or play in a decorative two feeling as LaFaro did. The Vitous contributions to Weather Report included fragmented melody statements, bowed sustained tones, and syncopated interjections. He could just as easily bow melody in unison with a sax line as feed rock style bass figures into the group texture. Vitous could play in unison with a rhythm the drummer was stating on ride cymbal or underscore a pattern being played on piano. He could quickly go back and forth, too. Vitous had cast off the restraints of traditional bass playing and become an improviser first and timekeeping bassist second. (His work made sense, too. It was not just the flashy playing of a gifted showoff.)

Airto Moreira brought an imagination of sweeping proportions to his use of Latin American percussion instruments. His rhythms made a compelling combination with those of Vitous and Mouzon.

Eric Gravatt soon took Mouzon's place, and Dom Um Romao took Airto's; these were the first of a long series of personnel changes. By the middle 1970s, even bassist Miroslav Vitous had left, and the only founding members who remained were Shorter and Zawinul.

Weather Report came on the scene with the standard instrumentation of sax, piano, bass, and drums. They also had an auxiliary percussionist, but that was not unusual; many 1950s and 60s jazz groups had employed conga drummers or other auxiliary percussionists to add a Latin American flavor to their groups. But Weather Report did not use its conventional instrumentation in conventional ways. It was rare for bassist Miroslav Vitous to walk, or for the drummer to play standard ride rhythms or close the high-hat sharply on the second and fourth beats of each measure. Zawinul usually did not comp for Shorter, and the auxiliary percussionist was not simply restricted to the conga drum. "Eurydice," on Weather Report's first LP, is one of the few pieces which contains walking bass, drummer playing ride rhythms and closing high-hat on second and fourth beats, sax solo followed by piano solo, etc. And even in that conventionally approached performance, there are portions which deviate from the standard bop roles.

For example, drummer Alphonse Mouzon often closed his high-hat on all four beats, and interjected musical comments to the point where instead of just keeping time and coloring the sound, he is heard in the forefront of the group. On "Eurydice" Miroslav Vitous often abandons the walking bass role and instead contributes embellishments to the ensemble. Zawinul does not always comp behind Shorter, either. He sets up delicate flourishes, plays counter-melodies, and sometimes lays out. Airto Moreira interjects colorful, speech-like sounds throughout the proceedings with his cuica, an instrument in which the player gently slides his fingers along a stick which in turn alters the tension of a specially connected drumhead and causes it to vibrate.

Collective Improvisation

On their first three LPs (*I Sing the Body Electric, Sweetnighter, Weather Report*), Weather Report explored an unusual approach to combo improvisation. Instead of adhering to roles consistent with bop formulas, the instruments in Weather Report were played in highly interactive ways. Spurts of melody might come from any member, not just from the sax. Rhythmic figures and fills could also be produced by any member, not solely by a drummer.

The kinds of interaction between members were so varied that in some pieces there was no distinction between soloist and accompanist. One player's sound might stand out momentarily from the ensemble texture, but it soon blended into the overall texture again. In this situation, every member had to be capable of playing melodically or of simply adding to the overall texture of the group sound. Weather Report's members developed special techniques for managing such tasks.

Solo choruses, as conceived in swing and bop, did not occur. A particular voice (sax, piano, arco bass, etc.) often held the focal point for a few moments. Call the few moments a solo if you wish. But regardless of how you label the event, it maintained much more continuity with the entire piece than conventional jazz solos usually did. Most conventional jazz solos came in sequence with other solos. They adhered to fixed chorus lengths and came strung together, one player directly following another. Each player did his own thing regardless of whether its mood or color continued or developed that of the preceding solo.

In Weather Report, each member's work contributes to the prevailing mood and color. The players do not usually feature themselves, but rather create notes primarily to serve the group sound. This approach helps produce a variety of consistently maintained musical feelings and flavors. There was a greater variety of texture and moods in Weather Report's music than was available to most bop, West Coast, and hard bop groups. Only bands led by such versatile composers as Duke Ellington, Charles Mingus, and Sun Ra had previously succeeded in achieving a comparable range of musical colors.

In Ellington's music, composition played a more important role than improvisation. For Mingus and Sun Ra the relative proportions of composition and improvisation vary considerably from piece to piece. Weather Report employs a certain amount of composition and works out quite a few rhythms and instrument effects in advance also. But much of the balance and distinctive feeling in their music is produced spontaneously. The fact that their spontaneous musical efforts work out so well is a credit to the sensitivity and discretion of Weather Report's members.

Good examples of collective improvisation are "Seventh Arrow" and "Umbrellas," on Weather Report's first album, *Weather Report*, "Surucucu," on *I Sing the Body Electric*, and "125th Street Congress," on *Sweetnighter*. Prewritten figures pop up at the beginning and end and occasionally within the pieces, but otherwise the music seems spontaneous.

Prior to 1970, modern jazz had produced very few recordings of collective improvisation in which solos were of secondary importance. In 1949, Lennie Tristano, Lee Konitz, and their group recorded "Intuition" and "Digression." Occasional attempts at improvised counterpoint were made during the 1950s by Dave Brubeck and Paul Desmond, John Lewis and Milt Jackson, and Gerry Mulligan and Bob Brookmeyer. In 1960 Ornette Coleman, Eric Dolphy, Freddie Hubbard, Don Cherry, et al. recorded *Free Jazz*, which contained moments when all musicians participated in spontaneous, collective improvisation. The 1965 LP, *Ascension*, which included John Coltrane, Pharoah Sanders, and others, had moments similar to those in *Free Jazz*. Yet in spite of the high-level improvisatory skills possessed by Tristano, Konitz, Coltrane, and others, the quality of their collective improvisations rarely equalled the overall quality produced in noncollective contexts by those same men. But Weather Report's collectively improvised performances stand out as highly successful examples. It was not that Joe Zawinul or Wayne Shorter were improvisers superior to Tristano, Konitz, or Coltrane, but in the context of Weather Report, Zawinul and Shorter have been able to collectively improvise music which, to many listeners, is consistently more successful than the collective improvisations of Tristano, Ornette Coleman, John Coltrane, etc. It is worth noting that the earliest forms of jazz placed great emphasis on the interplay between melodic voices (trumpet, clarinet, trombone). Often no single player had the lead. Over the years, jazz lost its interest in the collectively improvised approach. Weather Report might represent a return to that approach, indicating that jazz has come full circle.

Orchestral Approaches

Although they did not entirely abandon collective approaches, much of Weather Report's work after their third LP, *Sweetnighter*, left collectively improvised approaches in favor of more orchestral techniques, in which repeated, prewritten themes and preset Latin American and rock rhythm section figures dominate the sound. (Weather Report's exploration of Latin American rhythms has been extremely fresh.) Their *Mysterious Traveler, Tale Spinnin',* and *Black Market* all contain careful mixing of prearranged material and jazz improvisation. Their creative use of both acoustically and electrically produced tone colors achieved as broad a scope as any non-symphonic style rooted in the jazz tradition.

Both Shorter and Zawinul seem attracted to the compositional style of impressionist composers Claude Debussy and Maurice Ravel. This is reflected in sustained tone melodies which seem to float by and conjure up pastoral scenes. Some notable examples occur in "Orange Lady" (*Weather Report*) where Shorter's soprano sax and the bowed bass of Vitous state the melody in unison, "Dr. Honoris Causa" (*Zawinul*) where the soprano sax states a serene melody in unison with flute and trumpet, and "Will" (*Sweetnighter*) where English horn and bass play the theme in unison over Latin American rhythms. Though their music is sometimes reminiscent of Debussy, Ravel, Vaughan Williams, Aaron Copland, or Morton Gould, Weather Report's creations are set off from the works of those classical composers by the complex layers of rhythm patterns underlying the melodic lines.

CHICK COREA   Chick Corea followed Herbie Hancock as pianist in the 1968 Miles Davis Quintet. Corea had previously worked with Willie Bobo, Blue Mitchell, Cal Tjader, Herbie Mann, Mongo Santamaria, and Stan Getz. Along with Hancock, Bill Evans, and McCoy Tyner, he became a leading pianist of the 1960s and 70s (see Figure 15.7).

The piano style created by Corea was an interesting blend of McCoy Tyner, Bud Powell, Bill Evans, and others. The mid-1960s recordings he made with Blue Mitchell (*Boss Horn, The Thing to Do*) show the influence of bop piano styles, which he might have absorbed from Powell and Horace Silver. His work with Mann (*Monday Night at the Village Gate*) and Tjader (*Soul Burst*) points up his use of Evans and Tyner as sources. He favored the voicing in fourths (see Figure 15.6) and flashy lines which typify Tyner. His composition "Litha" (Stan Getz—*The Chick Corea/Bill Evans Sessions*) uses

Figure 15.6. Piano keyboard illustration of a chord voiced in fourths.

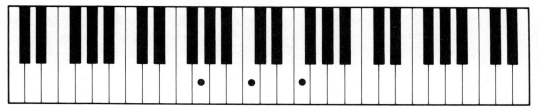

Figure 15.7. Chick Corea playing electric keyboards and wearing shirt with his group name: Return To Forever. *Warren Browne*

fourths in the melody line, and his left-hand comping on the album *Now He Sings, Now He Sobs* uses fourths. Corea may have absorbed ideas for the use of fourths from Horace Silver, also. Prior to 1959, Corea had studied Silver solos and compositions. In fact, he demonstrated a few typical Silver devices in his work on Blue Mitchell's album *The Thing to Do*. Corea also displayed Evans characteristics, having memorized some of Bill Evans's solos while developing his own style. The influence of Evans is most noticeable in Corea's work on the Stan Getz album *The Chick Corea/Bill Evans Sessions,* and in Corea's unaccompanied acoustic piano solos on his *Piano Improvisations Vols. 1 & 2* and *Where Have I Known You Before?*

Another prominent source from which he drew was Latin American music. Four of Corea's previous employers, Willie Bobo, Cal Tjader, Herbie Mann, and Mongo Santamaria, were quite fond of Latin American rhythms. Corea's playing, even in otherwise conventional modern jazz contexts, bears a distinctly double-time feeling, and that feeling is a prime characteristic of Latin American music. It is as though each beat is being subdivided over and over. Corea's crisp, percussive attack enhances the Latin feel. (The percussive aspect of his style may be related to the fact that he also plays drums.) He is very precise and even in his execution. Corea loves to play swift, multinoted lines. His comping is bright and very spirited. Corea does not pace his improvisations quite as well as Hancock or Evans, but is, by far, a match for the best hard bop pianists.

Chick Corea's piano style was a strong force during the 1970s. Hundreds of pianists admired his approach. Jan Hammer, Richard Beirach, and Masabumi Kikuchi were among those who exhibited his influence. But, as with Hancock, it is uncertain whether pianists sound like Corea because they have studied his work or because their styles stem from the same sources as his: Evans, Tyner, etc.

On and off between 1969 and 1972, Corea led a trio with bassist Dave Holland and drummer Barry Altschul (*A.R.C.*). In some situations they were joined by saxophonist Anthony Braxton, a player who brings an odd combination of Lee Konitz and Eric Dolphy to his work. With Braxton, the group was called Circle. They were heard more in Europe than in the United States. Braxton became a creative leader on his own during the 1970s.

Bassist **Dave Holland** has played with Miles Davis as well as Chick Corea's trio. He has an imagination which rivals Scott La Faro's, the firm foundation of Ron Carter's playing and a sweeping conception all his own. His playing exudes strength and confidence. His tone glows with a unique color and the vibrato he gives to each long note. Holland chooses notes with great care, yet seems not the least bit calculating. Naturalness is a pervasive feeling in his sound. He can take racing tempos and still swing and sound pretty. Ballads are a joy for his approach (*A.R.C.*).

After Circle disbanded, Corea formed a new group with bassist Stanley Clarke, Airto Moreira—a Brazilian drummer who had been with Miles Davis at the same time as Corea—and singer Flora Purim, Airto's wife. Airto had played auxiliary percussion with Davis and Weather Report, but he used a conventional drum set with Corea's new group. The group's sound was light and happy, full of Latin American rhythms and Spanish themes. It was a very energetic band, whose flashy technical feats impressed musician and non-musician alike. The group was called Return to Forever, also the title of their first album (*Return to Forever*). Their second LP was titled *Light as a Feather*. After Corea disbanded the group, he retained the Return to Forever group name.

The group Chick Corea carried through the middle 1970s was strongly influenced by rock, often displaying the insistent, machine-like sound of hard rock. In fact, he employed rock-influenced electric guitarists. The first was Bill Connors, then Al Dimeola took his place.

Corea retained bassist Stanley Clarke, now playing Fender electric bass guitar more than acoustic string bass. Drummer Lenny White rounded out the group. White's style was a very full, active approach which seemed to blend aspects of the Tony Williams techniques with those of modern rock drummers. He also had played with Miles Davis. Some of the group's material was orchestral, very involved, highly imaginative, slipping back and forth from rock to classical to jazz idioms (*No Mystery*). White and Dimeola left Corea during the summer of 1976. During 1977, Corea toured with a nine-piece band which, in addition to himself and bassist Stanley Clarke, included a vocalist-pianist, a drummer, two trumpeters, two trombonists, and saxophonist-flutist Joe Farrell. The Return to Forever group name was retained.

Like Wayne Shorter, Corea was an influential composer during the 1960s and 1970s. His style was quickly absorbed by many others. He liked the interval of a fourth which Shorter had used in his "E.S.P." and Eddie Harris in his "Freedom Jazz Dance." The interval of a fourth became as common in the construction of improvised lines as in voicing chords which accompanied the lines.

Voicing chords in fourths was especially appropriate for the electric piano. The overtones produced by an electric piano make chords voiced in the manner of bop pianists sound muddy. The open quality of voicing in fourths partly eliminates this problem and, to my ears, the fourth voicings actually sound better on electric than on acoustic piano (see Figure 15.7).

KEITH JARRETT   When Chick Corea left Miles Davis, pianist Keith Jarrett took his place. Like a few other Davis sidemen, Jarrett had also played with Art Blakey (1965 *Buttercorn Lady*). But Jarrett's widest pre-Davis exposure had come as a member of saxophonist Charles Lloyd's quartet beginning in 1966. In recordings with Lloyd, Jarrett had proven himself a powerful improviser paralleling Herbie Hancock and Chick Corea. Jarrett has as much or more command over the piano as they, but more importantly, he had his own distinctive approach. He was a piano original. Jarrett's playing demonstrated imagination of enormous scope. His sources were numerous and separated by wide gaps of idiom. Keith Jarrett seems able to draw from any musical idiom and incorporate its elements in a convincing way. To hear Jarrett play was to hear bits of Bill Evans, twentieth-century classical composers Béla Bartók, Alban Berg and Arnold Schoenberg, American gospel music, country music, and Ornette Coleman.

Like Herbie Hancock and Chick Corea, Jarrett is a prolific and quite original composer. He has written mounds of material for his own albums and contributed significantly to the records of Charles Lloyd and Norwegian saxophonist Jan Garbarek (*Belonging*). Some of

Figure 15.8. Keith Jarrett.

his albums contain extended performances with little or no improvisation; in these compositions the line between classical music and jazz is blurry.

Between 1970 and 1976, Jarrett, saxophonist Dewey Redman, bassist Charlie Haden, and drummer Paul Motian often performed and recorded as a quartet (*Backhand*). The group's sound reflected a combination of influences just as unusual as Jarrett's own piano style. Some of Jarrett's tunes sound like Ornette Coleman's, and both Redman and Haden were regulars in Coleman's groups. Drummer Paul Motian had been in the innovative Bill Evans trio with bassist Scott La Faro; however, Motian's playing was considerably more active with Jarrett.

During the 1970s, Jarrett made many albums and concert appearances as an unaccompanied solo pianist (*Facing You*). His improvisations were more spontaneous than those of most jazz pianists because he simply sat down at the piano and played whatever he felt like playing, rarely using prewritten melodies or preset chord progressions. His playing could be funky, earthy and gospelish, or pretty and orchestrally lush. Sometimes he clearly stated a tempo. Other times he implied only a momentum. He was one of the few jazz pianists who did not play electric piano.

Often Jarrett's lines project a singing quality (and sometimes you can hear Jarrett humming the lines as he plays them). These lines have the sweep of an inspired human voice or a surging saxophone improvisation. In fact, Jarrett plays soprano saxophone in many of his concerts. He is quite accomplished on sax. The long, legato sax lines he creates are mirrored by his long, legato, sax-like piano lines. (Chick Corea is far more crisp and percussive in his approach than Jarrett. Perhaps this is due to Corea's experience as a drummer, whereas Jarrett's preference for legato lines could be related to his saxophone playing.)

Though it is difficult to pin down his influence on other pianists, I am reminded of Jarrett's style when I listen to the playing of Art Lande (*Red Lanta,* with Jan Garbarek) and Richard Beirach (David Liebman's *Forgotten Fantasies*).

chapter 16
BIG BANDS & JAZZ EDUCATION IN THE 1960s & 1970s

STAN KENTON One of the few jazz names to become a household word after Louis Armstrong and Duke Ellington was Stan Kenton. That name, unlike Ellington's or Armstrong's, represented a huge number of different composers, arrangers, and soloists. Kenton's main contribution to jazz was his skill at public relations and organization. He himself was not particularly innovative as a jazz piano soloist or a composer, but he was very productive in the role of bandleader, talent scout, and contractor. His bands provided work for hundreds of musicians who may not have otherwise received much exposure. Though he started during the big band era in 1941, Kenton continued to lead when big bands were not in fashion—the post World War II years and into the 1970s.

Kenton's bands have a reputation for being the loudest of big bands, partly because of their preponderance of brass instruments. It is not unusual, for example, to have five trumpets and five trombones in a Kenton band, while Ellington had only four trumpets and three

TABLE 16.1. Big Bands of the 1960s and 70s

Stan Kenton	Gerald Wilson
Woody Herman	Count Basie
Maynard Ferguson	Duke Ellington
Buddy Rich	Gil Evans
Thad Jones—Mel Lewis	Sun Ra
Toshiko Akiyoshi—Lew Tabackin	Don Ellis
Gerry Mulligan	Kenny Clarke—Francy Boland

trombones. (Some Kenton bass trombonists have doubled on tuba.) One version of his band had a section of mellophoniums, brass instruments specially made for him which were a trumpet–French horn hybrid (*Adventures in Jazz*). Another had a French horn section.

Just as the general feeling of the Basie band can be described as easy swinging, the general feeling of the Kenton bands is massive power and intensity. Whether slow or fast, his pieces are usually massive sounding. Much of the book is solemn and weighty. Rich, modern harmonies are exposed vividly throughout the Kenton repertory. Two or three moving parts can often be heard simultaneously, one of which is occasionally improvised.

Although the ensemble emphasis is on brass, most of Kenton's best soloists have been saxophonists. Art Pepper, Charlie Mariano, Bud Shank, and Lee Konitz have played alto sax with him. (Konitz played a little over one year.) Another good alto saxophonist, Lennie Niehaus, contributed many arrangements to the band. One of Kenton's best composer-arrangers, Bill Holman, played tenor sax with him. Richie Kamuca, Vido Musso, Lucky Thompson, Bill Perkins, and Bob Cooper are some of Kenton's other good tenor soloists.

The sax section has occasionally been called upon to augment the band's massiveness, employing the unusual combination of two baritone saxophones. In many pieces, saxes play against brass and percussion and are swallowed in the resulting sound.

Though he has had good soloists, Kenton has not had a Johnny Hodges or a Lester Young (two of the many great soloists, employed by Ellington and Basie, respectively). Nor did Kenton's bands of the 1950s have soloists capable of the originality found in Thad Jones of the Basie band or Clifford Brown of the Hampton band. Few of Kenton's improvisers were strikingly innovative. The innovations Kenton was associated with were concepts of writing. (The list of Kenton arrangers includes Dee Barton, Bob Curnow, Russ Garcia, Robert Graettinger, Bill Holman, Bill Mathieu, Lennie Niehaus, Johnny Richards, Gene Roland, Pete Rugolo, and Bill Russo, as well as Kenton himself. For the recordings associated with each arranger, see Discography at the end of the text.) The Kenton bands have been for writers more than for soloists. In fact, some solo improvisations were not solos in the conventional sense, but embellishment of the ensemble sound. Muted trumpet noodling in the background is a trademark of certain Kenton ballad styles. Swallowing a soloist in ensemble sound is another Kenton characteristic (though not in ballads).

A few of the big names in the Kenton idiom are soloists. Trumpeters Conte Candoli and Marvin Stamm, trombonist Frank Rosolino, and saxophonists Boots Mussulli and Lee Konitz all improvised well (*New Concepts of Artistry in Rhythm*). But the biggest names in the Kenton idiom have been those of composers and arrangers, and

Kenton is one of the few leaders who properly credits his arrangers and gives them star billing on his album covers (for example, *Stan Kenton Conducts the Jazz Compositions of Dee Barton*).

Being an arranger's band, the Kenton ensemble performs a service to modern composers. Much of Kenton's music is ambitious twentieth-century classical music scored for trumpets, trombones, and saxophones, plus rhythm section. Some recordings additionally employ French horns, tuba, strings, and mellophoniums. The band's emphasis is more on elaborate arrangements than on the simple, swinging typified by Count Basie. The Basie band of the late 1930s was almost a "big combo" in the sense that solo improvisation was primary. The Kenton bands contrast markedly, sounding more like brass choirs than big jazz combos.

The big bands which remained on the road almost continuously throughout the 1950s were those of Ellington, Basie, Woody Herman, Lionel Hampton, and Harry James. Kenton rarely kept a single band intact for more than a few years, but was on the road more than any bands not contained in that small list. Ellington and Basie always had quite stable personnel. Herman, Hampton, and Kenton generally experienced high turnover in sidemen and tended to have much younger sidemen. Kenton's pattern was to go on tour, disband, get more new arrangements, promote another banner such as "Innovations in Modern Music," "New Concepts," or "Progressive Jazz," and form another band for eight to twelve months on the road again. Several sidemen reappeared in successive editions while hundreds of anonymous others filled the sections only briefly.

Stan Kenton tried to maintain a resident orchestra in Los Angeles from 1964 to 1967, commissioning new works and calling it the Los Angeles Neophonic Orchestra. During the 1970s, he launched a very ambitious project to put the means of production, advertising, and distribution of recordings into the hands of the musicians themselves. Kenton set up a mail-order record company. At first he simply repressed his old albums, bought from Capitol record company when it had refused to keep them on the market. Then he began making new records and marketing them himself (for list of Stan Kenton recordings, see Discography). His tours concentrated on promotion of "membership" in the enterprise he called Creative World. By 1973, they had a 100,000-name mailing list, a music publishing house which sold primarily to high school and college stage bands, and a promotional set-up that filled hundreds of auditoriums with new and old fans, auditoriums which were unable to break even with Ellington or Basie.

It should be noted that Kenton was neither the first nor the only jazz musician to run his own record company. Dizzy Gillespie started one in 1951 called Dee Gee. Charlie Mingus started his own Debut label in 1952. George Shearing, Denny Zeitlin, Sun Ra, Gene Perla,

Ahmad Jamal, Cecil Taylor, and others have tried to run their own companies. Strata-East was one of the most diverse musician-run companies of the 1970s, recording Charles Tolliver, Stanley Cowell, Frank Strozier, George Coleman, Sam Rivers, Clifford Jordan, Billy Harper, and others.

WOODY HERMAN

Woody Herman is one of those rare jazz musicians who has both good business sense and great skill at putting together all-star big bands. His band has not only survived the decline of big bands, but produced some of the better improvisers in a field otherwise dominated by Ellington and Basie musicians. Although a good clarinetist and alto saxophonist (a Johnny Hodges disciple), Herman's continuing contribution to jazz is a string of modern jazz big bands filled with topnotch improvisers playing lean, driving arrangements in a no-nonsense way.

Whereas Kenton and Maynard Ferguson find young sidemen who are simply good, Herman has had a knack for finding men almost the equal of those with Ellington and Basie. Like Kenton, though, he does have high turn-over of personnel. Also like Kenton, his best improvisers have been his saxophonists. In fact, Herman's sax section during the 1940s had some of the best disciples of Lester Young in jazz: Stan Getz, Herbie Steward, Zoot Sims, Al Cohn, and Gene Ammons. One of the great bop baritone saxophonists, Serge Chaloff, also played with him (*Early Autumn, Woody Herman's Greatest Hits*).

Instead of the five-man sax section (two altos, two tenors, and baritone) common to the Ellington and Basie bands, Herman uses four saxes (three tenors and baritone). Jimmy Giuffre wrote the piece "Four Brothers" for that original instrumentation, the "brothers" being Getz, Sims, Steward, and Chaloff. Some arrangements use Herman on alto, thus making a five-man section (alto, three tenors, and baritone). Until the early 1970s, when it gained several tenors with the Joe Henderson–John Coltrane sound, his four man sax section produced a distinctly light sound.

During the 1940s, trombonist **Bill Harris** was probably Herman's strongest brass soloist. Bill Harris is often thought to be a transitional figure in the development of modern jazz trombone, coming after J. C. Higginbotham and before J. J. Johnson. He had a broad, thick tone and quick vibrato which remained for the duration of each tone. Harris played with pronounced authority and employed good high range, by 1940s standards. Harris's solos made use of staccato, punching figures in addition to slides and smears. The construction of his solos was clearly thoughtful.

During the 1950s and 60s, much of the Herman band's quality was due to pianist-composer-arranger Nat Pierce. Although previously employing Shorty Rogers, Neal Hefti, Ralph Burns and Jimmy Giuffre, Herman was quite fortunate having Pierce on the road with him, providing and rehearsing new arrangements (see Chapter 9 for discussion of Giuffre and Rogers). A similar role was later filled by pianist-composer-arranger Alan Broadbent.

Herman has also had some of the best big band drummers in jazz: Dave Tough during the 1940s and Jake Hanna from 1962 to 1964. Jake Hanna is the drummer on Maynard Ferguson's classic recording of "Frame for the Blues," where his impeccably placed fills are responsible for much of the controlled tension in that performance.

The Four Brothers Band sound was distinctly Herman's and was retained into the 1950s. After that, Herman's band lost some of its uniqueness, but gained a versatility which Maynard Ferguson, Count Basie, or Stan Kenton lacked. Herman began recording tunes by composers as diverse as Horace Silver, Charlie Mingus, Henry Mancini, Herbie Hancock, Keith Jarrett, Chick Corea, and The Beatles. By 1968 the band was using rock-derived material and electric instruments. The Herman band became stylistically varied and remained that way in the 1970s. The Herman band of the early 1970s was as good or better than his great bands of the late 1940s. Pianist-arranger Alan Broadbent, saxophonists Frank Tiberi, Gregory Herbert, Steve Lederer, and a string of outstanding trumpeters and trombonists led many listeners to believe that, thirty years after "Woodchopper's Ball," he was leading his best band ever.

MAYNARD FERGUSON

Jazz has known many musicians with astonishing instrumental facility: pianist Art Tatum, bassist Jimmy Blanton, drummer Tony Williams, saxophonist John Coltrane, and others. Some of those men are also known for innovative concepts of improvisation, but spectacular facility is often talent enough.

Trumpeter Maynard Ferguson is known both as an astounding high-note artist and as a leader of several exciting post-bop bands. Maynard's almost freakish mastery of the trumpet extends throughout its entire range. No register is the least bit awkward for him. His facility takes him to B above double high C. What is even more important is that on most nights he does not simply squeal those incredibly high notes, but actually plays them with good intonation and large tone. Most big band high-note artists play few if any improvised solos, restricting their playing to trumpet-section lead work in order to keep their lips set specifically for those high parts. Maynard amazes brass players by not only playing high-register lead parts, but also improvising solos on nearly every tune. In addition to that, his endurance is as phenomenal as his range, and he can switch to trombone or French horn right in the middle of a piece, making an immediate adjustment to it. In fact, he is a master not only of the trumpet, but of all the brass instruments. He plays most of the reed instruments, too.

Although he had previously led his own bands and had played with Charlie Barnet, Maynard became better known as lead trumpet with Stan Kenton from 1950 to 1952, and as a leader of his own thirteen-piece band formed during 1957. Although his band was characterized by Kenton's emphasis on loud, flashy brass, it had a different feel: it swung. The band had a precise, hard-driving style that carried a lot of tension with it. Whereas Basie's effect is a subtle glow and Kenton's a massive brass choir, Ferguson's band was a happy fire, crackling away.

The 1957 to 65 Ferguson band had an instrumentation more compact than the usual big band (*Echoes of an Era, Maynard '62*). Instead of a sax section containing two altos, two tenors, and a baritone, his had an alto, two tenors, and a baritone. They tended to have a biting sound which was almost brassy. Rather than the usual three to five trombones, Maynard had only two. His thirteen piece band had a tight, polished sound that was filled with raw excitement. It seemed to thrive on fast tempos and loud playing; it had few slow or subdued arrangements.

Unlike Kenton, Maynard gave his sidemen plenty of unhindered solo time. Few of those sidemen became important after leaving Maynard, but many continued to play in road bands and do studio work. Among the exceptions are: trumpeter-composer-arranger Don Ellis, who formed his own musically successful big bands; reedman Joe Farrell, who later played with several leading modern combos of the late 1960s and early 70s; Pepper Adams, one of the few jazz baritone saxophone soloists; and Wayne Shorter, who became prominent with the combos of Art Blakey, Miles Davis, and Weather Report.

Many written arrangements came from within the Ferguson band. Trombonist Slide Hampton wrote "Frame for the Blues," a dramatic arrangement of well-paced bluesy figures. Trombonist Don Sebesky's arrangement of "Maria" was a gorgeous feature for Maynard's ballad style (*Maynard '62*). Sebesky later achieved recognition writing accompaniments for guitarist Wes Montgomery and alto saxophonist Paul Desmond at A & M Records during the 1960s and 70s. But some of his best work has been for a wide variety of soloists at C.T.I. Records: Freddie Hubbard, Hubert Laws, Milt Jackson, and others. Two sidemen-arrangers who were not with Maynard for long, but became prominent jazz figures, are pianist Joe Zawinul and trombonist Billy Byers. Zawinul later wrote for Cannonball Adderly and Miles Davis, and then formed his own group, Weather Report. Byers wrote all the arrangements for several Count Basie albums.

During the mid-1960s, Maynard was forced to disband. Then during the early 1970s, he formed a new band in England which made several albums of showy, rock-tinged material. Some of their pop tune arrangements, "MacArthur Park," for example, became popular with a.m. radio disc jockeys, a portion of the media usually unfriendly to jazz. Although several old arrangements were reworked for it ("L-Dopa," "Airegin," "Got the Spirit," and "Maria"), and it bore the Ferguson stamp of high energy, bright tone colors, and lack of solemness, his new band was different. Much of its book was like good, show band writing which was superimposed over rock rhythms. Instrumentation for that band started out with four trumpets, three trombones, alto, two tenors, and baritone saxophone, but later cut down to four trumpets (plus Ferguson), two trombones, one alto, one tenor, and one baritone saxophone. Like the 1957 to 65 band, Maynard's early 70s band gained a wide audience, especially with people who were otherwise non-jazz listeners.

THAD JONES—
MEL LEWIS

Despite the large audience acquired by Kenton, Herman, and Ferguson, many listeners considered the best big band of the 1970s to be the one co-led by trumpeter Thad Jones and drummer Mel Lewis. Though the band toured, it was not a road band in the fifty weeks per year sense that Kenton's, Herman's, or Ferguson's was. The Jones–Lewis band depended heavily on free-lance jazz musicians living in New York. For over ten years, most Monday nights found the band at the small New York night club called the Village Vanguard.

At various times since its formation in 1965, the Jones–Lewis band has had better soloists than Kenton, Herman, or Feguson had at the same time. Many players featured by Jones and Lewis are very strong, well-established jazz musicians, such as saxophonists Joe Farrell, Eddie Daniels, Lew Tabackin, Billy Harper, Frank Foster, Jerome Richardson and Pepper Adams, pianists Roland Hanna, Hank Jones, and Walter Norris, bassists Richard Davis and George Mraz, trombonists Jimmy Knepper and Bob Brookmeyer, and, of course, the leaders themselves, Jones and Lewis. Both are considered among the very highest rank in their respective styles.

The Jones–Lewis band was one of the first big bands after the Basie group of the 1930s both to achieve a flexible interaction between improvising soloist and rhythm section and to offer plenty of uncluttered solo space. During certain moments in a performance the Jones–Lewis band sounds like an up-to-date, modern jazz combo, indistinguishable from the quality combos of its period. This poses a striking contrast to the sound of the Kenton, Herman, and Ferguson bands. Those are rooted in earlier styles and usually characterized by both short solos and screaming ensemble figures which regularly engulf the improvising soloists who are trying to play sensitively and be heard.

A large portion of the Jones–Lewis arrangements represent the most distinctly original big band approach of the 1970s. Thad Jones had written provocative scores for Basie during the 1950s and in the Jones–Lewis band has expanded greatly upon many of the concepts exhibited in that earlier work (*Central Park North, New Life, Presenting Thad Jones–Mel Lewis and the Jazz Orchestra, Thad Jones–Mel Lewis*). In addition, Jones had impressed fans of the Mingus and Basie groups of the 1950s with his improvisational originality. He continued to invent intriguingly unpredictable lines as a soloist in his own band.

JAZZ EDUCATION AND THE BIG BANDS

Prior to the 1950s, jazz musicians had been forced to learn their craft by trial and error, reading the few technical articles jazz magazines provided, talking with older musicians, and studying classical music. Except for a few rare jazz musicians who had the skill necessary to teach selected young players privately, there was no formal jazz education. During the 1940s, formal education began for jazz musicians and jazz-oriented players and arrangers. Since 1942, Gene Hall had been teaching big band arranging at North Texas State College in Denton, Texas. In 1947, what had been a casually run dance band became a "dance band laboratory." This term was eventually shortened to lab band, a label adopted by many college jazz groups. Hall went to Michigan State University to teach in 1959. Michigan State became one of the best places for a college student to play jazz (others are Illinois, Indiana, and Denver). Leon Breeden took over Gene Hall's job at North Texas State, and built the program to the size of twelve complete big bands, in addition to courses in arranging and improvisation. Until 1967, North Texas State was the only college offering a jazz major (though it was actually called "Dance Band" in the course catalog).

Two schools have been devoted almost exclusively to jazz and jazz arranging—the now defunct Westlake College in Los Angeles and the still active Berklee School of Music in Boston. Berklee was started in 1945 by Lawrence Berk, who combined Berk and his son's name, Lee, into Berklee. It offers a four-year college program, and includes instruction in instrumental proficiency, improvisation, combo playing, big band playing, and arranging. And for years, Berklee has also offered an excellent correspondence course in big band arranging.

The late 1950s and early 1960s saw the growth of jazz ensembles in high schools and colleges. School dance bands had been common for decades, but these new groups were run primarily for listening and for the benefit of their participants. The most common label assumed by these thirteen-to-nineteen-piece jazz ensembles was "stage band." At the beginning of the 1960s, there were approximately five thousand high-school stage bands. By the 1970s, jazz ensembles were also appearing in junior high schools, and some colleges had more than one band.

Stage bands of the 1960s and 70s emphasized ensemble playing more than improvising. They were more like swinging concert bands than jazz groups. In most bands, only two or three members were given room for extended improvisation. Improvisation was not discouraged, but neither was it made very convenient. The skills of ensemble playing were taught, but improvisation instruction was often a low priority, usually not getting taught at all. Learning tunes, chord changes, and how to improvise with them was done outside of school, sometimes in rock bands, sometimes in combos which played for wedding receptions, dances, and parties.

A great opportunity for members of school stage bands was the chance to attend a summer clinic. These clinics offered teaching and playing sessions held on college campuses and were usually run by professional jazz musicians. Stan Kenton ran clinics which employed Kenton and his band members as teaching staff. (You can well imagine how exciting an experience that must have been for a very young musician.) Eventually, the clinics were run year-round and were brought directly to schools instead of requiring students to meet at a central location. Instruction books and teaching methods were developed so that a school band director could help his students improvise even if he did not improvise himself.

Since 1959, Stan Kenton has been a prime mover in the attempt to bring jazz to formal music education. He and Gene Hall helped establish summer band clinics held on college campuses. And they opened them to students regardless of age. The sessions were originally known as the National Stage Band clinics (later some were called the Kenton clinics). Kenton also donated large portions of his band library to North Texas State University. Thousands of young musicians who have never heard of Lester Young or Charlie Parker, know Kenton quite well.

Portions of most Kenton tours are devoted to clinics followed by an evening concert. The entire Kenton band becomes artist-in-residence at high schools and colleges. The practices of Kenton's educational campaign have been copied by many other professionals, mostly in big band formats. Don Ellis, Maynard Ferguson, and Woody Herman all have large followings among young stage band musicians. Due to the consolidation of music educators and jazz musicians during the 1970s, more jazz was being played in the nonprofit high schools and colleges than in such traditional, profit-motivated settings as night clubs, concert halls, and ballrooms.

A Very Abbreviated Outline of Jazz Styles—Not strictly chronological; many styles overlap the same time periods.

	Hornmen	Pianists	Composers-Arrangers	Rhythm Section Musicians
Early Jazz	Louis Armstrong Sidney Bechet Bix Beiderbecke	James P. Johnson Earl Hines	Jelly Roll Morton W.C. Handy	Baby Dodds Zutty Singleton Pops Foster
Swing	Coleman Hawkins Roy Eldridge Johnny Hodges Benny Carter	Art Tatum Teddy Wilson	Duke Ellington Fletcher Henderson Sy Oliver	Chick Webb Cozy Cole Sid Catlett Walter Page Israel Crosby Gene Krupa
Transition to Bop	Lester Young Don Byas	Nat Cole		Count Basie Rhythm Section 1937–43 Jimmy Blanton
Bop	Charlie Parker Dizzy Gillespie Dexter Gordon Stan Getz	Thelonious Monk Bud Powell Al Haig	Thelonious Monk Tadd Dameron John Lewis	Kenny Clarke Max Roach Oscar Pettiford
Transition to Cool & West Coast	Lee Konitz Miles Davis	Lennie Tristano	Claude Thornhill Gil Evans	
West Coast	Gerry Mulligan Chet Baker Art Pepper	Dave Brubeck	Gerry Mulligan Shorty Rogers Bill Holman	Chico Hamilton
Hard Bop	Clifford Brown Sonny Rollins Thad Jones John Coltrane Cannonball Adderly Miles Davis	Tommy Flanagan Horace Silver Red Garland	Horace Silver Benny Golson Cannonball Adderly Jackie McLean Oliver Nelson Gigi Gryce	Art Blakey Philly Joe Jones Paul Chambers Sam Jones Wilbur Ware
Later Styles	Ornette Coleman Albert Ayler John Coltrane	Bill Evans McCoy Tyner Cecil Taylor	Charles Mingus Sun Ra Wayne Shorter	Bill Evans Trio with Scott LaFaro John Coltrane Rhythm Section 1961–65

	Hornmen	Pianists	Composers-Arrangers	Rhythm Section Musicians
Later Styles	Eric Dolphy Miles Davis Wayne Shorter Don Cherry Joe Henderson Anthony Braxton Freddie Hubbard	Herbie Hancock Chick Corea Keith Jarrett	Ornette Coleman Cecil Taylor Herbie Hancock Chick Corea Keith Jarrett John Coltrane McCoy Tyner Joe Zawinul Carla Bley	Miles Davis Rhythm Section 1963–68 Sunny Murray Airto Moreira Jack DeJohnette

PART V

appendix

chapter 17
ELEMENTS OF MUSIC

In describing the nature of jazz and the characteristics of different styles, several basic musical terms are quite helpful. This chapter is devoted to defining some of these terms, and I urge all readers, including those who are musically knowledgeable, to examine them carefully.

When people think of jazz, they usually think of rhythm first. But because the word rhythm is often used to describe a large variety of musical characteristics, some uses convey inaccurate or contradictory meanings. Much of the confusion can be avoided by first understanding three related terms for which rhythm is often mistaken: beat, tempo, and meter.

Beat   Music is often said to have a pulse. The unit of pulse is called a beat. When you tap your foot to music, you are usually tapping with the beat. Here is a visualization of the pulse sequences we call beats.

Tempo   Tempo refers to the speed or rate at which the beats pass. If you describe a piece of music as fast, you probably mean it has a rapid tempo, not that it occupies a short time span. When the beats continue at a regular rate, we say the tempo is constant. A clock's ticking is a good example of constant tempo. If the passage of beats is rapid, the speed is called up tempo. Medium tempo means medium fast; down tempo means slow.

Meter The beats in music are rarely undifferentiated. They are usually heard as being grouped. Meter describes the type of grouping. Our perception of grouping results when sequences of beats are set off from each other. This occurs in several ways. Every third or fourth beat may be louder or longer than the others. It may be distinctive because it has a different pitch or tone quality. Those differences are perceived as emphasis or accent. If we hear a sequence of beats grouped in fours, it may be due to a pattern of accents which creates this effect: **ONE** two three four **ONE** two three four. That pattern represents a meter which musicians simply call "four."

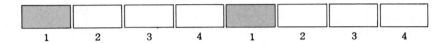

If the beats fall into the pattern, **ONE** two three, **ONE** two three, **ONE** two three, musicians say that the music "is in three" or in waltz time.

Meters of four and three are quite common, but there are also meters of five, six, seven, and others. A meter of five might sound like **ONE** two three four five **ONE** two three four five, **ONE** two three four five, with a large accent on the first beat and no other accents. Or there may be a strong accent on the first beat and a smaller accent on the fourth: **ONE** two three FOUR five **ONE** two three FOUR five **ONE** two three FOUR five; or a smaller accent on the third beat: **ONE** two THREE four five **ONE** two THREE four five **ONE** two THREE four five. A meter of six usually feels like **ONE** two three FOUR five six **ONE** two three FOUR five six.

Each group of beats is called a **measure**. When the meter is three, there are three beats in a measure; when the meter is four there are four beats in a measure.

Rhythm In the broadest sense, rhythm simply refers to the arrangement of sounds in time, and therefore encompasses beat, tempo, and meter. But rhythm has come to mean something more specific than these features. In fact, beat, tempo, and meter furnish the framework in which rhythm is described.

Imagine a continuous sequence of beats occurring at a constant tempo, with four beats to a measure. The steady beat which in musical notation is represented by a string of quarter notes can also be visualized as a series of boxes, representing equal amounts of time. Our meter would be called "four." Each beat is called a quarter note, and each unit of four beats constitutes a measure.

The sound within a measure can be distributed in an infinite number of ways, one of which includes "filling" the measure with silence. Rhythm is the description of how that measure or a sequence of measures is filled with sound.

Let us take a few examples, numbering the four parts of the measure one, two, three, and four, respectively. We shall create rhythms by using a single sound mixed with silence. First, divide a measure into four equal parts, filling only the first and third with sound.

We have a rhythm. It is not complex, but it does what a rhythm is supposed to do: it describes the distribution of sound over time. In fact, this is the bass drum part in numerous marches, and it is the string bass part in many slow dance pieces.

Now, instead of taking just one measure, take two measures as a unit of repetition. In other words, the rhythm is two measures long.

Finally, repeat a one measure rhythm to fill two measures worth of time. This might be heard as a two measure rhythm or as two one measure rhythms.

Rhythm is the distribution of sound over time, but rhythm also refers to the way sounds are accented. Usually, the first beat of a measure is accented. An example would be the typical OOM pah pah accompaniment for a waltz. In a measure of four, the first and third beats are often accented, as in the BOOM chick BOOM chick drum pattern used in much popular music.

Examining our use of accents can lend understanding to a rhythmic element called *syncopation,* a crucial aspect of jazz feeling. For example, if we expect to hear a sound on every beat but only hear it in a few odd places, the upset we feel is the result of syncopation. This upset can be very stimulating and contribute a prime component of jazz feeling.

Examine this manner of filling two measures.

Note that the sounds which occur, bordered by silence, in positions other than on the first and third beats seem to stand out. They seem to be self accenting. If we additionally stress these odd positions by making the sounds in those positions louder than the sounds in other positions, syncopation is enhanced: one TWO three four ONE two three FOUR.

The concept of syncopation partly depends on a listener's expectations. For example, if we are expecting to hear *ONE* two THREE four, but we actually hear one *TWO* three FOUR, we are experiencing syncopation. Jazz drummers often keep time by playing boom CHICK boom CHICK (one TWO three FOUR) instead of BOOM chick BOOM chick. This syncopation is part of what makes a performance sound like jazz. Another frequently used syncopation occurs when we hear one two three FOUR when we are expecting to hear ONE two three four. So you see that rhythm involves the arrangement of stresses in addition to just describing the arrangement of sound over time. We have also seen that a phenomenon called syncopation results when the sounds are arranged or stressed in unexpected ways. Of course, what is expected depends on what the listener is accustomed to hearing. Therefore the statement that syncopation consists of unexpected accent is inadequate. Perhaps a more useful definition involves the accent of beats other than the first and, in measure of four beats, also the third beat. Silence can also be syncopating. For example, if we encounter silence at a time when we are expecting to hear ONE, the feeling of syncopation results.

To understand more complex syncopations and another essential element of jazz feeling, the swing eighth note, requires an acquaintance with ways in which beats are divided into smaller units. Here is a measure in four, with four quarter notes to the measure. We can divide each quarter note in half to produce eighth notes.

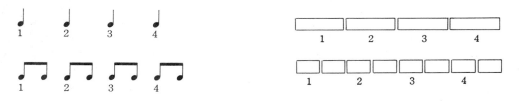

There are two eighth notes for every quarter note. If we place accents on the eighth notes according to the way we previously accented the measure of quarter notes, we have *ONE* two three four

FIVE six seven eight. The time span for a measure of eight eighth notes is identical to that in a measure of four quarter notes, but keeping track of eight eighth notes is cumbersome. So we express the eighth notes in terms of subdivided quarter notes, saying "and" for the second half of each quarter note (every other eighth note): one and two and three and four and. Each word, whether it is the name of a number or the word "and," represents an eighth note.

Syncopation occurs when any of the "and's" receives more emphasis than the numbered units. Accenting the "and's" is essential to rhythms frequently employed in jazz. The final two beats in a measure are often divided into eighth notes with the last one accented the most: three and four AND (for notations of this and other syncopations, see Chapter 18). Many notes which appear in written form on the first beat of a measure are played on the and of the fourth beat in the preceding measure when given a jazz interpretation. The practice of playing a note slightly before or slightly after it is supposed to be played is a syncopating device which jazz musicians apply to pop tunes in order to lend jazz feeling to a performance.

The quarter note can also be divided into three equal parts to produce what are called eighth-note triplets.

Here, each quarter note is divided into four equal parts, called sixteenth notes.

So far we have examined equal divisions of the quarter note. But it is also possible to divide it into notes of unequal value, for instance, a long note and a short note. One such pattern consists of a dotted eighth note followed by a sixteenth note. A dot after a note means that the note receives one and a half times its usual value; therefore the dotted eighth note has the combined value of an eighth note and a sixteenth note.

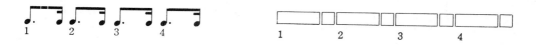

Another long-short pattern is based on the triplet division of the quarter note. The pattern is called a tied triplet figure. Here, the first note has the value of two-thirds of a quarter note, and the second has the value of one-third.

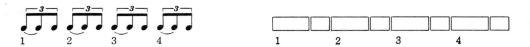

Jazz has one rhythmic quality which, to my knowledge, is not found in any other kind of music: jazz swing feeling. A discussion of it appears in the "What Is Jazz?" chapter, but that discussion hinges on the swing eighth note which is examined next.

Having heard the term swing eighth note, you might wonder how, if an eighth note is simply half the duration of a quarter note, we can have different types of eighth note, swing eighth note being one of them. Strictly speaking, you cannot have different types. An eighth note is an eighth note. Our descriptive language is loose enough, however, that we can use the term to label notes of slightly more or less duration than the eighth note is understood to receive.

This looseness in applying the term eighth note is not exclusive to jazz musicians. Non-jazz musicians often use terms such as legato and staccato which mean long, slurred together, connected and short, abruptly separated, respectively. A legato eighth note equals a full value eighth note as conceived in the preceding discussion. A staccato eighth note, on the other hand, has variable duration depending upon the style of the performance, and it may actually last less than half the duration of a full value eighth note. It can be called an eighth note only because it is immediately followed by silence which fills up the remaining time a full value eighth note requires. Actually it should be called a sixteenth note, or it should have a durational label which is more precise than that of staccato eighth note.

Quarter notes

Eighth notes

Eighth note triplets

Tied eighth note triplet figures

Dotted eighth— sixteenth note figures

So you see that a legato eighth note is equivalent to half a quarter note, a dotted eighth note is equivalent to one and a half eighth notes, a staccato eighth note represents less than a full value eighth note, and a tied triplet eighth note has two thirds the value of a quarter note.

Now that you understand several types of eighth notes, you might accept the claim that strings of eighth notes can be played in several different ways. Prior to the late 1920s influence of trumpeter Louis Armstrong, jazz musicians subdivided the beat into eighth notes and dotted eighth-sixteenth figures. But Louis Armstrong and his followers developed a more flexible and swinging approach to rhythm. Their solos might fluctuate between straight eighth notes, dotted eighth-sixteenth note figures, and the swing eighth note figures discussed next.

The long-short, tied triplet figure helps describe swing eighth note figures. Where the short member of a tied triplet figure receives the most accent (dark portion), we have a sequence resembling the swing eighth note sequence.

Tied triplet figures accented

The second member of the swing eighth note figure is shorter than the second member of the tied triplet, but it is longer than the second member of the dotted eighth-sixteenth note figure. In other words, the notes in swing eighth note sequences are uneven in emphasis as well as duration: dooo BE dooo BE dooo BE dooo BE.

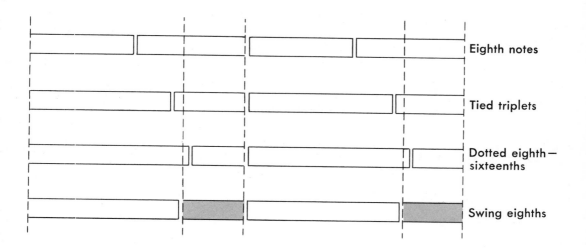

Eighth notes

Tied triplets

Dotted eighth—sixteenths

Swing eighths

An important aspect of jazz rhythmic feeling is the tendency for melodic lines to consist primarily of connected notes instead of brief, separated ones. This is called legato style. Most swing eighth notes are played in a legato manner. When staccato notes are used, they provide contrast.

It is important to remember that the concept of the swing eighth note is not a hard and fast one like that of the quarter note or the triplet. The swing eighth note is subject to lengthening and shortening relative to a player's style. Duration and loudness vary not only according to style, but also according to the feeling of the player at the moment of performance. Even the name swing eighth note lacks standard use among musicians. In fact, much of what is called a swing eighth sequence is often simply a sequence of triplet eighth note figures with accents on the short members, or it is only a sequence of legato eighth notes with accents on the "and's." What some would call a sequence of swing eighth notes, others call a shuffle rhythm, and for some people what is called a shuffle rhythm is definitely not a sequence of swing eighth notes. (In notating jazz, swing eighth notes are usually indicated by simple eighth note patterns; it would be almost impossible to put down on paper all the rhythmic nuances which are described by the term swing eighth note.)

Swing eighths as notated

Not all jazz musicians use swing eighth notes exclusively. Most mix them with straight eighth notes and dotted eighth-sixteenth note figures. And, the faster they are played, the more swing eighth notes sound like straight eighth notes.

To appreciate the rhythms which typify jazz, we should keep in mind the fact that several rhythms are usually played simultaneously. *Polyrhythm* (meaning *many rhythms*) is very important to jazz. When you listen carefully to a modern jazz performance, you should be able to hear several different rhythms at the same time. These include the rhythm in the melodic line, that of the bassist, the rhythm played by each of the drummer's four limbs, and each of the pianist's two hands.

Polyrhythms are often created by patterns which pit a feeling of four against a feeling of three. In other words, two measures can be played at the same time, with one being divided by multiples of two and the other being divided by multiples of three. In addition to that, the onset of one pattern is often staggered in a way which results in something less than perfect superimposition atop another pattern. Pitting three against four and staggering the placement of rhythms can project the feeling that the rhythms are tugging at each other. The resulting combination of stresses can be extremely provocative, and it can produce new syncopations in addition to those already contained in the separate patterns.

You can now understand why to say that jazz is quite rhythmic is to make an almost meaningless statement. All music has rhythm, and most music has syncopated rhythms. What sets jazz apart from many other types of music is the preponderance of syncopated rhythms, the swing eighth note sequences, and the constant presence of polyrhythm.

SCALES, KEYS, TONALITY, AND MODALITY

Understanding scales is basic to appreciating chord progressions, and an acquaintance with scales and chord progressions aids our knowledge of the rules which guide jazz improvisation. Everyone is familiar with musical scales. No one has been able to live very long without hearing a friend, neighbor, or family member practice "his scales."

Scales comprise the rudiments of beginning practice routines for singers and instrumentalists alike. Even people who cannot read music are familiar with the sequence *do* (pronounced dough), *re* (pronounced ray), *mi* (pronounced mee), *fa, sol, la, ti* (pronounced tee), *do*. Those eight syllables do not represent exact pitches as C, D, E, F, G, A, B, C; they are only the names of acoustic relationships. (Do not let that term, acoustic relationships, scare you. It is one of the simplest concepts in music. It means only that no matter what frequency of so many vibrations per second is assigned to *do*, the remaining seven pitches are determined by set multiples of it, for example twice the frequency, 1½ the frequency, and so forth.)

"*Do re mi fa sol la ti do*" numbers eight elements, the eighth element carrying the same name as the first, *do*. Its relationship to the first is exactly double the frequency of the first. For example, if the first *do* were 440 vibrations per second, the next higher *do* would be 880. It is no more complicated than that. That last *do* ends one sequence and begins another. The relationship between the bottom *do* and the top *do*, the first and eighth steps of the scale, is called an *octave*. The sound of two notes an octave apart is so similar that if they are played simultaneously, you can easily mistake the pair for a single tone. Most naturally produced tones contain an octave as one component of all the frequencies that combine to give a tone its own characteristic color or quality. The octave is called a harmonic or an overtone of the tone's fundamental pitch. That is the reason two tones an octave apart sound like one when they are played at the same time.

Since the interval of an eighth, from *do* to *do,* represents a doubling of frequency, you have probably guessed that those intervals between the first and the eighth must be fractions. You guessed correctly. The ratio of the fifth step (*sol*) to the first step (*do*) is $\frac{3}{2}$, that of the third (*mi*) to the first (*do*) is $\frac{5}{4}$, etc.

The seven note scale has many labeling systems. We have already used three of them: a) do, re, mi, fa, sol, la, ti, do; b) first, second, third, fourth, fifth, sixth, seventh; and c) the frequency ratios: re/do $= \frac{9}{8}$; mi/do $= \frac{5}{4}$; fa/do $= \frac{4}{3}$; sol/do $= \frac{3}{2}$; la/do $= \frac{5}{3}$; ti/do $= \frac{15}{8}$. Next is the system which uses alphabet letters A, B, C, D, E, F and G.

Look at the diagram of the piano keyboard printed here.

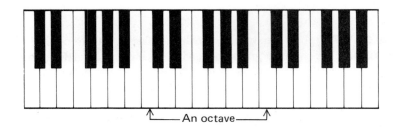

It is constructed so that the pattern of eight white keys and five black keys recurs again and again. The distance, or interval, between the beginning of one pattern and the beginning of the next is called an octave. The scale which beginners usually learn first is the C scale; the C scale is obtained by playing eight of the white keys in succession, starting with the one labeled C. That scale, C, D, E, F, G, A, B, C, contains the same note relationships which we know as do, re, mi, fa, sol, la ti, do. Play the notes of the C major scale in the order in which they are numbered in the diagram.

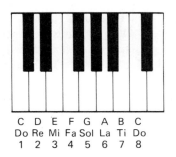

Look again at the piano keyboard.

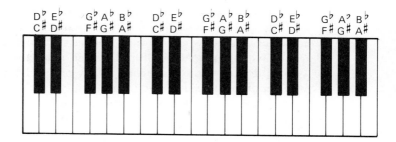

The black keys are known as sharps and flats. Sharp is symbolized ♯ (like the number sign on a typewriter) and flat is symbolized ♭ (like the lower case b on the typewriter). The black keys derive their names from the white keys which are next to them. The black key to the right of A is called A-sharp because it is slightly higher than A. But it is also referred to as B-flat because it is slightly lower than B. If we want only a C scale, going up an octave from C to C, we use none of the black keys. But if we want scales which begin on any note other than C, we have to employ at least one (and sometimes all) of the black keys. For instance, to play a major scale on D, it is necessary to make use of two sharps, F-sharp and C-sharp.

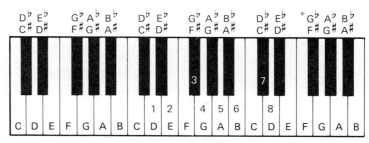

D major scale

A scale may be played starting from any black or white key. Altogether there are twelve such scales. Going up (moving left to right) from C, they are the scales of C, C-sharp, D, D-sharp, E, F, F-sharp, G, G-sharp, A, A-sharp, and B. Or, naming them in descending order, C, B, B-flat, A, A-flat, G, G-flat, F, E, E-flat, D, and D-flat.

When musicians say that a tune is in a certain key, for instance, the key of C, they mean that the song is played with the notes of the major scale beginning on C.

The relationship of the notes of the major scale gives a song a particular kind of sound and structure which is called **tonality.** Although tonality is a complicated idea, it can be understood as the feeling that a song must end on a particular note or chord. A key defines a scale which, in turn, defines that key. If a piece of music has the feeling of reaching for the same note, the key note, or it seems loyal to some note more than to any other, the overall harmonic character of the piece is called *tonal*.

There is another term interchangeable with scale but not interchangeable with key. The term is **mode.** Like a scale, a mode describes a sequence of acoustic relationships. Some modes even have the same number of elements as the scales we just explored. In fact, the C scale has a mode name: Ionian. But if we use the notes in the C scale and start the sequence on D, we produce another mode, Dorian. In other words, if we go from D to D in the key of C, we have constructed the Dorian mode.

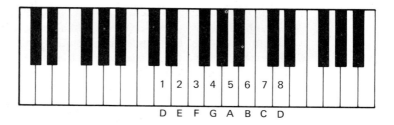

For each of the seven scale steps in a key, there is a corresponding mode. The major scale itself has a mode name: Ionian; beginning on the second step produces the Dorian mode; the third step, the Phrygian mode; fourth, the Lydian mode; fifth, the Mixolydian mode; sixth, the Aeolian mode; and seventh, the Locrian mode. Each has different sound because each has a different sequence of acoustic relationships which results from starting on different steps of the scale. I urge you to find a keyboard and play these modes. The concepts outlined here mean little without the sounds they describe.

We have seen that there are twelve keys, C, C♯ (or D♭), D and so forth. We also know that for each key there is a corresponding seven note scale starting on the note which bears the name of the key (C D E F G A B for the C scale). Within each key there are modes, one mode beginning on each of the seven steps. The mode constitutes an octave of its own. Scales (modes) of fewer than seven notes and greater than seven notes also exist (see Chapter 18). The most common scale constructed of more than seven notes is the *chromatic,* simply that sequence of all the piano keys in an octave, white ones and black ones. Scale is a poor name because the chromatic scale is actually just another way of dividing an octave into twelve equal parts. It does not indicate a key as the C scale and the B♭ scale do. The chromatic scale is only a sequence of very small intervals called half steps.

The chromatic scale has twelve steps: C, C♯ D, D♯ E, F, F♯, G, G♯, A, A♯ and B. Unlike the modes, which have to be started on certain scale steps to guarantee their unique qualities, the chromatic scale can be started on any note, proceed through an octave and create the same identifiable chromatic quality no matter what note is chosen for its starting position. That means the C chromatic scale is identical to the C♯ chromatic scale (and all others). Perhaps it should be called "chromatic scale starting on C" or "chromatic scale starting on C♯," specifying exactly what tone is to be the reference note.

The chromatic scale is very important because it expands the number of acoustic relations possible. Given twelve different tones in place of only seven, we have the option of raising and lowering (sharping and flatting) virtually any note we wish. Most Western European music of the past two centuries uses the chromatic scale instead of limiting itself exclusively to notes within one key at a time or, what is even more restrictive, only one mode at a time. Music was produced during the twentieth century which used all twelve tones equally and discarded the feeling of particular keys. Tonal music, you remember, is simply music which seems to be loyal to a certain note, always reaching for that note. Music without tone center is called *atonal*.

Most music has key feeling even when employing all twelve tones in the chromatic scale. This is just another way of saying that most music has tonality. During improvised music, tone centers might shift, but they usually remain long enough for their effect to be perceived. Most jazz employs tone center. It is extremely difficult to improvise without at least implying temporary tone centers and key feelings. The twelve tones are usually employed to enrich the conventional do re mi tonal orientation instead of providing a harmonic orientation all their own, one of atonality. Keep in mind that some music employs more than one key at once, but this type of music is not generally termed atonal. It is called *polytonal* which means many keys.

If you play within the do re mi scale and enrich your melody with chromatic tones, the character of your playing can be partly described by how often you employ certain chromatic tones. Many people consider *bluesy quality* essential to jazz. A central component of bluesy quality is the frequent use of chromatics, three chromatics in particular: the *flat third, flat fifth* and *flat seventh* notes of the scale. In other words, chromatic scale tones are employed to enrich the seven tones already available.

In the key of C, the blue notes are E-flat, G-flat, and B-flat. Remember the C scale consists of C, D, E, F, G, A, and B; there are no sharps or flats (none of the piano's black keys). To create a blue note we lower the third step of the scale. In the key of C this means changing E (a white key) to E-flat (a black key). We use both E *and*

E-flat in constructing jazz lines, but the E-flat stands out because it is not one of the notes in the C major scale.

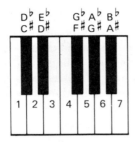

C scale without any blue notes

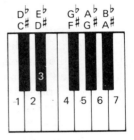

C scale with the flat third blue note

The second most common blue note is achieved by lowering the seventh step of the scale. In the key of C, this means changing B (a white key) to B-flat (a black key). Again we use both B *and* B-flat for our lines, but the B-flat is more distinctive because it is not in the key of C.

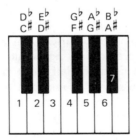

C scale with the flat seventh blue note (B-flat)

Note that the concepts of regular third step and blue third step are like the concepts of major chord and minor chord (the sounds of which you can demonstrate for yourself, using the following keyboard diagram as a guide to positioning your first, third, and fifth fingers).

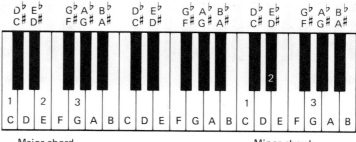

Major chord   Minor chord

The third most used blue note is the lowered fifth. Its use was not frequent until modern jazz began in the 1940s, but thereafter it became a standard device to convey a bluesy feeling, much as the lowered third and seventh had been in early jazz. In the key of C, a flat fifth is achieved by lowering G (a white key) to G-flat (a black key).

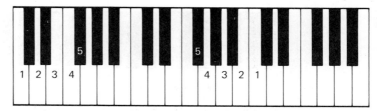

Going up to the flat fifth (G-flat)   Coming down to the flat fifth (G-flat)

CHORDS AND CHORD PROGRESSIONS

Familiarity with the concept of scales allows us to explore the concept of chords and chord progressions, which, in turn, is essential to appreciating the harmony that jazz improvisers follow. These concepts are quite simple, but they have far-reaching applications, not only in jazz, but in all music which uses harmony.

A chord is obtained by sounding three or more notes simultaneously. It does not matter what notes are chosen. Any notes will do. Try these:

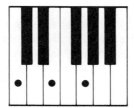

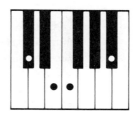

299

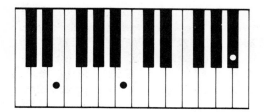 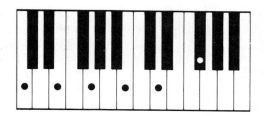

Although chords can be constructed from any tones, they are usually described in terms of scale notes and given Roman numeral names. The most common chord, one alternately described as a tonic chord, a major triad, the key chord, or a I (Roman numeral for 1) chord, employs the first, third, and fifth notes of the scale: *do, mi,* and *sol.* In other words, this chord is produced by simultaneously sounding do, mi, and sol in any key, any register, with any loudness or tone color.

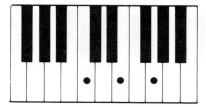

I chord in key of C

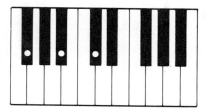

I chord in key of F-sharp

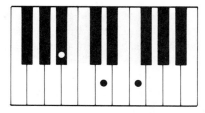

I chord in key of B-flat

Chords are named for the scale step on which they are based. A I chord is based on the first step of the scale, do; a II chord is based on the second step, re; a III chord on the third step, mi; a IV chord on fa; a V chord on sol; a VI chord on la; and a VII chord on ti. This system of naming is very handy for describing chord progressions (see Chapter 18 for notations of chord progressions).

A chord change is simply what it says, changing a chord. If we move from one chord to another, we have executed a **chord change.** We have moved forward, progressed, from one chord to another. In other words, **a chord progression** has been made. If the chords involved are those based on the first and second steps of the scale, respectively, we could describe the chord change as a I-II progression. If we move from a chord based on the first step to a chord based on the fourth, we create a I-IV progression. The reverse of that is a IV-I. If we move from the I chord to the V chord, and then back to the I chord, we create a I-V-I progression.

To hear the sound of a very common chord progression, the I-IV-I-V-I blues progression, find a piano, an organ, an accordion, or any other keyboard instrument and strike all the keys simultaneously, the number of counts (1234, 2234, etc.) indicated in the diagram on page 302. You need not worry about what fingers to place on what keys. In fact, go ahead and use fingers from both hands if necessary. Try to keep a steady rate for striking the keys. If you can keep a steady rate, you may find that you are sounding like you have heard pianists and guitarists in rhythm and blues bands sound.

Chord Voicing Most music uses chords which have been **voiced.** (For notated examples see Chapter 18). The concept of voicing is a very simple concept. It involves the fact that the keyboard is a succession of repeating octaves.

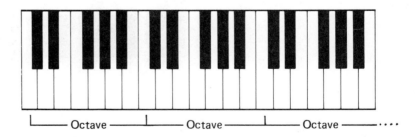

With the resulting repetition of notes available, we can pull each chord note away from the position it holds within a single octave and spread the chord over the range of the keyboard. We can also include additional notes and/or omit some of the original notes. All these manipulations fall under the heading of voicing.

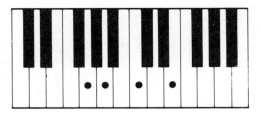

1234 2234 3234 4234 (I chord for 4 measures)

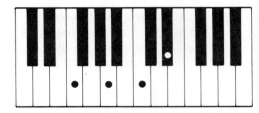

1234 2234 (IV chord for 2 measures)

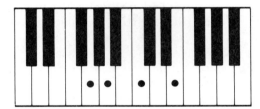

1234 2234 (I chord for 2 measures)

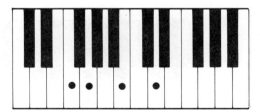

1234 2234 (V chord for 2 measures)

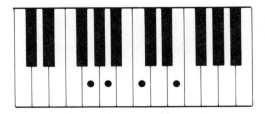

1234 2234 (I chord for 2 measures)

The same chord (three notes) arranged in different positions across the keyboard.

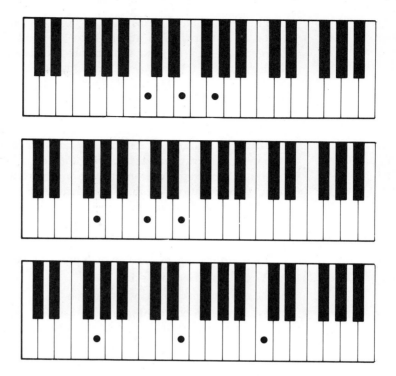

Jazz pianists can often be identified by the way they voice chords, and characteristic preferences in piano voicing are important components of the style in almost every period of jazz. In recent jazz, for example in the work of pianists McCoy Tyner and Chick Corea, **voicing in fourths** is quite common. Voicing in fourths means that chords are made up of notes four steps away from each other. In other words, a chord voiced in fourths might contain do, fa and ti instead of do, mi and sol. (The interval between do and fa is called a perfect fourth. To create a perfect fourth between fa and ti, the ti must be flatted. In building a chord composed of perfect fourths, each successive note is considered do of a new scale and the fourth note, fa, in that scale is used.) You can hear the sound of a chord voiced in fourths by playing this:

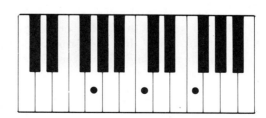

The term voicing also refers to how the notes of a chord are assigned to instruments in an orchestra or band. The ranges of the instruments as well as their tone colors are taken into consideration in voicing chords. Characteristic voicings serve to identify the work of different arrangers. Duke Ellington, for instance, voices chords in a manner distinguishable from Stan Kenton. Both Ellington's chords and his choice of instruments differ.

Voicing is also a term used to identify the instruments playing a melody. For example, we might say Duke Ellington voiced the lead (the melody) for clarinet, trumpet, and tenor sax, meaning that those instruments played a unison passage in a particular Ellington arrangement. Orchestration, scoring, and arranging are terms used synonymously. Voicing is an important aspect of all three.

The Blues   The term "the blues" has several meanings. It can describe

1) a sad feeling, or music which projects a sad feeling;
2) a rhymed poetic form;
3) a slow, funky, earthy type of music;
4) a type of chord progression, usually contained in twelve measures, which has certain predictable chord movements in the fifth, seventh, ninth, and eleventh measures;
5) any combination of the above.

Blues poetry is so common in popular music, that a technical description of the positions of accent and rhyme is not necessary in order for you to recognize the form. A single, very characteristic example, can serve to illustrate the structure of blues poetry:

> My man don't love me, treats me awful mean. (pause)
> My man don't love me, treats me awful mean. (pause)
> He is the lowest man I've ever seen.   (pause)

The I, IV, and V chords are basic elements of harmony used in the blues. In the twelve-bar blues, which is the most common blues form, these chords are distributed over twelve measures in a particular way. Although many variations are possible, the basic form is always the same. The chords and their respective durations are shown in the following chart. Each slash (/) indicates one beat. Perhaps it is helpful for you to think of a chord played on each beat by a rhythm guitarist. Note that the principal chord changes occur in the fifth, seventh, ninth and eleventh measures.

I   IV   I   V   I
//// //// //// //// //// //// //// //// //// //// //// ////

Although the chord relationships of the fifth, seventh, ninth, and eleventh measures usually hold, the remaining measures are the scene of countless alterations. Modern jazz blues progressions often employ more than one chord in a single measure and at least one change every measure. It is not unusual to have ten to twenty chord changes in the space of twelve measures. Sometimes the principal chords of the fifth, seventh, ninth, and eleventh measures are also altered (see Chapter 18 for typical modern jazz blues progressions). When the blues is sung, the words are often distributed in a standard way over the twelve-bar progression (Figure 17.1).

A blues can be fast or slow, happy or sad. It may have lyrics or it may be a purely instrumental piece, and its chord progressions may be simple or complex. For a piece to be a blues, the only requirement is that the I-IV-I-V-I chord progression or a variant of it be presented in a twelve-measure form.

The Thirty-Two Bar AABA Tune

Another form on which jazz musicians often improvise is the thirty-two-bar AABA tune. The thirty-two bar tune is made up of four eight-measure sections. The opening eight measures, called the A section, is repeated in the second section. The third part is the B section, sometimes referred to as the bridge, release, inside, or channel. The last eight bars bring back the material of the first eight. So the tune falls into what is called AABA form. Thousands of pop tunes composed during the 1920s, 30s, 40s, and 50s were thirty-two bars long in AABA form.

Listening for the Twelve Bar Blues and Thirty Two Bar Forms

To gain a practical familiarity with chord progressions, glance at the list of tunes in Table 17.1. These are categorized as twelve-bar blues or thirty-two-bar tunes in AABA form. Go to a record collection and find performances of tunes on the list, and choose one of them. Listen to approximately the first thirty seconds to determine whether this rendition has an introduction or begins immediately with the tune itself. Also determine how fast the beats are passing. A clue can often be found in the bass playing. If the bass is walking, there is a bass note for every beat, four beats to the measure. Listening to that sound, you should be able to hear the pulse as though the bassist were a metronome. The sound of the drummer's ride cymbal may also be a good indication of where the beats lie (see Table 17.1).

Having listened long enough to determine the tempo, you will also have discovered whether or not there is an introduction, and the point at which it ends and the tune begins. If you are not sure whether the beginning of the piece is an introduction or part of the tune itself, wait a while and listen for it to recur. If it does not recur it is probably an

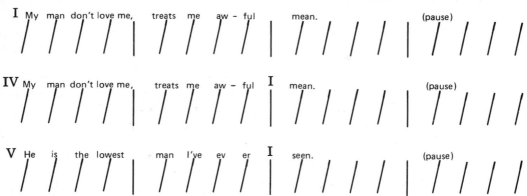

I My man don't love me, treats me aw-ful mean. (pause)

IV My man don't love me, treats me aw-ful **I** mean. (pause)

V He is the lowest man I've ev-er **I** seen. (pause)

Figure 17.1. Blues poetic form in relation to the 12-bar blues chord progression. The lyrics shown are from Billie Holiday's "Fine and Mellow." Copyright: *Edward B. Marks Music Corporation. Used by permission. Photo courtesy of Bettmann Archive.*

TABLE 17.1. Compositions in Twelve-Bar Blues and Thirty-Two Bar A-A-B-A Forms

Twelve-Bar Blues Compositions

"Bags' Groove"
"Barbados"
"Billie's Bounce"
"Bloomdido"
"Bluesology"
"Blue Monk"
"Blues in the Closet"
"Blue 'n' Boogie"
"Blue Trane"
"Cheryl"
"Cool Blues"
"Cousin Mary"

"Footprints"
"Freddie the Freeloader"
"Goodbye Porkpie Hat"
"Jumpin' with Symphony Sid"
"Mr. P. C."
"Now's the Time"
"One O'Clock Jump"
"Sid's Ahead"
"Soft Winds"
"Straight, No Chaser"
"Walkin' "
"Woodchopper's Ball"

Compositions with Thirty-Two Bar A-A-B-A Construction

"Ain't Misbehavin' "
"Angel Eyes"
"Anthropology"
"Birth of the Blues"
"Blue Moon"
"Body and Soul"
"Budo" ("Hallucinations")
"Darn That Dream"
"Don't Blame Me"
"Don't Get Around Much Anymore"
"Easy Living"
"52nd Street Theme"
"Flamingo"
"Four Brothers"
"Good Bait"
"Have You Met Miss Jones"
"I Can't Get Started"
"I Cover the Waterfront"
"I Love You"
"I'm Beginning to See the Light"
"It's Only a Paper Moon"
"I Want to Talk About You"
"Jordu"

"Lady Be Good"
"Lover Man"
"Lullaby of Birdland"
"Makin' Whoopee"
"The Man I Love"
"Midnight Sun"
"Misty"
"The More I See You"
"Moten Swing"
"Move"
"Oleo"
"Over the Rainbow"
"Perdido"
"Robin's Nest"
"Rosetta"
" 'Round Midnight"
"Ruby, My Dear"
"Satin Doll"
"September Song"
"Take the 'A' Train"
"Well, You Needn't"
"What's New?"
"What Is This Thing Called Love?"

introduction. In AABA form the first part, A, is immediately repeated, AA, before a new section, B, occurs. The routine for most twelve-bar blues tunes consists of repeating the entire twelve bars before beginning improvisation. Musicians occasionally use the same music for an ending that they used for the introduction. So if you hear something familiar at the end which does not seem to fit exactly in twelve or thirty-two bars, it may be the introduction attached for use as an ending.

By now you should know both the tempo at which to count beats and the moment to begin counting. Start when the tune itself starts (right after the introduction, in most cases). For a twelve-bar blues count: "1234, 2234, 3234, 4234, 5234, 6234, 7234, 8234, 9234, 10 234, 11 234, 12 234." Listen and count until you can detect the chord changes in measures five, seven, nine, and eleven:

$$^I //// \mid //// \mid //// \mid //// \mid ^{IV} //// \mid //// \mid ^I //// \mid //// \mid ^V //// \mid$$
$$//// \mid ^I //// \mid //// \mid$$

If your counting is accurate, you will eventually be able to anticipate these important chord changes. That should provide some insight into harmonies that the jazz musician uses in his improvisation.

Count like this for a thirty-two-bar AABA tune:

	"1234, 2234, 3234, 4234, 5234, 6234, 7234, 8234,
repeat	234, 2234, 3234, 4234, 5234, 6234, 7234, 8234,
bridge	234, 2234, 3234, 4234, 5234, 6234, 7234, 8234,
back to A	234, 2234, 3234, 4234, 5234, 6234, 7234, 8234."

Listen and count over and over until you cannot only hear the bridge and the repeated sections, A-A, when they occur, but anticipate them. Do not become discouraged if you find it necessary to start and stop many times. Counting beats and measures requires practice. It is very important because it may be your only clue to the tune's form once a soloist has begun improvising. Learning to count accurately may take a few minutes, a few hours, or even a few days, but it is essential to an understanding of jazz improvisation. It will be well worth the effort. You might get especially good at anticipating the B section. If you know the tune, or can learn it by listening a few times, try humming it while listening to the soloists improvise on its chord changes. This will help clarify the relationship between the improvisation and the original tune. It will also help you keep your place.

Not all tunes fit into the twelve-bar blues form or the thirty-two-bar AABA form. "I'll Remember April" is a forty-eight-bar ABCDAB form. "I've Got You Under My Skin" is a fifty-six-bar ABACDEF form. Together, the twelve-bar blues form and the thirty-two-bar AABA form probably describe more tunes than any other single form, but they actually describe less than forty percent of all tunes written between 1910 and 1960. Let us examine a few other forms.

The twelve-bar blues is a particular set of chord progressions (I-IV-I-V-I) in a twelve measure package. There are twelve-bar forms which are not blues simply because they do not follow the I-IV-I-V-I progression or any variation of it. For example, Richard Rodgers' "Little Girl Blue" is an AAB form in which each section is twelve bars long, but it is not a blues. It is also not uncommon in pop tunes to find a twelve-bar section which is actually an eight-bar progression with an extra four-bar progression connected to it.

The word "blues" in a song title does not necessarily signify the twelve-bar blues form. Both musicians and nonmusicians use the term "blues" to describe any slow, sad tune regardless of its chord progression. "Birth of the Blues" is a thirty-two bar AABA tune and "Sugar Blues" is an eighteen-bar tune. The "St. Louis Blues" is actually a twelve-bar blues plus an eight-bar bridge and an additional twelve-bar blues. Performers sometimes choose to repeat, delete, and reorder sections of "St. Louis Blues" when they play it.

Some people use the terms "eight-bar blues" and "sixteen-bar blues." Usually the tune they are describing has the I-IV movement in the first five bars and deviates from the twelve-bar I-IV-I-V-I progression thereafter. Some tunes of lengths other than twelve bars sound very much like twelve-bar blues simply because they contain the I-IV-I-V-I progression, but the durations of a few chords may be changed, and certain sections may be repeated. Herbie Hancock's "Watermelon Man," for example, has been called a "sixteen-bar blues."

Unlike the twelve-bar blues the thirty-two bar AABA form is not always based on the same basic chord progression. Many different chord progressions have been used in the AABA form. Fats Waller's "Honeysuckle Rose" and Erroll Garner's "Misty" are both thirty-two-bar AABA tunes, yet they have almost completely different chord progressions.

The form AABA does not always contain thirty-two bars nor does each section necessarily have the same number of measures. In "Girl from Ipanema," which is AABA, the A section has eight bars while the bridge has sixteen. In "Secret Love," another AABA tune, the A section has sixteen bars while the bridge has only eight.

There are also elongated versions of the basic twelve-bar blues and thirty-two-bar AABA forms. Lee Morgan's "Sidewinder" is a twenty-four-bar blues: each chord lasts twice as long as it would in a twelve-bar blues. Another example is the sixty-four-bar AABA form in which each section is sixteen bars long instead of eight. Ray Noble's "Cherokee" and Lerner and Loewe's "On the Street Where You Live" are both sixty-four bar AABA tunes. Charlie Parker's "Ko Ko," is based on the chord changes of "Cherokee"; consequently it is also a sixty-four-bar AABA tune. There are shortened versions of the thirty-two-bar AABA, too. Sonny Rollins's "Doxy" is a sixteen-bar AABA tune; each section is only four bars long.

AABA is not the only common thirty-two bar form for pop tunes. Numerous tunes fit an ABAC form (both the C section and the B section differ from the A section). "My Romance," "On Green Dolphin Street," "Indiana," "Sweet Georgia Brown," and "Out of Nowhere" all fall into a thirty-two bar ABAC form. In addition to the thirty-two bar AABA and ABAC, there is also the thirty-two bar ABAB. "How High the Moon" is an example. There are shortened versions of these, also. "Summertime" is a sixteen-bar ABAC tune. "Autumn Leaves" is a sixteen-bar AABC tune. Each section is four bars long in those tunes.

Hundreds of tunes fit into sixteen measures. "Peg o' My Heart" is a sixteen-bar pop tune. Horace Silver based his "The Preacher" on the sixteen-bar pop tune "Show Me the Way to Go Home." Wayne Shorter has written many sixteen-bar tunes, including "E.S.P.," "Nefertiti," "Prince of Darkness," etc. Some chord progressions are used in sixteen-bar tunes almost as often as the I-IV-I-V-I progression appears in the twelve-bar blues. Certain sixteen-bar progressions have become standard.

Verse and Chorus. It is important to note that the forms we have been examining refer only to chorus length. A large number of tunes consist of two major parts, a verse followed by a chorus. The verse traditionally differs from the chorus in tempo, mood, and harmony:

1) The chorus might be played at a faster tempo than the verse.
2) Verses are often performed freely, with accelerations and decelerations of tempo.
3) The verse might feel as though it is leading up to something, whereas the chorus usually has the stamp of finality to it.
4) There may be little similarity between chord progressions used in the verse and those in the chorus.
5) The key of the verse is sometimes different from that of the chorus.
6) Choruses are repeated, but once a verse is played, it is usually over for the entire performance.
7) The chorus is the section of the tune jazz musicians usually choose as basis for improvisation.

Breaking into Multiples of Two. When you are listening to performances and trying to detect forms, be aware that arrangements of thirty-two-bar AABA, ABAC, and ABAB tunes sometimes depart from strict repetition of those thirty-two bars. Arrangements sometimes contain four-, eight-, and sixteen-bar sections, formed by omitting or adding to portions of the original thirty-two-bar tune. Note also that many tunes, especially pre-1930s Dixieland tunes, have long, elaborate forms similar to those of marches and of nineteenth-century European dance music (such as the quadrille). Forms for many tunes in pre-1920s jazz were derived from march music. A piece might have a series of sections consisting of multiples of eight bars. Designating each section by a letter of the alphabet, a piece might conceivably follow a pattern like this:

$$A-A-B-B-C-D-E-F-C-D-E-F$$
$$16-16-16-16-16-16-24-32-16-16-24-32.$$

When listening for form, keep in mind that even in the most intricate pieces, forms can usually be broken down into two-bar segments. So if you are unable to divide a piece neatly into either four-bar or eight-bar sections, try using a few two-bar sections. "Sugar Blues" can be heard as 18 or as 8+10 or as 8+8+2. That form poses problems for the improviser because it tends to break the flow of ideas conceived in four- and eight-bar melodic units. It is like being forced to walk left, right, left, right, left, left, right. The form of the original "I Got Rhythm" is

$$A - A - B - A + tag$$
$$8 - 8 - 8 - 8 + 2 \text{ or}$$
$$8 - 8 - 8 - 10.$$

When jazz musicians improvise on its chord progression, they omit the two-bar tag. If included, the tag would interrupt the flow of the improvisations and again be like having to take two steps with your left foot before going back to an alternation of right with left. Another popular tune that has an unusual structure is "Moonlight In Vermont." It follows the form:

$$A - A - B - A + tag$$
$$6 - 6 - 8 - 6 + 2.$$

Modal Forms   During the late 1950s and especially during the 60s and 70s, modal forms practically eliminated the "change" part of "chord change." In modal music, improvisations are based on the extended repetition of one or two chords. Those chords contain so many notes that they either include or are compatible with all the notes in a scale. The term mode is synonymous with scale, hence the term "modal music." Although this is not the definition of modal employed by classical composers and in textbooks on classical music, it is what jazz musicians and jazz journalists have come to mean by "modal" (see Chapter 18 for further discussion of modes). In most instances, jazz musicians also employ notes which are not contained in the mode or in the repeated chords. Some of John Coltrane's work, for example, is not strictly modal, but has the flavor of music which is.

In modal music the entire improvised portion of the performance is often based on a single chord and scale. Usually the chord and its scale are minor, Indian, Middle Eastern, or in some way more exotic-sounding than the chords used in most pop tune progressions. Because it is based on a single scale, the music has no real chord changes, just a drone.

Sometimes a melody containing chord changes of its own precedes the improvised section of a modal performance. John Coltrane's recordings of the Rodgers and Hammerstein tune "My Favorite Things" are a good example. Coltrane played the original melody while his rhythm section played the appropriate chord changes. Then the entire group improvised only on the primary chord of the tune (and of course, the scale compatible with that chord). Near the end of their improvisations, they switched to another chord, which lent the piece a slightly different character. Coltrane could have retained the chord progressions of the tune and used them as the basis for improvisation, but he chose not to.

Some modal music does have chord changes, or "mode changes." One rich chord (or scale, depending on how one cares to conceive it) is the basis for four, eight, or perhaps sixteen measures. Then a different chord is in effect for another similar duration. The Miles Davis tune "Milestones" is based on one mode for the first sixteen bars, a different mode for the second sixteen bars, and returns to the original mode for the final eight bars. The melody has the form AABBA, and each section is eight bars long. Herbie Hancock's "Maiden Voyage" has a thirty-two bar AABA construction; here each mode lasts for four bars. The A section is based on two different modes, each lasting only four bars. The B section makes use of another two modes also lasting four bars each. If each mode were labeled by letter name, "Maiden Voyage" could be described as X-Y-X-Y-Z-W-X-Y. "So What" (on the Miles Davis album *Kind of Blue*) has a melody in thirty-two bar AABA form, and the use of modes corresponds to that form: there are sixteen bars of one mode, eight of another, and a return to the original mode for the last eight bars. John Coltrane's "Impressions" not only takes the same form as "So What" but also uses exactly the same modes. (See Chapter 18 for the modes used in "Milestones," "Maiden Voyage," and "So What.")

Much jazz of the 1960s and 70s was based on infrequent chord changes (another way of saying modal) instead of the frequent chord changes found in most twelve-bar blues and thirty-two-bar forms. Many groups abandoned both the blues form and the thirty-two-bar forms. Some groups used complex melodies and intricate rhythm section figures, yet their improvisations were based almost exclusively on one or a small number of chords ("Freedom Jazz Dance," for example).

The Effects of Form on Improvisation

Song forms of four and eight bar sections tend to break improvisations into small segments of similar length. Divisions of form, in other words, can influence the flow of improvised lines. This is not necessarily a disadvantage, however. The divisions in form can frame well-chosen melodic figures, and they can provide a means of transition from one figure to another. This creates more continuity than a solo might contain without chord progressions. Forms based on single modes sounding indefinitely tend to free the improviser, enabling him to create lines that are as long or short, tense or relaxed as he desires. No preset tension-relaxation devices in the form of chord progressions are there to suggest construction patterns for his improvised lines.

Bridges. The B section of an AABA tune is called the bridge. It bridges the gap between repetition of A sections, and it usually provides a contrast to the material in the A sections. The bridge can break up or lift the mood established by repeated A sections. Many bridges are placed a few keys higher than the A section. A key change can be a boost in any situation, but is especially effective after the repeated A sections.

The bridge is important to improvisers because a good improviser can capitalize on the bridge's natural capacity to provide contrast. Some of the greatest solo segments in jazz are those improvised over the chord progressions of a tune's bridge. The rhythm section also takes advantage of the bridge and is often especially active just before the bridge is entered and just before it is exited. Heightened rhythmic activity can announce the arrival or departure of the bridge.

Combos often use the bridge as a container for solo spots. Sometimes a tune's melody will be played for the final time in the performance, and when the bridge occurs, everyone stops playing except the drummer. It becomes his feature. Then the entire band returns precisely on the first beat of the final A section.

In some jazz tunes the bridge consists only of chord changes. Such pieces require improvisation during the bridge but return to the written melody when the final A section is reached. Sonny Rollins's tune "Oleo" is an example. Many groups also use that approach on "The

Theme," a popular up-tempo number for jazz combos of the late 1950s and early 60s.

Turnarounds. Another important part in the construction of standard tunes is the turnaround (also known as the turnabout or turnback). In many, perhaps in most songs, the seventh and eighth measures of each section are occupied by a single sustained tone or two long tones (see Figure 17.2). That part of the tune might be considered dead space due to the lack of melodic movement, but the jazz musician uses that space. (See Chapter 18 for common turnaround chord progressions.) He fills it with chord changes which lead directly to the beginning of the next section. Jazz musicians are expected to know a variety of chord progressions common to turnarounds. The manner in which they fill that space with chord changes and improvised lines is the art of the turnaround.

The whole combo digs in when a turnaround comes up. Drummers tend to kick more and, thus, tie together the musical statements of one section and bring in the next. Those bassists who almost invariably walk are more likely to vary this pattern in a turnaround. Tension can be built during a turnaround and resolved by the onset of the next section of the piece.

Phrasing in Relation to Form

Jazz musicians prior to the mid-1940s tended to improvise phrases which coincided with the tune structure. Most progressions consist of two- and four-bar units, and improvised solos often proceeded in phrases of similar length. Furthermore, soloists tended to make larger silences at or near the end of an A section or B section. They rarely connected tune sections by continuing phrases through the turnarounds. They stopped at or before the turnarounds, and then started anew at the beginning of the next section. They treated the eighth bar line as a barrier. Twelve-bar blues solos often contained phrases which started at the beginning of each chorus regardless of what happened at the end of a previous chorus, thus treating the twelfth bar line as a barrier.

One characteristic of modern jazz (beginning in the 1940s) and the music of the players who most influenced it, was the use of phrases which began somewhere within an eight-bar section and continued into the next section without a pause. There was no lull during the turnaround.

A characteristic of some modern jazz during the 1960s and 70s was the absence of preset chord progressions. That free approach significantly loosened the tendencies of jazz phrasing. Although players retained patterns common to preceding jazz eras, they were free to phrase with greater variety due to the lack of underlying chord movements. Some jazz of this type projects a feeling of expansiveness quite unlike the crowded feeling often projected by modern jazz of the 1940s and 50s.

Some tunes which appeared during the 1960s, especially those of Wayne Shorter, were sixteen or more bars without any repeated sections. The A section was not repeated, there was no bridge, no turnaround. These tunes were "all A." That form enabled improvisers to play with great continuity yet without the crowded, segmented feeling which sometimes characterizes improvisations based on standard AABA and ABAC forms with the usual turnarounds and bridges. Sometimes a free, floating feeling could be projected by improvisers using these "all A" forms.

TONE COLOR An important element of music, usually the first to be perceived, is tone quality or tone color. The term tone *color* is preferable because quality can imply that a tone is good or bad. But because musical beauty is a subjective perception, the term quality is less appropriate

Figure 17.2. Turnarounds in 32-bar A-A-B-A and 12-bar blues.

In 32-bar A-A-B-A form:

A ———————	A ———————	B ———————	A ———————
8 ———————	8 ———————	8 ———————	8 ———————
turnaround	turnaround		turnaround
6 + 2 ———————	6 + 2 ———————	8 ———————	6 + 2 ———————

In 12-bar blues form:

——————— 12 ———————	12 ———————	12 ———————
turnaround		turnaround
——————— 10 + 2 ———————	10 + 2 ———————	10 + 2 ———————

than that of color, a neutral term. This element is also known as timbre (pronounced tamm'burr).

How can you tell the difference between the sound of a flute and the sound of a trumpet if they each play only one note, and it is the same note? The difference is tone color. What is tone color? It is traditionally defined as the spectrum of frequencies generated by each instrument in its own unique way.

This definition is an oversimplification of a complex situation in which many factors come into play.

The spectrum of frequencies produced by an instrument is not fixed. The spectrum varies depending on the pitch and the forcefulness with which it is played. The ways in which a player starts and stops a note, the attack and release, also are important in determining tone color. The attack and release are accompanied by temporary changes in a tone's frequency spectrum.

Another complication arises from our tendency to associate an instrument's tone color with the aggregate effects of all the notes being played on it rather than the spectrum of frequencies present in a single note.

Finally, when sounds come to our ears, they are modified by room acoustics and by recording and playback techniques. The way our ears deal with that variability is quite involved.

Tone color varies greatly from one instrument to another, and there are also especially discernible differences in tone color among jazz musicians playing the same instrument. For example, to speak of the tenor sax tone color of John Coltrane or Stan Getz is to describe sounds so unique that some inexperienced listeners could differentiate them as easily as they could distinguish flute from trumpet. The evolution of jazz tenor saxophone playing reflects not only changes in the phrasing and rhythms, but also changes in tone color.

Tone color is a very personal characteristic of a player's style. Jazz musicians place great emphasis on creating the particular tone colors they want. A jazz musician's attention to tone color is comparable to an actor's concern for costume, make-up, and voice quality combined. Tone color is so important to saxophonists that many spend lifetimes searching for the perfect mouthpiece. They also experiment with different methods of blowing and different ways of altering the vibrating surface of the cane reeds that are attached to their mouthpieces.

Because the tenor saxophone is capable of producing an exceptionally wide variety of tone colors, it is easier to differentiate jazz tenor saxophonists by tone color alone than it is to recognize a particular trumpeter or pianist. That is not to say that differences are absent from trumpeter to trumpeter or from pianist to pianist. The differences are just more subtle.

Two pianists can play the same piece on the same piano and produce quite different sounds. No two pianos have the same tone color, and one piano can produce distinctly different tone colors, depending on how hard the keys are struck. The use of the pedals and a pianist's timing in releasing one key and striking the next are crucial to the sound. A key may be released before, after, or at the same time as the next is struck. When a note is short and ends well before the next note begins, we call it a staccato note. If one key is released after the next is struck, the two sounds overlap in time. Notes played smoothly one after the other are said to be legato. The amount of overlap influences the clarity of attack and the dimension of legato-staccato. Our ears hear sounds in combined form rather than as single tones. Whatever is left in the air from a preceding sound mixes and colors the subsequent sound. The relationship between consecutive sounds, ranging from complete separation to extreme overlapping, are resources which contribute to the personal character of a pianist's style. Count Basie's touch and tone color differ remarkably from Duke Ellington's. Perhaps you will perceive Basie's touch as lighter than Ellington's. No matter how you describe the sound, you will notice a difference if you listen carefully.

Guitarists' interest in tone color is manifested by their search for different types of picks, guitar strings, and amplifiers. Guitar amplifier dial settings are essential to the control of tone color. Bass players are also concerned with many of the same factors.

Trumpeters and trombonists explore available tone colors by experimenting with mouthpiece changes, methods of blowing, mutes, and instruments which represent different manufacturers and models (see Figure 17.3).

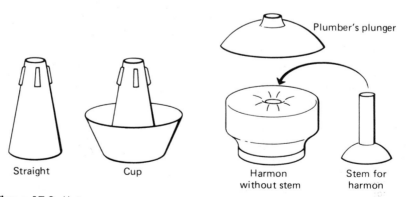

Figure 17.3. Mutes.

Another aspect of tone is **vibrato.** Vibrato is simply a repeating fluctuation of a tone's pitch. The tone of most singers, violinists, saxophonists, trumpeters, and trombonists does not remain at a constant pitch. The controlled changes of pitch constitute vibrato.

To understand vibrato, imagine a sustained tone as a straight line.

Now imagine the pitch of that tone oscillating, that is, becoming alternately higher and lower. The up and down motion of the line represents the slight changes in pitch which constitute vibrato.  We often tend to take vibrato for granted, because it can be almost imperceptible. But if you listen carefully to sustained tones in the work of most singers, violinists, saxophonists, trombonists, and trumpeters, you will hear it.

Vibrato can be present or absent, fast or slow, regular or irregular. Jazz players tend to start vibrato slowly and then increase its rate so that it is fastest at the end of the note.

Musicians in symphony orchestras tend to maintain an even rate of vibrato through a tone's complete duration. They employ different rates of vibrato for different styles of composition, however.

Vibrato is considered an expressive device. It can also be a prime characteristic for differentiating styles. Early jazz players tended to use much quicker vibratos than modern jazz players. The fast vibrato was undoubtedly a characteristic contributing to the popular description of early jazz as "hot," while modern jazz with its slower vibrato was "cool." During the 1960s and 70s, many jazz saxophonists employed faster vibrato than was common during the 1940s and 50s. If you compare music from these periods, you will notice a strong difference in feeling, part of which is due to the quickened vibrato rate.

Intonation is also an important aspect of tone. Intonation refers to playing in tune, playing sharp or flat. Playing sharp means playing at a pitch level somewhat higher than the average pitch of the ensemble. Playing flat refers to playing a pitch somewhat lower than that of the ensemble. Do not confuse the terms sharp and flat with words describing actual note names such as C-sharp and B-flat. These notes are raised (sharped) and lowered (flatted) by a larger amount than is usually the case in out-of-tune playing. That is, the interval between C and C-sharp is greater than the interval between C and that of a performer playing C a bit sharper than his fellow ensemble members. Small deviations of pitch occur all the time even in the best ensembles, but larger deviations lead listeners to comment "someone is playing out of tune."

Why is intonation described in this section on tone color? Intonation affects the tone color of both the soloist and the ensemble as a whole. If a group of musicians played the same piece twice, once without listening or adjusting to each other's pitch (perhaps by pre-tuning their instruments and then wearing ear plugs for the performance), and then a second time, listening carefully to each other's pitch and continuously adjusting accordingly, you would hear two performances, each having distinctly different tone colors. Ensembles which lack precision tuning have a thicker, rougher sound than precisely tuned ensembles. One element of a slick ensemble sound is careful and consistent tuning.

For tone color reasons, some soloists systematically play a little "high," meaning a bit sharp. Intonation is a musical resource for them. This is common in most types of music, including symphonic, but it is especially true for jazz soloists. A tone cuts through an ensemble if it is a bit sharper than the average pitch of that ensemble. Some jazz soloists seem to play at the average pitch. Others tend to different degrees of sharpness. That is another component of tone color which helps us identify a particular player's work.

Personal Perception of Tone Color

Sounds are described along several dimensions, labels for which lack standard use. A major difficulty is that the description of sound does not yet have its own vocabulary. To describe sounds, we borrow words ordinarily used to describe perceptions of sight and touch. Jazz musicians like to use words like color, width, texture, penetration, edge, and core. Other associated terms which you might find helpful include those concerned with variations in compactness or thinness, brightness or dullness (part of color), and softness or hardness.

I recently undertook a study in which forty people listened to recorded samples of several distinctly different tenor saxophone styles. Asked to write tone color descriptions for each style, the people produced these adjectives: light, aspirated, cutting, runny, brassy, pinched, bright, fuzzy, thin, fluid, deep, nasal, piercing, full, clear, smooth, raspy, muffled, round, jagged, sharp, hard, throaty, breathy, broad, shimmering, silky, biting, sweet, dusty, blunt, watery, tinny, cool, harsh, burry, airy, sour, screeching, lush, luxurious, velvety, bell-like, and others. You are probably impressed by the variety of labels. But can you believe that there was no strong agreement on which adjectives fit each saxophonist's tone?

A group of people was also asked to describe tones in terms of these dimensions: hard—soft, much buzz—no buzz, full-bodied—hollow, rough—smooth, dark—bright, and raw—mellow. Agreement was a little better, but still far from consistent in the application of these adjectives.

The lack of concurrence regarding tone color perceptions is only one aspect of individual differences in listening experience. Some recordings are perceived as warm by some, just as definitely as they are perceived as cool by others. What one person experiences as joyful music is described by another as angry music.

From this we are reminded that the application of words to musical sensations is very personal. Although distinctions between sounds definitely exist, people describe, and perhaps perceive, sounds in different ways. Bear this in mind when you read my descriptions of jazz sounds.

chapter 18
FOR MUSICIANS

This section is designed to give musically literate readers a chance to experience some of the musical elements discussed in the text. It is possible to learn more by playing the examples at the piano than by simply reading the attached explanations. After you have played these figures yourself, they will be easier to hear in jazz recordings.

Chords and Chord Progressions

We can imagine chords as being built by tones in major scales (B♭ C D E♭ F G A B♭ or C D E F G A B C or D E F♯ G A B C♯ D). Beginning with a single tone, the chord is made by adding every other tone in the scale. In other words, the first, third, and fifth tones are used when the beginning tone is the key note (first tone of major scale). The second, fourth, and sixth tones are used when the chord is based on the second step of the scale. The third, fifth, and seventh tones are used when the chord begins on the third step of the scale.

If a chord is based on the first tone of the major scale, it is called the "one chord," symbolized by the Roman numeral for one, I. (Roman numerals are used for chord names.) The chord based on the second step of the major scale is a II chord. The labeling system continues through the VII chord.

Of course, there is more to it than that. Before you can apply chord knowledge to studying improvisation, you must become acquainted with the construction of many types of chords: dominant sevenths and major sevenths; major, minor, diminished, and augmented chords; chords with added ninths, elevenths, and thirteenths; chords with added fourths and sixths, flat fifths, raised ninths, etc. And there is a collection of different chord labeling systems which also must be confronted.

Twelve-Bar Blues Progressions Though basically a I-IV-I-V-I progression, the twelve-bar blues may contain a huge assortment of chord progressions. Here are three possibilities for a blues in the key of C.

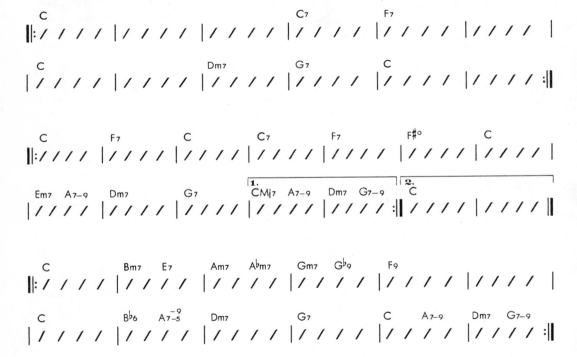

Turnarounds Turnarounds are the chord progressions occurring in the seventh and eighth, fifteenth and sixteenth, thirty-first and thirty-second bars of a thirty-two-bar chord progression, and in the eleventh and twelfth bars of a twelve-bar blues progression. Some turnarounds occupy more or less than two measures, however. Turnarounds provide an opportunity for numerous variations, which depend on the preferences and era of soloist and rhythm section.

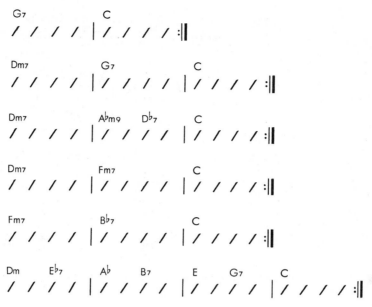

Voicing Rarely is a chord played with its tones contained in a single octave, the root on the bottom, the third in the middle, and the fifth on the top.

Usually chords are voiced. This means that the positions of a chord's tones are scattered over the keyboard; the tones may be altered, doubled, added to, missing, and so forth. Instead of having the root on the bottom and the fifth on the top, a chord might have its root on top and fifth on the bottom.

Or perhaps the third is on the bottom with the fifth next and the root on top.

In some voicings, the root is doubled by being duplicated in different octaves.

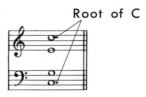

Root of C

Quite frequently the sixth is added to enrich major triads.

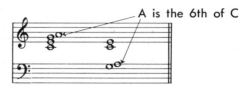

A is the 6th of C

Instead of being voiced in thirds (every other step in a major scale), some chords are voiced in fourths.

There are a great variety of possibilities available in voicing chords. Only a few simple examples have been cited as an introduction. In addition to striking force, phrasing, speed, and precision, an important characteristic of a jazz pianist's style is his preference in voicings. For instance, McCoy Tyner often uses an interval of a fifth in the left hand together with a chord voiced in fourths in the right hand.

Right hand (4ths)

Left hand (5th)

Modes Though used for centuries in classical music, modes just recently became popular harmonic bases for jazz improvisation. Modes are constructed using the tones of the major scale, and different modes are produced by starting on different notes of the scale. Each mode's unique sound is the result of its particular arrangement of whole steps and half steps. For example, in the Ionian mode (also known as the major scale), half steps occur only between the third and fourth tones and the seventh and eighth (an octave up from the first) tones.

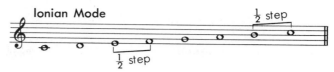

Ionian Mode

½ step

½ step

The Dorian mode is constructed from the same tones as the Ionian, but it begins on the second tone of the major scale. The Dorian mode has half steps between its second and third and its sixth and seventh tones.

Dorian Mode

½ step

½ step

There is a mode for each step of the major scale. Each mode has a distinct musical personality because its half steps fall in different places.

Examine the following modes, play them and listen carefully. Find the position of the half steps in each mode. Once you know a mode's pattern of whole and half steps, you should be able to begin it on other notes. Remember that the interval between B♭ and C is defined as a whole step as is that between E and F♯. Remember also that the interval between B and C is a half step as is that between E and F.

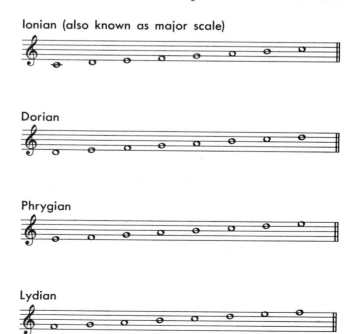

Ionian (also known as major scale)

Dorian

Phrygian

Lydian

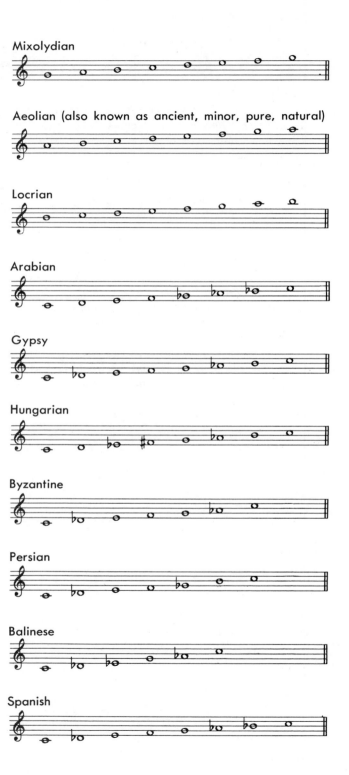

Chinese

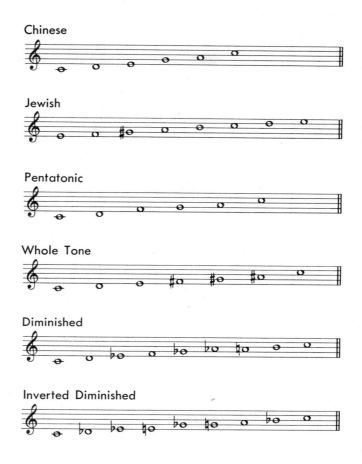

Jewish

Pentatonic

Whole Tone

Diminished

Inverted Diminished

Modal Construction for "So What" and "Impressions"

Dm⁷ (Dorian mode)   E♭m⁷ (Dorian mode)   Dm⁷ (Dorian mode)

‖: 8 bars :‖   ‖ 8 bars ‖   ‖ 8 bars ‖

Mode for first sixteen bars of "So What" and "Impressions"

Dm⁷

Mode for bridge of "So What" and "Impressions"

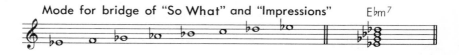

E♭m⁷

Modal Construction of "Milestones"

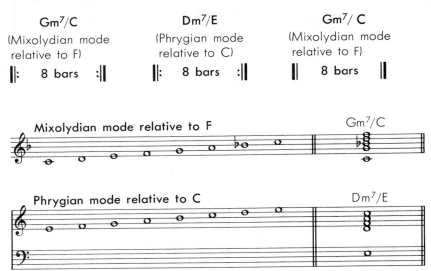

Gm⁷/C
(Mixolydian mode relative to F)

||: 8 bars :||

Dm⁷/E
(Phrygian mode relative to C)

||: 8 bars :||

Gm⁷/ C
(Mixolydian mode relative to F)

|| 8 bars ||

Mixolydian mode relative to F   Gm⁷/C

Phrygian mode relative to C   Dm⁷/E

Modal construction of "Maiden Voyage"

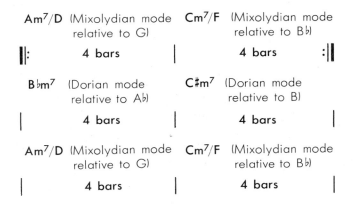

Am⁷/D (Mixolydian mode relative to G)   **Cm⁷/F** (Mixolydian mode relative to B♭)

||: 4 bars | 4 bars :||

B♭m⁷ (Dorian mode relative to A♭)   **C♯m⁷** (Dorian mode relative to B)

| 4 bars | 4 bars |

Am⁷/D (Mixolydian mode relative to G)   **Cm⁷/F** (Mixolydian mode relative to B♭)

| 4 bars | 4 bars |

Comping   Here is one example of a piano accompaniment, or comping, for a modern jazz twelve-bar blues solo in the key of C. Comping is accompaniment simultaneously composed and performed to fit the style of a piece, and harmonic and rhythmic directions of the solo line. Comping usually contains pronounced syncopation.

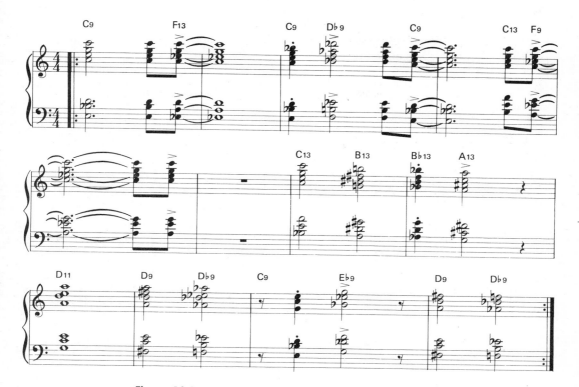

Figure 18.1. Piano comping for 12-bar blues in the key of C (conceived and notated by Willis Lyman).

Note that these chords have been voiced. Comping involves countless ways to voice chords, alter chord progressions, and design rhythms. But basically, comping is meant to accompany and complement the solo line by producing syncopated, unpatterned bursts of chords. Patterned chording, by definition, cannot flexibly enhance a spontaneously conceived solo line. Prewritten patterns (and accompanying figures which sound prewritten) cannot sensitively interact with solo improvisation. The improvising soloist might just as well be playing with a big band using written arrangements. (For examples of comping which sensitively interact with and enhance improvised solos, listen to Tommy Flanagan and Herbie Hancock. For examples of accompanying which are not comping in the sense used above but are more like prewritten material, listen to post-1960 Horace Silver and to John Lewis's work with the Modern Jazz Quartet.)

Walking Bass Lines Walking is meant to provide timekeeping in the form of tones chosen for their compatibility with the harmonies of the piece and style of the performance. Ideally, the walking bass complements the solo line.

Three choruses of walking bass are shown here. They display three levels of complexity.

Figure 18.2. Walking bass lines for the 12-bar blues in the key of C (conceived and notated by Willis Lyman).

Rock Bass Lines   Jazz bassists of the 1970s incorporated many devices which were previously used mainly by rock bassists. A number of rock bass figures are notated here to illustrate the material from which many 1970s jazz bassists drew.

Figure 18.3. Rock bass figures (notated by Richard Straub).

Latin American Bass Line

During performances of many jazz pieces of the 1950s and 60s, including the first eight bars of "On Green Dolphin Street" and "I'll Remember April," bassists employed a figure like the one below which was called a "Latin bass figure."

Figure 18.4. Typical Latin bass figure of the 1950s.

Syncopations

The rhythms common to jazz contain many syncopations. Here is a collection of examples.

Figure 18.5. Syncopations.

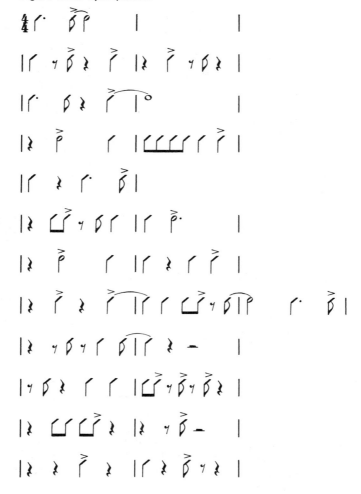

Ride Rhythms   Ride rhythms are used by drummers to keep time and propel a performance. These rhythms contribute to jazz swing feeling, accomplishing in the high register (cymbals or snare drum) what the walking bass does in the low register.

Figure 18.6. Common ride rhythms. Note the strong back beat in Blakey's playing, especially accented on the snare drum and high hat.

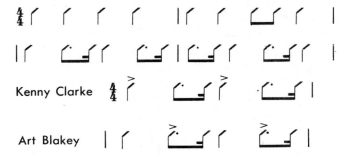

Kenny Clarke

Art Blakey

Some Variations

Two-beat feeling

Four-beat feeling

Turning the time around and back again

chapter 19

MY PERSONAL FEELINGS ABOUT DESCRIBING JAZZ SOUNDS

Music is difficult to describe. We can write about poetry and include the actual poetry being discussed. We can write about economics, including charts and graphs which describe the subject. World history can be studied by reading books filled with names and dates and concepts. Art books can include samples of the subject matter. But the different frames of reference which listeners carry and the endless connotations which adjectives assume pose overwhelming difficulty for describing music. With lyrics, you can express explicit messages through music. But lacking lyrics, musical messages are open to diverse interpretations. Words can convey contradictory messages also, but poetry and prose are less open to interpretation than wordless music.

Unless a book's audience can read musical notation and imagine the pitches, rhythms, and tone colors of a score, little information regarding the sounds of music can be clearly conveyed. Even if its readers understand musical notation, a book on jazz remains difficult to write because we have not yet perfected a system of notating the subtle, but essential, nuances of timing, tone color, and pitch which characterize jazz.

The best that an author can do is (1) explain the techniques of music's production, (2) tell the reader where he can find samples of the music to hear, and (3) include the author's own personal perceptions of the music. For these reasons, the single most important part of this book is the list of recommended records.

Records provide your principal access to the music described here for several reasons. (1) They make it possible to hear important jazz figures of the past. (2) Some great living musicians may never play in your town. (3) Jazz radio and television programs are rare. (4) Some players have undergone style changes, making it impossible to hear them play in person as they were at the time of their greatest impact.

Eliminating External Factors in the Enjoyment of Jazz

Biographical details are kept to a minimum in this book because I believe a man's music transcends his personal life, and knowledge of the personal details which commonly fill jazz books can bias and blur our perceptions of his music. For example, do you really think knowing a famous player's favorite foods and drinks tells us something concrete about the notes he plays? How about his opinions regarding race relations or government? What about the number of wives he has had or his religious affiliation? Does it genuinely help you appreciate his style if you know whether he uses addictive drugs or was ever hospitalized for an emotional disorder? Does your insight into his musical skills increase if you know whether he died by a bullet from a jealous girl friend or an auto accident during a rainy night on the Pennsylvania turnpike? I admit that personal intimacies fascinate all of us. But do you not agree that, in addition to failing to provide useful musical information, many of them constitute a disrespectful invasion of his privacy?

The way I feel about nonmusical factors in relation to individual jazz musicians is similar to the way I feel about the treatment of larger jazz styles. Discussion of cultural, social, economic, and political factors might spice up the reading and color it a bit. But I doubt that much in the way of nonmusical factors would substantially explain the actual notes played, innovations of harmony and rhythm adopted, or the amount of proficiency attained by improvisers. If the origins of styles can be explained in terms of musical elements and trends in preceding styles, there is no need for appealing to the vaguely defined and questionably related cultural factors which appear in discussions of jazz history (such as "frantic times bring frantic music," "repression and hardship created this style," "jazz is an expression of black American culture," "the untroubled joy of Dixieland music corresponds to the mood of a nation just before World War I," "the restlessness of the 1920s in America came to life in the style of Chicago jazz," "the big bands of the swing era embodied the standardization of life in industrialized America of the 1930s," and "cool jazz of the 1950s reflected the resignation of men who lived well, yet knew that H-bombs were being stockpiled"). It is unlikely that any music can truly represent the "feeling of the times" unless it has lyrics. And most "times" have so many different "feelings" that to characterize a period of history by a single cluster of feelings is bound to be both imprecise and inaccurate. I cannot deny that some connections exist between social factors and instrumental music, but I find far more direct understanding of music available within music itself, particularly within the evolution of jazz styles. Instrumental music can change by itself. It does not need the stimulus of social movements. It has its own set of cycles, and it draws upon other types of music rather than gaining its prime inspiration from the social environment of its time. To attach social significance to improvised instrumental music is to thrust your perceptions on listeners who, if left unbiased, would probably form their own quite different ideas of what the sounds represent, if indeed they represent anything more than sounds to be heard for their own sakes.

Over the past several years I have exposed hundreds of people to jazz recordings and have asked these people for written descriptions of their perceptions. Where very little introductory material accompanied the music, I found that, from reading one person's impressions and then another's, it was impossible to tell that all the people were describing the same music.

Our inability as listeners to accept musical sounds as they are, without labels, leads to tune titles which have meanings that are only arbitrarily related to the way music might sound to a particular listener. It also leads to album covers which have paintings, poetry, and essays unrelated to many of the ways in which listeners would probably interpret the contents otherwise. Record companies would probably give the listener more freedom of interpretation if they sold their products in plain wrappers.

It is our rigid expectation that music must *mean* something and our impatience with the abstract that leads us to thrust wild interpretations on sounds, saying for instance, that the instrumental jazz of certain groups in the late 1950s represented protest (why not joy or solidarity?), that the music of certain early 1950s groups represented a cool detachment reflecting the cold war (why not relaxed tenderness? or sensitive contemplation?), that combo jazz of the 1920s indicated the social abandon of the prohibition era (why not just the musical pleasure of the musicians?), and that modern jazz of the 1940s captured the nervous restlessness of its social period (why not the outpouring of a dynamic musical creativity?). Assumptions regarding the nonmusical sources of jazz styles may have some validity, but chances are slight. Even if they are correct, they have little relevance to a strictly musical understanding of the work, and can easily prejudice your perceptions or unfairly limit your imagination.

No one can be certain what inspires a piece of instrumental music: political or religious movements, love or hate, sexual feelings or hunger. People have claimed that repression, poverty, and prejudice are roots of jazz. Many jazz books and magazines contain extensive discussion of race relations. Discussions of Jim Crow, a term for antiblack prejudice, and Crow Jim, a term attached to reverse discrimination and the belief that black musicians are inherently superior to white jazz musicians, can provide emotional reading, but they probably shed little light on the actual chords and rhythms used in jazz.

Players sometimes attribute the creativity of one night's performance to a religious experience or a new love affair. But no matter how much they insist that a certain experience inspired a certain improvisation, you might hear those same passages played in the same way before or after the occasion. A religious experience, a new love affair, or a good meal, for that matter, may energize the creative processes, but they probably have little control over the actual sequence of notes.

What influences the choice of notes is the general style of the improviser, the patterns he has learned and practiced, and the type of music expected of him by the performing group. If his notes were totally different, each night depending upon the direct control of a different religious experience or new love affair, his playing would nightly be so completely original and unpredictable that we could not recognize it as part of a style. Recurrent sound patterns are necessary for us to recognize music as part of a style.

Music without lyrics is not like verbal communication. After it leaves its creator and strikes your ear, music is abstract. No matter what meaning its creator intended, if he intended any at all, the music is no more than sound. You will impose your own interpretation on it. Wordless music means something different to each listener, unless, of course, he has been told what it is supposed to mean or he has taken its title seriously.

Having been an active jazz musician for many years, I have taken the opportunity to question a great number of my fellow musicians. One of the most interesting things I have discovered is that only a minority of pieces were written with a title in mind, a picture to be painted musically, an emotion to be recreated with sound, a thought to be evoked by the arrangement of sounds. Usually, jazz pieces are created and then given titles later, often on the demand of a listener, publisher, or recording company. Most musicians are satisfied to create interesting sounds and leave it at that. In fact, they often only number the pieces ("Opus 1"), or distinguish them by the name of the key or style ("C-Jam Blues," "Blues in C♯ Minor"), or by the composer's name ("Bernie's Tune," "Ahmad's Blues," "Trane's Blues").

Humorous titles can reflect musicians' irreverence regarding tune titles. A Charles Mingus tune based upon the harmonies of "All the Things You Are" was named "All the Things You Could Be by Now If Sigmund Freud's Wife Was Your Mother." A group including bassist Arnold Fishkin recorded "Fishin' Around." Their alto saxophonist was named Lee Konitz (pronounced "cone-its"), and so they named another tune "Ice Cream Konitz." Their tenor saxophonist was named Warne Marsh, and so they named a tune "Marshmallow." They continued their play on words using Konitz's first name, Lee, for another tune title, "Subconscious-Lee" (subconsciously?). Tenor saxophonist Dexter Gordon has released albums with tune titles such as "Clear the Dex" and "Dextivity." One band had a four man saxophone section, calling its sax feature "Four Brothers"; then tunes appeared such as "Five Brothers" and "Four Mothers." Records by saxophonist Don Byas have contained such tunes as "Byas a Drink" and "Donby."

This book contains my personal impressions of numerous jazz sounds, but that aspect is meant only for readers who wish to be stimulated by both music and descriptions of that music. You might benefit most, however, by first concentrating on acquiring recommended records and forming your own perceptions, then by reading the "Elements of Music," "What Is Jazz," and "Appreciating Jazz Improvisation" chapters, and finally, perhaps, by glancing at my impressions for an interesting comparison with your own.

chapter 20
GUIDE TO
RECORD BUYING

Confusing Album Titles

Buying albums with which you are unfamiliar often raises a general problem: Taking album titles seriously. This applies especially to the category of albums bearing titles such as "The Best of ——," "The Indispensible——," "The Essential ——," and "—— at His Very Best." The biggest drawback is that such a set usually contains only a single record company's recordings, and that particular company may not have recorded the artist during his creative peak. Another company may have. And, of course, both companies may have released LPs called "The Best of ——." We must remember that many artists have had several different styles during their careers and a creative peak for each. They may have been recording for a different company during each important period.

Another problem is that the choice of selections usually represents only an opinion, and that opinion is limited by the person's taste and knowledge in addition to the dictates of the record company.

John Coltrane is a case in point. He made important recordings for at least three different companies (Prestige, Atlantic, and Impulse). Each of them happened to document a major portion of one stage in his career. In addition, some of his best work was with Miles Davis for Columbia, a fourth company. An Atlantic LP titled "The Best of John Coltrane" is not going to contain the best work from all three periods— although it might contain his best Atlantic sessions. Miles Davis has recorded at least four different group styles—one each for Capitol, Prestige, and Columbia, among others. How much of either man's career could an LP from only one company possibly represent? And, again, a company such as Impulse released more than thirty LPs of Coltrane's work. How could a "Best of" chosen by one producer represent even the best of Coltrane's Impulse period?

Occasionally an LP is appropriately titled. I can think of one, *Duke Ellington at His Very Best* (Victor LPM 1715). It has some of "his very best" work from one of his most creative periods, the 1940s. The listener must remember, though, that Ellington recorded from the middle 1920s to the middle 1970s. Picking a few selections from an important period constitutes only that: a few selections from an important period. It does not represent the definitive Ellington collection. Neither can it possibly contain what a group of critics consider Ellington's best sixteen recorded performances. A truly definitive Ellington LP would have to include not only Victor sessions of the early 1940s but also some of his earlier work on Decca and some of his late 1950s work for Columbia. Other listeners might also insist that his work for Fantasy, Reprise, and Atlantic be included. Similarly, you should not think you own "the best of Count Basie" just because you bought a two LP set called *The Best of Count Basie* (MCA 4050). To say you own "the best of Count Basie," you would have to include at least a few of his combo dates of 1936–41 on Columbia, his Roulette big band sessions from the 1950s, and some selections offered in the MCA set.

Another point to consider is that many players made some, or perhaps all, of their best recordings as sidemen in other men's bands, not as leaders on their own record dates. Lester Young probably did his best work as a sideman with the 1936–41 combos and big bands associated with Count Basie (reissued by Columbia-Epic and Decca). His own subsequent combo dates as leader sound unlike the Lester Young of the 1936–41 Basie groups. An Emarcy LP of some 1943–44 sessions called *Pres At His Very Best* is probably not his very best. A Verve LP of 1950s sessions called *The Essential Lester Young* is probably "essential" only to those Lester Young collectors who already have much of his earlier work. Both those LPs contain good playing, but if you are limited to a single album of Lester Young, neither of them would be appropriate, so their titles are misleading.

There are other examples of the confusion arising from album titles and varied careers. In the 1960s pianist Herbie Hancock and saxophonist Wayne Shorter both made records for Blue Note as leaders of their own recording groups. During much of that time they were also recording for Columbia in the Miles Davis Quintet. Most of their playing on the Davis recordings is superior to that on their own records. But since they were leaders on the Blue Note sessions, those sessions, instead of the Columbia ones, will probably provide the pool from which LPs titled "The Best of ——" will be chosen. I am not saying that Hancock's or Shorter's Blue Note work is poor. On the contrary, it is excellent music and it also features the beautiful composing that Hancock and Shorter are known for. The point is that, when heard strictly as piano and saxophone improvising, the Hancock and Shorter Blue Note work may not truly represent the absolute best of either man as claimed by an album title.

Another confusing album title is "Greatest Hits." It is usually misleading because, in addition to all the previously mentioned problems, a player's greatest hits measured by sales figures alone may not even appear on an LP titled "——'s Greatest Hits." For example, the largest-selling Miles Davis Columbia recording, his 1969 *Bitches Brew* (GP 26), is not represented on the Columbia album *Miles Davis' Greatest Hits* (PC 9808). Again, by sales figures alone, the 1964 Verve recording of "Girl From Ipanema" was Stan Getz's greatest hit. Yet there is a Prestige LP titled *Stan Getz' Greatest Hits* (Prestige 7337) drawn from 1949 and 1950 sessions. The Prestige material is excellent, perhaps better than the Verve material, yet it does not include his largest selling hits as the album title deceptively implies.

In summary, superlatives are rarely applied accurately in naming jazz records. You might be able to avoid confusion by reading album liner notes, carefully looking for recording dates and personnel, and consulting authorities to determine what companies were recording the artist during critical portions of his career.

Minimizing Risk in Selecting Albums

In seeking record buying advice, try not to assume that a newspaper, book, or magazine is an authority in itself. We may think their endorsements represent knowledge and understanding somehow greater than that of a single individual. Usually, however, a record review or list of recommended listening reflects only one individual's preferences and his own understanding or lack of understanding.

You may perhaps feel that it is impossible to make good choices without extensive previous knowledge. But the situation is not quite that desperate. Listening to records before you buy them is always a wise practice. Friends, libraries, jazz courses, and radio programs can often help here. Many albums list musicians and tunes which look great but turn out sounding less than great. Unless you want a record purely for academic reasons or historical perspective, you might realize too late that you have spent your money on something you do not enjoy. That point might seem elementary, but, unless you can afford to experiment expensively, it is worth keeping in mind.

Since advance listening will be impossible for many albums, you will have to collect opinions from friends, music teachers, and jazz journalists. If there is a jazz radio station near you, do not hesitate to phone and ask them to play a particular album. College radio stations not only broadcast more jazz than commercial stations, but they are also more likely to be interested in your requests. Another strategy is to phone the station just after it has broadcast something you enjoyed and ask for the album title and record company name.

If you have the luxury of advance listening, you ought to give a record at least three complete plays before deciding whether to buy it. The first play might help you get over what could be a shock to your expectations. The second could give you a chance to notice aspects you were unable to catch while experiencing the initial surprise. The third play could put the record in perspective once you were accustomed enough to listen carefully and notice more.

Try to avoid record buying as an impulse purchase. Decide what records you really want, write down their titles, labels, catalog numbers, and carry that list with you. Prepare yourself for the frustration, common to jazz fans, of rarely seeing a desired album in the record racks. (Most current jazz albums must be special-ordered, and all out-of-print albums must be obtained through very special sources.)

Those strategies are not guaranteed to always bring records you like. Even if you follow all this advice, you may end up with a record you do not enjoy. This is quite understandable because jazz represents an enormous variety of styles. It is reasonable to expect that you may dislike at least one of them. You may dislike several entire styles plus many players within additional styles. You should also remember that many players had several different periods during their careers. You may enjoy their playing from one period but not from another. Of course, when you do not have access to a large record collection, your opinion of a particular style or player may be based on only one recording. If that single example is either not stylistically representative or not typical of the quality of improvisation, you run the risk of unintentionally dismissing some area of music entirely.

How to Locate Records   Many people think certain records are available only in big city stores. But actually, no matter where you live, most records can be obtained by mail. It might be more practical to get records by mail even if you live in or near a big city which is full of record stores, such as New York or Los Angeles. Bus fare, or the price of gas and parking, could amount to a substantial fraction of the price of a record. Even then, a record store often orders your request by mail anyway. That leads us to the main point: most of the jazz records mentioned in this book will not be found in average record stores. If they are available to a store, they will probably require a special order. You therefore ought to phone ahead. Then you will know whether traveling an inconvenient distance will be worthwhile. Some stores accept special orders over the phone. You then have only to call the store periodically and find out whether it has arrived.

Usually jazz records quickly disappear from "the catalog" and are not available to the average record store even through special order. "The catalog" refers to *Schwann-1,* a paperback book listing the records in print for a particular month. Together with *Schwann-2,* its semiannual supplement, the catalog manages to list most records currently being distributed. When looking for a record, you should check both the latest *Schwann-1* and the latest *Schwann-2* before deciding how to get it. (The catalogs are often available in record stores. But if you are absolutely unable to find a store copy, Schwann will mail you one for a small fee. The address is listed at the end of this section.) If you want a record which does appear in the catalog, you ought to get it as soon as possible since it may soon disappear from the listing. Several jazz magazines specialize in taking mail orders for records listed in the Schwann catalogs. (Their addresses are also listed at the end of this section. A small service fee might be necessary for ordering.)

A service similar to Schwann is provided by Trade Service Publications. Their monthly publication, *Monthly Popular Guide—Titles and Artists,* and their weekly report of new releases, *Phonolog Reports,* are valuable. Many record stores subscribe, so you should look there first, especially because the guides are expensive. But if unavailable there, write the addresses provided at the end of this section.

Many of the records you will want can be obtained neither through average record stores nor through mail-order companies which supply from Schwann listings. Numerous records will appear in neither *Schwann-1* nor *Schwann-2.* Sometimes an in-print record simply fails to appear in the catalog. Schwann is not infallible. Occasionally out-of-print recordings appear by mistake. Some excellent jazz records also fail to appear because they are made by companies so small that Schwann is unaware of them. Records which have never been released have also been known to appear. Usually a record fails to appear because it is no longer being distributed. It is out of print. But do not despair. The problems are so common that entire magazines of record auction listings are printed. Specialty record stores exist for the same reason.

About Reissues   Many jazz recordings which have disappeared from the Schwann listings return later in altered form. This includes the category known as reissues, re-releases, and repackages. Before I discuss them, here is a bit of relevant history. Prior to the widespread use of twelve-inch, 33 1/3 rpm (revolutions per minute) LP (long play) records, most jazz was issued on ten-inch, 78 rpm records. (Remember those heavy black discs which almost invariably broke into pieces when you dropped them?) Twelve-inch 33s were not common until the 1950s, so many bop and West Coast style bands—in addition to Dixieland and swing bands—were initially presented on 78s. Several forms of recording material exist including paper, wire, tape, and plastic disc. (In addition to the ten-inch 78s and twelve-inch 33s, there have been twelve-inch 78s, ten-inch 33s, seven-inch 45s, twelve-inch 16s, etc.)

Due to the size of the record and the speed of rotation, most 78s could accommodate only about three minutes of music per side. An album consisted of several records packaged much like a book or a photo album, each record having a separate pocket or sleeve. The set was often bound in leather or cardboard. Then when the LP arrived, many of the three-minute jazz instrumentals originally on 78 were issued again (reissued) on 33 1/3 rpm albums. This time, the word album meant a single record containing many selections. All the records in this book's premodern section and a few modern records are to be found in this kind of "reissue." Later on, LPs themselves began to be reissued, re-released, and repackaged. This is the altered form in which you can often find music originally available on records which have "disappeared" from the catalog.

Do not assume that the music on a reissue is identical to what you are seeking just because it seems to be the same. As in the illustrations which follow, you cannot be sure of what you are getting until you have carefully checked tune titles, personnel listings, recording dates, and the name of the original company. Only if all those factors match are you likely to be getting what you think you are getting. Groups frequently recorded several versions of the same tunes, and many players did certain tunes with several different groups. Since you are a jazz fan, your interest lies not necessarily in listening to the tunes themselves but to particular improvisations. You must find the actual performances you want. The improvisation on other versions might not even resemble what you want.

The most common reissue situation is that not only are album titles changed, but material from certain recording sessions is scattered over several different albums. Another common problem is that the original recordings may have belonged to companies which later sold their material. Sometimes whole companies are bought by other companies. Countless jazz record companies have gone out of business. Knowing the original company's name consequently helps you identify reissued material because the reissue might be titled in reference to its original package. Often a set of performances is identified by the name of its most famous tune. Sometimes it is identified by the place it was recorded. The latter is especially true for performances before live audiences. The most useful information to have when seeking an out-of-print record is complete personnel, tune titles, recording dates, original album title, and catalog number. Personnel listings can be especially helpful when material is reissued under the name of a musician who was not leader on the original record date. He may have become important enough to justify an album presenting his work as a sideman.

You can keep up with what is being reissued by reading jazz magazines and visiting record stores. If you do not want to wait for a particular out-of-print record to be reissued (and some never are), contact importers, rare record stores, and record auctioneers (listed at the end of this section).

It is not very difficult to illustrate the usefulness of having personnel, tune titles, and dates. The music on Charlie Parker's 78s for Dial Record Company has been sold in several forms, sometimes by obscure companies. If you want his famous Dial recording of "Embraceable You," for example, it is likely to be found in collections which bear at least some of these vital facts: recorded in 1947 for Dial; personnel included pianist Duke Jordan, bassist Tommy Potter, and drummer Max Roach. Among the records which have reissued it are: Roost 2210, Spotlite 104, and *The Smithsonian Collection of Classic Jazz*. Parker recorded many different versions of "Embraceable You." In fact, he made two different versions at that very session.

If you are looking for the original Lester Young solo on "Lester Leaps In," you need some of this information: recorded in 1939; group name was Kansas City Seven; personnel included trumpeter Buck Clayton, trombonist Dickie Wells, pianist Count Basie, guitarist Freddie Green, bassist Walter Page, and drummer Jo Jones. Among the records which have included it are: *Lester Young Memorial Album Vol. I* (Epic LN 3576), The Folkways Collection (simply titled *Jazz*) 2810, and the *Smithsonian Collection*. Two versions were recorded at that 1939 session. There are other Lester Young recordings of "Lester Leaps In" not made at that session. Some were made years later. All of them contain distinctly different improvisations.

The problem of a single tune recorded many times by the same artist increased substantially during the 1960s and 70s. This was due to increases in: (1) legitimate reissue programs by major firms, (2) illegitimate releases (called bootleg or pirate records) by numerous small firms, and (3) the discovery, or, in many cases, rediscovery, of a seemingly endless variety of broadcast performances, called air shots or air checks. (Music of the 1930s and 40s, unlike that of the 50s and 60s, is well documented by air checks because most jazz groups made live radio broadcasts in those days.)

Beginning in the 1960s, record companies began massive distribution of repackaged material. Hundreds of albums with new titles were introduced. Many contained music originally on 78s. Other albums had music originally available on LPs. Some of the albums featured alternate, but originally rejected, versions of tunes. These are called alternate takes. (Some are labeled as alternate takes, but for others, you have to hear both versions to know whether they differ. They sometimes have improvisation equal or superior to the versions originally issued.)

Albums flooded the market from companies, both American and foreign, which operated without the consent of the recorded artists (or of their estates, in the case of deceased artists). Those albums constitute the illegitimate releases mentioned earlier. The companies were small and disappeared quickly. Some of their material had appeared previously on other records, but much of it had never been available before. A lot of it presumably came from homemade recordings of night club appearances and radio broadcasts. Many albums have incorrect tune titles. Few contain complete personnel listings and recording dates. Many display poor sound fidelity. But if you can tolerate all those weaknesses, you might be well rewarded by the music itself. It also may be worthwhile knowing about bootleg recordings because the appearance and distribution of them is a very common phenomenon and likely to continue.

Many albums unavailable in the United States are frequently available in foreign countries under the same titles. Usually, however, you must match tune titles, personnel, and dates to determine whether a foreign release is the same as the record you want. A list of importers and their addresses is provided at the end of this section.

Many Versions of the Same Tune

With the bootleg material added to the legitimate releases and reissues, it became possible to own more than eighty albums of Charlie Parker, more than one hundred of Duke Ellington, etc. The record collector might be confronted with five to ten Parker versions of "Confirmation" and "Ornithology" and just as many Ellington versions of "Mood Indigo" and "Sophisticated Lady." Keeping track of recording dates and personnel became essential to discussing particular performances of these frequently recorded tunes.

Although not nearly as confusing as the cases of Parker and Ellington, a few major figures of the 1950s and 60s also recorded several versions of certain tunes. John Coltrane has at least three versions of "I Want to Talk about You." Sorting them should again illustrate the importance of noting personnel and recording dates. His first version was made with pianist Red Garland, bassist Paul Chambers, and drummer Art Taylor in 1958. It was released on an LP called *Soul Trane* (Prestige 7142). Another version was made with pianist McCoy Tyner, bassist Jimmy Garrison, and drummer Elvin Jones at Birdland in 1963 and was released on an LP called *Live at Birdland* (Impulse A 50). Still another version was recorded with Tyner, Garrison, and drummer Roy Haynes at the Newport Jazz Festival in 1963. It was released on an LP called *Selflessness* (Impulse AS 9161). The title track of this album (that is, the selection which bears the same name as the album itself)* was recorded by *different* personnel on a *different* date. So you see that Coltrane not only made three different versions, but that two of them were made the same year, 1963. Of these two, the most obvious differentiating factor was the drummer: Roy Haynes played on one, Elvin Jones on the other. Additional Coltrane recordings of "I Want to Talk About You" and other favorites continue to be released on both legitimate and bootleg records.

Clearly, then, it is important to know what version of a tune you want before you begin searching for a recording of it. During the 1950s and 60s, Miles Davis recorded several versions of "Walkin'," "'Round Midnight," "Stella by Starlight," "My Funny Valentine," "Milestones," "Four," "All of You," "Bye Bye Blackbird," "Autumn Leaves," "There Is No Greater Love," "Well, You Needn't," "Oleo," and at least seven versions of "So What." The versions usually represent different groups, but occasionally several recordings of one tune were made with exactly the same personnel. "Joshua," for example, was recorded at least three times with tenor saxophonist George Coleman, pianist Herbie Hancock, bassist Ron Carter, and drummer Tony Williams. It was made twice in 1963. One version was released on *Seven Steps to Heaven* (Columbia CS 8851 or CL 2051), and the other was released on *Miles Davis in Europe* (Columbia CL 2183 or CS 8983). Then it was made again in 1964 and released on *Four and More* (Columbia CS 9253 or CL 2453).

---

* Confusion occasionally arises in discussing the performance of a tune when people think you are actually referring to an entire LP of the same name.

TABLE 20.1. A Small Basic Record Collection

Louis Armstrong and Earl Hines 1928, Smithsonian (2 LP set)*

Sidney Bechet—Master Musician, RCA (Bluebird), AXM2-5516 (2 LP set)

The Bix Beiderbecke Story Vol. 2—Bix and Tram, Columbia, 845 (1 LP)

This Is Duke Ellington, RCA, VPM 6042 (2 LP set)

Count Basie—The Best of Count Basie, MCA, 4050 (2 LP set)

Benny Goodman—Carnegie Hall Jazz Concert Vols. 1–3, Columbia, 814–6 (3 LP set)

Dizzy Gillespie—In the Beginning, Prestige, 24030 (2 LP set)

The Genius of Bud Powell 1949–51, Verve, 2506 (2 LP set)

Charles Christopher Parker, Jr. Bird—The Savoy Recordings, Savoy, 2201 (2 LP set)

Thelonious Monk—Complete Genius, Blue Note, LA 579 (2 LP set)

Woody Herman's Greatest Hits, Columbia, CS 9291 (1 LP)

Miles Davis—The Complete Birth of the Cool, Capitol, M 11026 (1 LP)

Lennie Tristano—Crosscurrents, Capitol, M 11060 (1 LP)

Gerry Mulligan—With Tentette, Capitol, M 11029 (1 LP)

Stan Kenton—New Concepts of Artistry in Rhythm, Creative World, ST 1002 (1 LP)

Dave Brubeck—The Fantasy Years, Atlantic, SD2-317 (2 LP set)

Sonny Rollins—Saxophone Colossus and More, Prestige, 24050 (2 LP set)

Clifford Brown—The Quintet Vol. 1, Emarcy, 403 (2 LP set); Vol. 2, Emarcy, 407 (2 LP set)

Art Blakey—A Night at Birdland Vols. 1 & 2, Blue Note, BST 81521-2 (2 LP set)

Charles Mingus—Better Git It in Your Soul, Columbia, CG 30628 (2 LP set)

Ornette Coleman—The Shape of Jazz to Come, Atlantic, 1317 (1 LP)

Miles Davis—Kind of Blue, Columbia, PC 8163 (1 LP)

John Coltrane—Giant Steps, Atlantic, 1311 (1 LP)

Bill Evans—The Village Vanguard Sessions, Milestone, M 47002 (2 LP set)

John Coltrane—Live at Birdland, Impulse, S-50 (1 LP)

The Heliocentric Worlds of Sun Ra Vols. 1 & 2, ESP DISK, 1014 & 1017

Albert Ayler—Spiritual Unity, ESP DISK, 1002 (1 LP)

Miles Davis—Sorcerer, Columbia, PC 9532 (1 LP)

John Coltrane—Interstellar Space, Impulse, ASD 9277 (1 LP)

The Best of Herbie Hancock, Blue Note, 89907 (2 LP set)

Miles Davis—Live-Evil, Columbia, CG 30954 (2 LP set)

Chick Corea, Blue Note, LA 395 (2 LP set)

Cecil Taylor—Silent Tongues, Arista, AL 1005 (1 LP)

Keith Jarrett—Backhand, Impulse, ASH 9305 (1 LP)

Weather Report—I Sing the Body Electric, Columbia, PC 31352 (1 LP)

The Smithsonian Collection of Classic Jazz, Smithsonian (6 LP boxed set)*

* To order, write: Smithsonian Collection, Division of Performing Arts, Smithsonian Institute, Washington, D.C. 20560.

TABLE 20.2. A List of Jazz Magazines, Record Dealers, and Other Record Information

Jazz Magazines		Importers and Rare Record Dealers	Discographies* and Current Record Information
Coda Box 87 Station J Toronto, Ontario M4J 4X8 Canada	Journal of Jazz Studies Transaction Periodicals Consortium Rutgers University New Brunswick, N.J. 08903	International Records Box 717 Mentone, Ca. 92359	British Institute of Jazz Studies 47 London Road Wokingham Berkshire RG11 1YA England
Crescendo P.O. Box 187 Williston Park, N.Y. 11596	N.A.J.E. Educator Box 724 Manhattan, Kansas 66502	Jazz Etc. P.O. Box 393 Bergenfield, N.J. 07621	Jorgen Grunnet Jepsen c/o Karl Emil Knudsen 39 Dortheave; DK-2400 Copenhagen NV Denmark
Down Beat 222 W. Adams St. Chicago, Ill. 60606	Radio Free Jazz! U.S.A. 3212 Pennsylvania Ave. SE Washington, D.C. 20020	Jazzway P.O. Box 142 Radnor, Pa. 19087	Brian Rust c/o Storyville Publications 66 Fairview Drive Chigwell, Essex I 1 G76 HS England
Cadence Rt. 1 Box 345 Redwood, N.Y. 13679		Import Record Service P.O. Box 343 South Plainfield, N.J. 07080	
Jazz Magazine Box 212 Northport, N.Y. 11768		Rare Records 417 East Broadway Glendale, Ca. 91205	W. Schwann, Inc. 137 Newbury St. Boston, Mass. 02116
Jazz Journal International 7 Carnaby St. London W1V1PG England		The Jazz and Blues Record Center 893 Yonge St. Toronto, Canada	Trade Service Publications One-Spot Publishing Division 701 E. Prospect Ave. Mt. Prospect, Ill. 60056
		International Association of Jazz Record Collectors P.O. Box 50440 Nashville, Tennessee 37205 (IAJRC members buy, sell, and trade records)	Trade Service Publications Phonolog Publishing Division 2720 Beverly Blvd. Los Angeles, Ca. 90057

* A discography is a listing, often in the form of a book or pamphlet, that tells you who played on a particular record, when it was recorded, and how many versions ("takes") were made at a particular recording session and that can give you a list of nearly every record issued by a particular player and the additional catalog numbers under which a record was issued.

There are two major jazz discographies, the Rust and the Jepsen, and many other smaller ones. The Rust discography is primarily a study of early jazz and swing. The Jepsen discography takes up approximately where the Rust leaves off. Jepsen is the tireless dean of jazz discographers. He periodically compiles supplements to his book-size discographies and publishes them in jazz magazines, often in Down Beat yearbooks.

GLOSSARY

attack the very beginning of a sound (opposite of release).

antiphonal an adjective describing a common pattern of interaction between improvisers or between sections of a band, taking the form of a question and answer or a call and response.

arco the technique of playing a stringed instrument with a bow.

big band an ensemble of ten or more players.

blues 1) a simple, funky style of black music separate from but coexistent with jazz; beginning at least as early as the turn of the century, probably much earlier; exemplified by such performers as Blind Lemon Jefferson, Leadbelly, Lightnin' Hopkins, Muddy Waters, T-Bone Walker and Robert Johnson. It has been and continues to be an influence on jazz and rock. The majority of blues compositions employ the I-IV-I-V-I chord progression or a variation of it.
2) a piece characterized by any one or any combination of the following—
a) the I-IV-I-V-I chord progression or some variation of it in a twelve-measure package
b) a sad feeling
c) a slow pace
d) poetry in the form of paired couplets in iambic pentameter

e) many lowered third, fifth, or seventh intervals
(see page 297 for further explanation)

bomb a pronounced accent played by the drummer.

bop (bebop) the style associated with Charlie Parker, Dizzy Gillespie, Thelonious Monk, Bud Powell, Dexter Gordon, and Sonny Stitt.

break 1) the portion of a piece in which all band members stop playing except the one who improvises a solo.
2) the solo itself.

bridge the B part of an A-A-B-A composition; also known as the channel, the release, or the inside (see page 313 for further information).

broken time 1) a style of rhythm section playing in which explicit statement of every beat is replaced by broken patterns which only imply the underlying tempo, exemplified by the 1961 Bill Evans trio with Scott LaFaro and Paul Motian.
2) the manner of playing bass or drums in which strict repetition of timekeeping patterns is not maintained, but constant tempo is; exemplified by the 1960s and 70s playing of Elvin Jones.

chops instrumental facility

chorus 1) once through, the set of chord changes being used for improvisation.
2) a jazz solo, regardless of its length.
3) the part of a pop tune performed in constant tempo and repeated several times after the verse has been played, usually the only portion of a tune's original form used by the jazz musician (see page 310 for further explanation).

comping syncopated chording which provides improvised accompaniment for simultaneously improvised solos, flexibly complementing the rhythms and implied harmonies of the solo line (see page 28 for further explanation).

cool 1) an adjective often applied to describe the subdued feeling projected by the music of Bix Beiderbecke, Lester Young, Claude Thornhill, Gil Evans, Miles Davis, The Modern Jazz Quartet, Gerry Mulligan, Lee Konitz, and Jimmy Giuffre.
2) sometimes used as a synonym for West Coast style.
3) sometimes used to denote modern jazz after bop.

counterpoint two or more lines of approximately equal importance sounding together.

double-time the feeling that a piece of music or a player is going twice as fast as the tempo, although the chord progressions continue at the original rate.

fill in general, anything a drummer plays in addition to basic timekeeping patterns; in particular, a rhythmic figure played by a drummer to—
1) fill a silence
2) underscore a rhythm played by other instruments
3) announce the entrance or punctuate the exit of a soloist or other section of the music
4) stimulate the other players and make a performance more interesting.

free jazz a label loosely applied to jazz that is free of any one or any combination of—
1) preset key
2) preset chord progressions
3) constant tempo
4) conventional methods of playing musical instruments

5) prewritten melody
6) conventional distinctions between solo and accompaniment
(see page 200 for further explanation).

funky 1) earthy or dirty
2) mean, "low down," evil, or sexy
3) bluesy
4) gospel-flavored
5) containing a predominance of lowered third, fifth, and seventh steps of the scale
(*Note: During the 1970s this adjective was applied to describe rhythms as well as melody, harmony, and tone color characteristics.*)

hard bop the jazz style associated with Horace Silver, Art Blakey, and Cannonball Adderly (see page 157 for further explanation).

high-hat (sock cymbal) an instrument in the drum set which brings two cymbals together by means of a foot pedal (see page 30 for illustration).

horn general label for any wind instrument; sometimes includes stringed and percussion instruments as well (the most general term for all instruments is ax).

jam session a musical get-together where improvisation is stressed and prewritten music is rare (jam means to improvise); may refer to a performance which is formally organized or casual, public or private, for profit or just for fun.

laid back an adjective used to describe a feeling of relaxation, laziness, or slowness; often describes the feeling that a performer is playing his rhythms a little later than they are expected, almost after the beat or "behind" the beat.

lay out to stop playing while other players continue.

legato a style of playing in which the notes are smoothly connected with no silences between them.

lick a phrase or melodic fragment.

locked-hands style a style of piano playing in which a separate chord parallels each note of the melody because both hands are used as though they are locked together, all fingers striking the keyboard together; also known as

block chording, playing the chord notes as a block instead of one at a time. (See sections on Milt Buckner, Lennie Tristano, George Shearing, Ahmad Jamal, Red Garland, and Bill Evans.)

modal music in which the melody and/or harmony is based on an arrangement of modes. In jazz, the term can mean music based on the extensive repetition of one or two chords or music based on modes instead of chord progressions (see page 296 for further explanation).

mode 1) the manner of organizing a sequence of tones, usually an ascending sequence of an octave.
2) the arrangement of whole steps and half steps common to scales.
(see page 296 for further explanation).

mute an attachment which reduces an instrument's loudness and alters its tone color (see page 317 for illustrations).

pizzicato the method of playing a stringed instrument by plucking instead of bowing.

ragtime 1) a popular turn-of-the-century style of written piano music involving pronounced syncopation.
2) a label often applied to much pre-1930 jazz and pop music, unaccompanied solo piano styles as well as band styles, improvised as well as written music.
3) the style of music associated with composers Scott Joplin and Tom Turpin.

release 1) the manner in which a sound ends or decays (opposite of attack).
2) the bridge of a tune.

rhythm section the combination of—
1) piano, bass, and drums
2) bass and drums
3) piano, bass, drums, and guitar if the guitarist is creating a chorded accompaniment for solo lines instead of creating solo lines himself
4) organ, guitar, and drums
5) organ and drums
6) any of the above plus additional drummers, bassists, guitarists, and pianists (see page 26 for further explanation).

ride cymbal the cymbal suspended over a drum set, usually to the player's right, struck by a stick held in the drummer's right hand; used for playing timekeeping patterns called ride rhythms (see page 28 for illustration).

ride rhythm the pattern a drummer plays on the ride cymbal to keep time, the most common being ching-chick-a-ching-chick-a.

riff 1) phrase
2) melodic fragment
3) theme.

rubato free of strict adherence to constant tempo.

scat singing jazz improvisation using the human voice as an instrument with nonsense syllables (dwee, ool, ya, bop, bam, etc.) instead of words.

sock cymbal see **high-hat.**

staccato brief and separated (opposite of legato).

swing 1) a word denoting approval—"It swings" can mean it pleases me; "to swing" can mean to enjoy oneself; "he's a swinging guy" can mean he is an enjoyable person.
2) the noun indicating the feeling projected by an uplifting performance of any kind of music, especially that which employs constant tempo (see page 14 for further explanation).
3) the feeling projected by a jazz performance which successfully combines constant tempo, syncopation, swing eighth notes, rhythmic lilt, liveliness and rhythmically cohesive group playing (see page 16 for further explanation).
4) the jazz style associated with Count Basie, Duke Ellington, Jimmie Lunceford, Benny Goodman, Art Tatum, Roy Eldridge, and Coleman Hawkins, as in the "swing era" (see Chapter 5).

syncopation 1) stress on any portion of the measure other than the first part of the first beat (and, in meter of four, other than the first part of the third beat), i.e. the second half of the first beat, the second half of the second beat, the fourth beat, the second half of the fourth beat, the second beat, etc.
2) stress on a portion of the measure least expected to receive stress (see page 287 for further explanation).

synthesizer any one of a general category of electronic devices (Moog and Arp, for example) which produces sounds or alters the sounds created by other instruments.

Third Stream a style which combines jazz improvisation with the instrumentation and compositional forms of classical music (see page 135 for further explanation).

tone color (timbre, tone quality) the characteristic of sound which enables the listener to differentiate one instrument from another, and, in many cases, one player from another.

tremolo 1) fluctuation in the loudness of a sound, usually an even alternation of loud and soft.
2) a manner of playing a chord by rapidly sounding its different notes in alternation so that the chord retains its character, but also sustains and trembles.
3) the means of sustaining the sound of a vibraharp (see page 138).
4) an expressive technique for use by instruments in which vibrato is very difficult (flute, for example) or in which the variation of pitch necessary for vibrato may not be wanted (some styles of oboe playing, for example).
5) the rapid reiteration of the same note.

turnaround (turnback, turnabout) a short progression within a chord progression that occurs just prior to the point at which the player must "turn around" to begin another repetition of the larger progression (see page 314 for further explanation).

two-beat style a rhythm section style which emphasizes the first and third beats of each four-beat measure, often leaving the second and fourth beats silent in the bass; sometimes called boom-chick style.

vamp a short chord progression (usually only one, two, or four measures long) which is repeated many times in sequence. Often used for introductions and endings. Much jazz and pop music of the 1960s and 70s used vamps instead of more involved chord progressions as the basis for melody and improvisation.

vibrato the slight fluctuation of a tone's pitch, alternating above and below its basic pitch; used as an expressive device, varied in speed and amplitude by the performer to fit the style and feeling of the music (see page 317 for further explanation).

voicing 1) the manner of organizing, doubling, omitting, or adding to the notes of a chord.
2) the assignment of notes to each instrument. (see page 301 for further explanation).

walking bass a style of bass line in which each beat of each measure receives a separate tone, thus creating a moving sequence of quarter notes in the bass range.

West Coast style the jazz style associated with Gerry Mulligan and Chet Baker during the 1950s (see **cool** and page 152 for further explanation).

DISCOGRAPHY (Index of Cited Recordings)

REGARDING FOOTNOTED RECORDINGS

Throughout the book, it has been necessary to cite out-of-print records. Recommending only current issues can often be a disservice to the musician who has no work currently in print or whose best work is yet to be reissued. Given a choice between an out-of-print record representing a player's best work and a current one which does not do the player justice, I always list the out-of-print one. Personnel, tune titles and recording dates are attached so that when a valuable item is reissued, you will recognize it. You should look for the original copy in libraries, rare record dealers and the cut-out bins which frequently appear in record stores, supermarkets, drugstores and department stores.

Many of the records listed as current may be out of print by the time you read this, but the attached information remains your key to finding the recommended works. Chances are good that within a few years of the book's publication, many important works that may be out of print—denoted by an asterisk (*)—will be reissued. For helpful strategies in obtaining jazz records, consult the Guide To Record Buying and Tables 20.1 and 20.2.

HENRY "RED" ALLEN

see ANTHOLOGIES AND COMBINATIONS—*Trumpeter's Holiday.*

see LUIS RUSSELL—*Luis Russell and His Louisiana Swing Orchestra.*

CANNONBALL ADDERLEY

Cannonball and Coltrane, Limelight, 86009 (1 LP); also Archive of Folk and Jazz, 216 (1 LP)

1959; with Adderley, John Coltrane, Wynton Kelly, Paul Chambers, and

Jimmy Cobb; includes "Limehouse Blues," "Stars Fell on Alabama," "Grand Central," etc.

Mercy, Mercy, Mercy, Capitol, ST 2663; also SM 2663; (1 LP)
late 1960s recordings (some live) with Cannonball, Nat Adderley, Joe Zawinul, Victor Gaskin, and Roy McCurdy; recommended not for its popular title track, "Mercy, Mercy, Mercy," but for some blazing solos and driving rhythm section on "Fun" that seems to evidence roots in both the hard bop style of the 1950s and Coltrane's methods of the 1960s.

Them Dirty Blues, Riverside, RLP 322 (1 LP); available as a Japanese import
1960; with Adderley, brother Nat, Barry Harris and Bobby Timmons trading off, Sam Jones, and Louis Hayes; includes "Jeannine," "Dat Dere," and "Del Sasser."
see ANTHOLOGIES AND COMBINATIONS—*The Smithsonian Collection of Classic Jazz.*

see MILES DAVIS—*Basic Miles, Kind of Blue,* and *Milestones.*

LOUIS ARMSTRONG

Armstrong and Hines, 1928, Smithsonian Collection (2 LP set).

Louis Armstrong and King Oliver, Milestone, M 47017 (2 LP set).
1923 "Dippermouth Blues," with King Oliver, Louis Armstrong, Honore Dutrey, Johnny Dodds, Baby Dodds, etc.; 1924 "Cakewalking Babies from Home," with Sidney Bechet, Armstrong, Lil Hardin, and Charlie Irvis; 1924 "Tom Cat Blues" duet between King Oliver and Jelly Roll Morton.

The Louis Armstrong Story Vols. 1–4, Columbia, CL 851-4 (1 LP each).
see ANTHOLOGIES AND COMBINATIONS—*The Smithsonian Collection of Classic Jazz.*

ART ENSEMBLE OF CHICAGO

People in Sorrow, Nessa 3 (1 LP)
1969; with Mitchell, Jarman, Bowie, and Favors. If you cannot find this LP or others by the Art Ensemble of Chicago, contact: The Jazz Record Mart, 4243 N. Lincoln, Chicago, Illinois 60618

ALBERT AYLER

Albert Ayler Trio—Spiritual Unity, ESP-DISK, 1002 M (1 LP)
1964; with Ayler, Gary Peacock, and Sonny Murray; "Ghosts—First and Second Variations," "The Wizard," and "Spirits"; all tunes composed by Ayler.

My Name Is Albert Ayler, Fantasy, 86016 (1 LP)
1963; with Ayler, Neils Bronsted, Neils-Henning Orsted Pedersen, and Ronnie Gardiner; includes "Billie's Bounce."

* *Note:* out-of-print recordings are denoted by an asterisk.

CHET BAKER

see GERRY MULLIGAN—*Revelation, Timeless,* and *With Tentette.*

COUNT BASIE

The Best of Count Basie, MCA, 2-4050 (2 LP set); formerly Decca, DXSB 7170
    1937–39 big band; "One O'Clock Jump," "Jumpin' at the Woodside," "Topsy," "Jive at Five," and "Cherokee."

see ANTHOLOGIES AND COMBINATIONS—*The Smithsonian Collection of Classic Jazz.*

see BENNY GOODMAN—*Carnegie Hall Jazz Concert.*

see LESTER YOUNG—*Lester Young Memorial Album—Lester Young with Count Basie and His Orchestra.*

(the following list of Basie LPs is organized by Basie arrangers)

BILLY BYERS

Basie Land, Verve, V-8597
    "Basie Land," "Rabble Rouser," "Instant Blues," etc.

More Hits of the 50's and 60's, Verve, V-8563
    "The Second Time Around," "I'll Never Smile Again," "In the Wee Small Hours," "Come Fly with Me," etc.

BENNY CARTER

Kansas City Suite/Easin' It, Roulette, RE 124 (2 LP set)
    "Vine Street Rumble," "Katy Do," "The Wiggle Walk," etc.

The Legend, Roulette, R52086 (1 LP)
    "The Swizzle," "The Trot," "The Legend," etc.

NEAL HEFTI

Basie Plays Hefti, Roulette, SR 52011
    "Cute," "Ponytail," "Sloofoot," etc.

Fantail, Roulette, SR 42009

On My Way and Shoutin' Again, Verve, V-8511
    "I'm Shoutin' Again," "Jump for Johnny," "Skippin' with Skitch," "Ducky Bumps," etc.

QUINCY JONES

Basie, One More Time, Roulette, R52024
    "For Lena and Lennie," "Jessica's Day," "The Midnight Sun Will Never Set," etc.

Li'l Ol' Groovemaker, Verve, V-8549
    "Li'l Ol' Groovemaker," "Nasty Magnus," "Count 'Em," etc.

THAD JONES

Count Basie—Chairman of the Board, Roulette, R 52032; also Emus, 12023 (1 LP)

> Thad Jones wrote "The Deacon," "Mutt and Jeff," "Speaking of Sounds," and "Her Royal Highness."

SAMMY NESTICO

Have a Nice Day, Daybreak, DR 2005

> "Have a Nice Day," "Scott's Place," "You 'n' Me," etc.

Straight Ahead, Dot, DLP 25902

> "Basie—Straight Ahead," "Switch in Time," "The Queen Bee."

ERNIE WILKINS

Hall of Fame, Verve, MGV 8291

> "Blues Inside Out," "Big Red," "Trick or Treat," "Flute Juice."

Sixteen Men Swingin', Verve, VE 2 2517 (2 LP set)

> "Sixteen Men Swingin' " and "She's Just My Size."

SIDNEY BECHET

Sidney Bechet Jazz Classics Vol. 1, Blue Note, 81201 (1 LP)

> 1945, includes "Milenberg Joys" with Bunk Johnson and Pops Foster; 1939, "Summertime" with Meade Lux Lewis, Teddy Bunn, Sid Catlett, etc.

Sidney Bechet—Master Musician, RCA (Bluebird), AXM 2-5516 (2 LP set)

> 1930s and 40s; includes "Blues in Thirds" with Earl Hines, "Shag," "I've Found a New Baby," "Weary Blues" and "Maple Leaf Rag" with Willie "The Lion" Smith; "When It's Sleepy Time Down South" with Gus Aiken and Sandy Williams; "The Sheik of Araby" with Bechet playing every instrument on it (clarinet, soprano sax, tenor sax, piano, bass, and drums).

BIX BEIDERBECKE

The Bix Beiderbecke Story Vol. 2—Bix and Tram, Columbia, CL 845 (1 LP)

> The second of a 3-volume Beiderbecke set; this volume includes 1927–28 sessions by Beiderbecke with Frankie Trumbauer, Joe Venuti, Eddie Lang, and others; "Singin' the Blues," "Mississippi Mud," "A Good Man Is Hard to Find," etc.

The Bix Beiderbecke Story Vol. 3—Whiteman Days, Columbia, CL 846 (1 LP)

> The third of the 3-volume Beiderbecke set; includes sessions of Bix with the 1928–29 Paul Whiteman Orchestra, including "Sweet Sue" and "China Boy," a piano solo by Beiderbecke called "In a Mist," and 1928–29 combo dates, including "Margie" with Frankie Trumbauer.

see ANTHOLOGIES AND COMBINATIONS—*The Smithsonian Collection of Classic Jazz.*

BUNNY BERIGAN

°*Bunny Berigan and His Orchestra—The Great Dance Bands of the 30's and 40's,* RCA, LPM 2078 (1 LP)
    1937, "I Can't Get Started" with Berigan's big band; 1937, "Caravan" with his big band; 1938, "Jelly Roll Blues" with his big band, etc.

CHU BERRY

    see CAB CALLOWAY—*16 Cab Calloway Classics.*

    see FLETCHER HENDERSON—*A Study in Frustration.*

    see TEDDY WILSON—*Teddy Wilson and His All Stars.*

    see LESTER YOUNG—*The Tenor Sax—Lester Young, Chu Berry, and Ben Webster.*

ART BLAKEY

°*Art Blakey with the Original Jazz Messengers,* Odyssey, 32160246 (1 LP)
    Formerly an Epic LP titled *The Jazz Messengers;* 1956, Donald Byrd, Hank Mobley, and Horace Silver; excellent Byrd work and two Silver compositions. This LP is recommended for some of the most well-constructed solos of Hank Mobley's career; includes "Ecaroh," "Nica's Dream," both by Silver, and "Carol's Interlude," "Hank's Symphony," and "Infra-Rae," all by Mobley.

Buttercorn Lady, Trip, 5505 (1 LP)—formerly Limelight, LM, 82034 (1 LP)
    1966; Keith Jarrett and Chuck Mangione; "The Theme" and "Buttercorn Lady."

°*Indestructible,* Blue Note, 84193 (1 LP)
    early 1960s; with Wayne Shorter and Curtis Fuller.

Mosaic, Blue Note, 84090 (1 LP)
    similar personnel and period as *Indestructible.*

A Night at Birdland Vols. 1–2, Blue Note, 1521 (1 LP); also 1522 (1 LP); also BST 81521 (1 LP); also BST 81522 (1 LP)
    1954 live recordings with Clifford Brown, Lou Donaldson, Horace Silver, Curly Russell, and Blakey; includes "Split Kick," "Confirmation," "Once in a While," "Night in Tunisia," "Quicksilver," etc.; some volatile moments in Blakey's drum style. Silver's piano style is more Bud Powell-like here than the leaner conception Silver employed during the 1960s and 70s.

PAUL BLEY

Paul Bley at the Hillcrest Club, Inner City, 1007 (1 LP)
    1958; with Ornette Coleman, Don Cherry, Charlie Haden, and Billy Higgins; includes Parker's "Klactoveesedstene"; available from: Inner City Records, 43 W. 61st St., New York, N.Y. 10023

    see JIMMY GIUFFRE—*Free Fall* and *Fusion.*

MICHAEL AND RANDY BRECKER

see HORACE SILVER—*In Pursuit of the 27th Man.*

BOB BROOKMEYER

see JIMMY GIUFFRE—*Travelin' Light* and *Western Suite.*

see THAD JONES—*Presenting Thad Jones-Mel Lewis and the Jazz Orchestra.*

see GERRY MULLIGAN—*The Concert Jazz Band.*

CLIFFORD BROWN

Clifford Brown—The Quintet Vols. 1 and 2, Emarcy, EMS–2 403 and 2
407 (both 2 LP sets)
    1954; with Brown, Harold Land, Richie Powell, and George Morrow;
Duke Ellington's "What Am I Here For?" Victor Young's "Delilah,"
Duke Jordan's "Jordu," Bud Powell's "Parisian Thoroughfare," Clifford
Brown's "Daahoud," "Joy Spring," and "Blues Walk." Vol. 2 has Sonny
Rollins on several selections.

see ART BLAKEY—*A Night at Birdland Vols. 1–2.*

see J.J. JOHNSON—*The Eminent Jay Jay Johnson Vols. 1 and 2.*

see SONNY ROLLINS—*Saxophone Colossus and More.*

DAVE BRUBECK

Dave Brubeck—The Fantasy Years, Atlantic, 2-317 (2 LP set)
    originally *Jazz at Oberlin*, 1953 concert; includes "These Foolish
Things," "Perdido," "How High the Moon"; with Paul Desmond.

Dave Brubeck—Gone with the Wind/Time Out, Columbia, CG 33666
(2 LP set)
    includes "Georgia on My Mind," "Basin Street Blues," "Take Five," and
"Blue Rondo Ala Turk"; with Desmond, Wright, and Morello.

* *The Dave Brubeck Octet*, Fantasy, 3-239 (1 LP)
    1946 and 1948–9; with Dick Collins, Bob Collins, Paul Desmond, Bob
Cummings, Dave VanKriedt, Bill Smith, Dave Brubeck, Ron Cotty, and
Cal Tjader; includes "The Way You Look Tonight," "Love Walked In,"
"What Is This Thing Called Love?" "September in the Rain," "Prelude,"
"Fugue on Bop Themes," "Let's Fall in Love," "IPCA," "How High the
Moon," "Serenades Suite," "Playland-at-the-Beach," "Prisoner's Song,"
"Schizophrenic Scherzo," "Rondo," "I Hear a Rhapsody," "You Go to
My Head," "Laura," and "Closing Theme"; some of these arrangements
sound like the *Birth of the Cool* arrangements, historically interesting in
light of the fact that these were made before the Miles Davis Nonet
recorded.

WILLIE BRYANT

Willie Bryant and Jimmie Lunceford and Their Orchestras, RCA (Bluebird), AXM2 5502 (2 LP set)

1934; Lunceford big band recordings, including "White Heat," "Jazz-nocracy," Sy Oliver's "Swingin' Uptown," etc.; the majority of the selections in this set is 1935–36 Willie Bryant big band material.

MILT BUCKNER

see LIONEL HAMPTON—*Lionel Hampton—"Steppin' Out" Vol. 1.*

KENNY BURRELL

Kenny Burrell/John Coltrane, Prestige, 24059 (2 LP set)
1958; with Tommy Flanagan, Paul Chambers, and Jimmy Cobb; includes "Lyresto," "Big Paul," etc.
see THAD JONES—*Detroit-N.Y. Junction.*

DON BYAS

see ANTHOLOGIES AND COMBINATIONS—*The Smithsonian Collection of Classic Jazz.*

see DIZZY GILLESPIE—*The Greatest of Dizzy Gillespie.*

DONALD BYRD

see ART BLAKEY—*Art Blakey with the Original Jazz Messengers.*

CAB CALLOWAY

°16 Cab Calloway Classics, CBS 62950 (1 LP); French import
1939–41; Calloway big band with Dizzy Gillespie, Jonah Jones, Chu Berry, and others; includes "Ghost of a Chance," featuring Berry, "Pickin' the Cabbage" and "Bye Bye Blues," featuring Gillespie, and "Jonah Joins the Cab," featuring Jones.

CONTE CANDOLI

see STAN KENTON—*New Concepts of Artistry in Rhythm.*
see CHARLIE VENTURA—*In Concert* and *It's All Bop to Me.*

BENNY CARTER

see ANTHOLOGIES AND COMBINATIONS—*Alto Saxes.*
see COUNT BASIE—list of Basie arrangers, BENNY CARTER.
see DUKE ELLINGTON—*The Greatest Jazz Concert in the World.*

RON CARTER

see MILES DAVIS—*Miles in Berlin, Miles in Europe, E.S.P., Miles Smiles, Sorcerer, Miles in the Sky, Nefertiti, Filles de Kilimanjaro, Four and More, Seven Steps to Heaven,* and *Miles in Tokyo.*
see ERIC DOLPHY—*Eric Dolphy—Magic.*

see STAN GETZ—*Stan Getz—The Chick Corea/ Bill Evans Sessions.*

see HERBIE HANCOCK—*Maiden Voyage.*

see JOE HENDERSON—*The Kicker, Power to the People, and Tetragon.*

see WES MONTGOMERY—*Wes Montgomery—While We're Young.*

see WAYNE SHORTER—*Speak No Evil.*

PAUL CHAMBERS

see MILES DAVIS—*Miles Davis, Kind of Blue, In Person at the Blackhawk, At Carnegie Hall, Someday My Prince Will Come, Milestones, Basic Miles,* and *Workin' and Steamin'.*

see JOHN COLTRANE—*Soultrane, Giant Steps.*

see KENNY BURRELL—*Kenny Burrell/ John Coltrane.*

see CANNONBALL ADDERLY—*Cannonball and Coltrane.*

TEDDY CHARLES

**Teddy Charles-Shorty Rogers Collaboration: West* Prestige 7028 (1 LP) 1953; with Jimmy Giuffre, Teddy Charles, Rogers, Curtis Counce, and Shelly Manne; "Etudiez Le Cahier" employs mode-based improvisation; "Variations on a Motive by Bud" uses a tone center-based improvisation instead of conventional chord progression-based improvisation.

DON CHERRY

Complete Communion, Blue Note, BST 84226 (1 LP) 1965; with Cherry, Leandro "Gato" Barbieri, Henry Grimes, and Eddie Blackwell; includes "Complete Communion," "Elephantasy," etc. This LP is recommended for Cherry's compositions and his work as a leader, and for some of tenor saxophonist Gato Barbieri's best playing on record.

see ANTHOLOGIES AND COMBINATIONS—*The Smithsonian Collection of Classic Jazz.*

see PAUL BLEY—*Paul Bley at the Hillcrest Club.*

see ORNETTE COLEMAN—*Ornette Coleman—The Shape of Jazz to Come, Free Jazz,* and *Something Else!*

THE CHICAGOANS

**The Chicagoans "The Austin High Gang"* 1928–30, Decca, DL 9231 (1 LP) 1928–30; Chicago-style combo recordings featuring Frank Teschemacher; includes the 1929 "Prince of Wails" by Elmer Schoebel and His Friar's Society Orchestra, with Dick Feige, Jack Read, Floyd Towne, Elmer Schoebel, Charlie Berger, John Kuhn, and George Wettling.

CHARLIE CHRISTIAN

Charlie Christian, Archive of Folk and Jazz Music, FS 219 and Upfront, UPF 181 (1 LP)

1941; live jam session performances. If you cannot find Archive of Folk and Jazz music records, write to: Everest Records, 10920 Wilshire Blvd., Suite 410, Los Angeles, Calif. 90024.

Solo Flight—The Genius of Charlie Christian, Columbia, CG 30779 (2 LP set)
> includes the majority of available performances by guitarist Charlie Christian in the context of the Benny Goodman big band and sessions with Goodman sidemen between 1939 and 1941.

see HOT LIPS PAGE—*Trumpet at Minton's.*

KENNY CLARKE

> see ANTHOLOGIES AND COMBINATIONS—*Strictly Bebop.*
>
> see J.J. JOHNSON—*The Eminent Jay Jay Johnson Vols. 1 & 2.*
>
> see MILES DAVIS—*Dig, Birth of The Cool, Tallest Trees.*
>
> see DIZZY GILLESPIE—*In the Beginning.*

JIMMY COBB

> see CANNONBALL ADDERLY—*Cannonball and Coltrane.*
>
> see KENNY BURRELL—*Kenny Burrell/John Coltrane.*
>
> see MILES DAVIS—*Kind of Blue, Someday My Prince Will Come, In Person at the Blackhawk,* and *At Carnegie Hall.*

NAT COLE

Trio Days—Capitol Jazz Classics Vol. 8, Capitol, M 11033 (1 LP)
> 1944–47 with Oscar Moore and Johnny Miller; 1949 with Irving Ashby and Joe Comfort.

GEORGE COLEMAN

> see MILES DAVIS—*Miles in Europe, Four and More, Seven Steps to Heaven* and *My Funny Valentine.*
>
> see HERBIE HANCOCK—*Maiden Voyage.*

ORNETTE COLEMAN

Free Jazz, Atlantic, 1364 (1 LP)
> 1960 recording of one, uninterrupted, collective improvisation employing very little preset structure; with Ornette Coleman, Eric Dolphy, Don Cherry, Freddie Hubbard, Scott LaFaro, Charlie Haden, Billy Higgins, and Ed Blackwell.

Ornette Coleman—The Shape of Jazz to Come, Atlantic, 1317 (1 LP)
> 1959; Coleman, Don Cherry, Charlie Haden, and Billy Higgins; includes "Lonely Woman," "Congeniality," "Peace."

Ornette Coleman Trio—At the Golden Circle Vol. 1, Blue Note, 84224 (1 LP)

1965 concert by Coleman, David Izenzon, and Charles Moffett; includes "Faces and Places," "European Echoes," "Dee Dee," and "Dawn."

°*The Music of Ornette Coleman,* RCA, LSC-2982 (1 LP)
1968; includes Coleman's "Forms and Sounds," played by the Philadelphia Woodwind Quintet, trumpet interludes played by Coleman, and "Saints and Soldiers" and "Space Flight," played by the Chamber Symphony of Philadelphia Quartet.

Skies of America, Columbia, KC 31562 (1 LP); also CG 33669 (2 LP set)
1972; Coleman's writing performed by the London Symphony Orchestra, conducted by David Measham; includes "Skies of America," "Native Americans," "The Good Life," "Birthdays and Funerals," "Dreams," "Sounds of Sculpture," "Holiday for Heroes," "All of My Life," "Dancers," "The Soul Within Woman," "The Artist in America," "The New Anthem," "Place in Space," "Foreigner in a Free Land," "Silver Screen," "Poetry," "The Men Who Live in the White House," "Love Life," "The Military," "Jam Session," and "Sunday in America."

Something Else!, Contemporary, S7551 (1 LP)
1958; with Coleman, Don Cherry, Walter Norris, Don Payne, and Billy Higgins; all tunes composed by Coleman; includes "Invisible," "The Blessing," "When Will the Blues Leave?" etc.

see ANTHOLOGIES AND COMBINATIONS—*The Smithsonian Collection of Classic Jazz.*

see PAUL BLEY—*Paul Bley at the Hillcrest Club.*

JOHN COLTRANE

Africa/Brass, Impulse, 6.

Ascension, Impulse, 95.

°*Avant-Garde,* Atlantic, S 1451.

Coltrane, Impulse, 21.

Giant Steps, Atlantic, 1311.

Impressions, Impulse, 42.

Interstellar Space, Impulse, 9277.

Kulu Sé Mama, Impulse, 9106.

Live at Birdland, Impulse, 50.

Live at the Village Vanguard, Impulse, 10.

Live in Seattle, Impulse, 9202.

Love Supreme, Impulse, 77.

Meditations, Impulse, 9110.

My Favorite Things, Atlantic, 1361.

Olé Coltrane, Atlantic, 1373.

Plays the Blues, Atlantic, 1382.

Soultrane, Prestige, 7531 (1 LP); also *John Coltrane,* Prestige 24003 (2 LP set)

> 1958; with Coltrane, Red Garland, Paul Chambers, and Art Taylor; includes "Good Bait," "Theme for Ernie," "I Want to Talk About You," etc.

Sun Ship, Impulse, 9211.

see CANNONBALL ADDERLY—*Cannonball and Coltrane.*

see ANTHOLOGIES AND COMBINATIONS—*Great Moments in Jazz Vol. 2: Alto Masters* and *The Smithsonian Collection of Classic Jazz.*

see TADD DAMERON—*Mating Call.*

see MILES DAVIS—*Miles Davis, 'Round About Midnight, Kind of Blue, Milestones,* and *Workin' and Steamin'* for Coltrane's pre-1960 playing with Davis.

see DIZZY GILLESPIE—*Dizzy Gillespie/Dee Gee Days.*

CHICK COREA

A.R.C., ECM 1009 (1 LP) 1-1009

> 1971; with Corea, Dave Holland, and Barry Altschul; includes "Nefertiti," "Ballad for Tillie," "Thanatos," etc.

Chick Corea, Blue Note, LA 395 (1 LP set); also °*Now He Sings, Now He Sobs,* Solid State, SS 18039 (1 LP)

> Blue Note set has material from the 1968 Solid State LP; with Corea, Miroslav Vitous, and Roy Haynes; includes "Matrix," "Steps-What Was," and "Now He Sings, Now He Sobs."

Piano Improvisations Vols. 1 & 2, ECM 1014 (1 LP) and 1020 (1 LP)

> early 1970s unaccompanied solo piano improvisations; all tunes written by Corea except Thelonious Monk's "Trinkle Tinkle" and Wayne Shorter's "Masqualero."

see MILES DAVIS—*Black Beauty.*

see STAN GETZ—*Stan Getz—The Chick Corea/Bill Evans Sessions.*

see HERBIE MANN—*Herbie Mann Plays The Roar of the Greasepaint—The Smell of the Crowd, Monday Night at the Village Gate,* and *Standing Ovation at Newport.*

see BLUE MITCHELL—*Boss Horn* and *The Thing to Do.*

see CAL TJADER—*Cal Tjader—Soul Burst.*

see RETURN TO FOREVER—*Return to Forever* and *Return to Forever—No Mystery.*

KENNY COX

°*Kenny Cox and the Contemporary Jazz Quintet—Multidirection,* Blue Note, 84339 (1 LP)

> 1969; with Charles Moore, Leon Henderson, Kenny Cox, Ron Brooks, and Danny Spencer; includes "Spellbound," "Snuck In," "Multidirection," "What Other One," and "Gravity Point." This music displays the influence of the mid-1960s Miles Davis quintet.

TADD DAMERON

Mating Call, Prestige, 7745 (1 LP)
  1956; with Coltrane, John Simmons, Philly Joe Jones; all tunes composed by Dameron: "Soultrane," "On a Misty Night," etc.

see ANTHOLOGIES AND COMBINATIONS—*Strictly Bebop—Capitol Jazz Classics Vol. 13.*

see DIZZY GILLESPIE—*The Greatest of Dizzy Gillespie.*

see DEXTER GORDON—*Dexter Gordon/ Long Tall Dexter.*

see FATS NAVARRO—*Fats Navarro—Prime Source.*

MILES DAVIS

Agharta, Columbia, PG 33967.

At Carnegie Hall, Columbia, PC 8612.

At The Fillmore, Columbia, CG 30038.

Basic Miles, Columbia, KC 32025.

Big Fun, Columbia, PG 32866.

Bitches Brew, Columbia, PG 26.

Black Beauty, CBS-Sony, SOPJ 39–40 (2 LP set, Japanese import)
  1970 LP made at San Francisco's Fillmore West with Davis, Steve Grossman, Chick Corea, Michael Henderson, Jack DeJohnette, and Airto Moreira. In my opinion, this set is superior to *Big Fun, At The Fillmore, In Concert, Jack Johnson, On the Corner,* and *Get Up With It.* It provides the only recorded examples of extended improvisation by Chick Corea while he was with Davis, and it might be the most exciting playing of Chick's career. The concert was one of those nights when everything seemed to fall into place and forge ahead with blistering intensity. Unfortunately, this LP is only available as an import from Japan.

Collector's Items, Prestige, 24022 (2 LP set)
  1956; with Davis, Rollins, Flanagan, Paul Chambers, and Art Taylor; includes Dave Brubeck's "In Your Own Sweet Way," and Davis's "Vierd Blues" and "No Line"; also contains a 1953 session with Sonny Rollins, Charlie Parker (playing tenor and identified as Charlie Chan), Walter Bishop, Jr., Percy Heath, and Philly Joe Jones; also includes "Compulsion," " 'Round Midnight," and two takes of "The Serpent's Tooth."

Miles Davis, Prestige, 24001 (2 LP set); formerly *Cookin'* and *Relaxin'*
  1956; with Coltrane, Garland, Chambers, and Jones; includes "Oleo," "If I Were a Bell," "You're My Everything," "I Could Write a Book," "It Could Happen to You," "Woody 'n' You," "My Funny Valentine," "Blues by Five," "Airegin," "Tune Up," and "When Lights Are Low."

Miles Davis—The Complete Birth of the Cool, Capitol, M 11026 (1 LP)
  the 1949–50 Davis-led recording sessions featuring arrangers Johnny Carisi, John Lewis, Miles Davis, Gerry Mulligan, and Gil Evans; with soloists Davis, Mulligan, Konitz, etc.; includes "Jeru," "Boplicity," "Budo," "Moon Dreams," etc. Instrumentation consists of trumpet, alto

sax, baritone sax, trombone, French horn, tuba, piano, bass, and drums, often called the Miles Davis Nonet.

Dig, Prestige, 24054 (2 LP set)
 1951; with Davis, Sonny Rollins, Jackie McLean, Walter Bishop, Jr., Tommy Potter, and Art Blakey; includes George Shearing's "Conception," McLean's "Dig" (also called "Donna," based on the chord progressions of "Sweet Georgia Brown"), "Denial" (based on the chord changes of Charlie Parker's "Confirmation"), "Bluing," "Out of the Blue," and "It's Only a Paper Moon."

E.S.P., Columbia, PC 9150.

Filles de Kilimanjaro, Columbia, PC 9750.

Four and More, Columbia, PC 9253.

Get Up With It, Columbia, PG 33236.

In a Silent Way, Columbia, PC 9875.

In Concert, Columbia, PG 32092.

In Europe, Columbia, PC 8983.

In Person at the Blackhawk, Columbia, C2S 820.

Kind of Blue, Columbia, PC 8163.

Live-Evil, Columbia, CG 30954.

Miles Ahead, Columbia, PC 8633.

Miles in Berlin, CBS Sony, SOPL 163 (1 LP); Japanese import
 1964 concert with Davis, Wayne Shorter, Hancock, Carter, and Williams; includes "Milestones," "Autumn Leaves," "So What," "Walkin'," etc.

Miles in the Sky, Columbia, PC 9628.

Miles in Tokyo, CBS Sony, SOPL 162 (1 LP); Japanese import
 1964 concert with Davis, Sam Rivers, Hancock, Carter, and Williams; includes "If I Were a Bell," "My Funny Valentine," "So What," "Walkin'," and "All of You."

Miles Smiles, Columbia, PC 9401.

Milestones, Columbia, PC 9428.

Modern Jazz Giants, Prestige, S 7650 (1 LP); also *Tallest Trees,* Prestige, 24012 (2 LP set)
 1954; with Davis, Milt Jackson, Thelonious Monk, Percy Heath, and Kenny Clarke; includes "The Man I Love" (takes #1 and #2), "Swing Spring," and "Bemsha Swing."

My Funny Valentine, Columbia, PC 9106.

Nefertiti, Columbia, KCS 9495.

Porgy and Bess, Columbia, PC 8085.

'Round About Midnight, Columbia, PC 8649.

Seven Steps to Heaven, Columbia, PC 8851.

Sketches of Spain, Columbia, PC 8271.

Someday My Prince Will Come, Columbia, PC 8456.

Sorcerer, Columbia, PC 9532.

Tallest Trees, Prestige, 24012 (2 LP set)
 1954; with Davis, Jackson, Monk, Heath, Clarke; includes "Bags' Groove"; this LP also includes a 1954 session with Davis, Sonny Rollins, Horace Silver, Percy Heath, and Kenny Clarke, including the Rollins compositions "Oleo," "Doxy," and "Airegin," and Gershwin's "But Not for Me."

Workin' and Steamin', Prestige, 24034 (2 LP set)
 1956; with Davis, Coltrane, Garland, Chambers, and Jones; includes "It Never Entered My Mind," "Four," "In Your Own Sweet Way," "The Theme (Takes #1 and #2)," "Trane's Blues," "Ahmad's Blues," "Half Nelson."

see ANTHOLOGIES AND COMBINATIONS—*Music for Brass, The Smithsonian Collection of Classic Jazz,* and *Strictly Bebop.*

see CHARLIE PARKER—*The Savoy Recordings.*

PAUL DESMOND

***Two of a Mind—Paul Desmond—Gerry Mulligan,* RCA, LPM/LSP 2624 (1 LP)
 1962; includes "All the Things You Are," "The Way You Look Tonight," etc.

see DAVE BRUBECK—*The Dave Brubeck Octet, The Fantasy Years,* and *Gone With the Wind/Time Out.*

ERIC DOLPHY

Eric Dolphy—Last Date, Trip, 5506 (1 LP); also Limelight, 86013 (1 LP)
 1964 concert; with Dolphy, Misja Mengelberg, Jacques Schols, and Han Bennink; includes "Epistrophy," "South Street Exit," "Miss Ann," "The Madrig Speaks, The Panther Walks," and "You Don't Know What Love Is."

Eric Dolphy—Magic, Prestige, 24053 (2 LP set)
 includes selections originally available on *Far Cry,* Prestige, 8270 (also 7747); with Dolphy, Booker Little, Jaki Byard, Ron Carter, and Roy Haynes; includes "Bird's Mother," "Ode to Charlie Parker," "Far Cry," "Miss Ann," "Left Alone," "Tenderly," and "It's Magic."

see ORNETTE COLEMAN—*Free Jazz.*

see CHARLIE MINGUS—*Stormy Weather—The Charlie Mingus Jazz Workshop.*

JIMMY DORSEY

see ANTHOLOGIES AND COMBINATIONS—*Thesaurus of Classic Jazz.*

TOMMY DORSEY

This Is Tommy Dorsey Vol. 1, RCA, VPM 6038 and *Vol. 2* VPM 6064 (each is a 2 LP set)

The Best of Tommy Dorsey, MCA 2, 4074 (2 LP set)

ROY ELDRIDGE

see ANTHOLOGIES AND COMBINATIONS—*The Smithsonian Collection of Classic Jazz.*

see FLETCHER HENDERSON—*A Study in Frustration.*

see GENE KRUPA—*Gene Krupa—Drummin' Man.*

see ARTIE SHAW—*Artie Shaw Featuring Roy Eldridge.*

see TEDDY WILSON—*Teddy Wilson and His All-Stars.*

see LESTER YOUNG—*The Tenor Sax—Lester Young, Chu Berry, and Ben Webster.*

DUKE ELLINGTON

*At His Very Best—Duke Ellington and His Orchestra, RCA, LPM 1715 (1 LP)

includes seven performances from 1940, two from 1946, and one each from 1927 and 1944; 1940 sessions feature what probably was his best band: Cootie Williams, Tricky Sam Nanton, Johnny Hodges, Ben Webster, Barney Bigard, Harry Carney, Jimmy Blanton, etc.; includes "Jack the Bear," "Concerto for Cootie," "Warm Valley," "Harlem Airshaft," etc. The 1944 date is part of Ellington's lengthy work, "Black, Brown, and Beige"; 1927 "Creole Love Call" and 1946 "Transbluency" contain wordless vocals. The following selections from *At His Very Best* are available as imports from Peters International, Inc. 619 West 54th Street, N.Y., N.Y. 10019 within the French Black and White series (*The Works of Duke Ellington*): "Black, Brown and Beige" (in Vol. 19 FXM1 7302); "Warm Valley," "Chloe," "Across the Track Blues" (in Vol. 12 FXM1 7094); "Ko-Ko" and "Jack the Bear" (in Vol. 9 FPM1 7002); "Concerto for Cootie" and "Harlem Air Shaft" (in Vol. 10 FPM1 7047).

*Duke's in Bed, Verve, MGV 8203 (1 LP)

1956; with sidemen from the Ellington band: Hodges, Jimmy Hamilton, Harry Carney, Ray Nance, Clark Terry, Quentin Jackson, Billy Strayhorn, Jimmy Woode, and Sonny Greer; includes "A-Oddie-Oobie," "Meet Mr. Rabbit," "Duke's in Bed" (also known as "Cop Out" and "Cop Out Extension," an Ellington big band feature for Paul Gonsalves), "Just Squeeze Me" (by Ellington), "Ballad for Very Tired and Very Sad Lotus Eaters" (Strayhorn), "Confab with Rab," "It Had to Be You," "Black and Tan Fantasy," and "Take the 'A' Train."

Ellington at Newport, Columbia, CS 8648 (1 LP)

1956 recording, most of which was recorded live at the Newport Jazz Festival; soloists include Gonsalves, Carney, Hodges, Jimmy Hamilton,

Russell Procope, Ray Nance, Willie Cook, Clark Terry, Cat Anderson, Britt Woodman, Quentin Jackson, Jimmy Woode, and Sam Woodyard; includes "Blues to Be There," "Newport Up," "Jeep's Blues," and "Diminuendo and Crescendo in Blue."

Duke Ellington—The Bethlehem Years Vols. 1 and 2, Bethlehem, 6013 and 6014 (1 LP each)

1956 big band featuring Jimmy Hamilton, Nance, Hodges, Jackson, and Woodman; includes old Ellington tunes ("East St. Louis Toodle-oo," "Creole Love Call," "Stompy Jones," "The Jeep Is Jumpin'," "Jack the Bear," "KoKo," "In a Mellotone," "Unbooted Character," and "Stomp, Look and Listen") plus a new violin feature for Ray Nance, "Lonesome Lullaby," and two Billy Strayhorn pieces, "Midriff" and "Upper Manhattan Medical Group" (mistakenly credited to Ellington). Vol. 2 contains the Carney feature, "Frustration."

°*Duke Ellington—Cosmic Scene*, Columbia, 1198 (1 LP)

1958 recording with abbreviated instrumentation: Hamilton, Gonsalves, and Terry plus three trombones, piano, bass, and drums; includes Ralph Burns's "Early Autumn," W. C. Handy's "St. Louis Blues," Johnny Green's "Body and Soul" (featuring Gonsalves), Lionel Hampton's "Midnight Sun," Ellington's new melodies to the chord changes of "Avalon" and "Perdido," and three Ellington originals, "Bassment," "Jones," and "Spacemen."

The Ellington Era Vol. 1, Columbia, C3L 27 (3 LP set)

Ellington big band recordings originally made for Brunswick, Okeh, and Columbia; includes 1934 "Solitude," 1937 "Caravan," 1932 "Lightnin'," 1927 "East St. Louis Toodle-Oo," 1927 "Black And Tan Fantasy," 1938 "Mood Indigo," 1938 "Prelude to a Kiss," 1938 "Boy Meets Horn," 1936 "Clarinet Lament," 1936 "Echoes of Harlem," 1940 "Sophisticated Lady," 1932 "It Don't Mean a Thing If It Ain't Got That Swing," 1930 "Rockin' In Rhythm," and 1928 "The Mooch."

°*Duke Ellington—Festival Session*, Columbia, 1400 (1 LP)

1959 big band with Gonsalves, Terry, Hamilton, Hodges, Procope, and Nance; includes "Idiom '59," "Launching Pad," etc.

Ellington Indigos, Columbia, CL 1085 (1 LP); also CS 8053 (1 LP)

1957 big band featuring Hodges, Gonsalves, Hamilton, and Harold "Shorty" Baker; high points are the Hodges solo on "Prelude to a Kiss," the Gonsalves solo on "Where or When" and the Baker solo on "Willow Weep for Me." The music on the mono copy (CL 1085) of this album is not identical to that on the stereo copy (CS 8053); several different improvisations and a few alterations in ensemble playing occur. The mono copy also contains an entire tune not on the stereo copy although it is mistakenly listed on the stereo copy's album jacket. That tune, "The Sky Fell Down," is one of the prettiest Ellington compositions on the mono album and contains a gorgeous Ray Nance trumpet solo.

Duke Ellington—Mood Indigo, RCA (Camden), DL2-0152 (2 LP set)

contains very early example of comping in first chorus of Hodges's alto solo on Nov. 30, 1928, "The Mooch."

**Duke Ellington—Newport 1958*, Columbia, CS 8072 (1 LP)
> live 1958 jazz festival recording featuring Terry, Hamilton, Gonsalves, Nance, Mulligan, Carney, etc.

**Ellington Showcase*, Capitol, T679 (1 LP)
> 1953, 54, and 55 Ellington big band including a feature for Harry Carney ("Serious Serenade"), a feature for Cat Anderson ("La Virgen de la Macarena") and a new version of "Harlem Air Shaft" (with Clark Terry soloing in the spots where Cootie Williams and Barney Bigard had soloed, Quentin Jackson doing what had been Tricky Sam Nanton's part on the original 1940 version; it also has other interesting differences that help cast light on the original), etc.

The Greatest Jazz Concert in the World, Pablo, 2625–704 (boxed collection)
> 1967 concert with the entire Ellington band plus the Oscar Peterson Trio (Sam Jones and Louis Hayes), singer Ella Fitzgerald, and others; includes Ellington's "Chromatic Love Affair," featuring Harry Carney; "Swamp Goo," featuring Russell Procope; "Mood Indigo" and "I've Got It Bad and That Ain't Good," featuring Johnny Hodges; "C-Jam Blues," featuring Coleman Hawkins, Hodges, and Benny Carter with the Oscar Peterson Trio; "Now's the Time," featuring Clark Terry, Carter, Zoot Sims and the Peterson Trio; Ella Fitzgerald singing Billy Strayhorn's "Day Dream" with pianist Jimmy Jones, bassist Bob Cranshaw and drummer Sam Woodyard; Ella Fitzgerald singing and scat singing with Paul Gonsalves and the Ellington band on "Cottontail," etc.

Hi-Fi Ellington Uptown, Columbia Special Products, JCL 830 (1 LP)
> 1950 big band featuring Russell Procope and Jimmy Hamilton ("The Mooch"), Gonsalves ("Take the 'A' Train"), and Louis Bellson ("Skin Deep"), etc.

*In a Mellotone, RCA, LPM 1364 (1 LP)
> 1940–42 big band including "Take the 'A' Train" and "Cottontail," both of which are on VPM 6042; also includes "Sepia Panorama," featuring Jimmy Blanton, "All Too Soon," "Blue Serge," and "Just A-Settin' and A-Rockin'," featuring Ben Webster, "Mainstem," featuring Rex Stewart, Hodges, Nance, Bigard, Tricky Sam Nanton, Webster, and Lawrence Brown solos; also includes "I Don't Know What Kind of Blues I've Got" and "What Am I Here For?" Selections from *In a Mellotone* available in Black and White import series: "Take the 'A' Train" (in Vol. 15 FWML 7135); "Cotton Tail," "All Too Soon," "A Portrait of Bert Williams," "Rumpus in Richmond" (in Vol. 10 FPML 7047); "In a Mellotone" (in Vol. 11 FXML 7072); "Just A-Settin' and A-Rockin'" (in Vol. 16 FXML 7201); "Main Stem" and "What Am I Here For?" (in Vol. 18 FXML 7301).

**The Indispensable Duke Ellington*, RCA, LPM-6009 (2 LP set)
> 1940s big band; includes 1940 "Morning Glory," featuring Rex Stewart, 1940 "Bojangles"; two 1940 duets between Jimmy Blanton and Duke Ellington ("Pitter Patter Panther" and "Mr. J. B. Blues"); Billy Strayhorn's 1941 "Raincheck" and 1941 "Chelsea Bridge" (both featuring

Ben Webster); 1945 "Blue Cellophane," featuring Lawrence Brown; a 1945 version of Mercer Ellington's "Things Ain't What They Used to Be" with solos by Johnny Hodges, Lawrence Brown and Taft Jordan, 1942 "I Didn't Know About You," featuring Hodges; a 1945 version of "Mood Indigo" with a wordless vocal; 1945 "The Perfume Suite"; etc. Selections from *The Indispensable Duke Ellington* available in Black and White import series: "Chelsea Bridge" and "Raincheck" (in Vol. 17 FXML 7274); "Mr. J. B. Blues" and "Pitter Panther Patter" (in Vol. 11 FXML 7072); "Blue Cellophane," "I Didn't Know About You," "Carnegie Blues" (in Vol. 19 FXML 7302).

This Is Duke Ellington, RCA, VPM 6042 (2 LP set)
a variety from the 1920s, 30s, and 40s, including 1927 "Creole Love Call" with Bubber Miley, 1941 "Take the 'A' Train" with Rex Stewart and Ray Nance solos, 1940 "Cottontail" with Webster solo, 1934 "Solitude," 1940 "Don't Get Around Much Anymore (Never No Lament)," "Sophisticated Lady," "C-Jam Blues," "Mood Indigo," "Concerto for Cootie," etc.

The World of Duke Ellington, Columbia, KG 32564 (2 LP set)
1947 big band with Lawrence Brown, Tyree Glenn, Nance, Shorty Baker, Dud Bascomb, Jimmy Hamilton, Hodges, and Oscar Pettiford; includes "Boogie Bop Blues," which has some great bass work, "On a Turquoise Cloud," with a wordless vocal with clarinet and muted trumpet, also violin and bass clarinet, "Sultry Serenade" with solos by Tyree Glenn and Hodges, and "Golden Cress," featuring Lawrence Brown.

see ANTHOLOGIES AND COMBINATIONS—*The Smithsonian Collection of Classic Jazz.*

BILL EVANS

Bill Evans—New Jazz Conceptions, Riverside, 6073M (1 LP); Japanese import
1956; with Bill Evans, Teddy Kotick, and Paul Motian; includes "I Love You," "Five," "Easy Living," "Displacement," "Conception," "Speak Low," "Our Delight," "My Romance," and "I Got It Bad."

Bill Evans Trio (Motian, Peacock), Duo (Hall), Verve, Ve 2 2509 (2 LP set)
includes *Intermodulation,* Verve, 8655; 1966 duets with Jim Hall.

Bill Evans—The Village Vanguard Sessions, Milestone, 47002 (2 LP set)
formerly known as *Waltz for Debby* and *Sunday at the Village Vanguard;* 1961; includes "My Foolish Heart," "Waltz for Debby," "Alice in Wonderland," "Gloria's Step," and "Milestones."

Peace Piece and Other Pieces, Milestone, 47024 (2 LP set)
Riverside LP, *Everybody Digs Bill Evans,* plus other work; with Sam Jones and Philly Joe Jones; includes "Peace Piece," "Young and Foolish," "What Is There to Say?" etc.; Evans believes this to be among his very best recorded playing.

see ANTHOLOGIES AND COMBINATIONS—*Modern Jazz Concert.*

see MILES DAVIS—*Basic Miles* and *Kind of Blue.*

see STAN GETZ—*Stan Getz—The Chick Corea/Bill Evans Sessions.*

GIL EVANS

see MILES DAVIS—*The Complete Birth of the Cool, Miles Ahead, Porgy and Bess,* and *Sketches of Spain.*

see CLAUDE THORNHILL—*The Memorable Claude Thornhill.*

ART FARMER

see THE JAZZTET.

see GERRY MULLIGAN—*What Is There to Say?*

see WARDELL GRAY—*Central Avenue.*

MAYNARD FERGUSON

Message from Newport/Newport Suite—Echoes of an Era, Roulette, RE 116 (2 LP set)

   1958 recordings originally on Ferguson's *Message from Newport,* with Willie Maiden, Don Sebesky, Slide Hampton, Jake Hanna, and others; includes "Three Little Foxes," Slide Hampton's "Frame for the Blues," etc.; also includes 1960 recordings originally on Ferguson's *Newport Suite,* with Willie Maiden, Frank Hitner, and others, including "Ol' Man River," "Got the Spirit," etc.

**Maynard '62,* Roulette R52083 (1 LP)

   1962; with Don Menza, Willie Maiden, Mike Abene, Rufus Jones, and others; includes "Have You Met Miss Jones?" "Lazy Afternoon," Don Sebesky's arrangement of "Maria," etc.

see STAN KENTON—*New Concepts of Artistry in Rhythm.*

TOMMY FLANAGAN

see KENNY BURRELL—*Kenny Burrell/John Coltrane.*

see JOHN COLTRANE—*Giant Steps.*

see MILES DAVIS—*Collectors Items* and *Tallest Trees.*

see WES MONTGOMERY—*While We're Young.*

see SONNY ROLLINS—*Saxophone Colossus.*

JAN GARBAREK

Jan Garbarek—Keith Jarrett—Belonging, ECM, 1050 (1 LP)

   1974; with Garbarek, Jarrett, Palle Danielsson, Jon Christensen; all tunes by Jarrett, including, "Spiral Dance," "Blossom," "Long as You Know," "You're Living Yours," "Belonging," "The Windup," and "Solstice."

see ART LANDE—*Art Lande—Jan Garbarek—Red Lanta.*

RED GARLAND

see MILES DAVIS—*Milestones, Miles Davis,* and *Steamin' and Cookin'.*

see JOHN COLTRANE—*Soultrane* and *John Coltrane.*

ERROLL GARNER

Concert by the Sea, Columbia, CS 9821 (1 LP)
   1955 concert with Eddie Calhoun and Denzil Best; includes "I'll Remember April," "Red Top," "Autumn Leaves," "Where or When," etc.

STAN GETZ

Best of Stan Getz, Roulette, RE 119 (2 LP set)
   1950–51; with Raney, Haig, and Silver; includes "Rubber Neck," "Mosquito Knees," "Hershey Bar," etc.

Stan Getz—The Chick Corea/Bill Evans Sessions, Verve, Ve 2510 (2 LP set)
   1967; formerly available as *Sweet Rain,* Verve, V 8693; with Getz, Corea, Carter, and Tate; includes "Litha," "Windows," and "Con Alma."

Stan Getz—Focus, Verve, Ve 12528 (1 LP)
   1961; Eddie Sauter string arrangements; Getz improvises with no preset melody or chord progressions.

Stan Getz—Greatest Hits, Prestige, S 7337 (1 LP); also *Stan Getz,* Prestige, 24019 (2 LP set)
   1949–50; with Haig; includes "There's a Small Hotel," "Indian Summer," etc.

°Stan Getz and J. J. Johnson at the Opera House, Verve, MGV-8265 (1 LP)
   1957 live concert recording by Stan Getz, J. J. Johnson, Oscar Peterson, Herb Ellis, Ray Brown, Connie Kay. "Billie's Bounce," "My Funny Valentine," "Crazy Rhythm," "Yesterdays," "It Never Entered My Mind," "Blues in the Closet." Highlights include Getz ballad solo "It Never Entered My Mind" and just about every solo on every selection. Note that the stereo version (Verve 68490) of this album is not the same as 8265; it was recorded a week later in a studio and omits the J. J. Johnson feature, "Yesterdays." I prefer the solos on the mono version (8265).

see WOODY HERMAN—*Early Autumn* and *Woody Herman's Greatest Hits.*

DIZZY GILLESPIE

Development of an American Artist, 1940–46, Smithsonian Collection (2 LP set)
   Gillespie with his own groups and the bands of Les Hite, Cab Calloway, Coleman Hawkins, Billy Eckstine, Boyd Raeburn, and others.

Dizzy Gillespie/Dee Gee Days, Savoy, SJL 2209 (2 LP set)
   includes Gillespie combo's "We Love to Boogie," which contains 1951

example of John Coltrane's solo style; also has "Lady Be Good," "Pop's Confessin'," "School Days," etc.

Dizzy Gillespie—The Sonny Rollins/Sonny Stitt Sessions, Verve, VE 2 2505 (2 LP set)

1957 recording with Gillespie, Stitt, Rollins, Ray Bryant, Tom Bryant, and Charlie Persip; includes "Eternal Triangle," "I Know That You Know," etc. This LP contains some of the fastest, most fluent tenor sax playing on record; Rollins, Gillespie, and Stitt keep up with each other at their fiery best on "Eternal Triangle."

The Greatest of Dizzy Gillespie, RCA, LPM 2398 (1 LP); also LJM 1009 (1 LP)

four combo tracks, eight big band tracks; 1946 combo with Don Byas, Bill DeArango, Milt Jackson, Al Haig, Ray Brown, and J. C. Heard; includes "Anthropology," "52nd St. Theme," "Ol' Man Rebop," and "Night in Tunisia"; 1947 and 49 big band dates include George Russell's "Cubano Be" and "Cubano Bop," Gillespie's "Manteca," featuring conga drummer Chano Pozo, Tadd Dameron's "Good Bait," etc.

In the Beginning, Prestige, 24030 (2 LP set); also Phoenix *LP 2 & 4* (1 LP each); also Archive of Folk and Jazz Music, FS 272 & FS 301 (1 LP each)

1940s combos and big bands led by Dizzy Gillespie; Parker and Gillespie are together on a 1945 date with Al Haig, Curly Russell and Sid Catlett ("Salt Peanuts," "Hot House," "All the Things You Are," etc.). One of the big band tunes is "Things To Come" (interchanged with "Our Delight" in the mislabelling of Prestige set). Everest set mistakenly labels the Parker-Gillespie tracks' personnel as the Gillespie-Dexter Gordon personnel. To avoid confusion, just remember that "Blue 'n' Boogie" is the only Dexter Gordon selection on FS 272 and Parker-Gillespie tracks are "Groovin' High," "Dizzy Atmosphere," "All the Things You Are" and "Hot House."

The Newport Years Vol. 5, Verve, V6-8830 (1 LP)

1957 live recording made by Gillespie big band at Newport Jazz Festival; with Lee Morgan, Al Grey, Benny Golson, Billy Mitchell, and Wynton Kelly, etc.; includes "I Remember Clifford," "Dizzy's Blues," "Manteca," etc.; Gillespie considers his "Dizzy's Blues" solo to be one of his best on record.

see ANTHOLOGIES AND COMBINATIONS—*Strictly Bebop—Capitol Jazz Classics Vol. 13* and *The Smithsonian Collection of Classic Jazz.*

see CAB CALLOWAY—*16 Cab Calloway Classics.*

see CHARLIE PARKER—*First Recordings, Bird/The Savoy Recordings, Charlie Parker on Dial Vol. 1*, and *Charlie Parker—The Verve Years 1948–50.*

JIMMY GIUFFRE

Free Fall, Columbia, CL 1964 (1 LP); also CS 8764 (1 LP)

1962; with Giuffre, Paul Bley, and Steve Swallow; all tunes composed by Giuffre; includes "Yggdrasill," "Propulsion," "The Five Ways," etc.

Fusion, Verve, V-8397 (1 LP)
1961; with Paul Bley and Steve Swallow; includes Carla Bley's "Jesus Maria," "In the Mornings Out There," Giuffre's "Scootin' About," "Emphasis," "Cry Want," "Trudgin'," "Used to Be," "Brief Hesitation," and "Venture."

The Jimmy Giuffre Clarinet, Atlantic, 1238 (1 LP)
1956; unaccompanied clarinet solo: "So Low"; clarinet and celeste: "Deep Purple"; "The Sheepherder," with Buddy Collete and Harry Klee; and "Fascinatin' Rhythm," with Jimmy Rowles and Shelly Manne.

Jimmy Giuffre: Piece for Clarinet and String Orchestra/Mobiles, Verve, V6 8395 (1 LP)
1959; compositions and clarinet solos by Giuffre.

Travelin' Light, Atlantic, 1282 (1 LP)
1958; with Giuffre, Bob Brookmeyer and Jim Hall: includes "Travelin' Light," "Forty Second Street," "Show Me the Way to Go Home," "California Here I Come" and the Giuffre compositions "The Swamp People," "The Green Country (New England Mood)," "Pick 'Em Up and Lay 'Em Down," "The Lonely Time."

Western Suite, Atlantic, 1330 (1 LP)
1958; with Giuffre, Brookmeyer, and Jim Hall; includes Eddie Durham's "Topsy," Thelonious Monk's "Blue Monk," and Giuffre's "Western Suite."

see TEDDY CHARLES—*Collaboration: West.*

see WOODY HERMAN—*Woody Herman's Greatest Hits.*

see SHELLY MANNE—*"The Three and "The Two."*

see SHORTY ROGERS—*Shorty Rogers and His Giants.*

BENNY GOLSON

see THE JAZZTET.

BENNY GOODMAN

The Complete Benny Goodman Vol. 1. 1935, RCA (Bluebird), AXM2-5505 (1 LP)
1935; variety including "After You've Gone" and "Body and Soul" by the Benny Goodman Trio (Goodman, Teddy Wilson, and Gene Krupa), and big band recordings including Fletcher Henderson's arrangements of "Sometimes I'm Happy," "King Porter Stomp," "Japanese Sandman," and "Blue Skies."

Benny Goodman—A Jazz Holiday, MCA 2-4018 (2 LP set)
combos led by Red Nichols and Adrian Rollini, plus the 1931 Venuti-Lang "Farewell Blues" and "Beale St. Blues," with Jack Teagarden, Frank Signorelli, Joe Tarto, and Neil Marshall; 1928 "Muskrat Ramble" with Goodman, Wingy Manone, Bud Freeman, Joe Sullivan, Herman

Foster, Harry Goodman, and Bob Conselman; 1928 "That's a' Plenty" and "Clarinetitis," with Goodman, Mel Stitzel, and Conselman.

Carnegie Hall Jazz Concert Vols. 1–3, Columbia, OSL 160 (3 LP boxed set)

1938; "Don't Be That Way," "One O'Clock Jump," "Shine," etc.; with Basie, Lester Young, Lionel Hampton, Harry James, Gene Krupa, Teddy Wilson, etc.; "Avalon," "Blue Reverie," "Blue Room," etc. with Johnny Hodges, Teddy Wilson, Gene Krupa, Harry James, etc.

see CHARLIE CHRISTIAN—*Solo Flight—The Genius of Charlie Christian.*

DEXTER GORDON

Dexter Gordon—The Dial Sessions, Polydor, 582 735 (1 LP); import

1947; with Red Callender on all selections, Chuck Thompson on some, Roy Porter on others, Charles Fox, Jimmy Rowles, Jimmy Bunn, Teddy Edwards, and Wardell Gray; includes "Lullaby in Rhythm," "The Chase," "Sweet and Lovely," "The Duel," etc.

Long Tall Dexter, Savoy, SJL 2211 (2 LP set)

1945; with Argonne Thornton, Gene Ramey, Ed Nicholson ("Blow, Mr. Gordon," "Dexter's Deck," etc.); 1946 session with Leonard Hawkins, Bud Powell, Curly Russell, Max Roach ("Long Tall Dexter," "Dexter Rides Again," etc.); 1948 session with Leo Parker, Tadd Dameron, Curly Russell, Art Blakey ("Settin' the Pace I and II," "Dexter's Riff," etc.).

see DIZZY GILLESPIE—*In the Beginning.*

see WARDELL GRAY—*Wardell Gray—Central Avenue.*

WARDELL GRAY

Wardell Gray—Central Avenue, Prestige, 24062 (2 LP set)

1950 live jam session with Gray and Dexter Gordon ("Move"); a 1949 studio session with Al Haig, Tommy Potter, and Roy Haynes ("Twisted" —this was the improvisation later transcribed by singer Annie Ross who recorded it with lyrics she composed, then recorded during the 1970s by pop singer Joni Mitchell; "Easy Living," "Southside," "Sweet Lorraine"); 1950 studio date with Phil Hill, Johnny Richardson, Art Mardigan ("Blue Gray," "Grayhound," "A Sinner Kissed an Angel," "Treadin'"); 1953 studio date with Teddy Charles, Frank Morgan, Sonny Clark, Dick Nivison, and Lawrence Marable ("So Long Broadway," "The Man I Love," etc.); 1951 studio date with Art Farmer, Hampton Hawes, Harper Cosby, Lawrence Marable, and Robert Collier ("Farmer's Market," "Lover Man," "Sweet and Lovely," etc.).

see DEXTER GORDON—*The Dial Sessions.*

see FATS NAVARRO—*Prime Source.*

BOBBY HACKETT

The Hackett Horn, Columbia Special Products, JEE 22003 (1 LP)

1938–40; with Hackett in combos and big bands; includes 1939 "Embraceable You" and "Ain't Misbehavin'" with big band, 1938 "Poor

Butterfly" and "Ghost of a Chance," with Brad Gowans, Pee Wee Russell, Ernie Caceres, Dave Bowman, Eddie Condon, Clyde Newcombe, and Andy Picardi.

AL HAIG

see STAN GETZ—*The Best of Stan Getz* and *Stan Getz—Greatest Hits.*

see DIZZY GILLESPIE—*The Greatest of Dizzy Gillespie* and *In the Beginning.*

see CHARLIE PARKER—*The Verve Years* (1948–50).

JIM HALL

see BILL EVANS—*Trio/Duo.*

see JIMMY GIUFFRE—*Travelin' Light* and *Western Suite.*

CHICO HAMILTON

°*Spectacular! The Chico Hamilton Quintet,* World Pacific Jazz, ST-20143 (1 LP)
    1955; with Buddy Collette, Jim Hall, Fred Katz, Carson Smith, and Hamilton; includes "My Funny Valentine" and "I Want to Be Happy," arranged by Hamilton, Jim Hall's "Spectacular," Fred Katz's "The Sage," Hamilton's "The Morning After," arranged by Hall, Buddy Collette's "A Nice Day," "Blue Sands," and "Buddy Boo," and "Walking Carson Blues," arranged by Carson Smith.

see GERRY MULLIGAN—*Timeless* and *With Tentette.*

JAN HAMMER

Jan Hammer—The First Seven Days, Nemperor, 432 (1 LP) selections "Light/Sun" and "Fourth Day" display Bill Evans influence.

Piano Jazz in Czechoslovakia, Supraphon, SUA 15991 (1 LP); a Czech import, listed under "Piano Jazz," not under Hammer
    1968; the Jan Hammer Trio selections, "Responsibility" and "Autumn Leaves," display Bill Evans influence.

LIONEL HAMPTON

°*Lionel Hampton—"Steppin' Out" Vol. 1,* Decca, DL 79244 (1 LP)
    1942, 44 and 45 recordings of groups led by Hampton; included only for good examples of the locked hands, block chording that pianist Milt Buckner popularized: "Royal Family" (1942) and "Blues in the News" (1942).

see BENNY GOODMAN—*Carnegie Hall Jazz Concert Vol. 1.*

HERBIE HANCOCK

The Best of Herbie Hancock, Blue Note, 89907 (2 LP set)

Death Wish, Columbia, C 33199 (1 LP)
    1974 film score by Hancock; includes "Death Wish," "Suite Revenge,"

"Fill Your Hand," etc. Much of the writing was arranged by Jerry Peters; this LP is included as an example of Hancock's versatility as a composer. The first three selections on its second side, "Suite Revenge," are beautiful classical type pieces in the manner of Erik Satie and other early twentieth-century composers.

Herbie Hancock—Maiden Voyage, Blue Note, BLP 84195 (1 LP)
1965; pianist-composer Hancock leading the Miles Davis group of 1963, with trumpeter Freddie Hubbard instead of Davis; with George Coleman, Ron Carter, and Tony Williams; all tunes composed by Hancock. It contains some of Hubbard's best recorded solos, and it showcases Hancock's writing; includes "Maiden Voyage," "Dolphin Dance," "Little One," etc.

Herbie Hancock—The Prisoner, Blue Note, BST 84321 (1 LP)
1969; with solos by Johnny Coles, Joe Henderson, Garnett Brown, and Hancock; the interplay between pianist Hancock, bassist Buster Williams, and drummer Al Heath on "He Who Lives in Fear" is as skillful and imaginative as the Bill Evans-Scott LaFaro-Paul Motian interactions.

Thrust, Columbia, PC 32965 (1 LP)
1974; with Hancock (electric piano and synthesizers), Bennie Maupin (soprano and tenor sax, saxello, bass clarinet, alto flute), Paul Jackson (electric bass), Mike Clark (drums), and Bill Summers (auxiliary percussion); all compositions written by Hancock; includes "Spank a Lee," "Butterfly," "Actual Proof," "Palm Grease." This LP is included as an example of Hancock's very popular mid-1970s band, which was heavily influenced by rock. Hancock has stated that, along with his playing on the Miles Davis *My Funny Valentine* LP, *Thrust* represents his best work.

*Treasure Chest, Warner Brothers, 2WS2807 (2 LP set)
contains many selections from *Fat Albert Rotunda* (1834), *Mwandishi* (1898), and *Crossings* (2617).

see MILES DAVIS—*Miles in Berlin, Miles in Tokyo, E.S.P., Filles de Kilimanjaro, Four and More, Miles in Europe, Miles Smiles, Miles in the Sky, My Funny Valentine, Nefertiti, Seven Steps to Heaven,* and *Sorcerer.*

see JOE HENDERSON—*Power to the People.*

see WAYNE SHORTER—*Speak No Evil.*

COLEMAN HAWKINS

*Body and Soul: A Jazz Autobiography, RCA, LPV 501 (1 LP)
a broad selection of performances covering 34 years of Hawkins's career; includes the 1939 "Body and Soul," solos with the Fletcher Henderson big band, and a bop date ("Half Step Down, Please"), etc.

Coleman Hawkins and the Trumpet Kings, Trip, 5515 (1 LP); also Emarcy, 26011 (1 LP)
1944 sessions with Teddy Wilson, Hawkins, Shavers, Billy Taylor, and Denzil Best; includes "My Man" and "El Salon de Gutbucket."

see ANTHOLOGIES AND COMBINATIONS—*The Smithsonian Collection of Classic Jazz.*

see DUKE ELLINGTON—*The Greatest Jazz Concert in the World.*

see FLETCHER HENDERSON—*all items.*

ROY HAYNES

see CHICK COREA—*Chick Corea.*

see ERIC DOLPHY—*Magic.*

see STAN GETZ—*Greatest Hits.*

see WARDELL GRAY—*Wardell Gray—Central Avenue.*

see BUD POWELL—*The Amazing Bud Powell.*

FLETCHER HENDERSON

The Complete Fletcher Henderson 1927–36, RCA (Bluebird), AXM2 5507 (2 LP set)
includes 1931 "Sugar Foot Stomp," 1934 "Hocus Pocus," 1936 "Sing, Sing, Sing."

Developing an American Orchestra 1923–37, Smithsonian (2 LP set)
contains some material on *A Study in Frustration* (see below).

°A Study in Frustration, Columbia, C4L19 (4 LP set)
1923–38; Fletcher Henderson big band recordings; includes "Sugar Foot Stomp," with solos by Rex Stewart and Coleman Hawkins, 1928 "King Porter Stomp," with solos by Hawkins and Jimmy Harrison, and 1936 "Christopher Columbus," with solos by Roy Eldridge and Chu Berry.

see BENNY GOODMAN—*The Complete Benny Goodman Vol. 1 1935.*

see COLEMAN HAWKINS—*Body and Soul: A Jazz Autobiography.*

JOE HENDERSON

If You're Not Part of the Solution, You're Part of the Problem, Milestone, 9028 (1 LP)
1970; with Woody Shaw, George Cables, Ron McClure, and Lenny White; includes "Caribbean Fire Dance," " 'Round Midnight," "Mode for Joe," and "Blue Bossa." The rhythm section style resembles that of the mid-1960s Miles Davis Quintet.

In Pursuit of Blackness, Milestone, 9034 (1 LP)
1971; Curtis Fuller, Pete Yellin, George Cables, Stanley Clarke, Lenny White; includes "No Me Esqueca," "Invitation," "A Shade of Jade," "Gazelle," "Mind Over Matter." The rhythm section style resembles that of the mid-1960s Miles Davis quintet.

The Kicker, Milestone, 9008 (1 LP)
1967; Mike Lawrence, Grachan Moncur, Kenny Barron, Ron Carter, Louis Hayes; includes "Mamacita," "The Kicker," "Chelsea Bridge," "Nardis," "Without A Song," "O Amor En Paz," "Mo' Joe." The rhythm section style resembles that of the mid-1960s Miles Davis quintet.

Power to the People, Milestone, 9024 (1 LP)
1969; with Herbie Hancock, Ron Carter, Jack DeJohnette, and, on two

tunes, Mike Lawrence; includes "Black Narcissus," "Power to the People," "Lazy Afternoon," etc. Four of the tunes are written by Henderson, one by Carter.

Tetragon, Milestone, 9017 (1 LP)
1967–68; with Henderson, Kenny Barron, and Don Friedman (they trade off from one tune to another), Ron Carter, Louis Hayes, and Jack DeJohnette (they also trade off); includes "Invitation," "Tetragon," etc.

WOODY HERMAN

Early Autumn, Capitol, M 11034 (1 LP)
1948–50; with Stan Getz, Zoot Sims, Gene Ammons, Al Cohn, Serge Chaloff, Bill Harris, etc.; includes Ralph Burns's 1948 arrangement "Early Autumn," Shorty Rogers's 1949 arrangement "Lollypop," Neal Hefti's "Great Lie," also a Gene Ammons feature, "More Moon," and the famous "Lemon Drop."

Woody Herman's Greatest Hits, Columbia, CS 9291 (1 LP)
1940s; with Sonny Berman, Pete Candoli, Bill Harris, Flip Phillips, Stan Getz, Zoot Sims, Herbie Steward, and Serge Chaloff; includes Jimmy Giuffre's 1947 "Four Brothers," featuring Getz, Sims, Steward, and Chaloff, and Ralph Burns's "Summer Sequence," featuring Getz.

J. C. HIGGINBOTHAM

see LUIS RUSSELL—*Louisiana Swing Orchestra.*

EARL HINES

Earl Hines—Monday Date, Milestone, 2012.

see ANTHOLOGIES AND COMBINATIONS—*The Smithsonian Collection of Classic Jazz.*

see LOUIS ARMSTRONG—*Armstrong and Hines, 1928.*

see SIDNEY BECHET—*Master Musician.*

see JIMMIE NOONE—*Jimmie Noone and Earl Hines "At the Apex Club."*

JOHNNY HODGES

Hodge Podge, Columbia Special Products, JEE 22001 (1 LP)
1938–39 recordings originally made for Vocalion; with Hodges, Otto Hardwicke, Cootie Williams, Lawrence Brown, Harry Carney, Duke Ellington or Billy Strayhorn, Billy Taylor (although Jimmy Blanton is on one selection), and Sonny Greer; includes "Jeep's Blues," "Dream Blues," "Empty Ballroom Blues," etc.

see DUKE ELLINGTON—*At His Very Best—Duke Ellington and His Orchestra, Duke's in Bed, Ellington Indigos, Ellington at Newport, The Indispensable Duke Ellington, In a Mellotone, The Greatest Jazz Concert in the World, This Is Duke Ellington,* and *The World of Duke Ellington.*

FREDDIE HUBBARD

see ORNETTE COLEMAN—*Free Jazz.*

see JOHN COLTRANE—*Olé Coltrane.*

see HERBIE HANCOCK—*Maiden Voyage* for some of Hubbard's best recorded solos; Hubbard is one of those players who seems to do his best work as a sideman rather than a leader.

see WAYNE SHORTER—*Speak No Evil.*

MILT JACKSON

see MILES DAVIS—*Miles Davis and the Modern Jazz Giants* and *Tallest Trees.*

see DIZZY GILLESPIE—*Development of an American Artist* and *The Greatest of Dizzy Gillespie.*

see THE MODERN JAZZ QUARTET—*The Modern Jazz Quartet* and *European Concert.*

see THELONIOUS MONK—*Thelonious Monk—Complete Genius.*

ILLINOIS JACQUET

°*Illinois Jacquet,* Imperial, 9184A (1 LP)
1947; originally recorded for Aladdin Record Company; with Fats Navarro, Miles Davis, Dickie Wells, Bill Doggett, and Shadow Wilson; includes "Big Dog," "You Left Me Alone," and "Jivin' with Jack the Bellboy."

KEITH JARRETT

Backhand, Impulse, ASH 9305 (1 LP)
1976; with Jarrett, Redman, Haden, Motian, and Franco; includes "In Flight," "Kuum," "Valpallia," and "Backhand."

Facing You, ECM, 1017 (1 LP); *note:* ECM is a German label marketed in the U.S. under Polydor.
early 1970s unaccompanied solo piano; all compositions by Jarrett; includes "In Front," "Ritooria," etc.

°*Somewhere Before,* Vortex, 2012 (1 LP)
1969; with Jarrett, Charlie Haden, and Paul Motian.

see ART BLAKEY—*Buttercorn Lady.*

see JAN GARBAREK—*Jan Garbarek—Keith Jarrett—Belonging.*

THE JAZZTET

°*The Jazztet at Birdhouse,* Argo, 688 (1 LP)
1961 live recording of Art Farmer, Benny Golson, Tom McIntosh, Cedar Walton, Tommy Williams, and Al Heath; includes "Junction," "Farmer's Market," "Darn That Dream," "Shutterbug," " 'Round Midnight," and

"November Afternoon." I think this LP contains the best recorded solos of Farmer and Golson and is representative of the Jazztet's tasteful, swinging style.

Meet the Jazztet, Cadet, 664 (1 LP); listed under Farmer-Golson in Schwann Catalog
> 1960; with Art Farmer, Benny Golson, Curtis Fuller, McCoy Tyner, Addison Farmer and Lex Humphries; includes such Golson compositions as "I Remember Clifford," "Killer Joe" (the same "Killer Joe" that Quincy Jones later recorded with singing), "Blues March" and "Park Avenue Petite."

JAMES P. JOHNSON

> see ANTHOLOGIES AND COMBINATIONS—*The Encyclopedia of Jazz on Records Vol. 1* and *The Smithsonian Collection of Classic Jazz.*

J. J. JOHNSON

> *The Eminent Jay Jay Johnson Vols. 1 and 2,* Blue Note, 81505 (1 LP) and 81506 (1 LP)
>> includes three separate sessions: 1953 with Clifford Brown, Johnson, Jimmy Heath, John Lewis, Percy Heath, Kenny Clarke ("Turnpike," "Lover Man," "Get Happy," "Sketch 1," "Capri," and "It Could Happen to You"); 1954 with Wynton Kelly, Charlie Mingus, Kenny Clarke, and Sabu ("Jay," "Old Devil Moon"); 1955 with Hank Mobley, Horace Silver, Paul Chambers.

> see ANTHOLOGIES AND COMBINATIONS—*Music for Brass.*
> see STAN GETZ—*Stan Getz and J. J. Johnson at the Opera House.*
> see SONNY STITT—*Bud's Blues.*

ELVIN JONES

> see JOHN COLTRANE—all Atlantic and Impulse LPs.
> see SONNY ROLLINS—*More from The Vanguard.*
> see WAYNE SHORTER—*Night Dreamer* and *Speak No Evil.*

PHILLY JOE JONES

> see JOHN COLTRANE—*Mating Call.*
> see MILES DAVIS—*Miles Davis Collectors Items, Miles Davis, Milestones,* and *'Round About Midnight.*
> see BILL EVANS—*Peace Piece and Other Pieces.*

THAD JONES

> *Detroit—New York Junction,* Blue Note, 1513 (1 LP)
>> 1956; with Jones, Billy Mitchell, Kenny Burrell, Tommy Flanagan, Oscar Pettiford, and Shadow Wilson; three of the tunes were written by Jones ("Tarriff," "Scratch," and "Zec"), the others by Richard Rodgers ("Blue Room," "Little Girl Blue").

*_The Magnificent Thad Jones_, Blue Note, 1527 (1 LP)
1956; with Jones, Billy Mitchell, Barry Harris, Percy Heath, and Max Roach; two of the tunes were written by Jones ("Billie Doo" and "Thedia").

see COUNT BASIE—_Chairman of the Board._

see THAD JONES-MEL LEWIS—*_Central Park North, Thad Jones-Mel Lewis, New Life,_ and *_Presenting Thad Jones-Mel Lewis and the Jazz Orchestra._

see CHARLIE MINGUS—_Trio and Sextet._

THAD JONES-MEL LEWIS

Central Park North, Solid State, SS18058 (1 LP)
1968-9; Jones wrote "Tow Away Zone," "Groove Merchant," "Big Dipper," etc.; with Jimmy Knepper, Roland Hanna, and Richard Davis.

Thad Jones-Mel Lewis, Blue Note, LA 392 (2 LP set)
Jones arrangements.

New Life, Horizon, 707 (1 LP)
1975; includes "Greetings and Salutations," "Little Rascal on the Rock," "Forever Lasting," "Love to One Is One to Love," "Cherry Juice"; all tunes composed and arranged by Jones.

Presenting Thad Jones-Mel Lewis and the Jazz Orchestra, Solid State, SM17003 (1 LP); also SS18003
1966; with Jones, Bob Brookmeyer, Joe Farrell, Eddie Daniels, Pepper Adams, and Richard Davis; includes "ABC Blues," "Mean What You Say," "Willow Weep for Me," etc.

WYNTON KELLY

see CANNONBALL ADDERLEY—_Cannonball and Coltrane._

see MILES DAVIS—_Kind of Blue, In Person at the Blackhawk, Someday My Prince Will Come,_ and _At Carnegie Hall._

see J. J. JOHNSON—_The Eminent Jay Jay Johnson Vols. 1 and 2._

STAN KENTON

Adventures in Jazz, Creative World, ST 1010 (1 LP)
1961, with mellophoniums; Kenton feels this to be one of his best recordings; includes Bill Holman's arrangement of "Malaguena," Dee Barton's "Turtle Talk" and "Waltz of the Prophets."

New Concepts of Artistry in Rhythm, Creative World, 1002 (1 LP)
1952; arrangements by Gerry Mulligan, Bill Russo, Bill Holman; solos by Conte Candoli, Lee Konitz, Maynard Ferguson, and Frank Rosolino; includes "23° N–82° W," My Lady," and "Portrait of a Count."

(the following list of Kenton LPs is organized by Kenton arrangers)

DEE BARTON

*_Stan Kenton Conducts the Jazz Compositions of Dee Barton,_ Creative World, ST 2932
includes "Man," "Lonely Boy," "Three Thoughts," etc.

BOB CURNOW

National Anthems of the World, Creative World, 1060-Q (2 LP set)

Stan Kenton Plays Chicago, Creative World, ST-1072 (1 LP)
   includes "Alone," "Inner Crisis," "The Rise and Fall of a Short Fugue," etc.

RUSS GARCIA

*Stan Kenton Conducts The Los Angeles Neophonic Orchestra, Capitol, SMAS 2424 (1 LP)
   includes "Adventure In Emotions" Parts I–V.

ROBERT GRAETTINGER

The City Of Glass & This Modern World, Creative World, ST 1006 (1 LP)

BILL HOLMAN

Contemporary Concepts, Creative World, ST 1003 (1 LP)
   includes "What's New," "Stella by Starlight," "Yesterdays," etc.

Kenton Showcase, Creative World, ST 1026 (1 LP)
   includes "Bags," "The Opener," "Solo for Buddy," etc.

STAN KENTON

Kenton/Wagner, Creative World, ST 1024 (1 LP)
   includes "Ride of the Valkyries," "Siegfried's Funeral March," "Prelude to Act I of Lohengrin," etc.

Collector's Choice, Creative World, ST 1027 (1 LP)
   includes "Southern Scandal," "September Song," "Artistry in Tango," etc.

The Jazz Compositions of Stan Kenton, Creative World, ST 1078 (1 LP)
   includes "Eager Beaver," "Opus in Pastels," "Concerto to End All Concertos," etc.

BILL MATHIEU

Standards In Silhouette, Creative World, 1049 (1 LP)
   includes "Willow Weep for Me," "Django," "When Sunny Gets Blue," etc.

LENNIE NIEHAUS

Adventures in Standards, Creative World, ST 1025 (1 LP)
   includes "Some Enchanted Evening," "Just in Time," "Come Rain or Come Shine," etc.

The Sophisticated Approach, Creative World, ST 1018 (1 LP)
   includes "But Beautiful," "You Stepped Out of a Dream," "Like Someone in Love," etc.

The Stage Door Swings, Creative World, ST 1044 (1 LP)
includes "Hey There," "Lullaby of Broadway," "On the Street Where You Live," etc.

JOHNNY RICHARDS

Adventures in Time, Creative World, ST 1011 (1 LP)
includes "Commencement," "March to Polaris," "Artemis," etc.

Back to Balboa, Creative World, ST 1031 (1 LP)
includes "Rendezvous at Sunset," "Out of this World," "I Concentrate on You," etc.

Cuban Fire, Creative World, ST 1008 (1 LP)
includes "Fuego Cubano," "El Congo Valiente," "Recuerdos," etc.

GENE ROLAND

Adventures in Blues, Creative World, ST 1012 (1 LP)
includes "Reuben's Blues," "Fitz," "Exit Stage Left," etc.

Viva Kenton, Creative World, ST 1063 (1 LP)
includes "Adios," "Opus in Chartreuse Cha Cha Cha," "Chocolate Caliente," etc.

PETE RUGOLO

A Concert in Progressive Jazz, Creative World, ST 1037 (1 LP)
includes "Cuban Carnival," "Elegy for Alto," "Impressionism," etc.

Stan Kenton Encores, Creative World, ST 1034 (1 LP)
includes "Peg O' My Heart," "He's Funny That Way," "Abstraction," etc.

The Kenton Touch, Creative World, ST 1033 (1 LP)
includes "Opus in Chartreuse," "Theme for Sunday," "Minor Riff," etc.

BILL RUSSO

Kenton Showcase, Creative World, ST 1026 (1 LP)
includes "A Theme for Four Values," "Blues Before and After," "Egdon Heath," etc.

Portraits on Standards, Creative World, ST 1042 (1 LP)
includes "Street of Dreams," "Under a Blanket of Blue," "Crazy Rhythm," etc.

ANDY KIRK

Instrumentally Speaking 1936–42, Decca, DL 9232 (1 LP)
1936 "Walkin' and Swingin'" with Mary Lou Williams and Dick Wilson; also "Moten Swing" and "Froggy Bottom"; 1942 "McGhee Special" and "Boogie Woogie Cocktail," featuring Howard McGhee.

Clouds of Joy, Mainstream, 399 (1 LP)
1936; with Mary Lou Williams.

ROLAND KIRK

The Best of Rahsaan Roland Kirk, Atlantic, 1592 (1 LP)
  1967–71 performances, including "One Ton," from 1968 Newport Jazz Festival.

LEE KONITZ

**Subconscious-Lee with Lennie Tristano*, Prestige, PR 7250 (1 LP)
  includes "Subconscious-Lee," "Judy," "Progression," "Retrospection" by Tristano, Konitz, Bauer, and others; also includes "Marshmellow," "Fishin' Around," "Tautology," and "Sound-Lee," by Konitz, Marsh, Sal Mosca, and others.

see ANTHOLOGIES AND COMBINATIONS—*The Smithsonian Collection of Classic Jazz*.

see MILES DAVIS—*The Complete Birth of the Cool*.

see GERRY MULLIGAN—*Revelation*.

see CLAUDE THORNHILL—*The Memorable Claude Thornhill*.

see LENNIE TRISTANO—*Crosscurrents*.

GENE KRUPA

Gene Krupa—Drummin' Man, Columbia, C2L29 (boxed 2 LP set)
  includes 1941 "After You've Gone," featuring Roy Eldridge.

see BENNY GOODMAN—*Carnegie Hall Jazz Concert* and *The Complete Benny Goodman Vol. 1 1935*.

ART LANDE

Art Lande—Jan Garbarek—Red Lanta, ECM, 1038 (1 LP)
  1973; with Lande and Garbarek; Lande's playing here suggests the work of Keith Jarrett.

JOHN LEWIS

see ANTHOLOGIES AND COMBINATIONS—*Music for Brass*.

see MILES DAVIS—*The Complete Birth of the Cool* and *Dig*.

see DIZZY GILLESPIE—*The Greatest of Dizzy Gillespie* and *In the Beginning*.

see MODERN JAZZ QUARTET—*all items*.

see CHARLIE PARKER—*Bird/The Savoy Recordings*.

MEADE LUX LEWIS

see ANTHOLOGIES AND COMBINATIONS—*The Smithsonian Collection of Classic Jazz*.

see SIDNEY BECHET—*Sidney Bechet Jazz Classics Vol. 1*.

DAVID LIEBMAN

David Liebman/Richard Beirach—Forgotten Fantasies, Horizon, 709 (1 LP)
1975; with Liebman and Beirach; portions of Beirach's playing here suggest the playing of Keith Jarrett.

JIMMIE LUNCEFORD

see ANTHOLOGIES AND COMBINATIONS—*The Smithsonian Collection of Classic Jazz.*

see WILLIE BRYANT—*Willie Bryant and Jimmie Lunceford and Their Orchestras.*

HERBIE MANN

°Herbie Mann Plays The Roar of the Greasepaint—The Smell of the Crowd, Atlantic, 1437 (1 LP)
with Chick Corea, Dave Pike, Potato Valdez, Earl May, and Bruno Carr; includes "The Joker," "Feeling Good," "Who Can I Turn To?" and "On a Wonderful Day Like Today." Contains good examples of early Corea.

°Monday Night at the Village Gate, Atlantic, 1462 (1 LP)
with Chick Corea, Dave Pike, Potato Valdez, Earl May, and Bruno Carr; includes "Away from the Crowd," "Motherless Child," "In Escambrum," "The Young Turks," and "You're Gonna Make It with Me." Good examples of early Corea.

°Standing Ovation at Newport, Atlantic, 1445 (1 LP)
1965; with Corea, Pike, Valdez, May, and Carr; includes "Potato," "Stolen Moments," "Mushi Mushi," and "Comin' Home Baby." Good examples of early Corea.

SHELLY MANNE

"The Three" and "The Two," Contemporary, M 3584 (1 LP)
1954; each side is a different group: side one has Shorty Rogers, Giuffre, and Manne; side two has Russ Freeman and Manne; "Abstract #1" is a "free" improvisation with no preset melody or chord progressions; also includes "Autumn in New York," Russ Freeman's "The Sound Effects Man," "A Slight Minority," "Speak Easy," etc.

see TEDDY CHARLES—*Collaboration: West.*

see SHORTY ROGERS—*Shorty Rogers and His Giants.*

JACKIE MCLEAN

°Right Now, Blue Note, BST 84215 (1 LP)
late 1960s; with McLean, Larry Willis, Bob Cranshaw, and Clifford Jarvis; includes "Eco," "Poor Eric," "Chistel's Time," and "Right Now."

see MILES DAVIS—*Dig.*

GLENN MILLER

The Complete Glenn Miller Vols. 1–3, RCA (Bluebird), AXM2 5512, AXM2 5514 and AXM2 5534 (each is a 2 LP set).

CHARLES MINGUS

Better Git It in Your Soul, Columbia, CG 30628 (2 LP set)
1958–9; with Shafti Hadi, John Handy, Booker Ervin, Jimmy Knepper, Horace Parlan, Roland Hanna, Dannie Richmond, and Charlie Mingus; includes "Better Git It in Your Soul," "Bird Calls," "Fables of Faubus," "Pussy Cat Dues," "Jelly Roll," "Open Letter to Duke," "Boogie Stop Shuffle," "Self-Portrait in Three Colors," "Diane," "Goodbye Pork Pie Hat," "Song with Orange," and "Far Wells, Mill Valley."

Charlie Mingus, Archive of Folk and Jazz, FS 235 (1 LP); also *Charlie Mingus—Trio and Sextet,* Trip, 5040 (2 LP set)
1954; with Thad Jones, Teo Macero, John LaPorta, Jackson Wiley, and Clem DeRosa; includes "Minor Intrusions," "Spur of the Moment," "Four Hands," and "Thrice Upon a Theme."

Charlie Mingus—Tia Juana Moods, RCA, APL1 0939 (1 LP)
1957 combo recordings that Mingus has stated to be among his best; with Clarence Shaw, Jimmy Knepper, and Shafti Hadi; includes "Flamingo," "Tia Juana Gift Shop," and "Dizzy Moods."

Mingus Revisited, Trip, 5513 (1 LP); also Limelight 86015 (1 LP)
previously called *Pre-Bird,* Mercury, SR 60627; 1960; with 5 trumpets, 4 trombones, tuba, cello, piano, oboe, flute, voice, etc.; all compositions by Mingus except Billy Strayhorn's "Take the 'A' Train" and Ellington's "Do Nothing Till You Hear from Me"; also includes "Prayer for Passive Resistance," "Eclipse," "Half-Mast Inhibition," etc.

Charles Mingus Presents Charles Mingus, Barnaby Candid, BR 5012 (1 LP)
1960 performance originally available on Candid; with Eric Dolphy, Ted Curson, Mingus, and Dannie Richmond; includes "What Love," "Original Faubus Fables," and "All the Things You Could Be by Now If Sigmund Freud's Wife Was Your Mother."

see ANTHOLOGIES AND COMBINATIONS—*Modern Jazz Concert.*

see MILES DAVIS—*Collector's Items.*

see J. J. JOHNSON—*The Eminent Jay Jay Johnson Vols. 1 and 2.*

BLUE MITCHELL

°Boss Horn, Blue Note, 84257 (1 LP)
with Chick Corea, Julian Priester, Junior Cook, Pepper Adams, Gene Taylor, and Mickey Roker; includes "Tones for Joan's Bones," "Straight Up and Down," etc.; includes some Bud Powell-influenced Corea solos.

°The Thing to Do, Blue Note, 4178 (1 LP)
with Chick Corea, Junior Cook, Gene Taylor, Al Foster (basically Horace Silver's band with Corea taking Silver's place); includes "Chick's

Tune," "Step Lightly," "The Thing to Do," "Mona's Mood," "Fungii Mama"; includes some Bud Powell-influenced Corea solos.

see HORACE SILVER—*Finger Poppin'*.

HANK MOBLEY

see ART BLAKEY—*Art Blakey with the Original Jazz Messengers.*

see MILES DAVIS—*In Person at the Blackhawk, Someday My Prince Will Come,* and *At Carnegie Hall.*

THE MODERN JAZZ QUARTET

European Concert, Atlantic, 2-603 (2 LP set)
  1960 concert by Milt Jackson, Percy Heath, John Lewis, and Connie Kay; includes "Django," "Bluesology," etc.

The Modern Jazz Quartet, Prestige, S 7425 (1 LP); also PR 24005 (2 LP set)
  early 1950s; includes "Concorde," "Milano," "Django," "La Ronde," "The Queen's Fancy," etc.; with Jackson, Lewis, Heath, and Clarke.

°The Modern Jazz Quartet and the Oscar Peterson Trio at the Opera House, Verve, MGV, 8269 (1 LP)
  1957 concert; one side is the MJQ doing "Now's the Time," the other is the Oscar Peterson Trio with Herb Ellis and Ray Brown; includes "Indiana," "Joy Spring," etc. This LP is included for Peterson's fastest solo, "Indiana."

MIFF MOLE

see ANTHOLOGIES AND COMBINATIONS—*Thesaurus of Classic Jazz.*

THELONIOUS MONK

Thelonious Monk—Complete Genius, Blue Note, LA 579 (2 LP set)
  1947–8; with Jackson, Blakey, and Sulieman; includes "Humph," "In Walked Bud," "Epistrophy," "Misterioso," "Well, You Needn't," "Off Minor," "Straight, No Chaser," "Evidence," and "Criss Cross."

It's Monk's Time, Columbia, CS 8984 (1 LP)
  early 1960s; with Rouse, Butch Warren, and Ben Riley; includes "Brake's Sake," "Lulu's Back in Town," and "Nice Work if You Can Get It."

Pure Monk, Milestone, 47004 (2 LP set)
  late 1950s unaccompanied solo piano; includes "Functional," "I Should Care," and " 'Round Midnight."

see ANTHOLOGIES AND COMBINATIONS—*The Smithsonian Collection of Classic Jazz.*

see MILES DAVIS—*Miles Davis and the Modern Jazz Giants* and *Tallest Trees.*

see HOT LIPS PAGE—*Trumpet at Minton's.*

see CHARLIE PARKER—*The Verve Years.*

WES MONTGOMERY

Wes Montgomery—While We're Young, Milestone, 47003 (2 LP set)
one LP in this set was recorded in 1960 with Tommy Flanagan, Percy
Heath, and Al Heath; other LP was recorded in 1961 with Hank Jones,
Ron Carter, and Lex Humphries (with Ray Barretto for five of the eight
selections).

AIRTO MOREIRA

see MILES DAVIS—*Black Beauty.*

see RETURN TO FOREVER—*Return to Forever.*

LEE MORGAN

see ART BLAKEY—*Indestructible.*

see DIZZY GILLESPIE—*The Newport Years Vol. 5.*

see WAYNE SHORTER—*Night Dreamer.*

JELLY ROLL MORTON

Jelly Roll Morton—King of New Orleans Jazz, RCA, LPM 1649 (1 LP)
1926–7; with Kid Ory, George Mitchell, and Johnny St. Cyr; includes
"Black Bottom Stomp" and "The Chant."

GERRY MULLIGAN

The Concert Jazz Band, Verve, V-8388 (1 LP)
1960; Mulligan big band featuring Mulligan and Bob Brookmeyer; includes "Sweet and Slow," "Out of This World," Duke Ellington's "I'm
Gonna Go Fishin'," and Mulligan's "Bweebida, Bobbida," etc.

Gerry Mulligan and Lee Konitz—Revelation, Blue Note, LA 532-H2 (2
LP set)
a live 1953 session with Mulligan, Chet Baker, Carson Smith (Joe
Mondragon substitutes on two numbers), and Larry Bunker; includes
"I Can't Believe That You're in Love with Me," "Broadway," "All the
Things You Are," "Almost Like Being in Love," and "Lover Man" (John
Mehegan transcribed the Konitz solo on this tune for Vol. 2 of his *Jazz
Improvisation* book).

Timeless, Pacific Jazz, PJ-75 (1 LP)
includes six selections with Mulligan and Baker together and six of
Baker without Mulligan; 1952 recordings of Mulligan compositions
"Walkin' Shoes" and "Soft Shoes," Baker composition "Freeway" with
Mulligan, Baker, Bob Whitlock, and Chico Hamilton; 1953 "Love Me or
Leave Me" and "My Funny Valentine" with Mulligan, Baker, Carson
Smith, and Larry Bunker; 1953 "Long Ago and Far Away" and "The
Thrill Is Gone" with Baker, Russ Freeman, Carson Smith, and Larry
Bunker.

What Is There to Say? Columbia Special Products, JCS, 8116 (1 LP)
1959; with Mulligan, Art Farmer, Bill Crow, and Dave Bailey; includes "What Is There to Say?" "Just in Time," "As Catch Can," etc. Mulligan feels this LP to be some of his best work.

With Tentette, Capitol, M-11029 (1 LP)
1953; the Gerry Mulligan tentette with Chet Baker, Pete Candoli, Bob Enevoldsen, John Graas, Ray Siegel, Bud Shank, Don Davidson, Mulligan, Joe Mondragon, Chico Hamilton, and Larry Bunker; includes "Walkin' Shoes," "Rocker," "Flash," etc.; solos by Mulligan and Baker. Mulligan considers this LP to represent some of his best work; the album also contains music by one of the few bop clarinetists, Stan Hasselgard; includes 1947 "Swedish Pastry," "Who Sleeps," etc. with Red Norvo.

see MILES DAVIS—*The Complete Birth of the Cool.*

see PAUL DESMOND—*Two of a Mind—Paul Desmond—Gerry Mulligan.*

see DUKE ELLINGTON—*Duke Ellington—Newport 1958.*

FATS NAVARRO

Fats Navarro—Prime Source, Blue Note, LA 507 H2 (2 LP set)
1948 with McGhee: "Double Talk" and "Boperation"; 1948 with Dameron: "Our Delight" and "Dameronia"; 1949 with Rollins and Powell: "Wail" and "Bouncin' with Bud"; and 1948 with Gray and Eager: "Lady Bird."

see ILLINOIS JACQUET—*Illinois Jacquet.*

see BUD POWELL—*The Amazing Bud Powell.*

FRANKIE NEWTON

Swinging on 52nd Street, Jazz Archives, JA-9 (1 LP)
1937–9; includes "Parallel Fifths" with Tab Smith, Kenneth Kersey, etc. and "Who's Sorry Now" with Ed Hall, Pete Brown, etc. Available from Jazz Archives, Inc., P.O. Box 194, Plainview, N.Y. 11803.

see ANTHOLOGIES AND COMBINATIONS—*Trumpeter's Holiday.*

RED NICHOLS

see ANTHOLOGIES AND COMBINATIONS—*Thesaurus of Classic Jazz.*

JIMMIE NOONE

*Jimmie Noone and Earl Hines "At the Apex Club," Decca, DL 79235 (1 LP)
1928; with Noone, Hines, Joe Poston, Bud Scott, Lawson Buford, and Johnny Wells; includes "Apex Blues," "My Monday Date," "King Joe," "I Know that You Know," and two versions each of "Every Evening" and "Sweet Lorraine."

see ANTHOLOGIES AND COMBINATIONS—*Encyclopedia of Jazz on Records Vol. 1.*

KING OLIVER

King Oliver's Jazz Band, 1923, Smithsonian Collection (2 LP set)
with Louis Armstrong, Johnny Dodds, Honore Dutrey, Lil Hardin, etc.;
includes "Snake Rag," "Sweet Lovin' Man," "High Society Rag," "Dippermouth Blues," "West End Blues," etc.

see ANTHOLOGIES AND COMBINATIONS—*The Smithsonian Collection of Classic Jazz.*

see LOUIS ARMSTRONG—*Louis Armstrong and King Oliver.*

THE ORIGINAL DIXIELAND JAZZ BAND

°*The Original Dixieland Jazz Band*, RCA, LPV-547 (1 LP)
usually considered the first recording of jazz, although this is now disputed; 1917 sessions featuring Nick LaRocca, Larry Shields, Eddie Edwards, Henry Ragas, and Tony Sbarbaro; includes "Livery Stable Blues" (1917), "Tiger Rag" (1918), "Clarinet Marmalade" (1918), etc.

ORAN "HOT LIPS" PAGE

Hot Lips Page and Joe Guy—Trumpet at Minton's, Xanadu, 107 (1 LP)
1941; with Charlie Christian and Thelonious Monk; *note:* if you have trouble find this or other Xanadu records, please write to: Don Schlitten, 3242 Irwin Ave., Kingsbridge, N.Y. 10463.

CHARLIE PARKER

Bird/The Savoy Recordings, Savoy, 2201 (2 LP set)
1944 with Grimes, Hart, Butts, West: "Tiny's Tempo" and "Red Cross"; 1945 with Davis, Thornton, Russell, Roach: "Billie's Bounce," "Now's the Time," "Ko Ko"; 1947 with Davis, Powell, Potter, Roach: "Donna Lee" and "Cheryl"; 1947 Davis, Lewis, Boyd, Roach: "Half Nelson" and "Sippin' At Bells"; 1947 with Davis, Jordan, Potter, Roach: "Blue Bird"; 1948 with Davis, Lewis, Russell, Roach: "Barbados" and "Parker's Mood."

° *First Recordings*, Onyx, 221 (1 LP)
1940; with Parker, William J. Scott, Bernard Anderson, Orville Minor, Bud Gould, Jay McShann, Gene Ramey, and Gus Johnson; includes "I Found a New Baby" and "Body and Soul"; 1940 session with almost same personnel: "Moten Swing," "Coquette," "Lady Be Good," "Wichita Blues," and "Honeysuckle Rose"; 1942 "Cherokee" by Parker with an unidentified rhythm section plus 1945 selections with Dizzy Gillespie.

Charlie Parker on Dial Vols. 1–6, Spotlite, 101-6 (1 LP each).
101: with Gillespie and Thompson, 1946 "Diggin' Diz"; 1946 with Davis, Thompson, Marmarosa: "Moose The Mooch," "Yardbird Suite," "Ornithology," and "Night In Tunisia"; 1946 with McGhee: "Lover Man"; 102: 1947 with Garner: "This Is Always," "Cool Blues," and "Bird's Nest"; 103: 1947 with McGhee, Gray, Marmarosa: "Relaxin' at

Camarillo" and "Cheers"; 104: 1947 with Davis, Jordon: "Dexterity,"
"Embraceable You," and "Dewey Square." If you cannot find Spotlite
records in stores, try Spotlite Records Box 1660 Escondido, California
92025.

Charlie Parker—The Verve Years 1948–50, VE 2 2501 (2 LP set)
    includes "April in Paris" and "Just Friends" with strings; "Star Eyes"
    with Hank Jones; and "Bloomdido" and "Relaxin' with Lee" with
    Gillespie, Monk, and Buddy Rich.

see ANTHOLOGIES AND COMBINATIONS—*The Smithsonian Collection of Classic Jazz.*

see DIZZY GILLESPIE—*In the Beginning.*

OSCAR PETERSON

Return Engagement, Verve, V3HB-8842 (2 LP set)
    assortment of Verve material previously issued.

*Tenderly, Clef, MGC 696 (1 LP)
    1950; with Ray Brown and Major Holley; includes "Tenderly," "Debut,"
    "Nameless," and "All the Things You Are."

see DUKE ELLINGTON—*The Greatest Jazz Concert in the World.*

see THE MODERN JAZZ QUARTET—*The Modern Jazz Quartet and the Oscar
Peterson Trio at the Opera House.*

BUD POWELL

The Amazing Bud Powell, Blue Note, 81503 (1 LP)
    1949–51; with Roach, Rollins, Navarro, Potter, and Haynes; includes "Un
    Poco Loco," "Bouncing with Bud," and "Dance of the Infidels."

The Genius of Bud Powell 1949–51, Verve, VE 2 2506 (2 LP set)
    with Russell, Roach, etc.; includes "Get Happy," "Hallucinations," "Tea
    for Two," etc.

see ANTHOLOGIES AND COMBINATIONS—*The Smithsonian Collection of Classic Jazz.*

see DEXTER GORDON—*Long Tall Dexter.*

see FATS NAVARRO—*Prime Source.*

see CHARLIE PARKER—*Bird/The Savoy Recordings.*

see SONNY STITT—*Bud's Blues.*

JIMMY RANEY

see STAN GETZ—*Best of Stan Getz.*

DJANGO REINHARDT

*The Best of Django Reinhardt, Capitol, TB 010226 (2 LP set)
    contains 24 selections including the 1945 "Swing Guitars," the 1939

"Montmarte," "Solid Old Man," "Finesse," and "I Know that You Know Cotton," the 1937 "Swinging with Django," "Paramount Stomp," "Japanese Sandman," "Minor Swing," and "Bolero."

Parisian Swing: Reinhardt/Grappelly, GNP Crescendo, 9002 (1 LP)
1935, 38, and 39; includes "Djangology," "Nocturne," "Louise," and "Improvisation."

Django Reinhardt—Swing It Lightly, Columbia, C 31479 (1 LP)
1953; with Maurice Vander, Pierre Michelot, and Jean Louis Viale; includes "Nuages," "Night and Day," "September Song," "I'm Confessin'," "Brazil," "Manoir de Mes Reves," "Insensiblement," etc.; additional accompaniments were dubbed in during 1968 re-recording.

RETURN TO FOREVER

Return to Forever, ECM, 1022 (1 LP)
1972; with Chick Corea, Stanley Clarke, Airto Moreira, Flora Purim, and Joe Farrell; all tunes composed by Corea; includes "Return to Forever," "Crystal Silence," "What Game Shall We Play Today?" and "Some Time Ago—La Fiesta."

Return to Forever—No Mystery, Polydor, PD6512 (1 LP)
1975; with Chick Corea (acoustic and electric piano, clavinet, Yamaha organ, synthesizers, snare drum, marimba, and vocal), Al Dimeola (electric and acoustic guitar), Stanley Clarke (acoustic and electric bass, Yamaha organ, synthesizer and vocal), and Lenny White (drums, marimba, conga, and percussion); Spanish flamenco and rock are the idoms, not primarily jazz, with little soft material, mostly hard feel; includes "Dayride" (Clarke), "Jungle Waterfall" (Corea-Clarke), "Flight of the Newborn" (Dimeola), "Excerpt from the Movement of Heavy Metal" (entire band), "No Mystery" (Corea), "Interplay" (Corea-Clarke), "Celebration Suite I and II" (Corea). This LP is cited to illustrate the mixture of acoustic and electric, jazz and rock styles, which typified Corea concerts of the mid-1970s.

see CHICK COREA—*all items.*

BUDDY RICH

see CHARLIE PARKER—*Charlie Parker—The Verve Years 1948–50.*

MAX ROACH

see ANTHOLOGIES AND COMBINATIONS—*The Smithsonian Collection of Classic Jazz.*

see CLIFFORD BROWN—*The Quintet Vols. 1 and 2.*

see MILES DAVIS—*Birth of the Cool.*

see DEXTER GORDON—*Long Tall Dexter.*

see THAD JONES—*The Magnificent Thad Jones.*

see CHARLIE PARKER—*Bird/The Savoy Recordings* and *Charlie Parker on Dial.*

see BUD POWELL—*The Amazing Bud Powell* and *The Genius of Bud Powell.*

see SONNY ROLLINS—*Saxophone Colossus and More.*

see SONNY STITT—*Sonny Stitt—Bud's Blues.*

SHORTY ROGERS

°Shorty Rogers and His Giants, RCA, 1195 (1 LP)
1953; with Rogers, Milt Bernhart, John Graas, Gene England, Art Pepper, Giuffre, Hampton Hawes, Joe Mondragon, and Manne; includes "Morpo," "Diablo's Dance," etc.

see TEDDY CHARLES—*Collaboration: West.*

see SHELLY MANNE—*"The Three" and "The Two."*

see WOODY HERMAN—*Early Autumn.*

SONNY ROLLINS

More from the Vanguard, Blue Note, LA 475 H2 (2 LP set)
1957; with Wilbur Ware and Elvin Jones; includes "A Night in Tunisia" and "I'll Remember April."

Saxophone Colossus and More, Prestige, 24050 (2 LP set)
1956; with Brown, Rollins, Richie Powell, George Morrow, and Roach; includes "Pent Up House," "Kiss and Run," and "Valse Hot"; Rollins has said that this is some of his best playing on record.

see CLIFFORD BROWN—*The Quintet Vol. 2.*

see MILES DAVIS—*Collector's Items, Dig,* and *Tallest Trees.*

see DIZZY GILLESPIE—*The Sonny Rollins/Sonny Stitt Sessions.*

see FATS NAVARRO—*Prime Source.*

see BUD POWELL—*The Amazing Bud Powell.*

GEORGE RUSSELL

see ANTHOLOGIES AND COMBINATIONS—*Modern Jazz Concert.*

see DIZZY GILLESPIE—*The Greatest of Dizzy Gillespie.*

see LENNIE TRISTANO—*Crosscurrents.*

LUIS RUSSELL

Luis Russell and His Louisiana Swing Orchestra, Columbia, PG 32338 (2 LP set)
1920s and 30s big band recordings featuring Henry "Red" Allen, J. C. Higginbotham, and others; includes "Plantation Joys," "Jersey Lightning," "Higginbotham Blues," etc.

PEE WEE RUSSELL

see ANTHOLOGIES AND COMBINATIONS—*Thesaurus of Classic Jazz.*

PHAROAH SANDERS

see JOHN COLTRANE—*Live in Seattle* and *Meditations*.

CHARLIE SHAVERS

see COLEMAN HAWKINS—*Coleman Hawkins and the Trumpet Kings.*

ARTIE SHAW

°*Artie Shaw Featuring Roy Eldridge,* RCA, LPV 582 (1 LP)
1944–5 big band and combo; with Eldridge, Shaw, Barney Kessel, Dodo Marmarosa, Morris Rayman, and Lou Fromm; includes "Scuttlebutt," "Mysterioso," "The Grabtown Grapple," and many other tunes by other personnel.

The Complete Artie Shaw Vol. 1, 1938–9, RCA Bluebird, AXM2 5517 (2 LP set)

This Is Artie Shaw, RCA, VPM 6039 (2 LP set)
1938 big band: "Begin the Beguine"; 1940 big band: "Star Dust," etc.; 1940 Gramercy Five combo recordings: "Summit Ridge Drive," "Cross Your Heart," "My Blue Heaven," etc.

GEORGE SHEARING

The Best of George Shearing, Capitol, SM 2104 (1 LP)
not necessarily his best, but a good survey, including his "Lullaby of Birdland"; nothing after 1964.

°*Touch of Genius,* MGM, E 3265 (1 LP)
1949–50; with Marjorie Hyams, Don Elliott, Chuck Wayne, John Levy, and Denzil Best; includes "My Silent Love," "I'll Never Smile Again," "Conception," "Carnegie Horizons," and "Midnight Moods."

°*You're Hearing George Shearing,* MGM, E 3216 (1 LP)
1949–50; with Marjorie Hyams, Don Elliott, Chuck Wayne, John Levy, and Denzil Best; includes "Tenderly," "Summertime," "East of the Sun," and "Changing with the Times."

ARCHIE SHEPP

Archie Shepp—Four for Trane, Impulse, 71 (1 LP)
1964; with Shepp, John Tchicai, Roswell Rudd, Alan Shorter, Reggie Workman, and Charles Moffett; includes "Syeeda's Song Flute," "Mrs. Syms," "Cousin Mary," "Naima," and "Rufus."

see CECIL TAYLOR—*Cecil Taylor—Air.*

WAYNE SHORTER

Night Dreamer, Blue Note, BST-84173 (1 LP)
middle 1960s; with Shorter, Lee Morgan, McCoy Tyner, Reggie Workman, and Elvin Jones; all tunes composed by Shorter; includes "Night

Dreamer," "Oriental Folk Song," "Virgo," "Black Nile," "Charcoal Blues," "Armageddon," and "House of Jade."

Speak No Evil, Blue Note, BST-84194 (1 LP)
middle 1960s; with Shorter, Freddie Hubbard, Herbie Hancock, Ron Carter, and Elvin Jones; all tunes composed by Shorter; includes "Witch Hunt," "Fee Fi Fo Fum," "Dance Cadaverous," "Speak No Evil," "Infant Eyes," and "Wild Flower."

Super Nova, Blue Note, 84332 (1 LP)

see ART BLAKEY—*Indestructible*.

see MILES DAVIS—*Miles in Berlin, Bitches Brew, E.S.P., Filles de Kilimanjaro, In a Silent Way, Miles in the Sky, Miles Smiles, Nefertiti,* and *Sorcerer.*

see WEATHER REPORT—all selections.

see JOE ZAWINUL—*Zawinul*.

HORACE SILVER

Finger Poppin', Blue Note, BST 84008 (1 LP)
1959; with Blue Mitchell, Junior Cook, Silver, Gene Taylor, and Louis Hayes; includes "Finger Poppin'," "Cookin' at the Continental," "Mellow D," etc.

In Pursuit of the 27th Man, Blue Note, LA054-F (1 LP)
1972; with Randy Brecker, Michael Brecker, David Friedman, Silver, Bob Cranshaw, and Mickey Roker; includes "Liberated Brother," "Kathy," "Gregory Is Here," "Summer in Central Park," "Nothin' Can Stop Me Now," "In Pursuit of the 27th Man," and "Strange Vibes." This LP is included because it contains the best recorded solos of the Brecker Brothers to date; it also hangs together very well, displays delightful Silver writing, and, on some tunes, an unusual format for Silver: vibes, piano, bass and drums.

see ART BLAKEY—*A Night at Birdland Vols. 1 & 2* and *Art Blakey with the Original Jazz Messengers.*

see MILES DAVIS—*Tallest Trees.*

see STAN GETZ—*Best of Stan Getz.*

JABBO SMITH

Jazz Makers, 1938–40, Swaggie, S1215 (1 LP); Australian import
1938, 39 and 40 recordings, including four 1938 selections by Jabbo Smith's band: "Rhythm in Spain," "Absolutely," "More Rain More Rest," and "How Could Cupid Be So Stupid?" Available from Swaggie Records, P.O. Box 125, South Yarra, Victoria, Australia.

PINETOP SMITH

see ANTHOLOGIES AND COMBINATIONS—*The Encyclopieda of Jazz on Records, Vol. 1.*

SONNY STITT

Sonny Stitt—Bud's Blues, Prestige, 7839 (1 LP); also *Genesis*, Prestige, 24044 (2 LP set)

> 1949; with Stitt, Bud Powell, Curly Russell, and Max Roach ("All God's Chillun Got Rhythm," "Bud's Blues," "Sonny Side," and "Sunset"; 1950: "Strike Up the Band," "I Want to Be Happy," "Taking a Chance on Love," "Fine and Dandy"; 1949 with Stitt, J. J. Johnson, John Lewis, Nelson Boyd, and Max Roach: "Blue Mode," "Teapot," "Afternoon in Paris," and "Elora."

see DIZZY GILLESPIE—*The Sonny Rollins/Sonny Stitt Sessions.*

SUN RA

Astro Black, Impulse, AS 9255 (1 LP)

> portions of this recording, side two of *Heliocentric Worlds of Sun Ra Vol. 2* (see below), and *Magic City* (see below) sound collectively improvised, free of preset chord progressions and tempos.

Atlantis, Impulse, AS 9239 (1 LP)

> much of side two of this LP and *Heliocentric Worlds of Sun Ra Vols. 1 & 2* resembles the work of Edgard Varese.

Bad and Beautiful, Impulse, ASD 9276 (1 LP)

> 1961 performance, including "Just in Time."

Heliocentric Worlds of Sun Ra Vols. 1 & 2, ESP-DISK, 1014 and 1017 (1 LP each)

Magic City, Impulse, AS 9243 (1 LP)

Nubians of Plutonia, Impulse, AS 9242 (1 LP)

> 1959 performances; the selections on side two resemble mode-based work of later John Coltrane and Pharoah Sanders pieces.

Sun Ra—The Futuristic Sounds of Sun Ra, Savoy, MG 12169 (1 LP)

> 1960–61; with John Gilmore, Marshall Allen, Pat Patrick, Bernard Mc-Kinney, Ronnie Boykins, and Willie Jones; includes "Bassism," "Of Sounds and Something Else," "What's That?" "Where Is Tomorrow?" "The Beginning," "China Gates," "New Day," "Tapestry from an Asteroid," "Jet Flight," "Looking Outward," and "Space Jazz Reverie."

Sun Song, Delmark, 411 (1 LP); also Transition, J 10 (1 LP)

> portions of this 1956 LP and *Super-Sonic Sounds* (see below) resemble updated Ellington big band styles.

Super-Sonic Sounds, Impulse, AS 9271 (1 LP)

> *Note:* if you cannot find these LPs or others by Sun Ra, contact The Jazz Record Mart, 4243 N. Lincoln Ave., Chicago, Ill. 60618.

ART TATUM

Art Tatum-Ben Webster Group Masterpieces, Pablo, 2310 737 (1 LP)

> 1956 ballad performances by Webster, Tatum, Red Callender, and Bill Douglass; includes "All the Things You Are," "Where or When," "My One and Only Love," etc.

Art Tatum Masterpieces, MCA2-4019 (2 LP set)
   with Tatum, Tiny Grimes, and Slam Stewart; includes an amazing 1944 version of "I Got Rhythm," and "Tea for Two," along with "Deep Purple," "Cocktails for Two," etc.

Piano Starts Here, Columbia, CS 9655 (1 LP)
   1933 and 1949; includes "Tea for Two," "Humoresque," "Tiger Rag," "St. Louis Blues," "Willow Weep for Me," "The Man I Love," "Yester-days," etc.

see ANTHOLOGIES AND COMBINATIONS—*The Smithsonian Collection of Classic Jazz.*

CECIL TAYLOR

Air, Barnaby, Z 30562 (1 LP); also Candid, M 8006 (1 LP); also Candid, S 9006 (1 LP)
   1960; with Archie Shepp, Taylor, Buell Neidlinger, and Dennis Charles; includes "Air," "This Nearly Was Mine," "Port of Call," "Eb," and "Lazy Afternoon."

In Transition, Blue Note, LA458-H2 (2 LP set)
   two of Taylor's earliest recordings; mostly standard pop tunes; 1955, with Steve Lacy, Buell Neidlinger, and Dennis Charles: "Bemsha Swing," "Charge 'Em Blues," "Azure," "Song," "You'd Be So Nice to Come Home To," "Rick Kick Shaw," and "Sweet and Lovely"; 1959, with Ted Curson, Bill Barron, Chris White, and Rudy Collins: "Get Out of Town," "Carol/Three Points," "Love for Sale," "Little Lees," and "I Love Paris."

Silent Tongues, Arista, 1005 (1 LP)
   unaccompanied piano solo improvisations recorded live at the Mon-treaux Jazz Festival in 1974; includes "Abyss," "Petals and Filaments," "Jitney #1 & #2," etc.

Unit Structures, Blue Note, 84237 (1 LP)
   1966 performances with Eddie Gale Stevens, Jr., Jimmy Lyons, Ken McIntyre, Taylor, Henry Grimes, Alan Silva, and Andrew Cyrille; in-cludes "Steps," "Unit Structure/As of a Now," etc.

see ANTHOLOGIES AND COMBINATIONS—*The Smithsonian Collection of Classic Jazz.*

JACK TEAGARDEN

King of the Blues Trombone, Columbia Special Products, JSN 6044 (3 LP set)
   1928–40; with Benny Goodman, Frankie Trumbauer, Bud Freeman and His Famous Chicagoans; includes 1933 "Texas Tea Party," 1939 "I Got a Right to Sing the Blues," and 1940 "47th and State."

LUCKY THOMPSON

Dancing Sunbeam, Impulse, 9307 (2 LP set)
   1956; with Thompson, Jimmy Cleveland, Hank Jones, Oscar Pettiford, and Osie Johnson: "Tom-Kattin'," "Old Reliable," and "Deep Passion,"

and "Translation"; with Thompson, Pettiford, and Skeeter Best: "Tricrotism," "Bo-Bi My Boy," "A Lady's Vanity," and "OP Meets LT."

see DIZZY GILLESPIE—*Development of an American Artist.*

see CHARLIE PARKER—*Charlie Parker on Dial Vol. 1.*

CLAUDE THORNHILL

The Memorable Claude Thornhill, Columbia, KG 32906 (2 LP set)
1941; featuring Lee Konitz; includes "Snowfall," "Hungarian Dance #5," "Traumerai," "Portrait of a Guinea Farm," "Where or When," "Night and Day," "Grieg's Piano Concerto," "There's a Small Hotel" (Gil Evans arrangement), "I Don't Know Why," "Moonlight Bay," "Buster's Last Stand," "Moments Like This," "A Sunday Kind of Love," "Warsaw Concerto," "Anthropology" (Gil Evans arrangement), "Robbin's Nest," "Lover Man," "Donna Lee" (Gil Evans arrangement), "For Heaven's Sake," and "Yardbird Suite" (Gil Evans arrangement).

CAL TJADER

*Cal Tjader—Soul Burst, Verve, 8637 (1 LP)
with Chick Corea, Jerome Richardson, Jerry Dodgian, Seldon Powell, Richard Davis, and Grady Tate; includes "Oran," "Curacao," "My Ship," "Manteca," and "Soul Burst"; includes some McCoy Tyner—influenced Corea soloing.

see DAVE BRUBECK—*The Dave Brubeck Octet.*

LENNIE TRISTANO

Crosscurrents, Capitol, M11060 (1 LP)
volume 14 of the Capitol Jazz Classics series; only one side contains Tristano; the other half is Buddy DeFranco in 1949 combo and big band settings; Tristano side includes 1949 "Wow," "Crosscurrent," "Yesterdays," "Marionette," "Sax of a Kind," "Intuition," and "Digression"; with Tristano, Lee Konitz, Warne Marsh, Billy Bauer, and others.

see ANTHOLOGIES AND COMBINATIONS—*The Smithsonian Collection of Classic Jazz.*

see LEE KONITZ—*Subconscious-Lee with Lennie Tristano.*

MCCOY TYNER

see JOHN COLTRANE—Atlantic and Impulse LPs.

see THE JAZZTET—*Meet the Jazztet.*

see WAYNE SHORTER—*Night Dreamer.*

CHARLIE VENTURA

In Concert, GNP Crescendo, GNP 1 (1 LP)
same tunes and personnel as *It's All Bop to Me* (see below).
*It's All Bop to Me, RCA, LPM 1135 (1 LP)
1949 studio recordings with Candoli, Boots Mussulli, Bennie Green and

vocalists Jackie Cain and Roy Kral; includes "Fine and Dandy," "Boptura," "Lullaby in Rhythm," etc.

MIROSLAV VITOUS

°*Infinite Search*, Embryo, SD 524 (1 LP); available as *Mountain in the Clouds*, Atlantic, 1622 (1 LP)

see CHICK COREA—*Chick Corea.*

see WEATHER REPORT—all items except *Black Market.*

FATS WALLER

Fats Waller Piano Solos/1929–41, RCA Bluebird, AXM2 5518 (2 LP set) includes 1929 "Numb Fumblin' " and "Valentine Stomp."

see ANTHOLOGIES AND COMBINATIONS—*The Smithsonian Collection of Classic Jazz.*

WEATHER REPORT

Black Market, Columbia, PC 34099 (1 LP)

I Sing the Body Electric, Columbia, PC 31352 (1 LP)
1971 and 72; one side is a live performance by Zawinul, Shorter, Vitous, Gravatt, and Dom Um Romao, including "Vertical Invader," "T.H.," "Dr. Honoris Causa," "Surucucu," and "Directions"; the other side is a studio date with Weather Report augmented by three singers, English horn (Andrew White), flute, trumpet, and 12-string guitar, including "Unknown Soldier," "The Moors," "Crystal," and "Second Sunday in August."

Mysterious Traveller, Columbia, PC 32494 (1 LP)

Sweetnighter, Columbia, PC 32210 (1 LP)

Tale Spinnin', Columbia, PC 33417 (1 LP)

Weather Report, Columbia, PC 30661 (1 LP)

CHICK WEBB

The Best of Chick Webb, MCA, 2 4107 (2 LP set)
1934–39 big band; includes "Blue Lou," "Don't Be That Way," "A-Tisket, A-Tasket," etc.

TONY WILLIAMS

see MILES DAVIS—*Filles de Kilimanjaro, Four and More, In a Silent Way, Miles in Berlin, Miles in Europe, Miles in the Sky, Miles in Tokyo, Miles Smiles, Seven Steps to Heaven, Sorcerer, Nefertiti,* and *E.S.P.*

see HERBIE HANCOCK—*Maiden Voyage.*

GERALD WILSON

°*Moment of Truth*, Pacific Jazz, 61 (1 LP)
1963 big band; seven of the nine selections were composed and arranged by Wilson; "Viva Tirado" features solos by Teddy Edwards, Joe Pass,

and Carmell Jones; "Latino" features solos by Joe Pass and Harold Land; "Nancy Jo" has solos by Harold Land, Carmell Jones, and Joe Pass; rhythm section includes Jack Wilson, Jimmy Bond, and Mel Lewis.

TEDDY WILSON

Statements and Improvisations 1934–42, Smithsonian (1 LP)
contains Columbia material (see below).

Teddy Wilson and His All Stars, Columbia, CG 31617 (2 LP set)
1936; with Roy Eldridge, Buster Bailey, Chu Berry, Bob Lessey, Israel Crosby, and Sid Catlett, including "Blues in C# Minor," "Mary Had a Little Lamb," and "Warmin' Up"; 1937, with Harry James, Red Norvo, and John Simmons, including "Ain't Misbehavin'," "Just a Mood," and "Honeysuckle Rose"; includes other sessions with numerous swing era standouts. Though some of the best Teddy Wilson is on Benny Goodman combo recordings, this LP is included for an outstanding 1936 session containing some of Roy Eldridge's most thoughtful solos.

see BENNY GOODMAN—*Carnegie Hall Jazz Concert* and *The Complete Benny Goodman Vol. 1 1935.*

LESTER YOUNG

*Lester Young Memorial Album—Lester Young with Count Basie and His Orchestra, Volume 1, Epic, LN 3576 and *Volume 2,* Epic, 3577; also Epic, SN 6031 (2 LP set)
1936, 1939, and 1940 Count Basie combo and big band; with Young, Buck Clayton, Dickie Wells, Freddie Green, Walter Page, and Jo Jones; includes "Shoe Shine Boy," "Lady Be Good," "Lester Leaps In," "Dickie's Dream," "Moten Swing," "Taxi War Dance," "Pound Cake," "Easy Does It," "Ham 'n' Eggs," etc.

The Lester Young Story Vol. 1, Columbia, CG 33502 (2 LP set)
includes 1936 "Shoe Shine Boy" (2 takes), "Boogie Woogie," and "Lady Be Good."

*The Tenor Sax: Lester Young, Chu Berry, and Ben Webster, Atlantic, SD2-307 (2 LP set); includes **Lester Young with the Kansas City Five,* Commodore, FL 30 014 (1 LP)
the Commodore FL material is combined with material by Berry, Webster, Hot Lips Page, and Roy Eldridge on the Atlantic issue; the Lester Young selections feature Young on clarinet and tenor saxophone, Buck Clayton, Eddie Durham, and Freddie Green (Green is not credited on the Commodore album jacket, however), Walter Page, and Jo Jones; selections include "Way Down Yonder in New Orleans," "I Want a Little Girl," "Countless Blues," etc. (1938); *Note:* alternate takes of "Shoe Shine Boy," "Lester Leaps In," and "Dickie's Dream" on Epic and the Buck Clayton-Lester Young sessions on Commodore are available on *Alternate Takes,* Tax, M-8000 (1 LP), an import and on **Young Lester,* Columbia, J 24 (1 LP).

see ANTHOLOGIES AND COMBINATIONS—*The Smithsonian Collection of Classic Jazz.*

JOE ZAWINUL

Zawinul, Atlantic, SD 1579 (1 LP)
1970; with Shorter, Earl Turbinton, Woody Shaw, George Davis, Hubert Laws, Zawinul, Hancock, Vitous, Walter Booker, Jack De-Johnette, Joe Chambers, Billy Hart, and David Lee; includes "Doctor Honoris Causa," "In a Silent Way," "Double Image," etc. This LP displays some of Zawinul's best composing and arranging.

see CANNONBALL ADDERLEY—*Mercy, Mercy, Mercy.*

see MILES DAVIS—*Bitches Brew* and *In a Silent Way.*

see WEATHER REPORT—all selections.

ANTHOLOGIES AND COMBINATIONS

°*Alto Saxes,* Verve, MGV 8126 (1 LP)
included for Benny Carter solos.

Changing Face of Harlem, Savoy, SJL 2208 (2 LP set)
included for Earl Bostic solos, which show possible origins of certain Coltrane devices.

The Encyclopedia of Jazz on Records Vol. 1, MCA, 2-4061 (1 LP)
includes "Boogie Woogie," by Pinetop Smith, "You've Got to Be Modernistic," by James P. Johnson, selections by Jelly Roll Morton, Johnny Dodds, Ellington, etc.

Great Moments in Jazz Vol. 2 Alto Masters, Swing Treasury, 109 (1 LP)
included for John Coltrane solo in 1954 with the Johnny Hodges combo.

°*Modern Jazz Concert,* Columbia, WL 127 (1 LP)
commissioned by the 1957 Brandeis University Festival of the Arts; with Hal McKusick and John LaPorta, Louis Mucci and Art Farmer, Jimmy Knepper, James Buffington, Robert DiDomenica, Manuel Zegler, Teddy Charles, Margaret Ross, Barry Galbraith, Bill Evans, Joe Benjamin, Fred Zimmerman, and Ted Sommer; includes "Revelations (First Movement)" by Charles Mingus, "Transformation" by Gunther Schuller, and and "All About Rosie" by George Russell, featuring Evans's solo.

°*Music for Brass,* Columbia, CL 941 (1 LP); also *Outstanding Jazz Compositions of the 20th Century,* Columbia, C 25831 (2 LP set)
1956; with the Brass Ensemble of the Jazz and Classical Music Society; six trumpets, three trombones, four French horns, tuba, two baritone horns, string bass, drums, and percussion; soloists include Davis, Joe Wilder, and J. J. Johnson; selections include "Three Little Feelings" by John Lewis and "Poem for Brass" by J. J. Johnson.

The Smithsonian Collection of Classic Jazz, Smithsonian (6 LP boxed set)
Critic-journalist Martin Williams has drawn from the vaults of many record companies to compile an ambitious 6-LP collection for the Smithsonian Institute. It is an excellent place to find one or two good examples of a particular musician's work without purchasing the albums

from which the selections were taken. It would take months, even years, to obtain the selections contained in this collection separately; however, it should not be purchased with the intention of gaining a well-balanced view of jazz history because of the lengthy list of historically significant players and groups omitted: tenor saxophonist Albert Ayler, pianist-composer-bandleader Sun Ra, The Original Dixieland Jazz Band, Stan Kenton's big bands, Woody Herman's big bands, Stan Getz, post-1964 John Coltrane, pianist-composer-bandleaders Herbie Hancock, Chick Corea, Keith Jarrett, combos led by composer-baritone saxophonist Gerry Mulligan, the combos of Art Blakey and Horace Silver, and combos led by Miles Davis during the 1960s and 70s, etc.

Of course, it is not what the collection omits that is important, but what it includes. The following is a partial listing of the set.

LOUIS ARMSTRONG

eight selections including 1928 "West End Blues," featuring Earl Hines; 1928 duet with Hines called "Weather Bird"; 1927 "Hotter Than That," with Johnny Dodds, Kid Ory, Lil Hardin Armstrong, Lonnie Johnson, and Johnny St. Cyr.

BIX BEIDERBECKE

1927 "Singin' the Blues," with Frankie Trumbauer.

DON BYAS

1945 "I Got Rhythm," duet between Byas and Slam Stewart.

ORNETTE COLEMAN

includes "Congeniality," "Lonely Woman," and an excerpt from his LP *Free Jazz*.

MILES DAVIS

includes "Boplicity" (*Birth of the Cool*) and "So What (*Kind of Blue*)," with Cannonball Adderly, John Coltrane, Bill Evans, Paul Chambers, and Jimmy Cobb.

DUKE ELLINGTON

eight big band selections including "Concerto for Cootie," "Harlem Air Shaft," and "KoKo," all from 1940.

ROY ELDRIDGE

1941 big band version of "Rockin' Chair."

DIZZY GILLESPIE

1945 "I Can't Get Started" and 1945 "Shaw 'Nuff," with Al Haig, Curly Russell, and Sid Catlett.

COLEMAN HAWKINS

famous 1939 "Body and Soul."

JAMES P. JOHNSON

1921 "Carolina Shout."

LEE KONITZ

1949 "Crosscurrent," with Konitz, Warne Marsh, Billy Bauer, and Lennie Tristano.

MEADE LUX LEWIS

famous 1937 "Honky Tonk Train Blues."

JIMMIE LUNCEFORD
1939 "Lunceford Special."

THELONIOUS MONK
six selections including "Criss Cross" and "Misterioso."

KING OLIVER
1923 "Dippermouth Blues," with Johnny Dodds and Louis Armstrong.

CHARLIE PARKER
seven selections including two 1947 versions of "Embraceable You," one version of "Parker's Mood," and one of his fastest performances, a 1945 version of "KoKo."

BUD POWELL
1947 "Somebody Loves Me," with Curly Russell and Max Roach.

SONNY ROLLINS
1956 "Blue Seven," with Tommy Flanagan, Doug Watkins, and Max Roach.

ART TATUM
1949 "Willow Weep for Me" and 1956 "Too Marvelous for Words."

CECIL TAYLOR
includes an excerpt from his *Unit Structures*.

FATS WALLER
1927 "I Ain't Got Nobody," solo piano piece.

LESTER YOUNG
1939 "Lester Leaps In" and 1939 "Taxi War Dance," with Count Basie.

You may order the Smithsonian Collection from: Division of Performing Arts, Smithsonian Institute, Washington, D.C. 20560.

Strictly Bebop—Capitol Jazz Classics Vol. 13, Capitol, M 11059 (1 LP)
1949, with Dameron, Davis, Navarro, and Clarke—mostly Dameron compositions; and 1949–50 Gillespie big band (5 selections)—included for Dameron's writing.

°Thesaurus of Classic Jazz, Columbia, C4L 18 (4 LP set)
boxed set including twelve 1927–30 recordings by Miff Mole and His Molers ("At the Darktown Strutters Ball," with Red Nichols and Jimmy Dorsey, "That's a Plenty," with Jimmy Dorsey and Eddie Lang, etc.); eleven 1927 recordings with Red Nichols and the Charleston Chasers ("Farewell Blues," with Jimmy Dorsey and Miff Mole, "Five Pennies," with Pee Wee Russell, etc.); and other tunes by other groups.

°Trumpeter's Holiday, Epic, LN 3252 (1 LP)
included for Frankie Newton's solos and Henry "Red" Allen's 1935 "Body and Soul"; also has Roy Eldridge's 1937 "After You've Gone."

SUPPLEMENTARY READING

Biographies

ARMSTRONG, LOUIS. *Satchmo: My Life in New Orleans*. Englewood Cliffs, N.J.: Prentice-Hall, 1954.
Louis Armstrong's autobiography.

CHILTON, JOHN. *Who's Who of Jazz: Storyville to Swing Street*. London: Chilton Book Co., 1972.
Available from The Bloomsbury Book Shop, 31-35 Great Ormond Street, London, W.C. 1. Biographies of hundreds of musicians born before 1920.

DANCE, STANLEY. *The World of Duke Ellington*. New York: Charles Scribner's Sons, 1970.

ELLINGTON, DUKE. *Music Is My Mistress*. Garden City, N.Y.: Doubleday, 1973. In DaCapo paperback
Duke Ellington's autobiography.

FEATHER, LEONARD. *The New Encyclopedia of Jazz*. New York: Bonanza, 1960.
Leonard Feather and Ira Gitler's monumental compilation with over two thousand biographies from A to Z.

FEATHER, LEONARD. *The Encyclopedia of Jazz in the Sixties*. New York: Horizon, 1966.

A follow-up to the above, this one including *1400* biographies.

FEATHER, LEONARD, and GITLER, IRA. *The Encyclopedia of Jazz in the Seventies*. New York: Bonanza, 1976.
A follow-up to the above.

FEATHER, LEONARD. *From Satchmo to Miles*. New York: Stein and Day, 1972.
Chapters on Louis Armstrong, Duke Ellington, Count Basie, Lester Young, Charlie Parker, Dizzy Gillespie, Miles Davis and others.

GITLER, IRA. *Jazz Masters of the Forties*. New York: Macmillan, 1966. In Collier paperback.
Approximately a chapter each on the music and colleagues of Dizzy Gillespie, Kenny Clarke, Charlie Parker, Dexter Gordon, Tristano–Konitz, Bud Powell, Tadd Dameron, Oscar Pettiford, and J. J. Johnson.

GOLDBERG, JOE. *Jazz Masters of the Fifties*. New York: Macmillan, 1965. In Collier paperback.
A chapter each on Miles Davis, Thelonious Monk, Gerry Mulligan, Charlie Mingus, John Coltrane, Sonny Rollins, Ornette Coleman, and Cecil Taylor.

HADLOCK, RICHARD. *Jazz Masters of the Twenties.* New York: Macmillan, 1965. In Collier paperback.
A chapter each on Armstrong, Beiderbecke, Earl Hines, Fats Waller, James P. Johnson, Fletcher Henderson, Eddie Lang, and The Chicagoans.

REISNER, ROBERT. *Bird: The Legend of Charlie Parker.* New York: Citadel, 1962. Reprinted by DaCapo Press.
Charlie Parker biography in the form of documents.

RUSSELL, ROSS. *Bird Lives: The High Life and Hard Times of Charlie Parker.* New York: Charterhouse, 1972. In Popular Library paperback.
Charlie Parker biography in the style of a novel by the man who created Dial Record Company for the express purpose of recording Parker. The book is filled with colorful anecdotes. Russell describes many significant recording sessions. Try not to take Russell's musical discussions too seriously, however. When listening to the actual music, you might find his descriptions and your impressions quite opposed. Russell also tends to confuse and misuse technical terms, but his inaccuracies are quite minor when compared to the biographical contribution his book makes.

SHAPIRO, NAT, and HENTOFF, NAT. *Hear Me Talkin' to Ya.* New York: Dover, 1955. Also Peter Smith. Also Greenwood.
Interviews with famous jazz musicians.

SHAPIRO, NAT, and HENTOFF, NAT. *Jazz Makers.* New York: Grove Press, 1959. Also Rinehart, 1957. Also Greenwood.
A chapter each on Jelly Roll Morton, Baby Dodds, Louis Armstrong, Jack Teagarden, Earl Hines, Bix Beiderbecke, Pee Wee Russell, Fats Waller, Art Tatum, Coleman Hawkins, Benny Goodman, Duke Ellington, Charlie Parker, Fletcher Henderson, Count Basie, Lester Young, Roy Eldridge, Charlie Christian, and Dizzy Gillespie.

SIMPKINS, C. O. *Coltrane: A Biography.* New York: Herndon House, 1975.

Available from Herndon House, Suite 17-D, 25 W. 132 St., N.Y., N.Y. 10037.

SPELLMAN, A. B. *Black Music: Four Lives.* New York: Schocken, 1966.
Biographical interviews with Ornette Coleman, Cecil Taylor, Jackie McLean, and Herbie Nichols.

STEWART, REX. *Jazz Masters of the Thirties.* New York: Macmillan, 1972. In Collier paperback.
A chapter each on Ellington, Hawkins, Henderson, Basie, Art Tatum, and Benny Carter.

SUDHALTER, R. M., EVANS, P. R., and MYATT, W. D. *Bix, Man and Legend.* New York: Schirmer Books, 1974.
An exhaustive biography of Bix Beiderbecke.

THOMAS, J. C. *Chasin' the Trane: The Music and Mystique of John Coltrane.* Garden City, New York: Doubleday, 1975. In DaCapo paperback.

ULANOV, BARRY. *Duke Ellington.* New York: Creative Age, 1946. In DaCapo paperback.

WILLIAMS, MARTIN. *Jazz Masters of New Orleans.* New York: Macmillan, 1970. In Collier paperback.
A chapter each on King Oliver, Jelly Roll Morton, Sidney Bechet, Louis Armstrong, and Original Dixieland Jazz Band.

Texts for Readers Familiar with Musical Notation

HODEIR, ANDRÉ. *Jazz: Its Evolution And Essence.* New York: Grove Press, 1956. In DaCapo paperback.
Technical analyses of various styles and recordings including an essay on trombonist Dickie Wells and one on Ellington's "Concerto for Cootie."

OSTRANSKY, LEROY. *The Anatomy of Jazz.* Seattle, Washington: University of Washington Press, 1960. Also Greenwood.

SCHULLER, GUNTHER. *Early Jazz: Its Roots and Musical Development.* New York: Oxford University Press, 1968.
Scholarly and quite technical examination

of the earliest jazz known, its possible sources in African music and nineteenth-century American popular music. Detailed analysis of Louis Armstrong, Jelly Roll Morton, assorted pre-swing players, Fletcher Henderson, Ellington's earliest recordings, Bennie Moten and bands of Kansas and Missouri during the 1920s and early 1930s.

Technical References

BAKER, DAVID. *Jazz Improvisation: A Comprehensive Study for All Players.* Chicago: Maher, 1969. A helpful instruction manual for intermediate and advanced as well as beginning jazz improvisers.

COKER, JERRY. *Improvising Jazz.* Englewood Cliffs, N.J.: Prentice-Hall, 1964.
Excellent explanation of chords, chord progressions, how to swing, and how to improvise melodically.

MEHEGAN, JOHN. *Jazz Improvisation 1. Tonal and Rhythmic Principles.* New York: Watson-Guptill Publications, 1959.

MEHEGAN, JOHN. *Jazz Improvisation 2. Jazz Rhythm and the Improvised Line.* New York: Watson-Guptill Publications, 1962.

MEHEGAN, JOHN. *Jazz Improvisation 3. Swing and Early Progressive Piano Styles.* New York: Watson-Guptill Publications, 1964.
The three volumes by Mehegan provide scholarly instruction series for the serious jazz student who has solid knowledge of the piano. The series is not exclusively for pianists, but any hornmen using it must have some acquaintance with the keyboard. Distributed by Amsco Music Publishing Co., 33 West 60th St., N.Y., N.Y. 10023. Distributed to schools and libraries by Hyperion Press, Inc. 45 Riverside Avenue, Westport, Connecticut 06880.

RIZZO, PHIL. *Creative Melodic Techniques Used in Jazz Improvisation.* Modern Music School, 101 Northfield Road, Bedford, Ohio 44146.
Manual for the beginning improviser.

Sources for Notated Jazz Solos

Jazz books and magazines often include notations. The Mehegan books, listed here under "Technical References," contain numerous solo transcriptions. *Down Beat* magazine, listed on page 350 under "Jazz Magazines," publishes entire books of transcriptions. The beginning of a projected series has a volume of trombone solos and a volume of alto saxophone solos. The most dedicated of all solo transcribers is Andrew White. Over two hundred John Coltrane solos and several Eric Dolphy solos are available through Andrew's Music, 4830 South Dakota Ave., N.E., Washington, D.C. 20017.

Solos by Freddie Hubbard, Miles Davis, Clifford Brown, Charlie Christian, Wes Montgomery and others are available through Giant Steps, 612 N. Sepulveda Blvd., Los Angeles, California 90049.

Approximately 250 Charlie Parker solos are transcribed and analyzed in THOMAS OWENS, *Charlie Parker: Techniques of Improvisation 1 and 2.* Doctoral Dissertation (1974) Catalog #75-1992. Available from University Microfilms International, P.O. Box 1307, Ann Arbor, Mich. 48106.

Fourteen Dizzy Gillespie solos are in *Dizzy Gillespie: A Jazz Master*—transcribed by Frank Paparelli. Published by Belwin-Mills, Melville, N.Y. 11746.

Four Charlie Parker solos are in *Bebop for Alto Sax.* Published by Criterion Music, 17 W. 60th St. New York, N.Y. 10023.

Seven Charlie Parker Solos are in *Sketch-Orks.* Published by Criterion Music, 17 W. 60th St. New York, N.Y. 10023.

Six Bill Evans solos are in *Bill Evans Plays.* Published by TRO Songways Service, 17 W. 60th St., New York, N.Y. 10023.

Four Bill Evans solos are in *Bill Evans 3.* Published by TRO Songways Service, 17 W. 60th St. New York, N.Y. 10023.

Louis Armstrong transcriptions can be found in *44 Trumpet Solos and 125 Jazz Breaks* published by Charles Hansen, 1860 Broadway, New York, N.Y. 10023.

INDEX

See Discography for index of cited recordings.
Page numbers in italics indicate illustrations.